Prose Fiction of the Cuban Revolution

Latin American Monographs, No. 37
Sponsored by the Institute of Latin American Studies
The University of Texas at Austin

Prose Fiction
of the Cuban Revolution

BY SEYMOUR MENTON

UNIVERSITY OF TEXAS PRESS • AUSTIN AND LONDON

Library of Congress Cataloging in Publication Data

Menton, Seymour.
    Prose fiction of the Cuban revolution.

    (Latin American monographs; no. 37)
    Bibliography: p.
    Includes index.
    1. Cuban fiction—20th century—History and
criticism. 2. Cuba in literature. I. Title.
II. Series: Latin American monographs (Austin,
Tex.); no. 37.
PQ7382.M4   863   75–5993
ISBN 0–292–76421–9

. . . nunca he sido incondicional de nada ni de nadie.

—Ernesto Sábato

. . . sin libertad de crítica y sin pluralidad de opiniones y grupos no hay vida política. Y para nosotros, hombres modernos, vida política es sinónimo de vida racional y civilizada.

—Octavio Paz

La literatura en general y la novela en particular, son expresión de descontento: el servicio social que prestan consiste, principalmente en recordar a los hombres que el mundo siempre estará mal hecho, que la vida siempre deberá cambiar.

—Mario Vargas Llosa

CONTENTS

ABBREVIATIONS

Used for Anthologies of the Cuban Short Story

AF-1   ANTOLOGÍA DEL CUENTO CUBANO CONTEMPORÁNEO, Ambrosio Fornet

AF-2   CUENTOS DE LA REVOLUCIÓN CUBANA, Ambrosio Fornet

AM   NUEVOS CUENTISTAS CUBANOS, Antón Arrufat and Fausto Masó

BS   NARRATIVA DE LA JOVEN CUBA, Bernardo Subercaseaux

CB   NARRATIVA CUBANA DE LA REVOLUCIÓN, José Manuel Caballero Bonald

CM   NARRATIVA CUBANA, Eduardo Congrains Martín

DA   NUEVOS CUENTOS CUBANOS, Dora Alonso et al.

GL   NARRADORES CUBANOS CONTEMPORÁNEOS, Cristóbal Garcés Larrea

JEM   ANTOLOGÍA DEL NUEVO CUENTO CUBANO, Julio E. Miranda

JMC   WRITERS IN THE NEW CUBA, John Michael Cohen

JMO   ANTOLOGÍA DEL CUENTO CUBANO, José Miguel Oviedo

JRF   CUENTOS: ANTOLOGÍA, José Rodríguez Feo

PR   PUNTO DE PARTIDA, Germán Piniella and Raúl Rivero

RF   AQUÍ 11 CUBANOS CUENTAN, José Rodríguez Feo

RLL   CUENTOS CUBANOS DE LO FANTÁSTICO Y LO EXTRAORDINARIO, Rogelio Llopis

RW   CRÓNICAS DE CUBA, Rodolfo Walsh

SC   CUBAN SHORT STORIES, 1959–1966, Sylvia Carranza and María Juana Cazabon

SCC   SELECCIÓN DE CUENTOS CUBANOS

UN   "LITERATURA CUBANA '67," *Unión* 6, no. 4 (December 1967)

PREFACE

Although social scientists, historians, and journalists have published many studies on the Cuban Revolution, relatively little has been written about its literature. Considering the unique and world-wide significance of the Revolution, it is nothing short of amazing that its literature should be so neglected. A study of the prose fiction in particular provides the emotional ingredient that is indispensable for a total understanding of history. Although I could draw upon quotes from several well-known authors to support this point of view, it is perhaps more appropriate to cite the words of one of the Revolution's more interesting (albeit little known outside Cuba) novelists and short-story writers, Ezequiel Vieta (1922):

History does not move nor does it horrify the reader; it addresses itself to the mind, not to the emotions. Particularly that kind of history which, in order to be objective, adheres to a given method and uses it to arrange data objectively. But, and perhaps herein lies the need for art, the human being's vital experiences are not exclusively intellectual: they contain an intense emotional ingredient, which is complementary and at times even becomes a determining force. In other words, nothing can give us a total picture of life if it does not take into account or is not specifically based on experience. Art provides us with this emotion . . . and, therefore, it is an indispensable element for the true understanding of history. When art delights us, whether with a painting or through music, or in a novel or a short story, or in the movies—as Fidel has graphically demonstrated—it is bringing to us the emotional ingredient that, when added to the rational exposition of History, brings us closer to a live contact with reality.[1]

[1] Ezequiel Vieta, *Vivir en Candonga*, p. 151.

The three main purposes of this book are:

1. To provide additional insights for an understanding of the complexities of the Cuban Revolution.

2. To record for posterity the over two hundred volumes of novels and short stories published since January 1959 in Cuba and elsewhere that are related in varying degrees to the Revolution and thus rescue them from the oblivion to which, with few exceptions, they have been condemned by the isolation of Cuba from the United States and the rest of Latin America. The question arises as to the value of preserving a certain number of those works that by aesthetic standards hardly merit being read. The answer is that inferior works of art are often quite important in illuminating national characteristics and trends, and that their sheer number attests to the vitality of a movement. Furthermore, all novels and short stories, regardless of their quality, help recreate the social history of the period with which they deal.

3. To establish for this large corpus of material some coherent pattern.

Because of the intrinsic differences between the novel and the short story and because of the disparity in their growth in prerevolutionary Cuba, I have chosen to treat them separately and somewhat differently. Almost one-half of the book is devoted to the Cuban novel of the Revolution divided into four chronological periods: 1959–1960, 1961–1965, 1966–1970, 1971–. This classification transcends generational as well as aesthetic considerations. The fact that we are dealing with only a fifteen-year period in which at least some members of each of four distinct literary generations participate greatly diminishes the usefulness of a generational classification. Nonetheless, significant generational differences will be discussed within each of the chronological periods. Although a limited number of novelists—Alejo Carpentier, José Lezama Lima, Guillermo Cabrera Infante, and Severo Sarduy—have achieved continental and indeed world renown, an overly preferential treatment for their works would result in a distorted picture of Cuba's total novelistic production and would necessarily involve some paraphrasing of what other critics have already said about *El siglo de las luces, Paradiso, Tres tristes tigres,* and *De donde son los cantantes.* Moreover, since the vast majority of the other authors have published only two or three novels and may still continue to produce, it is somewhat premature to establish a well-defined hierarchy based on artistic values.

Whereas almost each and every one of the seventy some novels will be studied individually and will be woven into the chronological pattern, I have relied to some extent on the anthologies to determine which are the most significant of the short stories. The anthological survey will, however, be supplemented by a more detailed study of the complete volumes of the six short-story writers who have clearly surpassed their colleagues: Guillermo Cabrera Infante, Calvert Casey, Humberto Arenal, Antonio Benítez, Jesús Díaz Rodríguez, and Norberto Fuentes.

Because the narrative has been responsive to changes in government policy, the second part of the book will trace the relationship between the artist in general and the revolutionary government, with greater emphasis on what has actually happened than on the theoretical aspects. Certain parallelisms will also be established between Cuba and other revolutionary societies. This part follows rather than precedes the discussion of the Cuban novel because the chronological groupings were derived from a reading of the novels themselves and only later were the Revolution's policy changes toward the arts seen as contributing factors.

The fast-growing number of novels and short stories written by Cuban exiles provide, of course, a very different interpretation of the Revolution and merit consideration despite their overall poor quality. The fact that this book is titled "Prose Fiction of the Cuban Revolution" rather than "Cuban Prose Fiction of the Revolution" will permit me to devote part five to twenty-two novels, one volume of short stories, and one other short story written by non-Cubans about the Revolution.

Given the recent emphasis on literary theory and criticism, it is incumbent upon me to state which critical approach I intend to apply to the works under consideration. If I beg the question by proclaiming myself an eclectic, it is because no single approach to literature is equally applicable to all works. While I share with the New Critics the belief that each work of art should be analyzed intrinsically with emphasis on structural unity and other formalistic features, I accept wholeheartedly the historical and sociological critics' insistence upon relating the work of art to the society in which it is created. As far as relating the work to the author's life, the lack of adequate biographical data would make this approach fruitless. Some pertinent information will be provided at times, but I shall not systematically include the minimal facts that are readily available in the anthologies and in Lourdes Casal's sociological article.[2] Archetypal criticism may be extremely valuable in explicating certain works—those of Alejo Carpentier are prime examples—but it is of rather limited use in the interpretation of most of the Cuban narratives. Although the general notions of structuralist criticism have affected my critical attitude, they are much more appropriate for an in-depth study of one author than for a synthetic study of the works of close to 150 authors. Casting myself in the role of the literary historian, I shall attempt to focus on the basic components of each work and relate it to both the literary and political environments inside as well as outside Cuba. That I shall do so with the greatest objectivity possible goes without saying. That perfect objectivity is unattainable is also quite apparent. With this in mind, I have preferred to express my biases clearly through the epigraphs by Ernesto Sábato, Octavio Paz, and Mario Vargas Llosa.

Because of the difficulty in obtaining Cuban books in the United States and Latin America, this study would have been impossible without the splendid cooperation of the staff of the *Handbook of Latin American Studies* and the Hispanic Foundation of the Library of Congress. I am also deeply indebted to Rosa Abella, bibliographer of the University of Miami Library, to Professor Julio Sánchez of McGill University, to Professor Roberto González Echevarría of Cornell University, to Julio Ortega, to Juan Mejía Baca, and to Dorothy Graham, Jacqueline Doyle, and Marion Buzzard of the University of California, Irvine, Library for supplying bibliographical information and for helping me locate many of the works. A vote of thanks is also due to Suzanne Bolliger, Victoria Groskreutz, Lorna Rocha, Margaret Ryan,

[2] Lourdes Casal, "La novela en Cuba, 1959–1967: Una introducción," *Exilio*, Fall-Winter 1969–Spring 1970, pp. 184–217.

Olaya Gonzales, and Celia Bernal for helping in the preparation of the final manuscript, and to my wife, Cathy, for sharing the labor pains. The completion of the major part of this project during the summer of 1972 was made possible by a grant from the Humanities Institute of the University of California.

Prose Fiction of the Cuban Revolution

Part One. The Cuban Novel
of the Revolution

I. The Struggle against Tyranny: 1959–1960

The first group of novels to be published in Cuba after the triumph of the Revolution in January 1959 reflect the tremendous and almost universal enthusiasm generated by the fall of dictator Fulgencio Batista. Although differences among all those who had collaborated to defeat Batista surfaced in the early months of 1959, the so-called honeymoon, or "romantic period of the Revolution,"[1] characterized by "espontaneidad y desorientación,"[2] lasted until the spring of 1961. This spirit of

[1] Ernesto F. Betancourt, "Exporting the Revolution to Latin America," in *Revolutionary Change in Cuba*, ed. Carmelo Mesa-Lago, p. 106.

[2] José Antonio Portuondo, "Corrientes literarias en Cuba," *Cuadernos Americanos* 26, no. 4 (July–August 1967): 197.

enthusiasm, spontaneity, and rebelliousness found a cultural outlet in *Lunes de Revolución*, whose avant-garde tastes were several years ahead of the times, as far as the Cuban novel was concerned.

Of the total of seven novels published in Cuba during 1959 and 1960, the four really significant ones deal with the Revolution from a remarkably similar point of view: *El sol a plomo* (1959) by Humberto Arenal (b. 1926), *La novena estación* (1959) by José Becerra Ortega, *Bertillón 166* (1960) by José Soler Puig (b. 1916), and *Mañana es 26* (1960) by Hilda Perera Soto (b. 1926).[3] Of all the novels published after 1960, only *El perseguido* (1964) by César Leante (b. 1928) shares their characteristics, and it will also be discussed here.[4] All five novels are short, episodic, exciting accounts of the struggle to overthrow Batista, which does not preclude but overshadows any concern for long-range revolutionary goals or for national consciousness.

The concentrated action in all five of these novels occurs during Batista's last two years in office, 1957 and 1958. Only in the final chapter of *Mañana es 26* is the action extended to January 1959 to include the triumphant entry into Havana of Fidel Castro, his small son, and Camilo Cienfuegos "como un Nazareno vigilante."[5] The plots of all five novels unfold in the city: four in Havana and *Bertillón 166* in Santiago. The constant theme of the five novels is the pitiless pursuit of the revolutionary conspirators by Batista's henchmen. The mere sight of a

---

[3] The other three are *El barranco* (1959), originally published in French (*Le ravin*) in 1958 by Nivaria Tejera (b. 1930), which recounts the author's tragic memories of the Spanish Civil War; *Y se salvaba el amor* (1959) by Miguel A. Macau, a poorly written sentimental novel with the thesis that, in spite of everything, orphans can be good children; *Alma hueca* (1960), which I have been unable to locate, by Ana María Amador Martz. Excluded are also those novels that were obviously written before the Revolution and are totally unrelated to it, such as the three Carlos Enríquez (1901–1957) novels published in 1960: *La feria de Guaicanama*, *Tilín García*, and *La vuelta de Chencho*.

[4] *Ciudad rebelde* (1967) by Luis Amado Blanco is similar in theme to this first group of novels, but it is much longer (433 pages), exalts Fidel Castro much more than do the early novels, and expresses more concern about what will happen after Batista is overthrown. Several other late novels similar in theme differ from the 1959–1960 novels because of their varying degrees of literary experimentation and will be discussed in subsequent chapters.

[5] Hilda Perera Soto, *Mañana es 26*, p. 227.

police jeep terrifies both revolutionaries and innocent bystanders, while many of the characters are killed by machine-gun blasts. More than anything else, Batista is criticized for the tortures carried out in the last year of his regime. The titles of two of the novels refer directly to the police state. "La novena estación" is the police station whose captain is particularly adroit at torturing his victims. "Bertillón 166" is the code term used by the newspapers to report the deaths of revolutionary conspirators. In *El sol a plomo*, Captain Fortuna[6] and his assistants wildly beat and kick a woman schoolteacher and send electric charges through another revolutionary's body. The protagonist of *El perseguido* is shot at close range after participating in the unsuccessful 1957 plot to assassinate Batista. *Mañana es 26*, perhaps because it was written by a woman, is the only novel of this group that does not describe directly the violence of Batista's police state.

The identity of the revolutionaries as well as the urban setting seem to confirm the now generally accepted view that the Cuban Revolution was not an agrarian or a proletarian uprising. These early novels also bear witness to the existence of more than one revolutionary organization. In all five novels, the revolutionaries are young; in four, their status as university students is emphasized; in two, they belong to the upper class, while in the others they are probably from the middle class. In *Bertillón 166* and *Mañana es 26*, the conspirators belong to Fidel Castro's Twenty-sixth of July Movement, but, in *El sol a plomo*, they are simply members of a movement, possibly the Twenty-sixth of July one; in *La novena estación* and *El perseguido*, they belong to another unnamed revolutionary group. Because of the protagonists' youth, one of the subplots of *Bertillón 166* and *Mañana es 26* is the lack of understanding on the part of the heroes' parents, some of whom had actively participated in the fight against dictator Gerardo Machado in the early 1930's. Realizing that the fall of Machado did not put an end to Cuba's ills, they respond to the new revolutionary movement with a cynicism that conflicts with their children's enthusiastic idealism.

Although the one and only clear goal of the revolutionaries is to overthrow the Batista regime, three of the novels reveal a small but

---

[6] The name is an obvious allusion to Esteban Ventura, one of Batista's most notorious police officers.

growing social concern, which, however, never reaches real prominence. In *La novena estación*, the government is criticized more for its
corruption than for its lack of programs to help the poor: "Cuba is
a booty divided up among the cheap politicians. Every public official,
from the highest to the lowliest, devours our country. The legislative
branch does not work; the executive branch is autocratic; the press,
with few exceptions, is venal . . ." The masses are also blamed for their
passivity and their lack of discipline: ". . . the people, complacent and
fearful, are disorganized and undisciplined; the most ignorant sell
their votes and the most cautious dare to criticize only at a restaurant
table."[7]

Only in one brief, contrived scene does an old peasant complain to
the revolutionary fugitives of the bad conditions in the sugar-cane
fields. Communism is mentioned two or three times as constituting
less of a threat to democracy than do the usurpers of democracy.

The revolutionary atmosphere is more intense in *Bertillón 166* because it takes place in Santiago. The protagonist Carlos proclaims that
he is fighting for a new government that will guarantee freedom and
justice "for the poor, for the workers, for the peasants, for the students."[8] The United States is criticized for having placed Batista in
power back in the 1930's and for supporting him in the 1950's with
arms: "Batista, Mr. Caffery made him Batista";[9] "We'll put an end to
the interference of the Americans, who are giving arms to Batista."[10]
American economic control of Cuba is also denounced: ". . . the land
and the monopolies belonged to the Americans."[11] Although two
Communists participate to some extent in the revolutionary movement, their roles are ambiguous. Quico the tailor, a former Communist
who is afraid of his shadow, nonetheless helps Carlos after the latter
kills a soldier. Quico and his wife, in turn, are both killed by the
police. A more important character is the Negro Communist from

[7] José Becerra Ortega, *La novena estación*, p. 13.

[8] José Soler Puig, *Bertillón 166*, p. 154.

[9] Ibid., p. 162. Jefferson Caffery succeeded Sumner Welles as ambassador to Cuba
in December 1933. Both men supported Batista against the leftist movement of Antonio
Guiteras and Ramón Grau San Martín.

[10] Ibid., p. 61.

[11] Ibid., p. 162.

Havana who is distrusted by the Santiago revolutionaries because of both his ideology and his color. By contrast, the revolutionaries feel quite close to the brave priest who hides them in the church and withstands interrogation from Batista's officers.

The most specific statement of revolutionary goals is to be found in *Mañana es 26*. In a dialogue with his uncle, the young revolutionary Rafael sees the need for restructuring the country's economy by instituting an agrarian reform and establishing protective tariffs. His concern for all of Spanish America and his perception of the political problem reveal more foresight about the Revolution than do the other novels: "Cuba is going to solve Spanish America's great dilemma: whether profound economic changes can be carried out through democratic institutions or whether, in order to carry out these changes, a dictatorship of the Left is inevitable."[12] Rafael's own political views are seen in his categorical affirmation that the Revolution is not communist; and "even the Communists know that."[13] When his uncle points out to him that the American press has already begun to prepare the country for another Guatemala-like intervention, Rafael affirms his faith in the American people: "*Time* magazine is not the American people, nor is the United Fruit Company the American people."[14] In addition to this discussion, the author's socioeconomic concerns are revealed in a peasant's description of his life, which, structurally speaking, is as gratuitous as the one in *La novena estación*. "Sometimes we ate, sometimes we didn't. Sometimes we had shoes, sometimes we didn't; sometimes we had medicine, sometimes we suffered without it; sometimes we managed to get a piece of meat, sometimes we didn't—and there I am plowing away, tied to the land, look at my hands! I raise my son to the age of 16—and one day they come and take him away for being a revolutionary."[15]

The fact that this peasant's appearance in a 1960 novel is so exceptional, along with the absence of lower-class characters in general, emphasizes the authors' point of view that the Cuban Revolution was not

[12] Perera Soto, *Mañana es 26*, p. 34.
[13] Ibid., p. 33.
[14] Ibid., p. 35.
[15] Ibid., p. 139.

at first primarily agrarian or proletarian. In the five novels, the urban masses are either indifferent to the Revolution, or they sympathize with Batista, or they even betray the revolutionaries. *Mañana es 26* is the only one of the five novels in which a plot involving the poor is interwoven with the main plot of the upper-class revolutionaries. The original idea of the author seems to have been to contrast the frivolous life of Doña Teresa with the miserable conditions in which her servants live. However, the author herself seems to lose control of her novel as Doña Teresa becomes a revolutionary heroine and her maids are really not mistreated. Although they come from large poor rural families, submit to examinations in the employment agencies by the wealthy ladies as though they were animals, and are considered easy prey by the men, they are not exploited by Doña Teresa. They are given their days off, they listen to the radio, Doña Teresa encourages them to attend night school, and the father of the illegitimate child is not Doña Teresa's husband but a Negro laborer who is working on a building in the neighboring lot.

The fact that the Negroes and mulattoes on the street and in the market are described as having a sinister appearance confirms the author's racist attitude,[16] in which she is not unique among the authors of the 1959–1960 novels. In *La novena estación*, the driver for Batista's secret police is a mulatto; the narrator comments that a dance hall is a place where the Chinese and the mestizos go to look for women; while police brutality is compared to that of "las tribus salvajes de Africa."[17] In *El sol a plomo*, the informer who reveals the whereabouts of the revolutionary kidnappers is a Negro. In *Bertillón 166*, the author is not expressing an opinion but merely reflecting reality when he has the Negro Communist sense the distrust of his cohorts because everyone says that "the Negroes don't start up with Batista."[18] The obvious

---

[16] This is surprising in view of José Antonio Portuondo's statement about her *Cuentos de Apolo*: "Hilda Perera Soto (1926) . . . has dealt tenderly and somewhat ironically with the themes of racial discrimination, in her delightful *Cuentos de Apolo*" (*Crítica de la época y otros ensayos*, pp. 155–156).

[17] Becerra Ortega, *La novena estación*, p. 74.

[18] Soler Puig, *Bertillón 166*, pp. 44, 126.

reason why the Negroes identified with Batista was because he himself was a mulatto.[19]

The relatively poor quality of the novels published in 1959–1960 may be explained by the author's inexperience and by the fact that they were written hurriedly during the height of the enthusiasm for the Revolution. They are all first novels that bear no resemblance whatsoever to the increasingly sophisticated Latin American novel and short story of the late 1950's. *La novena estación* is the most anachronistic of the group, bearing a strong resemblance to Argentine José Mármol's *Amalia* (1851): the struggle for democracy against a tyrannical dictator who relies on an elaborate espionage system; the upper-class heroes and their racist attitude, which reflects the author's own attitude; the convalescence of the hero in the country home of the heroine with whom he falls in love. In addition to these plot details, the two novels have in common a sentimental and melodramatic tone typical of romanticism as well as an excessive amount of moralizing on the part of the author.[20]

El sol a plomo and *El perseguido* are similar to the novels of the Mexican Revolution written during the 1930's in that action predominates over character development, only single historical episodes are involved, and suspense is not sacrificed for the sake of either moralizing or embellishing. Written and first published, and later translated, in New York, Humberto Arenal's *El sol a plomo* is a suspense-packed fictionalized version of the kidnapping of the Argentine automobile racer Juan Fangio (December 18, 1957), who, in the novel, is transformed into a Mexican boxer.[21] Although the author succeeds in cap-

[19] In Leonel López-Nussa's *Recuerdos del 36*, Batista is called "a good guy mulatto." The following opposing opinion of Batista comes from Reynaldo González's short story "Miel sobre hojuelas": "Because now what is most important is to overthrow Batista, because if we don't, that damn nigger will get in for another year" (DA, p. 287).

[20] José Becerra Ortega has not published any other novels, and I have been unable to unearth any clue at all about his identity.

[21] Humberto Arenal (b. 1926) has since distinguished himself more as a short-story writer with *La vuelta en redondo* (1962) and *El tiempo ha descendido* (1964). His second novel, *Los animales sagrados* (1967), has greater literary pretensions but is actually less successful than *El sol a plomo*.

turing the atmosphere of terror in the Havana of the late 1950's under Batista, the lack of character development reduces the novel's impact: "*El sol a plomo* could have been the novel of the clandestine struggle in the city, but its author failed in one essential point: he couldn't get to the core of the problem. When we close the book, we have somewhat the impression of having watched a fight among toy soldiers."[22] César Leante's *El perseguido* is based on the Directorio's unsuccessful attempt to assassinate Batista on March 13, 1957, but the author concentrates exclusively on the pursuit of the assailants. Although this novel may have been written earlier, the fact that it was published in 1964[23] could explain the greater probing of the protagonist's thoughts and feelings and the somewhat lesser historical immediacy than is found in *El sol a plomo*.[24]

Of this first group of novels, Soler Puig's *Bertillón 166* stands out because of its somewhat broader and more convincing presentation of the atmosphere of terror prevailing in Santiago in 1957–1958. The recipient of the first annual Casa de las Américas award for the best novel of the year, *Bertillón 166* has nevertheless certain imperfections, which may be attributed to the author's inexperience.[25] By attempting to manipulate too many characters in a relatively short volume, Soler Puig fails to create individual personalities; the priest, in spite of being the hero of the first chapter, hardly reappears; the novel is framed artificially by a deaf beggar on the steps of the cathedral, a scene reminiscent of Miguel Angel Asturias's *El Señor Presidente*, without, however, the beggar's ever cropping up again.

Although *Mañana es 26* is more ambitious structurally than the other 1959–1960 novels and is therefore somewhat closer to the main-

[22] Luis Agüero, "La novela de la Revolución," *Casa de las Américas* 4, nos. 22–23 (January–April 1964): 62.

[23] In March 1964, Marcos A. Rodríguez was tried and sentenced to death for informing on members of the Directorio who had participated in the attempted assassination of Batista. Rodríguez's relationship with some high-ranking members of the Communist party gave special importance to this trial.

[24] César Leante (b. 1928) is a literary critic who has subsequently published one other novel, *Padres e hijos* (1967).

[25] José Soler Puig (b. 1916) began his literary career relatively late but has published two other novels that reflect directly the changes in Cuban society wrought by the Revolution: *En el año de enero* (1963) and *El derrumbe* (1964).

stream of the Latin American novel, the author falls far short of justifying a socialist revolution, and she is less convincing in her portrayal of the Batista reign of terror than are Soler Puig and the others.[26]

Fidel Castro's April 1961 proclamation that the Revolution was Marxist-Leninist had a profound effect on the development of the Cuban novel. Between 1961 and 1965, with the aid of more sophisticated literary techniques, most of the novelists sought to justify this turn to the Left. Of the 1959–1960 novelists, only José Soler Puig was to participate in the new orientation.

II. Exorcism and Existentialism: 1961–1965

Whereas two novels of the 1959–1960 group have epigraphs by José Martí (*La novena estación*) and Jorge Mañach (*El sol a plomo*), Jaime Sarusky's *La búsqueda* (1961) has, significantly, an epigraph by Jean-Paul Sartre, whose visit to Cuba in March 1960 may have helped prolong existentialism as the primary literary influence for the next five years. Although traces of existentialism may be found in the stories of Lino Novás Calvo dating back to the early 1930's, it did not become a dominant tendency until the 1950's. For those writers born in the late 1920's and early 1930's, "French existentialism was widely read because it called for action and a committed literature."[27] Although this statement by Graziella Pogolotti confirms the influence of existentialism, the call to action is hardly a trait of the 1961–1965 novels, except by implication. While the 1959–1960 novels are characterized by romantic heroes who live melodramatically in a short novelistic period of less than a year, the protagonists of the second group of novels are anguish-laden individuals whose aimless prerevolution-

---

[26] Hilda Perera Soto (b. 1926) has published two volumes of short stories, *Cuentos de Adli y Luas* (1960) and *Cuentos de Apolo* (1943; 2d ed. 1960), and a second novel, *El sitio de nadie* (1972). She resides in Miami.

[27] Graziella Pogolotti, *Examen de conciencia*, p. 10.

ary lives justify the sweeping social reforms undertaken by the Revolution in the early 1960's. By placing the Revolution in historical perspective, the authors indicate a distinct awareness of the fact that by 1961 the overthrow of Batista was no longer considered the Revolution's main goal. The launching of the campaign against illiteracy and the establishment of the Committees for the Defense of the Revolution and the Schools of Revolutionary Instruction—all in the latter part of 1960—indicated that Cubans in all walks of life were being mobilized to create a new nation. Most novelists and short-story writers helped, wittingly or not, by exorcising the past. As late as 1966, Cuban critic José Rodríguez Feo was still pondering over the scarcity of works dealing with the post-1959 revolutionary changes. His partial explanation and use of the term *exorcismo* have been accepted and repeated by subsequent critics. Although he refers specifically to the short story, his words are totally applicable to the novel.

Why are there so few Cuban works that reflect in depth the changes that have occurred in Cuba since the triumph of the Revolution? I believe that one of the reasons is the fact that the majority of our most mature short-story writers are men who were born and who were formed intellectually in the prerevolutionary era. Therefore, their stories tend to reflect a world of the past, a world that they were familiar with and that they experienced directly. As a result, their historical vision has as its purpose not only to reveal the most abhorrent aspects of that past but also to arouse in us a commitment against several aspects of that Cuban reality that have endured up to the present. Only to the extent that that literature has a moral purpose can its existence be justified today. The best of that which is now being written in Cuba has as a goal not only to show us the innermost recesses of that society that we are abolishing. It also has the healthy effect—perhaps without directly proposing so—of fortifying our resistance to a return of that past. It amounts to a prelude, but a morally inevitable one, to that other literature which will focus on the violent changes produced by the Revolution and its effects on the society and on the new man that are emerging in Cuba. Many revolutionary writers have not yet touched many of the revolutionary themes that are waiting for them. But I insist that one of the reasons is that strong desire to liquidate the past, to settle accounts with a situation that still lingers in our memories like a nightmare. A large part of our literature is an exorcism of that terrible past which many of us had the ill fortune to live through.[28]

The Chilean critic Bernardo Subercaseaux, in his *Narrativa de la joven Cuba,* repeats some of Rodríguez Feo's exact words but also attributes to these writers a feeling of guilt for not having participated in the pre-1959 revolutionary struggle: ". . . *a feeling of guilt,* which manifests itself in parallel structures or narrative sequences, in a painful bourgeois past and in a revolutionary present or future conceived from without, and which is important according to the extent that it affects the conscience of the protagonist, who is usually an intellectual or a petit bourgeois of the past in the process of changing. Almost all the works of these 'interrevolutionary' writers strive to reflect a past world with which they were thoroughly familiar and to compare it simultaneously with the new world made possible by the Revolution."[29]

This same feeling of guilt had been identified more succinctly as early as March 1965 by Che Guevara: ". . . the feeling of guilt of many of our intellectuals and artists stems from their original sin: they are not authentic revolutionaries."[30]

Guevara's words were quoted by José Manuel Caballero Bonald in his 1968 anthology *Narrativa cubana de la revolución,* but he also attributed the avoidance of post-1959 themes to strict dogmatism and to a pernicious self-imposed censorship:

And, even so, the action of a tenacious and recalcitrant dogmatism—even though it was officially unmasked—provoked in many writers who were in complete agreement with government policy an attitude of cautious inhibition or a harmful self-censorship, both of which seemed to be a contradiction of a true revolutionary spirit. It is undeniable that this procedure was responsible to a great extent for the above-mentioned fact that Cuban literature, especially that produced between 1959 and 1962, systematically avoided an overall picture of the present and limited itself to sketching schematic denunciations of the bourgeois world that the Revolution had taken apart at the seams. The vague fear of exercising an honest criticism of

[28] RF, pp. 8–9.
[29] BS, p. 11.
[30] Ernesto Che Guevara, *Obra revolucionaria,* p. 636.

the immediate present was as negative as the sectarian tendency that provoked it.[31]

Although most of the 1961–1965 novels have in common the pre-revolutionary setting and the existentialist tone, they do show greater variety and more internal evolution than does the 1959–1960 group. In order to arrive at a series of common denominators, not every single one of the twenty-nine novels published during this period can be taken into account.[32] For example, César Leante's *El perseguido* (1964) has already been identified as an anachronistic novel of the first period. At the same time, Alejo Carpentier's *El siglo de las luces* (1962) and Severo Sarduy's *Gestos* (1963) anticipate the third group of novels, which corresponds to the 1966–1970 period. One other novel whose unique character defies group classification is *Birín* (1962), a romantic historical novel about the wars of Cuban independence from 1868 to 1898, by Eduardo Benet y Castellón (b. 1878).

The overriding consideration of the twenty-five remaining novels published between 1961 and 1965 was to justify the total transformation of Cuban society undertaken by Fidel Castro, not in political terms but rather in social and moral terms. Police brutality under Batista, which was the main theme of the 1959–1960 novels, is depicted in only three of the 1961–1965 novels: Edmundo Desnoes's *No hay problema* (1961), Noel Navarro's *Los días de nuestra angustia* (1962), and Raúl González de Cascorro's *Concentración pública* (1964). In the first two cases, however, the action is not limited to 1957–1958 but goes back respectively to Batista's March 1952 *golpe de estado* and Fidel Castro's attack on the Moncada Barracks of July 26, 1953, while the concerns of all three authors extend far beyond police brutality. Nineteen of the twenty-five novels under discussion take place either completely in the prerevolutionary period or in a variety of counterpoint presentations of life in Cuba before and after 1959. Although

---

[31] CB, p. 16.

[32] This number does not include Emma Armenteros's *Guamá* (1964) and Ramón Becali's *Los dioses mendigos* (1965), both listed in Rosa Abella's bibliography (*Revista Iberoamericana* 32, no. 62 [July–December 1966]: 307–318) and repeated in Lourdes Casal's annotated bibliography (*Abraxas* 1, no. 1 [Fall 1970]: 77–92), but which I have been unable to locate.

almost half of the authors to be discussed were born between 1908 and 1920, the more significant novels were written mainly by members of the generation of 1950, which has also been called the first revolutionary generation. Born between 1924 and 1937, these authors are the products of the moral degeneration of Cuba under Presidents Ramón Grau San Martín (1944–1948), Carlos Prío Socarrás (1948–1952), and Fulgencio Batista (1952–1959) and made their literary debuts in the late 1950's. Although Batista's 1952 *golpe de estado* was one of the key historical events in the formation of this generation, most of these contemporaries of Fidel Castro (b. 1926) did not participate actively in the struggle to overthrow Batista, either in the Sierra Maestra or in Havana, and many of them lived for several years in the United States.[33]

The Pre-1959 Existentialist Hero

The mainstream of the 1961–1965 novels is initiated by five works whose pre-1959 urban settings and existentialist heroes not only symbolize the unhealthy state of Cuban society but also bring them closer to those Latin American contemporaries headed by Uruguayan Juan Carlos Onetti who had established existentialism as one of the dominant trends in the prose fiction of the 1950's. In fact, two of these novels, *Pequeñas maniobras* (1963) by Virgilio Piñera (b. 1912) and *El sol ese enemigo* (1962) by José Lorenzo Fuentes (b. 1928), were actually completed by 1957. The preeminence of existentialism in Cuba in the late 1950's is corroborated by an analysis of the first post-1959 short-story anthology, *Nuevos cuentistas cubanos* (1961),[34] all of whose selections were written between 1954 and 1959. The influence of prevailing literary currents is further demonstrated by the fact that, in at least three of the five novels, the anguish-laden protagonist is less representative of the typical Cuban than he is of mankind in general in a bourgeois society.

[33] Lisandro Otero (b. 1932) seems to have been the outstanding exception. He "returned from Paris in 1956 and fought with the revolutionaries for three years" (Roberta Salper, "Literature and Revolution in Cuba," *Monthly Review*, October 1970, p. 23). Manuel Granados (b. 1931) was a member of the Columna 9 "Antonio Guiteras" del Tercer Frente Oriental.

[34] Antón Arrufat and Fausto Masó, *Nuevos cuentistas cubanos*.

Sartre's epigraph in *La búsqueda* (1961) by Jaime Sarusky (b. 1931), "Once upon a time there was a poor devil who was born into the wrong world by mistake," is applicable to the protagonists and other characters in each of the five novels. Regardless of their backgrounds, they are all alienated from society. Misunderstood by relatives and friends because of their introspective personalities, they refuse to allow themselves to get involved with either people or causes. They are extremely sensitive human beings who prefer to live alone so that no one will criticize their inaction and lack of goals. Each one of the five protagonists, however, is created by the author in a slightly different way.

Anselmo in Sarusky's *La búsqueda* is the most tragic of the characters in spite of being the least existentialist. Although he is every bit as lonely and nonaggressive as the others, his anguish stems from his inability to attain a goal. The fact that he even has a goal may be explained by his lower-class origins, a relatively unique phenomenon among existentialist heroes. A mulatto flutist in a dance band, his mother was a prostitute, and his ambition, or *búsqueda*, is to move up in the world by playing in a symphony orchestra. His failure is due both to his own inability to communicate with his fellow man and to the imperfections of Cuban society. When his friend Fico arranges interviews for him with a local politician and an American businessman, Anselmo fails to keep the appointments because he does not understand: "What did politics have to do with music?"[35] Anselmo's fiancée admires him for his sensitivity but finally tires of his lack of drive and leaves him. Her success as a secretary due to her catering to the boss's whims contrasts poignantly with her father's previous revolutionary activities against President Machado. Anselmo completes his isolation by going insane and fleeing when his roommate and only friend buys him a new flute. His anguish is reflected in the setting of the novel in the Havana of the late 1940's with emphasis on prostitutes, dope peddlers, corrupt police officers, American businessmen, and mean, selfish people in general. The author's rather strange intention of having a dance-band flutist symbolize all prerevolutionary

[35] Jaime Sarusky, *La búsqueda*, p. 67.

artists is borne out by the suicide of a poet, who has been unable to complete his essay "Cuba or the Truth about the Lack of Literary Tradition in the Largest Island of the Greater Antilles."[36] Luis Agüero succinctly summarizes the novel as "the story of the artist in a world that refuses to accept him."[37]

In contrast to Anselmo's *búsqueda*, Sebastián, the protagonist of Virgilio Piñera's *Pequeñas maniobras*, is determined *not* to succeed. Like Anselmo, he feels totally alienated from all human beings whether they be his parents, employers, fellow workers, neighbors, mistress-fiancée, or even those victims of society with whom he sympathizes, like the old dying janitor or some of the grotesque types he photographs in the street. However, whereas Anselmo fails in his quest, Sebastián eventually attains his goal of total isolation as a watchman and assistant for a group of spiritualists whose beliefs remove them from the problems of reality. Sebastián's "success" is reinforced by the untimely deaths of three dynamic, ambitious, and "successful" (in terms of a materialistic society) men. Written in 1956–1957, *Pequeñas maniobras* is the most refreshing of the existentialist novels within the 1961–1965 group, even though it is apparently less related to the Revolution. Piñera's professional virtuosity and his tempering the existentialist formula with a variety of techniques separate this novel from its contemporaries.[38] The picaresque job changes—from teacher to servant, to encyclopedia salesman, to street photographer, to spiritualist-watchman—help break the existentialist monotony. A few scenes of the absurd and conversations with the reader about the creative process also tend to inject some humor into the usually grim, lonely, and monotonous world of the existentialist hero with his tradi-

[36] Ibid., p. 58.

[37] Agüero, "La novela de la Revolución," p. 63.

[38] Even Rogelio Llopis, who criticizes the mixture of absurdist and existentialist elements, recognizes Piñera's skill in creating a complex Cuban society with an apparently effortless style: "The Cubanness of *Pequeñas maniobras* is not achieved through conventional techniques; it comes out effortlessly from the complex world that the author brings to us with an easy style that reveals a rare matureness in the handling of our peculiar brand of Spanish" (*Casa de las Américas* 5, no. 24 [January–April 1964]: 107).

tional symbols of cats, flies, and nausea. Although the novel is obviously set in the Havana of the 1930's and 1940's, local references are deemphasized in keeping with both the existentialist and the absurdist universal view of mankind.

The almost complete elimination of references to Cuba and a similar combination of existentialism and absurdism characterize *Después de la Z* (1964) by Mariano Rodríguez Herrera (b. 1935).[39] In an almost biblical, balletlike version of modern man's loneliness and exploitation, three sets of characters are alternated: the lonely drunkard and the mulatto *pícaro*, the misanthropic beggar, and the distraught widower who abandons his two sons to a sadistic plantation owner. No specific Cuban places or personalities are ever mentioned. The country is referred to only once, as a piece of land "surrounded by water on all sides."[40] The only other possible allusions to Cuba are the use of the word *guajiros*,[41] and the presence of "a Galician storekeeper"[42] and "the Chinese restaurant owner."[43] On the other hand, the author portrays the anguish of man in general by describing him as "an animal pursued . . . throughout the centuries."[44] Although *Después de la Z* shares with Piñera's *Pequeñas maniobras* the existentialist and absurdist tones, it reveals greater compassion for the poor and more social protest. God, religion, the wealthy landowner, and the rich in general are criticized, while the poor commit suicide, die, or are enslaved. It is also the only one of these five novels that is not completely urban.

Of the five existentialist novels with prerevolutionary urban settings, only *El sol ese enemigo* (1962) by José Lorenzo Fuentes (b. 1928) and *No hay problema* (1961) by Edmundo Desnoes (b. 1930) end

---

[39] Mariano Rodríguez Herrera's short story "Los pobres andan a pie" is included in the 1961 anthology *Nuevos cuentistas cubanos*. In 1962, he published a collection of science-fiction stories entitled *La mutación*. A native of Camagüey, Herrera migrated to the United States in the 1950's, returned to participate in the clandestine struggle against Batista, and was forced into exile. After the triumph of the Revolution, he entered the Policía Nacional Revolucionaria and worked in the "cuadro político juvenil" (Ambrosio Fornet, *En tres y dos*, p. 64).

[40] Mariano Rodríguez Herrera, *Después de la Z*, p. 62.

[41] Ibid., p. 87.

[42] Ibid., p. 31.

[43] Ibid., p. 65.

[44] Ibid., p. 97.

on optimistic notes. *El sol ese enemigo,* which is dated October–November 1957, is a first-person narration of the bitterness and anguish of a man condemned to a wheelchair as a result of a horseback-riding accident caused by a disillusioned love. This upper-class invalid lives in a Camus-like vacuum totally isolated from the rest of society. The completely unexpected optimistic ending is politically motivated: the invalid's hatred for his ex-fiancée's daughter is gradually converted into love and is identified with the impending triumph of the Revolution, to which no previous allusions had been made.

Desnoes's *No hay problema* is a much more successful blending of the existentialist hero with the revolutionary theme. Sebastián,[45] who has a Cuban father and an American mother, is a correspondent for a New York magazine in Havana. Like so many other existentialist heroes, he is an intelligent and sensitive young man who feels estranged from his parents, his friends, his mistresses, and even himself: "Nobody understands anyone."[46] There is a portrait of Sartre in Sebastián's apartment, and on the book jacket we are told that Desnoes's favorite authors are Dostoevsky, Martí, Kafka, and Baroja. The presence of Martí in this group reflects the novel's greater concern for Cuba's political reality and the final heroic stance of the protagonist. Unlike the other four existentialist novels, *No hay problema* has definite chronological limits: from Batista's March 1952 *golpe de estado* to the intensification of revolutionary activities in the Sierra Maestra in 1958. News of the attack on the Moncada Barracks led by "a lawyer with sad and feverish eyes"[47] starts the revolutionary movement, which ultimately engulfs Sebastián and some of his bourgeois friends. Sebastián is arrested, beaten, and tortured for having published two articles critical of Batista. Thoroughly intimidated, he is prevented by his fear

---

[45] The fact that this is the same name as the protagonist of Piñera's *Pequeñas maniobras* suggests a possible common source: the Christian martyr Saint Sebastian, who was condemned to death by archers, miraculously recovered, and was later beaten to death and his body thrown into a sewer. His martyrdom was described by the well-known Cuban poet Eugenio Florit (b. 1903) in "Martirio de San Sebastián," with which Piñera and Desnoes may well have been acquainted, since it was published in the collection *Doble acento* (1937), Florit's most important volume.

[46] Edmundo Desnoes, *No hay problema,* p. 139.

[47] Ibid., p. 67.

from actively joining the revolutionary movement. He leaves for Florida with his wealthy fun-loving American mistress, but, once there, he feels equally alienated by the excessively routinized, antiseptic, and sterile life of the Americans. In the short third, and final, part of the novel, Sebastián makes the heroic decision to return to Cuba even though he is undoubtedly risking more torture and death. This decision is sparked by the recognition of his friend Francisco with Fidel Castro in a *Life* magazine photograph. Francisco, the one positive character in the novel, is overwhelmingly outweighed by the protagonist and various representatives from other social classes: the son of a wealthy plantation owner, the mulatto maid who prefers prostitution over marriage to Sebastián, and the police sergeant who had been involved in the revolutionary activities against Machado in 1933. The latter's support for Batista stems from his conviction that "nobody can change Cuba . . . Cuba is a whore who needs to be set straight."[48]

Three other 1961–1965 novels with prerevolutionary urban settings are worthy of brief comment even though they are not really part of the mainstream. *El descanso* (1962) by Abelardo Piñeiro (b. 1927) is the only Cuban novel published between 1959 and 1965 in which the protagonists are clearly members of the proletariat. Written in 1958–1959, this poorly constructed novel condemns police intervention and the role of the courts in thwarting a bus drivers' strike during the Auténtico governments of Grau San Martín (1944–1948) and Prío Socarrás (1948–1952), without the exact date's being pinpointed. Working-class conditions seem to be realistically portrayed, but the author fails artistically in his Dos Passos–like attempt to intertwine the lives of too many characters.

Frutos del azote (1961), completed in 1958 by Raúl Aparicio Nogales (b. 1913) and published in Buenos Aires, goes back even further in Cuban history, but the author's epilogue, written in September 1960, is a weak attempt to relate the novel to the Revolution: ". . . in the second half of 1958, the Cuban people began to vibrate to the rhythm of Fidel Castro."[49] The main theme is the failure of the revolutionary movement of the 1930's, which led to the gangsterism of the 1940's,

---

[48] Ibid., p. 101.
[49] Raúl Aparicio Nogales, *Frutos del azote*, p. 125.

just as the Cuban War of Independence against Spain spawned the government corruption, immorality, and excessive American influence of the 1900–1930 period. This pessimistic view of Cuban history, accurate as it may be, is artistically inconsistent with the melodramatic acts of the two leading characters. Don Jobo atones for his cowardice during an 1898 battle against the Spaniards by actively joining his son Pedro in a violent strike in the 1930's, while the latter, a Latin teacher, miraculously escapes from a police ambush. As in the case of *La novena estación*, Pedro follows the example of the hero of *Amalia* by falling in love with Arelia, who helps him recover from his wounds. In spite of its weaknesses, this novel is significant for being the first Cuban novel to attempt the integration of different periods of history through the use, albeit limited, of the counterpoint technique.

Although *El caserón del Cerro*, by the well-known artist Marcelo Pogolotti (b. 1902), was written in 1940, the author's prologue is dated December 2, 1960, and it was published for the first time by the Universidad Central de Las Villas in 1961. Its critical view of high society during the Machado dictatorship links it in general terms to the above-discussed 1961–1965 novels. However, the social tableau is overshadowed by the psychological and financial problems of the upper-class heroine. The influence of Dickens in character portrayal and in the creation of mystery detracts from the novel's authenticity. Time moves too abruptly and the plot is occasionally melodramatic.

Historical Perspective and Literary Experimentation:
Sartre plus Dos Passos and Faulkner

Most of the following 1961–1965 novels either contrast the existentialist mood of pre-1959 Cuba with the post-1959 revolutionary exhilaration or trace in varying degrees the historical genesis of the Revolution. This change in perspective from the 1959–1960 novels occurred with amazing rapidity in comparison with the evolution of the Mexican novel of the Revolution. It was not until the 1940's, over twenty years after the end of the fighting, that José Revueltas, in *El luto humano* (1943), and Agustín Yáñez, in *Al filo del agua* (1947), were able to break away from the episodic accounts of the Revolution and utilize the techniques of Faulkner and Dos Passos to create more

panoramic and transcendental tableaux.[50] Of course, the major works
of these two Americans were not published until the late 1920's and
the 1930's: *The Sound and the Fury* (1929) and *As I Lay Dying*
(1930), *Manhattan Transfer* (1925) and the trilogy *U.S.A.* (1930,
1932, 1936, 1938).

In *Los muertos andan solos* (1962) by Juan Arcocha (b. 1927),[51]
the action apparently begins shortly before New Year's Day of 1959,
but, by means of a series of individual recollections, the author envelops the whole prerevolutionary epoch in a blanket of existentialism. Rosa, the nymphomaniac protagonist, surrounds herself with a
group of young people who are all "walking corpses" because of their
lack of idealism. Their lives consist of excursions to Varadero Beach,
social gossip, obsessions with the latest American fashions, and an occasional orgy. The Revolution at first hardly affects their lives, but
little by little the entire group is dissolved. In contrast to the authors
of the 1959–1960 novels, Juan Arcocha actively denounces racial prej-
udice and shows real concern for the lower classes. Scorned by the
protagonists, the poor mestizos, mulattoes, and Negroes arouse the
reader's sympathy. In a small café in Matanzas, the discussion by the
main characters of the picturesque aspects of the farmers' hovels is
made to appear ridiculous when a pregnant country girl arrives followed by her two sickly children. The tragic Judas-like Rogelio, the
son of a poor fisherman, desperately wants to be accepted into the
group of wealthy idlers, but the consequence of his class treachery is
suicide. By contrast, the novel's hero is Luis, a lawyer who succeeds
in saving himself by rejecting the nymphomaniac and embracing the
revolutionary-communist (here equated) cause. In the huge popular
rally in front of the national palace, he reacts positively to an unknown
Negro's admiring remark about Carmen, one of his Varadero friends:
"—Hey! Look a' dat little white gal! How she moves! Luis turned

[50] Mauricio Magdaleno's *El resplandor* (1937) was probably the first Mexican novel
to provide historical perspective by seeking out the colonial roots of the ruthless landowner, but technically he can hardly be called a forerunner of Revueltas and Yáñez.

[51] After a year spent in Paris as cultural attaché, Arcocha defected. His second novel,
A Candle in the Wind (1967), will be discussed in part four devoted to the antirevolutionary novel, along with his nonfiction novels, *Por cuenta propia* (1970) and *La
bala perdida* (1973).

around to the Negro and laughed together with him, sharing his joy."[52] In the epilogue, Luis indulges in another act of revolutionary comradeship by helping a half-mulatto, half-Indian soldier start an expropriated car. Feeling redeemed, he returns home where his wife, Esperanza, has begun to read communist books in order to improve her understanding of the Revolution. This idyllic ending detracts from what is otherwise a well-structured, cohesive novel with good character portrayal and a perceptive analysis of certain sectors of Cuban society.

In spite of the author's condemnation of prerevolutionary sexual immorality and his acceptance of the Revolution's communization, the novel was severely criticized by Rogelio Luis Bravet for its obscene language and its choice of characters. According to Bravet, a better revolutionary novel could have been written about the hard-working businessmen and honest professionals whose bourgeois sense of values made it difficult for them to accept communism:

> But, from the social point of view, there would be more dramatic interest in describing the conflict with the Revolution, not of the depraved bourgeois parasites, but rather of the hard-working businessmen and respected upper-class professionals who even fought against the dictatorship in one way or another and maintained "certain" principles of social justice, but who, when confronted with the real naked truth of the Revolution, fell back on their class interests and on their characteristic submission to American imperialism, betraying their country and their own people. The real live drama is there and not among the wealthy lumpen who used to organize orgies in Varadero Beach every weekend.[53]

Although the title of *Los días de nuestra angustia* (1962) by Noel Navarro (b. 1931) reflects the same Sartrian existentialism as does *Los muertos andan solos*, the use of Dos Passos's panoramic techniques gives the novel greater historical interest, but at the expense of character development. The book is divided into sixteen chronological periods that trace the history of the July Twenty-sixth Movement from the Moncada Barracks attack in 1953 to the sense of impending victory in 1958. Although most of the action takes place in Havana, this is

---

[52] Juan Arcocha, *Los muertos andan solos*, p. 90.
[53] Rogelio Luis Bravet, *Bohemia*, January 11, 1963, p. 18.

one of the few novels that relate the action of the guerrillas in the Sierra Maestra to the revolutionary goal of eliminating misery and social injustice in the rural areas. Newspaper clippings, classified ads, radio reports, official bulletins, camera-eye selections, and biographical sketches of Fidel, Che, and Camilo Cienfuegos increase the novel's historical authenticity. In spite of the emphasis on police brutality, this novel differs from those of the 1959–1960 group in its broader historical scope, its greater social concern, and its marked anti-Americanism. For example, racial discrimination in the Little Rock schools is contrasted with the pronouncements of economic prosperity by President Eisenhower, and two American tourists in Cuba are totally unaware of the revolutionary drama unfolding before their very eyes. Because of the constant references to historical figures and because of the Revolution's dynamic rhythm, the existentialist outlook on life of the novelistic protagonists is not nearly as effective as in Piñera's *Pequeñas maniobras*, Desnoes's *No hay problema*, and the other previously discussed existentialist novels. *Los días de nuestra angustia* was announced as the first volume of a trilogy, the second of which, *Los caminos de la noche* (1967), clearly falls into the 1966–1970 group.

Also the first volume of a still-incomplete trilogy,[54] *La situación* (1963) by Lisandro Otero (b. 1932) offers a much better fusion of an existentialist protagonist and Dos Passos–like technique. Awarded the 1963 Casa de las Américas first prize, *La situación* was widely praised as the best novel produced by the Revolution up to that point. The plots are well fused with the historical background, and the novel in general is solidly structured and well written.[55] The protagonist is Luis Dascal, the typical existentialist character, who senses everything that is wrong about Cuba in 1951–1952 but who feels totally incapable of remedying *la situación*. The novel opens with an interior monologue in which Dascal drinks one Scotch after another and introduces himself: "The horizon is red and I have no awareness of time. I am here in Varadero, across from this long Kawama pier and I exist. My name is Luis Dascal,

---

[54] The second volume, *En ciudad semejante*, was published in 1970.

[55] Luis Agüero, writing in 1964, calls Otero and Desnoes the only young Cuban writers who know how to structure a novel: "With Desnoes, Lisandro Otero is the other young Cuban novelist who knows how to put together a novel" ("La novela de la Revolución," p. 66).

that's ten letters, a conventional sign, a factory label to distinguish a manufactured product; it doesn't say, it doesn't pretend to say anything: Luis Dascal."[56] A university student, Luis himself succumbs to the temptation of improving his socioeconomic situation by having an affair with Cristina Sarría, wife of the wealthy sugar-plantation owner. Luis's existentialist refusal to take a firm political stand causes him to view Batista's March 1952 *golpe de estado* as an unimportant part of the totality of Cuban history in the first half of the twentieth century. "Nothing really important has happened today, thought Dascal, nothing important; nothing that might change this island flourishing in sugar cane and submerged in a sea of shit, floating toward nothingness, covered with dissipation, orgasms, and fetiches, a devotee of chance, ruined by inefficiency, filthy with quick violence . . . No one feels good for this, that, or the other thing . . . it is all the same: with a Prío for every day and a Batista for dawn and always a Machado, a Grau, a Zayas to break everything and to spend wastefully our remaining moments of life.

"Here nothing has happened."[57]

In spite of Dascal's pessimistic denial of the concept of historical progress, his allusions to Machado, Grau, and Zayas, purposely out of chronological order, serve ironically as a link to the two other sets of short alternating chapters, which are presented in clear chronological order. Printed in italics, *Oro blanco* and *Un padre de la patria* describe the history of the Sarría and Cedrón families, who represent respectively the sugar barons and the corrupt politicians from the War of Independence up to the novelistic present of 1951–1952. The chapters involving Luis Dascal are also dated exactly from August 26, 1951, through March 10, 1952. The novel's historical authenticity is strengthened in both past and present through the limited use of Dos Passos's technique of inserting newspaper headlines and dispatches as well as lines from popular songs. The entire period of Cuba's independent history up to 1952 is seen as plagued by American influence and Cuban public and private immorality and frivolity.

With less emphasis on history and greater concentration on one pro-

---

[56] Lisandro Otero, *La situación*, p. 1.
[57] Ibid., p. 280.

tagonist and one locale (Santiago) than has *La situación*, José Soler
Puig's third[58] and best novel, *El derrumbe* (1964), is a much bolder
and in some ways more successful attempt to capture the spirit of prerevolutionary Cuba.[59] Much more influenced by Faulkner than by Dos
Passos, *El derrumbe* consists primarily of a series of interior monologues and dialogues from different chronological periods with the
point of view varying from character to character. The protagonist's
drive to accumulate wealth in the 1940's and 1950's is equated with
his sexual drive, both of which lead him to corruption and immorality,
in complicity with the local military officers and politicians. In a switch
from Soler Puig's first novel, *Bertillón 166*, the clergy also comes in
for its share of criticism. In spite of the grotesqueness of his marrying
a mentally deranged adolescent for her money and his raping his own
goddaughter, Lorenzo Reyes de la Torre is sufficiently humanized so as
not to appear totally villainous. His whole world crumbles—thence
the title—with the triumph of the Revolution, and he loses his hardware store, his money, his servants, and his chauffeur. Equally devastating is the fact that his son, an aspiring poet, turns out to be a homosexual who leaves for Paris with Lorenzo's Negro business partner.

Much more obvious and, therefore, less successful attempts to contrast the revolutionary present with the past are *Concentración pública*
(1964) by Raúl González de Cascorro (b. 1922) and *Dos viajes*
(1965) by Víctor Agostini (b. 1908). Using a counterpoint technique, González de Cascorro contrasts the revolutionary exhilaration of
a huge crowd gathered in the Plaza de la Revolución to listen to Fidel
Castro with memories of the prerevolutionary era. In his choice of
characters and situations, he reveals the same panoramic goal that motivated Lisandro Otero in *La situación*. The villains are the corrupt
politicians with their mistresses and the frivolous absentee plantation
owner, while the victims are both peasants and urban workers. The
three revolutionary conspirators are equally representative: the medical

[58] For a discussion of his second novel, *En el año de enero*, see pp. 26–28.
[59] In José Antonio Portuondo's prologue to the novel, Soler Puig is singled out
as the "most outstanding representative" of the novelists of the Revolution, and *El
derrumbe* is considered clearly superior to his previous two novels (Prologue to *El
derrumbe*; reprinted in Portuondo, *Crítica de la época y otros ensayos*, pp. 197–208).

student and the Negro worker from Havana and the peasant from Oriente Province.

In Víctor Agostini's *Dos viajes*, there is no attempt at all to integrate past and present. In 1963, the protagonist volunteers as an interpreter for a group of foreigners who tour the island from Havana to Santiago with stops at new schools, factories, and Playa Girón. He himself overcomes his doubts about the Revolution as he experiences first-hand socialist comradeship with no racial or sexual discrimination. This second trip is the antithesis of his first one, twenty-five years before, to Santa Barbara, California, where the frivolity, immorality, and racism of the wealthy and arty are sharply contrasted with the misery of the Mexican *barrio*.

Post-1959 Settings: Socialist Propaganda and Remnants of Bourgeois Consciousness

Of the twenty-nine novels published between 1961 and 1965, only six take place exclusively during the post-1959 era and reflect varying degrees of identification with the Revolution. *Maestra voluntaria* (1962) by Daura Olema García (b. 1937) and Loló Soldevilla's *El farol* (1964) are clearly propagandistic with a bare minimum of novelistic conflict. Their purpose is to capture the tremendous revolutionary enthusiasm generated by the 1961 campaign to eliminate illiteracy. *Maestra voluntaria*, which was awarded the 1962 Casa de las Américas award for the best novel of the year, focuses, in documentary fashion, on the conversion to communism of a volunteer teacher. A young woman from Havana leaves her child with her mother in order to participate in the rigorous physical and mental training program. She attends indoctrination classes in which she studies, among other things, the political economy of the Soviet Union. Catholicism is replaced by faith in mankind, while the individual becomes subordinate to the group. Even the personality cult of Fidel Castro is reduced for the sake of achieving communism: "—The Revolution is in all of us, in the people, and don't forget that, although Fidel is very useful, he is not indispensable for the Revolution to forge ahead."[60]

[60] Daura Olema García, *Maestra voluntaria*, p. 102.

In *El farol*, on the other hand, published two years later in 1964, Fidel is constantly glorified. The teachers dedicate their efforts to him: "United, always united, let us march forward in this noble educational campaign: onward, comrades, literacy workers, let our song reach Fidel's ears";[61] "The clear and illuminating words of Fidel are like a sun at dawn of my Socialist Fatherland!"[62] Toward the end of the novel, a poor farmer in Oriente Province expresses his deep gratitude to both his teacher, a member of the Conrado Benítez Brigade, and to Fidel: "You can leave confident that you brought us happiness and also learning . . . How well equipped we feel to face life!"[63] "This light that dazzles me, the Heavens be thanked, I owe it to Fidel."[64] *El farol* also differs from *Maestra voluntaria* in that the emphasis is on the actual contact between the teacher and the illiterate farmer rather than on the training of the teacher.

The other four novels that deal exclusively with the post-1959 period are less doctrinaire than are *Maestra voluntaria* and *El farol*. They are concerned, in varying degrees, with the real problems of adjustment faced by different bourgeois sectors of the population. Soler Puig's *En el año de enero* (1963) is the least sympathetic to the antirevolutionaries because its action is limited to 1959, when the most outspoken opponents of the Revolution were the people who had been closely associated with the Batista regime. The plot pits five workers against the three owners of a copra factory near Santiago. While the three owners represent different gradations of the bourgeois mentality that prevents them from accepting social changes, the five workers gradually overcome their reservations as the Revolution proves that it is really on their side. Of the three factory owners, Felipe Montemayor is the most villainous. A rich landowner, he is shocked at the agrarian reform, which affects him directly. His former mistress, Niní, becomes a revolutionary convert from watching Fidel on television. Montemayor flees to Havana and takes refuge in a foreign embassy. One of

---

[61] Loló Soldevilla, *El farol*, p. 22.
[62] Ibid., p. 35.
[63] Ibid., p. 111.
[64] Ibid., p. 125.

his partners, Angel Rodríguez, is a relatively minor character who before 1959 sold supplies to the Moncada Barracks. The third partner, Capt. Alfredo Gómez, is a former Batista officer who feels secure because he left the army in 1958. In his eyes, the purpose of the Revolution was "to clean up the corruption in the government, and . . . to put an end to that gang of thieves who took control of Cuba on that tenth of March."[65] When he is recognized by a Negro revolutionary officer as the man who had beaten him in jail several years ago, Gómez's false sense of security comes to an end. His brother Guillermo was actually an officer in the July Twenty-sixth Movement, but he too turns against Fidel because of what he considers the communist measures adopted by the government. Guillermo's only ideal in fighting against Batista was to eliminate political corruption: "We tried to do away with the theft, the dirty deals, the murders, the arbitrariness . . . We fought to give the country a decent, honest, and clean government."[66] Guillermo is also offended by the government's elimination of racial discrimination: "Look what he [Fidel] has done with the question of the Negroes: he has made the whites distrustful and has made the Negroes think that Cuba belongs to them."[67]

The five workers, all of whose names begin with the letter *A*, develop their revolutionary consciousness gradually. Juan Armentero, who comes closest to being the novel's protagonist, little by little overcomes his cowardice, inspired by the example of his revolutionary son Pedrito. Anselmo allows his wife's cousin, a former Batista police officer, to hide in his home, but, with the aid of Arturo, he finally forces him to leave. Aparicio, a Negro, rejects his father, who was executed by the revolutionary government for having tortured political prisoners. The fifth worker, Arquímedes, is never given any distinguishing characteristics. The novel ends on New Year's Eve with the triumph of the workers through revolutionary solidarity as the copra factory is nationalized. In addition to its obvious didacticism, the novel is weakened by the author's inability to develop sufficiently the large number of

[65] José Soler Puig, *En el año de enero*, p. 108.
[66] Ibid.
[67] Ibid., p. 183.

novelistic threads that he attempted to interweave with the tumultuous events of 1959.

The book is actually divided chronologically, but unequally, into four trimesters. The first two are more than twice as long as the last two, when the novelistic plot is overshadowed by historical events: the defection of Air Force Comdr. Díaz Lanz and the resignation of President Urrutia in July, the disappearance of Camilo Cienfuegos in October, the appointment of Che Guevara as director of the Banco Nacional in November, and the sentencing of Hubert Matos in December.

Set in the early 1960's and published in 1965, Edmundo Desnoes's second and third novels, *El cataclismo* and *Memorias del subdesarrollo*, are more convincing portrayals of bourgeois reactions to the revolutionary changes. *El cataclismo*, the only one of Desnoes's novels that is not thoroughly autobiographical, presents the cataclysmic effects of the Revolution on two opposing segments of society. Whereas Soler Puig concentrated on the euphoric year of 1959, Desnoes deals with the more controversial period between July 1960 and April 1961. The historical allusions to the expropriation of urban property, the universal cutting of sugar cane, the guard duty of the *milicianos*, the exodus of the *gusanos*, and the Bay of Pigs invasion are much better integrated into the novel. Dr. Ricardo Castellanos supported the Revolution against Batista, but, when the hundred houses that his family owns are expropriated, he leaves for New York with his whole family except for his bored, dilettante wife. She moves into a hotel with Simón, a revolutionary bureaucrat, tries unsuccessfully to change her life style, and ultimately attempts suicide. At the other end of the social ladder, Simón's thirteen-year-old brother volunteers to teach in the literacy campaign and his father, Salvador, a stevedore, affirms that Fidel will establish socialism and put an end to foreign exploitation and illiteracy. In a third group of characters, Evelio, the unschooled *miliciano*, and Migdalia, the Castellanoses' maid, get caught up in the revolutionary fervor, marry, and face the future optimistically. The title of the novel is taken from a Fidel Castro speech, part of which constitutes the introduction to the novel: "A Revolution is a social cataclysm: it is also the overflowing masses, a Revolution that floods everything, invades everything, and is also capable of sweeping away all obstacles, everything in its path. That is a Revolution."[68]

In contrast to the contrived panoramic view of *El cataclismo*, the cataclysmic effects of the Revolution on the bourgeois are nowhere better presented than in Desnoes's *Memorias del subdesarrollo*, a first-person impressionistic account of events limited to one man, a former furniture-store owner and would-be writer. This very successful novel was republished in Argentina (1968), has been translated into English, French, Russian, Czech, and Bulgarian, and was made into a popular film in Cuba directed by Tomás Gutiérrez Alea. The English version, *Inconsolable Memories* (1967), which received significant reviews in the *New York Times*,[69] the *Nation*,[70] and the *New York Review of Books*,[71] includes elements not in the original: an expanded treatment of the missile crisis and a visit to Hemingway's former home, where Russian tourists were encountered. This additional material, which was written especially for the film version, was published in Spanish in Caballero Bonald's *Narrativa cubana de la revolución*,[72] and in the Unión Nacional de Escritores y Artistas Cubanos (UNEAC) anthology "Literatura cubana '67."[73]

The success of this novel is undoubtedly due to the great sincerity with which the antihero of the Revolution is portrayed. Although Desnoes shares the goal of most other 1961–1965 novelists of capturing the essence of prerevolutionary bourgeois society, he is more successful because, like Soler Puig in *El derrumbe*, he limits himself to the personal experiences of one man. Furthermore, these experiences are unobtrusively evoked within the framework of the revolutionary present of 1962. Like the protagonist of Desnoes's first novel, *No hay problema*, the narrator is the typical existentialist hero. His wife, relatives, and friends have left Cuba but he remains, lonely and alienated. Although he recognizes all the negative aspects of prerevolutionary bourgeois life and despises all its representatives, he cannot liberate

---

[68] Edmundo Desnoes, *El cataclismo*, p. 7.
[69] *New York Times Book Review*, June 11, 1967, pp. 4–5.
[70] *Nation*, October 16, 1967, pp. 378–380.
[71] *New York Review of Books*, May 23, 1968, pp. 37–41.
[72] CB, pp. 147–158.
[73] UN, pp. 173–177.

himself from his past and clings to such bourgeois habits as having a lower-class mistress and complaining about the shortage of consumer goods. Totally devoid of ideals, he simply exists from day to day with the usual existentialist symbols: "I feel as though I'm in the bottom of a well," "to vomit," "belches," "I crushed the cigarette butt in the bronze ashtray," and "I'm an insignificant cockroach."[74] Although the narrator writes in diary form, he does not indicate dates, because, in the words of the American popular blues song that he quotes, "[I'm] feeling tomorrow just like I feel today."[75]

In true existentialist style, the protagonist is so obsessed with his own inner world that outside reality is reduced to an apparently insignificant role. Nevertheless, Desnoes gives his novel historical significance by relating his own problems to an analysis of the Cuban national character and its possible consequences for the Revolution. Whereas Sebastián in *No hay problema* returned to Cuba in 1958 as an affirmation of revolutionary commitment, the nameless narrator of *Memorias del subdesarrollo* does not profess any faith in the Revolution and prefers to stand on the sidelines criticizing the Cuban stereotype, in his typical staccato style, rather than be disillusioned again: "All the Cuban's talent is spent in adapting to the circumstances of the moment. In appearances. People don't follow through, they settle for little. They abandon projects halfway through, they don't maintain for long the same feelings, they don't follow things through to their ultimate consequences. The Cuban can't suffer very long without bursting out into laughter. The sun, the tropics, the irresponsibility . . . can Fidel be that way? I don't think so, but . . . but I don't want to be disillusioned again. At best, I can be a witness. A spectator."[76]

By refusing to participate in the Revolution while at the same time collecting a monthly stipend from the Reforma Urbana, the narrator recognizes that he is really an enemy of the government: "I'm still not used to placing myself within the revolution,"[77] "I'm a worm."[78]

---

[74] Edmundo Desnoes, *Memorias del subdesarrollo*, pp. 17, 21, 17, 26, 92.
[75] Ibid., p. 16.
[76] Ibid., p. 39.
[77] Ibid., p. 49.
[78] Ibid., p. 51.

When he comments on a novel written by his friend Eddy, undoubtedly his own *No hay problema*, Desnoes presents the problem that has
preoccupied revolutionary Cuba throughout the past decade, the role
of the artist in a socialist revolution: "The artist, the true artist (you
know it, Eddy), will always be an enemy of the State."[79]

The same skepticism and cynicism expressed by Desnoes's antihero
also prevails in the Bohemian world of *Un cri sur le rivage* (1963) by
the French Cuban Eduardo Manet (b. 1927).[80] The time span is
specifically December 1960 until shortly after the Bay of Pigs invasion
of April 1961. The passionate love story of Gavilán and Elsa is well
integrated into a series of cocktail parties involving a variety of fun-
loving artists and intellectuals with different attitudes toward the
Revolution. Although they are reminiscent of the characters in Juan
Arcocha's *Los muertos andan solos*, the tone of the book is definitely
not existentialist. Only one minor character, Gustavo, leaves Cuba in
despair and commits suicide in Puerto Rico after writing on the wall
with his own feces: "I'm bored."[81] Some of the others prefer to continue listening to their American records of Billie Holiday and Frank
Sinatra while making snide remarks about the presence in Cuba of
Eastern European personnel and equipment and about various government policies. Homosexual Jorge Vega is critical as well as skeptical
of the Revolution's antihomosexual campaign: "I'm curious to see
how Communism is going to cope with the sexual appetites of our
compatriots. Have you noticed that, every time war is declared against

---

[79] Ibid., p. 44.

[80] Although the novel is written in French and Manet has lived in France for many
years, he has consistently been considered a Cuban by revolutionary writers. Before the
Revolution, Manet published in Havana a book of poetry and a volume of three plays.
Portuondo includes him in his list of fiction writers who emerged with the Revolution
(*Crítica de la época y otros ensayos*, p. 158), Luis Agüero mentions Manet's two
novels (*Un extraño en la viña* [*sic*] and *Al borde de la orilla*) in his brief survey of
the novel of the Revolution ("La novela de la Revolución," p. 62), and Manet's essay
on the revolutionary cinema was published in the UNEAC anthology, "Literatura
cubana '67." *Les étrangers dans la ville* (1960) portrays the life of Latin American
students and bohemians in Paris with relatively few references to Cuba. Manet's recent
absurdist play, *Las monjas*, was performed in Mexico City in late 1971 after a highly
successful run in Paris: ". . . one of the great hits of the last few theatrical seasons in
Paris" (*Revista de la Universidad de México* 26, no. 5 [January 1972]: 40–41).

[81] Eduardo Manet, *Un cri sur le rivage*, p. 197.

homosexuality, the campaign ends in two days? The number of people having important relations with the government who are arrested in the roundups must be so high that they don't dare continue."[82] Film maker Mathias ridicules censorship: "The Cinema Institute will no longer turn out scenarios that do not present positive heroes. And I wanted to make a film about a love affair between a syphilitic Greek sailor and a Cuban whore with cancer in her left breast."[83] However, this does not prevent him from accepting a position as art instructor. These antirevolutionary characters are neither praised nor condemned by Manet. They are presented as living out the last days of their bohemian existence before the Bay of Pigs invasion provokes a government crackdown on all antirevolutionary suspects. At the same time, the revolutionary patriotism aroused by the attempted foreign invasion leads Gavilán to terminate his love affair with Elsa because her brother was involved with the counterrevolutionary conspirators and her ex-husband took part in the invasion. Elsa and her brother Ricardo are portrayed as pleasure-seeking adventurers who, in spite of having contributed actively to Batista's downfall, are totally devoid of social consciousness: ". . . we wanted to kick Batista out. And I personally wasn't too sure why."[84] By contrast, Gavilán, in spite of his friends, never deviates from his revolutionary posture. As though he were born with the Revolution, nothing is told of his pre-1959 life. In December 1960, he holds a position in the Ministry of Foreign Affairs. He volunteers to cut sugar cane and he studies Konstantinov's *Les Fondements de la Philosophie marxiste.* Toward the end of the novel, he writes radio soap operas, which gives the author the opportunity to satirize socialist realism through the words of Elsa: "Listen: instead of killing Emilia and ending the story just to start another one, make a series with Emilia raped under the Batista regime; Emilia a prostitute-mother at the beginning of the Revolution; Emilia a poor farm girl in the country who becomes a factory worker in the city; then Emilia in the militia, and through Emilia you'll follow what is happening in the country, that is to say, Emilia Communist,

[82] Ibid., p. 106.
[83] Ibid., p. 50.
[84] Ibid., p. 141.

Emilia brigade commander if the Revolution continues, or Emilia wounded in battle, and then Emilia a prostitute under the American occupation . . ."[85]

The American invasion attempt does actually take place at the Bay of Pigs, and Gavilán forgets Elsa for the moment and works feverishly at the radio station sending personal letters to writers employed in radio stations all over South America. Shortly before, he sums up for Elsa the basic structural and ideological conflict of the novel: "Can we live like this in these times? Can we live only for the two of us?"[86] The obvious negative answer is spelled out when Gavilán decides once and for all to break with Elsa after finding out that she has gone to see her imprisoned ex-husband. In order to resist temptation, Gavilán volunteers for the literacy campaign, while Elsa subsequently attempts to commit suicide. The fact that the main course of the novel is periodically interrupted by brief, almost hour-by-hour accounts of Gavilán's race back to Havana in order to see Elsa before she dies does not alter the basic message that personal happiness cannot thrive in isolation from society and that, in times of national crisis, it must be sacrificed.

In spite of this revolutionary concept, *Un cri sur le rivage* has not yet been published in Cuba. The ridicule of "the austerity unleashed by the archangels of the Revolution,"[87] "the Puritans of the Party,"[88] the criticism of other aspects of the Revolution, albeit by negative anti-revolutionary characters, and the featuring of several unpuritanical love scenes suggest a certain similarity to *Memorias del subdesarrollo*. However, the air of irreverence is sufficiently stronger than in Desnoes's novel so as not to qualify for acceptance under the oft-quoted stricture "within the Revolution, everything; against the Revolution, nothing."[89]

Off the Beaten Path

Considering that one of the primary goals of the Revolution was the

[85] Ibid., p. 194.
[86] Ibid., p. 203.
[87] Ibid., p. 53.
[88] Ibid., p. 54.
[89] Fidel Castro, *Palabras a los intelectuales*, p. 11.

agrarian reform, the paucity of "novels of the land" seems amazing. Not one of the 1959–1960 novels, only five of the twenty-nine 1961–1965 novels, and only one or two of the 1966–1970 novels fall into this category. The explanation lies in the importance of existing international literary currents in determining the form and even the themes that any national literature is likely to adopt. If the Cuban Revolution of 1933 against Machado had been successful, the resultant novels might well have been primarily rural. However, by the 1960's, novels like *La vorágine, Don Segundo Sombra, Doña Bárbara, Huasipungo,* and *El mundo es ancho y ajeno* had fallen into relative disrepute in the face of the greater literary sophistication of writers like Borges, Onetti, Carpentier, and Fuentes. Therefore, those few rural novels written in Cuba during the 1960's constitute a small minority that is definitely out of the mainstream or, to use a rural image, off the beaten path.

Among the five 1961–1965 "novels of the land," there is great disparity. The best known is undoubtedly *Tierra inerme* (1961) by Dora Alonso (b. 1910). A recipient of the 1961 Casa de las Américas first-prize award, this novel is an anachronistic attempt to justify the agrarian reform—1960 was the *año de la reforma agraria*. The novel is anachronistic not because the conditions described were no longer prevalent but rather because they had already been presented more convincingly in the novels and short stories of Luis Felipe Rodríguez and Carlos Montenegro in the 1920's and early 1930's. In fact, the artistic failure of *Tierra inerme* may be attributed to the author's unsuccessful attempt to apply the Rómulo Gallegos novelistic formula to the Cuban landscape.[90] Several novelistic threads and a relatively large number of characters are interwoven, as in Gallegos's *Canaima,* but character development is weak, suspense is minimal, descriptions of nature are uninspiring, and the epic tone is missing. The names of the good *caciques*, the brothers Pablo Juan Montero and Juan Pablo Montero, recall Gallegos's penchant for pairs of similar names: the Arda-

---

[90] Rómulo Gallegos took refuge in Cuba in 1948 after being overthrown as president of Venezuela by a military coup. His novel *La brizna de paja en el viento* (1952) portrays the conflicts in Cuban society and criticizes political gangsterism in the University of Havana.

vín brothers, José Gregorio and José Francisco, in *Canaima* and Cecilio el viejo and his nephew Cecilio el joven in *Pobre Negro*.

As far as the actual portrayal of Cuban rural conditions is concerned, the author is particularly critical of Mr. Higgins, the American owner of the huge sugar plantation, and his compatriots who are constantly enlarging their holdings at the expense of the peasants. However, the only time that Mr. Higgins actually appears in the novel is when, on his way to extinguish a fire in his canefield, he fails to stop his car after running over a retarded child. The more immediate villain is the promiscuous old Spanish cattle rustler and *cacique* Pancho Capote, who rules the area in cahoots with the local military officers and politicians. The peasants work hard, are sickly and uneducated, and live in miserable huts. They are exploited by the local doctor and pharmacist, and even the prerevolutionary rural schoolteacher is criticized for her less than 100 percent devotion to her pupils. However, the effectiveness of the social criticism is greatly weakened because it is all presented through the eyes of Ernestina, the niece of the plantation owner, Clemente Muñoz. Although Muñoz's workers live in great misery, he is not held personally accountable. On the contrary, he is portrayed as a hard-working, positive character who even insists that his son look after the peasant girl whom he has made pregnant. On the other hand, the peon Andrés Pérez is represented as being lazy. Ernestina's personal problems also dilute the social protest.

A less pretentious but much more effective portrayal of prerevolutionary rural Cuba is presented by folklorist Samuel Feijóo (b. 1914) in *Juan Quinquín en Pueblo Mocho* (1964). Unlike *Tierra inerme*, the protagonist Juan Quinquín represents the poor farmer who suffers directly at the hands of the lecherous mayor, who is supported by the absentee landowner-politician and the *guardias rurales*. Those who work the land have to pay the landowner a certain percentage and have to buy supplies in the store controlled by the mayor. Their *cédulas* are periodically collected by the mayor in order to ensure the reelection of the *doctor*. If any of the poor dare protest, their homes are burned and they are beaten, hanged, or shot. If they leave the area, their families are constantly molested and they encounter hunger and unemployment wherever they go. Juan Quinquín finally becomes so exasperated at these conditions that he forms a small guerrilla band with his friends in Pueblo Mocho. After some initial successes against the army, his three best friends are killed and he is seriously wounded. Although this work seems to have all the ingredients of the typical Mexican novel of the Revolution, its Cuban flavor is unmistakable. The setting is the southern part of Las Villas Province, where Juan Quinquín, in spite of representing the oppressed poor farmers, is a bold, dashing, heroic *pícaro*, whose many occupations permit the author to temper his protest with much local color and humor. Juan Quinquín is an itinerant circus performer whose problems start when he falls in love at first sight with Teresa. He incurs the mayor's wrath by eloping with her. His hopes for achieving economic security by clearing a parcel of land and planting coffee trees are constantly threatened by the mayor. Undaunted, Juan also works cutting sugar cane, boxing, and cockfighting. The simplicity with which the characters are drawn, the lack of a complicated plot, and the straightforward unadorned style almost qualify the book for classification as children's literature. However, it is this very simple charm that makes the social protest that much more effective. Totally removed from the mainstream of the Cuban novel of the Revolution, *Juan Quinquín en Pueblo Mocho* is one of the most sincere and touching justifications of the Revolution. Although it has been made into an internationally acclaimed film, *Las aventuras de Juan Quinquín* (1967), Ernesto García Alzola is one of the very few critics, if not the only one, to grant this novel the recognition it deserves: ". . . for its language, its charm, its mood, the most Cuban novel of these nine years, perhaps the most native one of all times in Cuba linguistically and psychologically, is, in our opinion, *Juan Quinquín en Pueblo Mocho* by Feijóo."[91]

A similar formula is used by Samuel Feijóo in *Tumbaga*, also published in 1964 by the Universidad Central de Las Villas. However, whereas in *Juan Quinquín en Pueblo Mocho* the folkloric and humorous elements are gradually overshadowed by the social protest, the humorous escapades of the elephant Tumbaga predominate throughout the shorter work and prevent the criticism of the Cuban politicians and

[91] Ernesto García Alzola, "La novela cubana en el siglo XX," in *Panorama de la literatura cubana*, p. 207.

military officers, the Spanish storekeepers in Cienfuegos, and the American sugar plantation owners from assuming major proportions.

The same *costumbrista* picaresque tone of Feijóo's novels also characterizes *Tabaco* (1963) by Feijóo's contemporary Leonel López-Nussa (b. 1916). Although *Tabaco* goes back to the late 1920's and early 1930's to expose the abuses on a Pinar del Río tobacco plantation, the conditions are not that different from those presented in *Tierra inerme* and *Juan Quinquín en Pueblo Mocho*. Likewise, the revolutionary activities in Havana directed against Machado may be interpreted as the model for what was to happen twenty-five years later. The gap between city and country as well as a range of attitudes are bridged by the four Capote brothers and their exchange of letters. Adolescent Efrén's mischievous activities, including sex, plus his sympathy for the downtrodden peasants give him the leading role in the novel. In spite of his happy-go-lucky attitude, he becomes furious at the system when his friend Casimiro goes berserk and kills his whole family with his machete and then hangs himself after being dispossessed of his land by Efrén's lawyer brother Basilio. This intensification of rural violence is paralleled by the 1933 Havana strikes against Machado and the police machine-gunning of the protestors as reported in newspaper clippings and letters from oldest brother, Onelio, a revolutionary university student. Most of the latter's letters are answered by the fourth brother, Fernando, close to Efrén in age but worlds apart in everything else. Fernando is weak, sickly, religious, enamored of literature, pro-American, and somewhat effeminate. As novelistic characters, however, all four brothers are somewhat caricaturized in keeping with the author's *costumbrista* approach. For the same reason, the rural social protest is somewhat tempered, as in *Juan Quinquín en Pueblo Mocho*, by the author's desire to fill his tableau with the chief of police, the doctor, and the devout spinster. On the other hand, the countryside of *Tabaco* is far less isolated from the outside world than that in Feijóo's novel because the local color is balanced by Onelio's chronologically determining references to the Sacco-Vanzetti case, Charles Lindbergh, Babe Ruth, Sandino's guerrilla warfare against American troops in Nicaragua, and Rockefeller's opposition to the Diego Rivera mural in the RCA Building.

Almost the same time period, 1928–1933, is covered in the first part of *Primeros recuerdos* (1963), the only slightly novelized autobiography of Araceli C. de Aguililla (b. 1920), a self-taught "spontaneous, simple, popular writer."[92] Because of her own peasant background, the description of rural abuses is presented with a humorless but effective simplicity: "On a nearby plantation, property of a very rich man, they had killed a Negro because he didn't want to work; the men ran around intimidated; nobody wanted to become involved; the rural police patrolled the countryside and even the cockfights were dispersed with machetes."[93]

The balance between the countryside and Havana, which is achieved in *Tabaco* by means of letters, is more equitable in *Primeros recuerdos*. The second half of the book traces the narrator's move to Havana with her family and her experiences in business schools and in a variety of secretarial positions. Through her determination and moral fortitude, she manages to avoid falling into the common patterns of the innocent country-girl secretary's being seduced by the city-slicker boss. This first and only published volume of her memoirs ends in 1941 with her happy marriage to a divorced man. The pertinence of this work to the Revolution is made obvious when the narrator compares her own difficult situation in the Havana of the 1930's to that of the youngsters today with their educational opportunities and boundless hopes. Her vision of Havana as a "monster . . . weighing heavy on weak shoulders"[94] is very much in keeping with the revolutionary goal of decentralizing Cuba.

Although *Primeros recuerdos* is totally devoid of literary pretensions, it fits very neatly into the 1961–1965 group of novels by implicitly, and at times explicitly, contrasting pre-1959 conditions with the new revolutionary era. Whereas the 1961–1965 novels represent a broadening of the chronological and spatial vision of Cuba over the 1959–1960 works, it remained for the 1966–1970 novels to capture the totality of the Cuban nation through the use of a more up-to-date and more sophisticated artistry.

[92] Araceli C. de Aguililla, *Primeros recuerdos*, jacket flap.
[93] Ibid., p. 67.
[94] Ibid., p. 158.

III. Epos, Experimentation, and Escapism: 1966–1970

Between 1966 and 1970, the Cuban novel caught up with and joined the Latin American mainstream.[95] The highpoint of Cuban novelistic production, not only since the Revolution but also for the entire history of the island, was attained in 1967: fifteen titles in comparison with three in 1965, five in 1966, eight in 1968, and three in 1969. This relatively abrupt qualitative as well as quantitative spurt may be attributed to both domestic and international literary and political events.

In 1966, the publication of Lezama Lima's *Paradiso* and the awarding of the Casa de las Américas short-story prize to Jesús Díaz's *Los años duros* indicated a relaxation of official restraints on Cuban writers. The following statement, applicable to both the novel and the short story, was written in January 1967 by José Rodríguez Feo and clearly identifies 1966 as a major turning point in Cuban revolutionary literature.[96]

It should be pointed out that many of the most interesting themes that our narrators might treat in their works—like the abuse of power, the mistakes of some of our leaders, the dogmatism, and the other themes that our prime minister has repeatedly indicated in his speeches—are controversial because of the political problems that they touch on, and, therefore, many writers are inhibited for fear that their criticism could be interpreted as a lack of loyalty

---

[95] Of the more than thirty novels considered in the third group, only two, *El siglo de las luces* (1962) and *Gestos* (1963), were published before 1966, both outside Cuba. *Tres tristes tigres* was awarded the 1964 Seix Barral prize in Barcelona but was not published until 1967. Likewise, only four were published after 1970: Gustavo Eguren's short novel *En la cal de las paredes* (1971), Nivaria Tejera's *Sonámbulo del sol* (1972), Sarduy's *Cobra* (1972), and Carpentier's *El recurso del método* (1974), the latter three outside Cuba.

[96] Although the prologue is dated January 1966, the reference to *Los años duros* as having won the Casa de las Américas prize the previous year indicates that January 1966 is a typographical error (RF, p. 12).

to the Revolution. In this sense, several writers have exercised a self-censorship in the past because of groundless fears rather than because of objections
of our leaders.

One of the concerns of many of our writers has been to present the revolutionary reality with the greatest sincerity. This implies the realistic description of the way in which our people behave and speak. In some cases, this
has been tried through a conversational style that includes all forms of
expression. Since Cubans have a tendency to use many dirty words, these
stories have been considered offensive by certain cultural bureaucrats who
would like Cuban literature to be edifying at all times.

A false morality has on occasion prevented the publication of these "dar-
ing" stories in our literary journals. Not only the literal transcription of
popular speech but also the description of scenes involving the sexual act
have provoked the anger of certain bureaucrats who happened to be in office
at the time. When Jesús Díaz won first prize in the Casa de las Américas
contest last year, Cuban literature breathed a sigh of relief. The book is
written with a style full of dirty words and the most audacious situations. In
part, they are stories that describe the struggle against Batista, although he
also deals with the cutting of sugar cane by our volunteer workers and the
fight against the counterrevolutionary insurgents and the CIA infiltrators.
Díaz is a revolutionary, a professor of Marxism at the University of Havana.
He certainly could not be accused of writing pornographic literature or of
trying to pervert the masses. One of the members of the selection committee
that gave the award to his book, Los años duros, points out that "the exemplary way in which he deals with some themes opens up new perspectives for
the young Cuban prose-fiction writers." Jesús Díaz's case is encouraging because with his work it is now possible to focus seriously and bravely on
themes that, until very recently, our writers had avoided for fear of being
considered immoral.

For example, Edmundo Desnoes, in "Aquí me pongo," starts to discuss
problems, such as the participation of intellectuals in the tasks of the
Revolution, with a new criterion.[97]

This new freedom for the Cuban novelist reflected Cuba's assertion
of its independence from the Soviet Union. In January 1966, while
Moscow-oriented Communists throughout Latin America were disen-
gaging themselves from revolutionary guerrilla movements, Cuba was

---

[97] Ibid., pp. 11–12.

reacting against the 1965 landing of United States marines in the Dominican Republic and the escalation of the Vietnam War by founding the Organization for the Solidarity of the People of Africa, Asia, and Latin America as well as the Latin American Solidarity Organization. In late 1966, Che Guevara began his ill-fated Bolivian campaign. In June 1967, conciliatory talks were held in Glasboro, New Jersey, by Premier Kosygin and President Johnson. At the first OLAS conference in August 1967, Fidel Castro attacked the Venezuelan Communist party for its failure to cooperate with guerrilla leader Douglas Bravo. In October 1967, Che Guevara's guerrilla band in Bolivia was crushed and he was killed, at least partly because of the lack of cooperation from the Bolivian Communist party. In January 1968, Aníbal Escalante and other long-standing Cuban Communists were accused of microfactional activities and sentenced to prison. Cuba's short-lived independence from the Soviet Union came to an end in August 1968 with Fidel Castro's qualified approval of Soviet intervention in Czechoslovakia. Two months later at the UNEAC meeting in Cienfuegos, a new government policy toward the arts was formulated, which, however, did not succeed in shutting off the flow of avant-garde novels until the end of 1970.

The flourishing of the Cuban novel between 1966 and 1970, and especially between 1966 and 1968, coincided with the universal acclaim accorded to many Latin American novelists, like Julio Cortázar and Mario Vargas Llosa, who, at the time, were closely associated with the Revolution.[98] Just as 1967 was the highpoint for the Cuban novel, it was also the unprecedented highpoint for the Latin American novel: in June, Gabriel García Márquez's *Cien años de soledad* became an immediate best seller; in August, Mario Vargas Llosa's *La casa verde* was awarded the Rómulo Gallegos prize in Caracas amid an atmosphere of public enthusiasm formerly reserved for movie stars

---

[98] In a letter to Roberto Fernández Retamar, dated May 10, 1967, published in *Casa de las Américas* 8, no. 45 (November–December 1967) and republished in *Cuba por argentinos* and in *Ultimo round*, Cortázar affirms that "specific events have caused me in the past five years to renew my personal contact with Latin America, and that contact has been established through Cuba and from Cuba" (p. 201 of *Ultimo round*). Like Cortázar, Vargas Llosa was for several years an active collaborator of the Casa de las Américas.

and sports figures; in October, Miguel Angel Asturias was awarded the Nobel Prize for Literature.

The Latin American novels of the 1960's are distinguished from the majority of those of the preceding decade by their dynamic formal experimentation and their epic scope. Whereas the 1950's were dominated by the cosmopolitan philosophical short stories of Borges and Arreola and the existentialist novels of Onetti with their concentration on the anguish-laden urban dweller, the 1960's witnessed the emergence of the epic novel, which utilizes a variety of experimental devices to express a revolutionary interpretation of the geographic and historical totality of the individual nation, while at the same time creating psychologically complex characters whose experiences are patterned after universal myths: *Hijo de hombre* (1960) by Augusto Roa Bastos, *La muerte de Artemio Cruz* (1962) and *Cambio de piel* (1967) by Carlos Fuentes, *Entre héroes y tumbas* (1962) by Ernesto Sábato, *La casa verde* (1967) by Vargas Llosa, and *Cien años de soledad* (1967) by García Márquez. Paradoxically, it is probably Julio Cortázar's *Rayuela* (1963), outwardly the least nationally oriented of all these works, that has become the symbol of this revolutionary attitude, directed not only against Argentine society but also against Western society in general. The pervading absurdist sense of humor, the breakdown of the traditional genre boundary lines, and the aesthetic and metaphysical questioning of *Rayuela* reflect the world-wide crisis that manifested itself in the 1968 student revolts in France, Germany, Mexico, Japan, the United States, and so many other countries.

In addition to the intrinsic quality of the above-mentioned novels, their success has been converted into a boom by the unprecedented publicity campaign orchestrated to a great extent by Uruguayan critic Emir Rodríguez Monegal (b. 1921). It was mainly through the Paris-based journal *Mundo Nuevo*, which he directed between June 1966 and July 1968, that the works of Cubans José Lezama Lima, Guillermo Cabrera Infante, and Severo Sarduy became known to Hispanists throughout the world. Along with the universally respected Alejo Carpentier, these men constitute the core of the third group, the avant-garde novelists whose works indicate an artistic maturity and exuberance lacking in most of the earlier novels of the Revolution.

The newly found artistry and the example of their Latin American colleagues enabled several Cuban novelists to portray the Revolution with greater historical perspective than had previously been attempted. By 1966, the basic structures of the Revolution had been established, and the need to justify the transformation of Cuban life in terms of the immediate past was no longer paramount. Instead, more ambitious all-encompassing national murals were undertaken somewhat similar in intent to the Mexican novels *El luto humano* (1943) by José Revueltas, *Al filo del agua* (1947) by Agustín Yáñez, *Pedro Páramo* (1955) by Juan Rulfo, and *Cambio de piel* (1967) by Carlos Fuentes. The institutionalization of the Cuban Revolution and the greater artistic freedom also led many authors to apply the new experimental techniques both to noncontroversial subjects totally removed from the Revolution and to the already time-worn themes of the 1959–1960 and 1961–1965 novels.

Although most of the novels published between 1966 and 1970 were written by men born in the late 1920's and early 1930's, the strength of this movement is indicated by its absorption of four distinct generations, each of which is represented by its most important authors: Alejo Carpentier (b. 1904), José Lezama Lima (b. 1912), Virgilio Piñera (b. 1912), Guillermo Cabrera Infante (b. 1929), Severo Sarduy (b. 1937), and Reinaldo Arenas (b. 1943).

Linguistic Artistry and Epos

The oldest and best known of all Cuban novelists is undoubtedly Alejo Carpentier, who was born in 1904. Nurtured on the surrealism and the revolutionary politics of the 1920's, Carpentier, like his Guatemalan and Mexican contemporaries Miguel Angel Asturias (b. 1899) and Agustín Yáñez (b. 1904), made his literary debut in the early 1930's, with *¡Ecue-Yamba-O!* (1933), but did not publish his more famous works until the late 1940's and the 1950's. After spending eight years in France, Carpentier directed the radio station of the Ministry of Education in Cuba between 1939 and 1945 and then lived in Venezuela between 1945 and 1959. With the triumph of the Revolution, he returned to Cuba in June 1959 and organized the Festival del Libro Cubano. In March 1960, he was appointed assistant director of the Dirección de Cultura and, in 1961, vice-president of the Consejo Nacional de Cultura and executive director of the Editorial Nacional. He retained the latter position until 1967 when he was appointed cultural attaché in Paris.

Although Carpentier's pre-1959 novels and short stories reveal a strong predilection for the panoramic epic sweep with strong cosmopolitan overtones, the differences between *Los pasos perdidos* (1953) and *El siglo de las luces* (1962) reflect somewhat the change in the Latin American novel from the existentialist individual-urbanite-centered novel of the 1950's to the multiprotagonist national epics of the 1960's. Although *El siglo de las luces* was completed by 1958, the delay in its publication until 1962 was attributed by Carpentier to the need for additional polishing and to the excitement of the revolutionary changes that were taking place. "I carried in my suitcase a new novel, *El siglo de las luces*, which I had begun to write in Caracas in 1956 and finished two years later on the island of Barbados, but it needed some touching up, and the changes that were taking place in Cuban life and society were too engrossing to allow me to think of anything else. That's why it was not published until 1962."[99]

Ostensibly a historical novel set in the Caribbean, France, and Spain between the late 1780's and 1808, this highly artistic creation based on universal myths and archetypes and written in Carpentier's unique baroque style raises some doubts about revolutionary idealism that could well be applied to the Cuban Revolution, regardless of the author's intentions. This interpretation stems from Carpentier's penchant for erasing chronological boundaries, as seen in "Semejante a la noche" and *Los pasos perdidos*. Carpentier himself has said, "I'm obsessed with historical themes for two reasons: because for me modernity does not exist in the usual sense of the word; man is sometimes one and the same in different ages, and to place him in his past can be the same as placing him in his present."[100] In fact, in the beginning of *El siglo de las luces*, Carpentier purposely left the historical period undefined: "I, therefore, decided not to let the reader know that the story was taking place at the time of the French Revolution until at least

[99] Alejo Carpentier, *Bohemia*, July 9, 1965, p. 27.
[100] Ibid.

after the first eighty pages."[101] The atmosphere surrounding the arrival of the guillotine on the island of Guadeloupe in chapter 21 resembles that of the *paredón* executions in early 1959 and particularly the trial of Sosa Blanco in the large Havana sports stadium. Although it would be impossible to establish conclusively the relationship between the two events, the following phrases are certainly suggestive:

Soon, in order to shake off the horror that held them stupefied, many suddenly began to indulge in the merrymaking that would prolong that day which had already been converted into a holiday . . . and since the curiosity to witness the executions was kept alive in a place where everyone knew everyone else, at least by sight, if not from business dealings—one man held a grudge against another, while still another could not forget some humiliation he had suffered—the guillotine became the center of town.

But, in spite of the many novelties and amusements that were being introduced into the pastoral, cloistered life of the island, some people could see that the Terror was beginning to descend the rungs of the social ladder, and was now cutting at ground level . . .[102]

The similar "merrymaking" surrounding the 1959 Sosa Blanco trial makes a deep impression on the protagonist of Uruguayan Carlos Martínez Moreno's prorevolutionary *El paredón*: "As he drew near, he was welcomed by the hawkers, the multicolored whirling around of people selling or eating—in bleeding slices—papaya and other fruits. Small Cuban flags, July Twenty-sixth emblems, everything mixed together, was being offered in great abundance, in the midst of a great din of almost savage cries, of children's games, of music."[103] The fact that Cuba's Marxist critic José Antonio Portuondo denies any relationship between *El siglo de las luces* and the Cuban Revolution strengthens rather than weakens the suggestion.

After reading *El siglo de las luces*, we are left with a feeling of being dazzled by its stylistic richness, a pleasant dizziness that follows the contemplation of a vast historical film in which a large and effective movement of the masses jolts the protagonists and sucks them into the great central vortex only to return them to us at the end with a skeptical smile about the solidity

[101] Ibid.
[102] Alejo Carpentier, *El siglo de las luces*, 2d ed., pp. 131–132.
[103] Carlos Martínez Moreno, *El paredón*, p. 149.

and even the validity of their political ideals. We don't get to perceive the great importance of the Enlightenment or the profound consequences of the French Revolution in our lands. But the novel stands as an immense mural that portrays what those historical events meant for a certain sector of the native bourgeoisie.

As far as the Cuban Revolution is concerned, *El siglo de las luces* has only a simple chronological coincidence: they both developed together, without any causal relationship at all between them.[104]

The absence of any other points of contact between this novel and the Cuban Revolution, as well as the large number of published critical studies, obviates the necessity for any further discussion.[105]

Since at least 1963, Carpentier has been working on a trilogy, which when completed may well become known as *the* novel of the Cuban Revolution.[106] However, despite Klaus Müller-Bergh's report in 1967 that Carpentier had just finished the first volume, to be called *El año 59*,[107] thus far only three chapters have appeared in print. The first two, entitled "El año 59"[108] and "Los convidados de plata," [109] were published in Cuba in 1964 and 1965 respectively. In February 1970, the Mexican publishing house Siglo XXI advertised in *Siempre* the forthcoming publication of *El año 59*, but in a letter dated March 9, 1970, the Departamento de Promoción y Ventas indicated that "it would not be published for at least another year." On June 30, 1970,

104 Prologue to *El derrumbe* by Soler Puig, p. vi, and reproduced in Portuondo, *Crítica de la época y otros ensayos*, pp. 198–199. Salvador Bueno is equally unconvincing when he asks if Carpentier is not asking, "Don't revolutions progress through the mistakes of the revolutionaries? Don't revolutions fail when they revive old-line dogmatism and extremism? Don't revolutions fail when they no longer represent the desire for constant improvement that provided them with their initial impulse?" ("Alejo Carpentier y su concepto de la historia," in *El ensayo y la crítica literaria en Iberoamérica*, p. 261).

105 See Helmy Giacomán, ed., *Homenaje a Alejo Carpentier*, and Eugene R. Skinner, "Archetypal Patterns in Four Novels of Alejo Carpentier."

106 Interview between Alejo Carpentier and Luis Suárez in *Siempre*, November 20, 1963.

107 Klaus Müller-Bergh, "Alejo Carpentier: Autor y obra en su época," *Revista Iberoamericana* 33, no. 63 (January–July 1967): 23.

108 Alejo Carpentier, "El año 59," *Casa de las Américas* 4, no. 26 (October–November 1964): 45–50.

109 Alejo Carpentier, "Los convidados de plata," *Bohemia*, July 9, 1965, pp. 28–32.

Orfila Reynal indicated in a telephone conversation that he had no idea when Carpentier would submit the manuscript for publication. In June 1972, the Editorial Sandino of Montevideo published a 66-page volume entitled *Los convidados de plata*, which consists of the above-mentioned chapters preceded by a third one. In an interview with Silvia Lemus in Paris, reprinted in the July 25, 1973, issue of *Siempre*, Carpentier announced the fall publication of two novels, *Concierto barroco* and *El recurso del método*, and the mid-1974 publication of his longest novel, a 650-page epic work, which will apparently incorporate the three already published revolutionary chapters into a broader historical framework: from the Spanish Civil War to the Bay of Pigs invasion. Carpentier's optimism about the completion of this volume, however, must be tempered by his admission that roughly one-half of the book remains to be written.

—The theme of the third book on which I've been working for some time —a few parts, some individual chapters have already been published in Venezuelan magazines, in one in Montevideo, in the Cuban journal *Casa de las Américas*, etc.—is a novel that has already over three hundred pages written. We might say that the chronological setting of the novel comprises the following: it starts in an environment that has not been touched by the contemporary novel and that I consider to be of capital importance for our continent: the activities of the Latin Americans in the international brigades in which men like Pablo de la Torriente, some poets, some artists, and others fought; Mexican, Cuban, and Latin American friends of mine, and an atmosphere with which I was well acquainted and wanted to portray. The action starts there and ends with one of the most important events in the history of America, the victory at the Bay of Pigs. Because the Bay of Pigs marks a milestone, a key date in the history of America. Different characters appear: Hemingway is seen from a distance; profiles of the French surrealists are seen from a distance; Brancusi the sculptor appears there, in Paris at a given time; in short, even Picasso is included. In that novel there is a mixture of real and imaginary characters. The action runs, as I have indicated, from the Spanish War and the activities of the International and the Lincoln brigades up to the victory of the Cuban revolutionary forces against the Bay of Pigs invaders. That is to say, in a certain way, it ends with an epic chapter within a novel that aims to be an epic novel, a collective novel, of groups, of many characters, which is something of an innovation for me, since up to now in my novels I've always concentrated the action on two, three, or four main characters. Here they are masses on the march, armies on the march, groups on the march, they are collective struggles. On this, I've been working a long time. (Pp. 45–46)

El recurso del método was actually published in April 1974, but a June 26, 1974, letter from Siglo XXI indicates that Carpentier has not yet submitted the completed manuscript of his novel on the Cuban Revolution "nor is there any certainty that he will do so."

On the basis of the three published chapters and Carpentier's own remarks, this trilogy of the Revolution will have the same epic sweep as *El reino de este mundo* and *El siglo de las luces* and will apply basic archetypal myths to the gestation, birth, and growth of the Revolution. The style will continue to be Carpentier's plush woven tapestry replete with enumerations, appeals to all the senses, and a moderate use of the combined first-, second-, and third-person narrative point of view. Because of Carpentier's unique importance among Cuban novelists, an analysis of these chapters seems appropriate in spite of the uncertainty over the ultimate publication of the whole novel.

The two protagonists of "El año 59" are the city of Caracas and an anonymous Cuban exile who is waiting at the airport "huddled like a fetus at the foot of the wall" for the next flight to Havana.[110] The fact that he is referred to three times as *el ovillado* emphasizes his fetal position and identifies him as the symbol of the rebirth of the Cuban people. This rebirth is given cosmic dimensions by its interplay with the awakening of the city of Caracas at dawn on January 1, 1959, and the architectural recapitulation of its history from the "decadent" aluminum and glass skyscrapers back through the colonial churches to the prehistoric "Gran Arbol Genésico."[111] The vehicle for penetrating back through the geological layers of the earth to this nonbiblical Garden of Eden, "without stories of Serpents, or Apples,"[112] is the discovery of petroleum deposits, which are compared gratuitously to those of Ploesti and Baku. The scandalous prosperity caused by the discovery of petroleum has led to the decadence of Caracas, which, in future

---

[110] Carpentier, "El año 59," p. 47.
[111] Ibid., p. 48.
[112] Ibid.

chapters, will undoubtedly be contrasted with the vigorous rebirth of Cuba.

The musical accompaniment for the awakening of Caracas is supplied by a variety of insects, which are replaced later in the day by a variety of in-coming international flights with their respective hostesses. The references to KLM, Air France, Pan American, and others provide Carpentier the opportunity to expand the book's horizon beyond Latin America. Ironically, he also uses the flights to reduce the city of Caracas to the size of an architectural model and then proceeds to convert it into a toy world in the best tradition of magic realism. By referring to the toys as coming from Nuremburg, Carpentier evokes memories of nazism, which reinforces his vision of the world as a single unit without geographical or historical boundaries. The chapter ends with a return to historical reality. As dawn approaches on January 2, the Cuban *ovillado* is awakened and told that a plane will leave for Cuba within a half-hour and that they will arrive in time to see Fidel enter Havana.

In contrast to "El año 59," which represents the birth of the new revolutionary Cuba, "Los convidados de plata" represents the death of the old Cuba or, at least, of its most aristocratic sector. The protagonist, once again anonymous, is a revolutionary soldier who arrives in Havana in early January after having taken part in the battle of Santa Clara.[113] He returns to the home of his extremely wealthy and frigid spinster aunt only to find that his family has fled to Miami leaving behind their eleven servants. In contrast to the dynamic nature of "El año 59," "Los convidados de plata" is a static still-life description of the objects and the objectified human beings in the mansion. The period furniture, the paintings, and the sculptures transport the protagonist and the reader into the unreal world of art, which is extended to include the dancer Carmen Amaya and the theatrical troupe of Louis Jouvet. The protagonist transforms himself into a literary character at the begin-

---

[113] "My next novel, *El año* 59, inspired by the Cuban Revolution, will be, moreover, a novel without characters. Individual studies are no longer possible. The word has become a means of exploring certain groups, and a link between the particular and the universal" (Claude Fell, "Rencontre avec Alejo Carpentier," *Les Langues Modernes* 59, no. 3 [May–June 1965]:105).

ning of the chapter by commenting on the classical return of so many Italian and central European novels. He recalls that his brother used to say that the laundress's assistant, Carmita Regulez, had the name of a Juan Valera character. The literary process is also quite evident in the varied use of first-, second-, and third-person points of view.

The eleven servants provide Carpentier with the material to indulge in his favorite pastime of enriching his tapestry with international threads from different chronological periods. The Japanese gardener reads Nietzsche; the Spanish housekeeper's great-grandmother used to tell Queen Isabel II's fortune; the negress Mercedes's grandparents came from a continent called Guinea; the French chef speaks in French about the family's fear of Monsieur Fidel Castro and recalls the great revolution of Robespierre, Danton, and Marat. The presence of the French Revolution is further strengthened by the protagonist's discovery among his aunt's bric-a-brac of a woodshaving from the guillotine upon which Marie Antoinette was decapitated. The ultimate escape from reality is symbolized by the protagonist's shaving his beard (which makes him feel like Wells's "Invisible Man"), bathing, dressing with collar and tie, and sitting down to dinner alone at the table set for his whole family.

The third chapter of *El año 59* to be published is designated as chapter 1 in the slim volume *Los convidados de plata*. Its three long paragraphs and nineteen pages are similar stylistically to the previously discussed chapters, but its artistic creativity is substantially below that of the others. Without the characteristic touches of magic realism, chapter 1 focuses on the revolutionaries, "hombres de otra raza," in contrast with all the vestiges of prerevolutionary life in Havana.[114] The date is February 1959 and the narrator, undoubtedly an upper-class intellectual, realizes that although life continues as before—"The advocates continued to advocate; the toy stores continued to toy around with their toys; the Jaguar dealers continued to jaguarize; the merchants of Cuban souvenirs continued to cubansouvenir; the croupiers continued to roulette the roulette wheels installed in the fancy hotels, and the whores continued to whore"[115]—the presence of the old-fashioned

114 Alejo Carpentier, *Los convidados de plata*, pp. 10, 24.
115 Ibid., pp. 8–9.

clock with its Roman numerals and its grotesque figures marking the hours with their little hammers indicates that sweeping changes are imminent. Industrialists announce their support for agrarian reform and even Shell supports the Revolution, but alarm is beginning to spread among the automobile dealers: ". . . the fiaters of Fiat, the cadillackers of Cadillac, the chevroleters, the mercedesbenzers, the lincolnmercuriers."[116] Racial discrimination has been officially terminated by the Revolution but the Negroes are still timid about exercising their new rights. The dramatic framework for these observations is the customary sexual encounter between the narrator and his wealthy *novia*. However, even sex is no longer quite the same, as she wonders whether her father's collection of Spanish paintings will be nationalized and he tries to reassure her that the changes will not be too drastic. This wishful thinking is belied by the contrast that Carpentier stresses between the old and the new "races" as symbolized by "those who are lying down"[117] (the narrator and his *novia*) and the revolutionaries who are constantly on the go: "And they walked, they walked."[118]

Each of these three published chapters of *El año 59* is an artistic unit in itself, and, even if the complete first volume and trilogy are never published, they may be considered as significant contributions to the literature of the Revolution. The future publication of the entire work will reveal to what extent a superior artist is able to create a literary epic in the midst of a constantly changing political reality. In an interview published on February 2, 1969, in *Verde Olivo*, Carpentier himself recognized the opportunity as well as the difficulty: "There is, here, an *epos*, an epic element, which is certainly difficult to deal with because of its newness and because of the presence of real characters, but thrilling because of the magnitude of its context and its repercussions."

Although José Lezama Lima (b. 1912) shares with Carpentier his aestheticism, his lack of political commitment is partially attributable to his being eight years younger. Whereas Carpentier is basically a product of the 1920's, a revolutionary in both art and politics, and

[116] Ibid., pp. 20–21.
[117] Ibid., pp. 10, 16.
[118] Ibid., pp. 14 and 10, 12, 24.

participated actively in the struggle against Gerardo Machado, Lezama
Lima's generation turned completely away from politics when the
toppling of Machado in 1933 led only to the emergence of another
dictator, Fulgencio Batista, with strong American support. Lezama,
unlike Carpentier, remained in Cuba and rose to fame as the leader of
the esoteric poetry movement known as *transcendentalismo*, whose
journal *Orígenes* he directed from 1944 to 1956. Although he had
written some short stories, *Paradiso* (1966) was his first novel and
rapidly became an international success, due in great part to the very
favorable comments and analyses of Julio Cortázar,[119] Mario Vargas
Llosa,[120] and Emir Rodríguez Monegal.[121]

Undoubtedly one of the most unique novels in all Latin America,
Paradiso fits comfortably into the 1966–1970 grouping because of its
panoramic scope as well as its experimentation. The first seven chapters
are devoted to the childhood and adolescence of the protagonist, José
Cemí, who by his name, his various relatives, his date of birth, and his
social surroundings symbolizes prerevolutionary upper-class Cuban society. Whereas the name "José" indicates his Spanish heritage, "Cemí"
(although supposedly a Basque name) is the name of a Taíno Indian
god.[122] Since José Cemí was born around 1904, his childhood parallels
Cuba's early years of political independence.[123] The strong ties to the
United States are indicated by the fact that his father, a Cuban colonel,
moves to Pensacola, Florida, in 1917 for advanced training after

[119] Julio Cortázar, *La vuelta al día en ochenta mundos*, pp. 135–155; reprinted in
"Para llegar a Lezama Lima," *Unión* 5, no. 4 (December 1966): 36–60.

[120] Article published in the journal of Lima's Universidad Nacional de Ingeniería,
Amaru 1 (1967), and commented on by Emir Rodríguez Monegal in *Mundo Nuevo*,
no. 12 (June 1967), p. 91, and answered by Vargas Llosa in "Sobre el *Paradiso* de
Lezama," *Mundo Nuevo*, no. 16 (October 1967), pp. 89–95.

[121] *Mundo Nuevo*, no. 24 (June 1968), contains a series of critical articles on
Lezama, including a study of *Paradiso* by Rodríguez Monegal and a brief selection of
his poems, short stories, and interviews prepared by Severo Sarduy.

[122] J. J. Arrom, "Research in Latin American Literature: The State of the Art (A
Round Table)," *Latin American Research Review* 6, no. 2 (Summer 1971): 110.

[123] In chapter 6, José Cemí's father dies of influenza in Pensacola, Florida, during
World War I. Since Pershing is mentioned, this is probably 1917–1918. José Cemí
is challenged to fight by the fourteen-year-old Thomas whose sixteen-year-old sister,
Grace, has introduced José to some sexual play on the beach. This places José Cemí's
birthdate around 1904.

eliminating banditry from the Cuban countryside. Twenty-five years earlier, one of José Cemí's maternal great-grandmothers, the daughter of a judge of the Puerto Rican *audiencia*, had emigrated to Jacksonville to spare her family the hardships and dangers of the War of Independence (1895–1898), while another maternal great-grandmother had helped the insurgents. José's maternal grandmother was from Matanzas and her father was from Seville, Spain, while José's paternal grandmother from Pinar del Río was of English descent. Colonel Cemí's grandmother, Doña Munda, who raised him, was constantly lamenting the family move from the beautiful tobacco field to the sugar-cane field. Among the servants are Negroes and Chinese; other characters are Austrian, Danish, and Jewish.

Actually the first seven of the novel's fourteen chapters seem to parody the nineteenth-century *Bildungsroman*. Chapter 1 presents the protagonist as a young child; chapter 2 describes his environment at age ten; chapter 3 goes back to the time when his mother was ten years old and describes her family; chapter 4 describes his father's family; chapter 5 brings the two families together; chapter 6 describes the wedding of José Cemí's parents and brings José up to the age of fourteen and the time of his father's death; chapter 7 completes the first half of the book with the death of José's uncle and José's being sent to a *colegio*.

From this point on, all the many interesting family characters gradually drop out of sight, and the protagonist comes to rely more on his classmates. In chapter 8 he meets Ricardo Fronesis and in chapter 9 Eugenio Foción, who remain dominant through chapter 11. In the final three chapters, the most hermetic of all, José Cemí is abandoned by his two friends and finds himself alone with several strangers on a symbolic bus. Christian symbolism becomes more overt, and José Cemí's initials transform him into a symbol for every man's loneliness. When his mysterious protector, Oppiano Licario, dies in the final chapter, José Cemí no longer has anyone to protect him and is thus ready to begin life—"we can begin."[124]

Although José Cemí is certainly the pivotal character of the novel,

---

[124] José Lezama Lima, *Paradiso*, p. 490.

there is no doubt that the real protagonist is language.[125] Just as the abstract painters concentrate on the medium to the exclusion of representation, so do Lezama and other new novelists concentrate to varying degrees on the intrinsic value of the word. Equally important as the plot, if not more so, are the variations on the themes of sex, death, food, music, and religion. Besides abundant Christian symbolism, Greek, Oriental, and Nordic mythologies form an important part of the novel's texture. Lezama's prose, like Carpentier's, is dense and sensual and is even further enriched and complicated à la Góngora by an abundant use of recondite metaphors.

Every bit as experimental and epic as Carpentier's and Lezama's works, the novels of the generation of 1950 tend to be less cosmopolitan and more Cuban and also place greater emphasis on the American cultural influence in prerevolutionary Cuba. The two Cuban novels whose broad and experimental sweep most closely resembles that of the new Latin American epic novels are *De donde son los cantantes* (1967) by Severo Sarduy (b. 1937)[126] and *Los niños se despiden* (1968) by Pablo Armando Fernández (b. 1930). Both works attempt to capture the total essence of Cuba by enveloping a variety of geographic, ethnic, and historical elements in a highly experimental structure based to a great extent on myth, fantasy, and linguistic games.

Sarduy's *De donde son los cantantes*, his second novel,[127] was published in 1967 by Joaquín Mortiz in Mexico, shortly after the publication of the French translation *Ecrit en dansant*.[128] Like Carpentier's unpublished *El año 59* and Lezama Lima's *Paradiso*, *De donde son los cantantes* is a highly original vision of the Cuban nation, based on

[125] Julio Ortega, *La contemplación y la fiesta*, p. 91.

[126] Although Sarduy was born in 1937, his precocity—he published poetry in the journal *Ciclón* in 1955–1956 and short stories in *Bohemia* and *Carteles* in 1957—places him within the generation of 1950. Lourdes Casal makes 1937 the cut-off date for what she calls the first and second revolutionary generations; Sarduy and Daura Olema García (b. 1937) are placed in the first generation while Luis Agüero (b. 1938) is placed in the second ("La novela en Cuba, 1959–1967"). Portuondo lists Agüero's birthdate as 1937 (*Crítica de la época y otros ensayos*, p. 159).

[127] His first novel, *Gestos*, will be discussed later in this same chapter.

[128] Sarduy was sent by the Cuban government to Paris with a scholarship to study art criticism in 1960; he defected and continued living in Paris. His novels have not been published in Cuba.

three of its four main racial components: Spanish, Negro, and Chinese. Sarduy recognizes the Indian as one of the four integral parts of the Cuban population in the prologue to the novel, entitled "Curriculum cubense," but the novel is divided into three, not four, parts, and hardly any other allusions are made to the Indian, because, in Sarduy's eyes, the vestiges of Indian culture have disappeared: ". . . the group is a giant four-leaf clover, or a four-headed animal facing the four cardinal points, or a Yoruba sign of the four roads: the white man with his wig and dress coat,

> the Chinese girl with her 'charades' and catlike mouth
> the Wilfredo Lamesque Negress,
> and the last one—who was the first—:
> the fraudulent, the waxlike, the
> solitary Redskin girl."[129]

Earlier in the prologue, one of the ethnic snapshots shows the narrator among the Caduveo Indians, reading Boas, with a tape recorder at his side.

Although there is no traditional plot or character development and no fixed chronology or geography, Sarduy succeeds both in tracing Cuba's roots back to medieval Spain and in capturing the frivolity and corruption of prerevolutionary Cuba. The triumphant march of Fidel Castro from Santiago to Havana in the early days of January 1959 may have provided some of the inspiration for the highly fanciful religious procession, which reverts back to the medieval processions to Santiago de Compostela in Spain with its Mohammedan, Jewish, and Christian elements.[130] Part three actually goes back as far as tenth-century Moorish Spain in order to identify the Spanish component of Cuba's cultural heritage. The search for Mortal Pérez leads the two synonymously named protagonists, Socorro and Auxilio, through a variety of geographical regions (Aragón, Castilla, Toledo, La Mancha, Ronda, and

[129] Severo Sarduy, *De donde son los cantantes*, pp. 20–21. Although *pelirroja* means redhead, I have translated it as Redskin (*piel roja*) because of Sarduy's fondness for puns and because the original (*la primera*) Indian has become the last (*la última*) of Cuba's four racial components, represented by the four-leaf clover.
[130] A probable literary antecedent of this pilgrimage is Carpentier's short story "El camino de Santiago" (1958).

Cádiz), architectural styles (Mudejar, plateresque, baroque, churrigue-resque), and literary allusions from the Cid to Don Quixote. The constant traveling of Socorro and Auxilio, alternately mendicant pilgrims and prostitutes, allows Sarduy to paint a broad tableau of Spain before and during the conquest of America, which is somewhat reminiscent of Enrique Larreta's *La gloria de Don Ramiro*. Chronological fidelity is obviously not taken seriously.

After arriving in Cádiz, the girls sail to Santiago, Cuba. The rapidity of their voyage—less than one page—as well as the encounters with sirens and tritons are part and parcel of the author's goal of transforming reality into fantasy. Their more prolonged stay as organists in the cathedral of Santiago provides Sarduy with the opportunity to comment on colonial music and art and to allude to Fray Luis de León's immortal poem "Qué descansada vida."

With the discovery of an image of Jesus in the Santiago cathedral, the search for Mortal Pérez's origins ends. The symbolic meaning of his name as a kind of everyman identifies him with Jesus. After the pilgrimage moves out of Oriente Province, stops are made along the way to Havana, during which Sarduy tries to capture the linguistic flavor of each province: "It leaves from the interior of Cuba, from Santiago, traverses the provinces and the dialect of each one from East to West. Because this question about Cuba has changed for me into a question about language: how do we speak, that is, what are we like?"[131] The influence of the American consumer society[132] and its technology is apparent from the christening of Auxilio and Socorro in Santiago as "Las Cristo's Fans,"[133] their descent into the subway station in Las Villas Province by escalator and their ascent by elevator, and ultimately the photographing of Jesus as the procession arrives in Havana: "They take more pictures of him than they would of a bottle of Coca-Cola!"[134]

---

[131] Severo Sarduy, interview in *El arte de narrar*, by Emil Rodríguez Monegal, p. 279.

[132] Without suggesting any influence, *De donde son los cantantes* reflects the same application of contemporary cultural patterns to the story of Jesus as does the rock opera *Jesus Christ Superstar* (October 1970) by Andrew Lloyd Webber and Tim Rice.

[133] Sarduy, *De donde son los cantantes*, p. 119.

[134] Ibid., p. 138.

In Havana, Jesus is "recrucified" by a blizzard, with the finishing touches administered by a rain of bullets from a number of helicopters. Sarduy has stated that the blizzard is metaphorical, just as he defines the whole novel as a "*síntesis metafórica* . . . de la cubanidad."[135] If the title of this third and final part of the novel, "La entrada de Cristo en La Habana," was intended to refer to Fidel Castro's triumphant entry into Havana in January 1959, Jesus's second death may be Sarduy's enigmatic way of expressing the demise of the Revolution due to foreign elements.

The triumphant revolutionary march of part three is preceded by the satire of the corrupt Cuban politician, the same Mortal Pérez, before and during the Batista regime. Entitled "La Dolores Rondón," part two is the story of a mulatto chanteuse from Camagüey Province. The mistress of Mortal Pérez, she accompanies him on his ascent from local councilman to senator in Havana and on his fall from grace, which leads to the cemetery. Dolores's role as the representative of the Negro component of Cuban culture is reinforced by allusions to Afro-Cuban religious rites, mention of Haitian and Jamaican immigrants, and references to American musicians Duke Ellington, Ella Fitzgerald, and Eartha Kitt. The fact that Batista is a mulatto may have induced Sarduy to make politics the subject of the part devoted to the Negroes, just as he associated religion with the Spaniards in part three, but the constancy of the corrupt politician in prerevolutionary Cuba is emphasized by the phrase "toda tragedia es repetitiva"[136] and by the chronological disarray of the nine chapters dealing with the life of Dolores Rondón. The exclusive use of the dialogue form in part two helps create an air of superficiality, which, in Sarduy's view, characterizes the bombastic politicians. Negro culture is conceived by him as being theatrical, like a dialogue or a questioning: "The second part corresponds to the Negro stratum, to the black cultures. It is a lively, very dramatic part where there are no descriptions. Its sixty pages are pure dialogue. I conceive of Negro culture as essentially a dialogue, a questioning."[137]

[135] Rodríguez Monegal, *El arte de narrar*, p. 279.
[136] Sarduy, *De donde son los cantantes*, p. 79.
[137] Rodríguez Monegal, *El arte de narrar*, p. 278.

The first part of the novel, "By the River of Rose Ashes," is based on the Chinese component of Cuban culture and introduces the basic motifs of the whole novel. Although the Chinese component is generally not considered to be of the same magnitude as the Spanish and Negro components, Sarduy defends his allotting to it an equal third of the novel:

The Chinese have been very important in Cuba because, aside from their influence in the cultural spectrum, they are at the center of the Cuban's concept of the world. This Chinese flute is at the core of Cuban music. That's one part of it; as for the other, there is the Cuban sense of chance. I should mention that, in my country, chance reached diabolical proportions, since there were between eight and ten lotteries every day . . . The "charade" or the lottery and the gambling instinct in Cuban life are Chinese. And I think that the sense of chance has been very important in the history of Cuba.[138]

The scene is a Chinese cabaret in Havana where Auxilio Chong and Socorro Si-Yuen double as dancers in the chorus line and prostitutes. The Gallego Mortal Pérez, corrupt politician in part two and religious image in part three, is the prurient and impotent general in search of exotic sexual thrills in the midst of an "orange-colored smoke."[139] In addition to sex and cabaret shows, the Chinese influence is associated with the drug traffic and the numbers game, both dependent on the complicity of the police. American influence in Cuba is symbolized by the prostitute María's leaving the Cuban general for an American sailor. Phrases in English, German, and Italian also underscore the lack of national pride in prerevolutionary Cuba.

The dialogue between the author and the increasingly hypothetical reader,[140] only one of the novel's many commentaries on the creative process, is typical of *Rayuela* and many other works of the boom. In fact, as the title indicates, *De donde son los cantantes* is really a burlesque epic of Cuba in which language is as much a protagonist as are any of the characters. "De donde son los cantantes" is a line from a popular song sung by Socorro in Santiago and echoed by other popular songs, such as "Se acabó lo que se daba" and "Parece que va a llover."

[138] Ibid., p. 277.
[139] Sarduy, *De donde son los cantantes*, p. 47.
[140] Ibid., p. 49.

Like an opera, the three parts of the novel are introduced by an over-ture entitled "Curriculum cubense," in which most of the basic themes as well as a series of leitmotifs are "heard." Among the most fre-quently recurring ones are the phallic knives and serpents, hair and feathers, disguises and multiple identities, tropical fruits and colors (orange, green, and purple), and geometrical patterns, the latter stem-ming from Sarduy's personal contacts with the authors and critics of the new French novel. Part three has its own brief overture in the form of Socorro's panoramic vision of Spain framed by the serpent and the green light: ". . . la serpiente, la claridad verde . . . una serpiente, una claridad verde."[141]

Language is also one of the principal protagonists in the more offi-cial Cuban epic, *Los niños se despiden* by the poet Pablo Armando Fer-nández. In the words of the author himself, "nothing is superior to words."[142] Although character and plot development are subordinate to language, the strong emphasis on the Ten Years War (1868–1878) as the antecedent of the Revolution is a direct reflection of the official centennial celebration and undoubtedly contributed to the novel's be-ing designated the Casa de las Américas 1968 prize winner.[143]

The title, *Los niños se despiden*, reflects the author's broad and se-rious vision of Cuba's national roots. Literally, it refers to the many youths who used to emigrate to New York before 1959 in search of personal advancement. More deeply, however, it heralds the creation of a new Cuba by the Revolution. After years of being anchored to its traditions, the new Cuba is taking leave of its parents and is ready to chart its own course. The roots of prerevolutionary Cuba are traced as far back as the biblical stories of Adam and Eve and Noah's Ark. The equally distant African roots are constantly recalled through the stories of the Negro *nana* Ianita. By a typographical trick of changing 1948

---

[141] Ibid., pp. 91–93.

[142] Pablo Armando Fernández, *Los niños se despiden*, p. 528.

[143] The following year Fernández was awarded a prize for poetry, which led to his becoming embroiled in controversy: ". . . later in 1969 the Padilla affair was appar-ently repeated in the case of Pablo Armando Fernández who also won a prize, de-livered himself of some critical remarks about the Cuban cultural scene on television, and had the prize withdrawn. (But in this case, Castro intervened and insisted on the return of the award.)" (Hugh Thomas, *Cuba*, p. 1466).

to 1498, the children turn their thoughts to the original Indian inhabitants of Cuba and to the Spanish conquistadors. Occasional references are made to the sixteenth, seventeenth, and eighteenth centuries,
but more frequently evoked are the first two wars of independence of
1868–1878 and 1895–1898. The 1933 strike against President Machado and discussions about Mella and Guiteras are also presented as
antecedents of the Revolution.

This is, however, by no means a historical novel. The book's 547
pages are divided into two unequal parts, which portray life in the imaginary town of Sabanas, Cuba, and in New York City, mainly in the
1930's and 1940's. In part one, the different child narrators listen to
the conversations of their elders, remember their earlier years, and
dream, often in the form of interior monologues. A poetic and mythical atmosphere is created by the likening of their ancestors to biblical
characters: ". . . the purpose of creating a panoramic view of history
by poetizing it, by constructing myths, by finding the poetic elements
in myth."[144] Reality in this dreamlike world is concerned with the
children's first sexual experiences and the pervading American cultural
influence. Even more than in the Argentine novel *La traición de Rita
Hayworth* (1968) by Manuel Puig, Hollywood movie stars play a
predominant role in Cuban society. One of the author's favorite techniques is the mounting of collages based on the names of actors and
actresses, popular singers, and comic-strip characters from Ava Gardner and Ella Fitzgerald to Dick Tracy and Woody Woodpecker. He is
also fond of placing these stars in positions of importance in the sugar
industry: Charles Laughton, president; Buck Rogers, vice-president;
Frederic March, purchasing agent. Interspersed among the eleven
chapters of part one are five brief sections entitled "Miscelánea,"
whose statistics and technical information about the sugar industry
contrast with the Afro-Cuban folklore in the five "Baldío" sections.

In part two, the "Miscelánea" and "Baldío" sections are replaced
by seven "Jardín" sections, whose visions of the revolutionary Garden
of Eden contrast sharply with the fifteen chapters designed to present
New York City as the proverbial den of iniquity. Through Alejandro's

144 Reynaldo González, "La palabra, el mito, el mito de la palabra," *Casa de las
Américas* 9, no. 49 (July–August 1968): 149.

letters to his friends and relatives in Cuba, and through a variety of first-, second-, and third-person narrators, the collages are complemented by sordid stories of sexual degradation. According to Alejandro, living in New York City is "to be dead."[145] The idyllic "Jardín" sections, on the other hand, are highly poetic. The first one is a "Canto a las Antillas," while, in the sixth one, the revolutionary ship sails ahead with all Cubans knowing how to read and land being distributed in fulfillment of Martí's dreams. At the end of the twenty-sixth (in deference to the July Twenty-sixth Movement) and final chapter, the novel comes to an end with the seventh "Jardín" section deifying Fidel Castro and thus forming a new revolutionary Trinity: the Luz de Yara (1868), the martyr Martí (1895), and Fidel Castro (1959): "Here he is seated on a white horse and he is called Faithful and True and he judges justly and struggles."[146]

Unlike Carpentier, Lezama Lima, Sarduy, and Fernández who weave all-encompassing epic tapestries by manipulating language artistically, the authors of the following four novels separate the epic strands (*En ciudad semejante* and *Adire y el tiempo roto*) from the linguistic ones (*Tres tristes tigres* and *Recuerdos del 36*). The change in literary fashions is clearly illustrated by the relative degrees of experimentation in the first two volumes of Lisandro Otero's trilogy. Whereas *La situación* (1963) was considered the most experimental of the new Cuban novels in the early 1960's, *En ciudad semejante* (1970), in spite of being more experimental than *La situación*, seems almost conventional in comparison with *Paradiso*, *De donde son los cantantes*, and *Los niños se despiden*.

The basic six–and–one-half–month chronological plane of *La situación* is expanded in *En ciudad semejante* to the whole seven-year Batista dictatorship. Luis Dascal, the exclusive existentialist protagonist of volume one, is joined in the second volume by two revolutionary heroes, whose experiences are narrated in the second person, in two independent series of chapters: Raúl Figueroa in "Retrato de un héroe" and Julia Salazar in "La educación revolucionaria." As the revolutionary tempo increases, it becomes apparent that the author's goal in vol-

[145] Fernández, *Los niños se despiden*, pp. 396, 409.
[146] Ibid., p. 541.

ume two is to present a dynamic panorama of as many sectors of society, both contemporary and historical, as contributed to the January 1959 triumph. Even Gabriel Cedrón, the "padre de la patria" of *La situación*, now represents deposed President Carlos Prío Socarrás and contributes money and arranges for the shipment of arms to the guerrilla rebels in the Sierra. Nonetheless, he disapproves of his daughter María del Carmen's more active participation in the guerrilla movement and sends her off to Miami in 1958. It is through María del Carmen, his *novia*, that Luis Dascal allows himself to be drawn into the revolutionary group, but without ever truly committing himself. He makes a very weak attempt to distribute leaflets, occasionally provides transportation for the revolutionaries, and is even accidentally wounded when the police break up a student rally. Although he does make some progress from the beginning of the novel, when he works in the law office of a close associate of American textile tycoon Sheridan (a fictitious version of Dayton Hedges) and seeks entertainment in the plush nightclubs and gambling casinos, Dascal seems incapable of breaking completely with his past. He becomes disillusioned with his mentor, the highly respected but sanctimonious politician Dr. Pedroso, but he does not give up his idle friends: Arsenio, the cynical aesthete, and Octavio, the dogmatic and exclusively theoretical Communist. Even at the end of the volume, when Dascal visits the dying revolutionary heroine Julia Salazar, his attitude is ambivalent and there is no indication that his dilemma will be resolved in the as yet unpublished volume three.

The misgivings of Dascal and the other more or less negative characters toward the Revolution are overshadowed by the sincere devotion of a variety of revolutionaries, whose roots are traced back to the Ten Years War (1868–1878) and, somewhat more artificially, to the discovery and conquest of Cuba by the Spaniards. The two most representative heroes are Raúl Figueroa and Julia Salazar, who "escape" from their independently designated sections in the novel to play dominant roles in the main narrative, whose fifteen individually titled chapters constitute the bulk of the novel. Raúl is the university student who promotes revolutionary activities in Havana and finally makes his way to the Sierra where he becomes a captain in the guerrilla army.

Julia is the rural woman, daughter of an administrator of one of sugar baron Sarría's *centrales*. She moves to Havana, participates in the same Twenty-sixth of July Movement as Raúl, accompanies him to the Sierra, and is mortally wounded in one of the final skirmishes. In order to convey the impression that the Revolution did not depend on the efforts of any one individual, Fidel Castro's name is rarely mentioned and Raúl and Julia share the glory with several other companions. Police torture is inflicted on the persons of Ignacio, a studious poet, and Adelino, who takes cyanide to avoid being tortured a second time. Max Schwanthaler is expelled from the Movement because of his anarchist terrorism but also dies a hero's death after leading the police cars a merry chase through the streets of Havana—one of the constants of both pre- and post-1959 Cuban prose fiction. Tito appears to represent a different revolutionary group of university students (probably the Directorio), but he collaborates with Raúl and Julia and also dies a hero's death. A lesser role is played by the equally representative Berro, a Negro bootblack, who joins the revolutionaries more to improve his personal fortunes than out of political convictions. He, too, is killed. The impact of some of the violent and heroic scenes is increased by their being fragmented and alternated with fragments of scenes involving the less committed or noncommitted characters. One of the prime examples is the chapter "Ergástula, flor, ojo de sal," in which the torture of Adelino and Ignacio is contrasted with Dascal's reading *Le rouge et le noir* (ironically the colors of the July Twenty-sixth Movement) and Dr. Pedroso's pontificating on a television interview.

The impression of Cuba's being a land beset by violence is strengthened by a series of fifteen short historical sections entitled "El nacimiento de una nación." The antecedents of the Revolution, from the death of President Carlos Manuel de Céspedes in 1874 to the flight of Batista in the early hours of New Year's Day 1959, are narrated in a variety of manners, including a poem dedicated to the generation of 1930. A point is made of recalling that it was with twelve men that Céspedes[147] began the Cuban struggle for independence and that twelve men fell at General Antonio Maceo's side after he was shot off

[147] Lisandro Otero, *En ciudad semejante*, p. 21.

his horse.[148] The number twelve hearkens back to Jesus and his disciples and links these two heroes to Fidel Castro, who was one of the supposedly twelve survivors of the "Granma" landing that made it up to the Sierra Maestra.[149] An additional poetic touch that tends to mythify Cuban heroes Céspedes, Maceo, José Martí, Antonio Guiteras, Eduardo Chibás, and Fidel Castro is achieved by totally omitting the hero's name or by withholding the key identification clue until the last lines of the section. One of the historical heroes singled out for special treatment is the Negro Jesús (his last name, Menéndez, is never mentioned), a Communist leader of the sugar workers who rose from cane cutter to member of Congress. His murder (in 1947) is felt more personally because he had been befriended by Julia Salazar, in one of the sections devoted to her revolutionary education, after having been insulted by an administrator of the Sarría *central* and beaten by his two policemen accomplices.

The relationship between the fictitious Julia Salazar and her historical predecessors is tightened in the last of the "La educación revolucionaria" sections. Mortally wounded, Julia recalls Fidel Castro's attack on the Moncada Barracks and attributes the idea of a landing in Oriente Province to José Martí. Her thoughts whirl feverishly around the theme of who began the revolutionary process. Céspedes, Maceo, Gómez, Martí, and Castro are all confused with her own martyred cousin, Ciro, and Hatuey, the Indian rebel burned at the stake by the Spanish conquerors back in the sixteenth century. Ultimately, the originator of the revolutionary violence is identified as Mabuya, the god of the hurricanes, the god of violence, who "has always acted against those who violate the sweet Island."[150]

Although the revolutionary antecedents going back to President Céspedes are consistent with the overall plan and style of the novel, the poetic Indian references appear unexpectedly and give rise to speculation that Otero let himself be influenced at this point by Pablo Armando Fernández's *Los niños se despiden*. However, unlike Fer-

---

[148] Ibid., p. 38.

[149] For a further discussion of this religious symbolism, see the analysis of Cortázar's story "Reunión" on pp. 255–258.

[150] Otero, *En ciudad semejante*, p. 364.

nández's novel, language is definitely not one of the protagonists of *En ciudad semejante*. The latter's structure is experimental in the Dos Passos manner, interior monologues alternate effectively with rapid-fire dialogues, and the second-person narrative point of view, popularized by Carlos Fuentes, is utilized convincingly. Nevertheless, Otero's language is neither creatively artistic like that of Carpentier, Lezama Lima, and Fernández nor innovative like that of Sarduy.

Equally devoid of linguistic experimentation, *Adire y el tiempo roto* (1967) by Manuel Granados (b. 1931) anticipated the use in *En ciudad semejante* of male and female representative protagonists to trace the development of the July Twenty-sixth Movement from its inception to its victory. With less concern for historical perspective than had Otero, Granados begins his heroic quest with the July 26, 1953, attack on the Moncada Barracks and closes it with the struggle against the Escambray counterrevolutionaries in the early 1960's. *Adire y el tiempo roto* is distinguished not only from *En ciudad semejante* but also from all the novels of the Cuban Revolution in that the more important of the two protagonists is a poor Camagüey Negro, cast in the traditional mold of the marginal man, whose search for personal identification and security parallels the development of the Revolution. By concentrating on the Negro Julián and the prostitute Cira, with a relatively small supporting cast, Granados infuses a spark of life into his characters and prevents them from being overshadowed by the historical background. At the same time, Julián's personal experiences in the army and later with the *guerrilleros* in Santiago and the Sierra Maestra combine with Cira's personal experiences in Havana to provide a convincing panoramic view of the struggle against Batista.

The dominant factor in the development of Julián's psyche is his sexual relations with white women. In this respect he mirrors his literary prototypes in Peruvian Enrique López Albújar's *Matalaché* (1928) and Venezuelan Rómulo Gallegos's *Pobre negro* (1937). Julián's experiences with his childhood sweetheart, with the frustrated wife of a plantation owner, and with a French newspaperwoman convince him that he is regarded only as an instrument of pleasure and that social taboos prevent him from being loved as a complete human being. After the triumph of the Revolution, Julián marries the fourth white woman, the ex-prostitute Cira, whose rehabilitation helps her overcome her previous dislike for Negroes. In an obviously didactic ending, Julián dies fighting against the counterrevolutionaries while Cira will soon give birth to their child, Cuba's new revolutionary man.

In comparison with the other 1966–1970 novels, *Adire y el tiempo roto* is only mildly experimental. In fact, the title is one of the most enigmatic features of the novel and is clarified only in the glossary. A technique used in Nigeria to dye cloth, *adire* may be interpreted as referring to the changes in racial attitudes wrought by the Revolution. The second part of the title suggests a break with tradition as well as a cubistic treatment of time, which is really not carried out in the novel. Certain passages labeled with the letters of the alphabet from *A* to *K* and narrated in the third person indicate that perhaps Granados originally planned to use these sections to tell parts of the story in reverse chronological order, as in Carpentier's "Viaje a la semilla." In "A," Julián dies on May 24; "B" represents a May 23 conversation between *miliciano* Julián and his wife, Cira, who works in a bank; and, in "C," Julián's return to Camagüey stirs memories of his parents. However, from that moment on, the story leaps back in time to Julián's adolescence and then proceeds in normal chronological order despite the alternate labeling of the passages as "Paso en el tiempo," letters *D* through *K*, "Le pas d'un," "Pas de deux," or "Pas de quatre," and "Movimiento," "Movimiento último." The penultimate section of the novel is labeled "C (2)" and returns us to the point of departure shortly before Julián's death. The bulk of the novel is made up of the "Paso en el tiempo" passages narrated in the first person with a predominance of dialogue.

Prior to the publication of *Tres tristes tigres*, Cabrera Infante's literary reputation was based on one of the first and most highly praised collections of short stories to come out of revolutionary Cuba, *Así en la paz como en la guerra* (1960). The fifteen one-page vignettes that vividly portray the terror of the disintegrating Batista regime alternate with a variety of existentialist stories written between 1950 and 1958. The latter deal primarily with personal frustrations and the anxieties of the poor, like *La búsqueda, Pequeñas maniobras*, and many of the other 1961–1965 novels. The striking change from the existentialist stories of the 1950's to the rollicking linguistic experimentation of *Tres tristes tigres,* although somewhat anticipated by the film reviews published in *Carteles* (1954–1960) and *Revolución* (1959–1960) under the pseudonym G. Caín,[151] reflects Cabrera Infante's leap into the Latin American mainstream along with so many of his compatriots from 1966 on.

The 1964 version of *Tres tristes tigres,* which was awarded the Seix Barral prize in Barcelona, was entitled "Vista del amanecer en el trópico" and portrayed Havana night life as the symbol of the decadent Batista regime of the late 1950's. More in keeping with the 1961–1965 novels, the dissolute, antisocial lives of the protagonists were contrasted with the exemplary behavior of the urban and rural guerrillas. According to Cabrera Infante, "it turned out to be a book of absolute socialist realism,"[152] "a politically opportune book,"[153] which he has since morally repudiated. Because of the change in his attitude toward the Revolution, Cabrera Infante took advantage of the Spanish censors' puritanical objections to the prize-winning text to rewrite the book, utilizing fragments of the first version. Begun in mid-1961 and entitled "La noche es un hueco sin borde," this version was inspired by the Cuban government's confiscation of the twenty-five–minute film *P. M.* made by Cabrera Infante's brother Sabá.[154]

Be that as it may, and no matter how nostalgically the author may view pre-1959 Havana today, his reminiscences, like those of Edmundo Desnoes, are basically "memorias del subdesarrollo." Nowhere is this more obvious than in the novel's prologue, an introduction of the Tropicana Nightclub show, in "Spanglish," by the ingratiating and obsequious master of ceremonies. Although the hybrid language in itself would be sufficient to illustrate the Americanization of Cuba, the presence of soup-fortune heir William Campbell and fifteen-year-old debutante Vivian Smith Corona Alvarez del Real indicates that American influence had penetrated Cubans' eating habits, working habits

---

[151] Collected and published under the title *Un oficio del siglo XX.* The pseudonym is derived from the first two letters of each of the family names.

[152] Rodríguez Monegal, *El arte de narrar,* p. 64.

[153] Ibid., p. 66.

[154] For a full discussion of the controversial antecedents and consequences of *Tres tristes tigres,* see part two.

(typewriters), and even marital habits (marriage between an aristocratic Spanish family and a financially successful but plebeian American family).

The frivolous tone of the prologue is sustained throughout the
book's 451 pages, a length that reflects the proverbial Cuban loqua-
ciousness. Likewise, the lack of a tightly structured coordinating plot
exemplifies the spontaneity and improvisation that are usually associated with the Cuban national character. The only two novelistic threads
that run throughout the book (actually, the first two-thirds) are "Ella
cantaba boleros," the story of an enormous mulatto chanteuse, and the
confessions to a psychiatrist, in ten numbered installments, of an author's disturbed wife. The eleventh installment appears at the end of
"Bachata," the final third of the book, which is devoted to unrestrained
punning, often on the names of movie actors and authors, by television
actor Arsenio Cué and journalist Silvestre as they drive around Havana. The third of the "three trapped tigers," the concept of whose
multiple adventures Cabrera Infante attributes to his childhood reading of Petronius's *Satyricon*,[155] is the nightclub photographer Códac,
who narrates and takes an active part in the "Ella cantaba boleros" sections. A fourth friend, bongo player and commercial artist Eribó, narrates the story of another cabaret singer, Gloria Pérez, whom he discovered and rebaptized Cuba Venegas. The dependence of Havana
nocturnal life on American tourism is acknowledged by the author's
including in his composition a section called "Los visitantes," which
consists of the twice-told-by-Mr.-Campbell and the twice-corrected-by-
Mrs.-Campbell "Historia de un bastón."

Although these narratives constitute parts of the mosaic of the now
extinguished pre-1959 Havana nightlife—the book's epigraph is
Lewis Carroll's sentence "And he tried to imagine what the light of a
candle would look like after it was extinguished"—the sole protagonist, even more than in *Paradiso*, *De donde son los cantantes*, and *Los
niños se despiden*, is language. The puns, which predominate throughout the book, are inspired to a large extent by the "Tigres' " mentor,
Bustrófedon, who never appears in the flesh. They are supplemented
by a variety of typographical tricks, drawings, and blank pages remi-

---

[155] Rodríguez Monegal, *El arte de narrar*, p. 53.

niscent of the Spanish humorist Enrique Jardiel Poncela (1902–1952); by the reproduction of a letter full of orthographical mistakes and the phonetic transcription of a monologue in the Negro dialect; and by the parodies on the styles of Cuban authors José Martí, José Lezama Lima, Virgilio Piñera, Lydia Cabrera, Lino Novás Calvo, Alejo Carpentier, and Nicolás Guillén.

The choice of Trotsky's assassination as the subject for the stylistic parodies as well as the irreverent allusions to Stalin and Cuban Communist leader Blas Roca undoubtedly reflect Cabrera Infante's distaste for the route that the Cuban Revolution was following by the mid-1960's. In retrospect, he even ridicules Arsenio Cué's decision to join Fidel in the Sierra, by associating it with the Sierra Nightclub, Pancho Villa, the foreign legion, Ronald Colman, and Nicolás Guillén.[156] Fidel Castro himself is criticized in the untranslatable *Alice in Wonderland* Jabberwocky parody of one of José Martí's *Ismaelillo* poems:

> Váyala fiña di Viña
> deifel Fader fidel fiasco
> falla mimú psicocastro
> alfú mar sefú más phinas.[157]

Toward the end of the novel, Silvestre recounts a friend's dream in which Havana is destroyed by an apocalyptical fire out of which gallops a gray horse—Fidel's nickname is "El Caballo"—that stops below a miraculously intact balcony. Although Cabrera Infante identifies the rider as Marilyn Monroe, any doubt as to the interpretation of the dream is removed by Silvestre's comparing it to the dream Lydia Cabrera had just before Batista's 1952 *golpe*.[158]

Since Cabrera Infante's official defection in 1965, he has been working on a thousand-page autobiographical work to be called "Cuerpos divinos." The prologue, entitled "Delito por bailar el chachachá," criticizes the dogmatic attitudes of the revolutionary cultural bureaucrats.[159]

---

[156] Guillermo Cabrera Infante, *Tres tristes tigres*, 2d ed., p. 347.
[157] Ibid., p. 210.
[158] Ibid., pp. 421–422.
[159] Dated Brussels, December 1962; slightly corrected, London, 1968; published in the July 1968 issue of *Mundo Nuevo*, pp. 59–71.

The critical attitude toward communism in López-Nussa's *Recuerdos del 36* is more surprising than that of *Tres tristes tigres* since it was published in Cuba. This rarely mentioned novel deserves greater recognition, not because of its anticommunism, but because of its perceptive burlesque of Cuban society in the mid-1930's and because of its experimental approach to language and the novel form. The considerable increase in experimentation in *Recuerdos del 36* over the author's earlier novel *Tabaco* illustrates the extent to which the new Latin American novel of the 1960's influenced even the older Cuban novelists from 1966 on.

The first and last chapters of *Recuerdos del 36* are concerned respectively with the planning and successful execution of a Chicago-type holdup complete with the stolen getaway car. However, the possible identification of the target as a Catholic institution—"We entered brusquely. A fat priest said this can't be possible! No? Open the drawers. In the distance some bells began to ring"[160]—the lack of violence, and the total inexperience of the group convert the holdup into a parody that forms an absurd framework around the whole novel. The narrator himself terminates the final chapter of the book as though it were the end of a typical 1930's movie serial: "If you want to find out, reader, what Fernando wrote, what Efrén lived through, and what happened to Onelio and Basilio as well as Fernandina, don't fail to read 'THE FOREIGNER,' the next novel in this absurd series. Now the CURTAIN falls."[161]

The bulk of the novel is comprised of scenes and conversations involving each of the members of the holdup gang, with the purpose of painting a panoramic tableau of Cuban society in the mid-1930's. Tembeleque's family are wealthy landowners and former slaveholders who belong to the highly Americanized Havana upper class. They are rich and Catholic, read the *Diario de la Marina*, and travel often to Miami. In keeping with the novel's absurdity, the narrator of this section is Efrén, *el guajiro*, while Tembeleque reads Trotsky and is wounded in the Spanish Civil War. Efrén Capote, *el guajiro*, and his brother Fernando, the poet, are sent by their widowed mother from

[160] López-Nussa, *Recuerdos del 36*, p. 193.
[161] Ibid., p. 194.

their provincial city to Havana to join a third brother, Onelio, a Communist. The fourth brother, Basilio, an unscrupulous lawyer, remains in the provincial city and continues to cheat the peasants out of their lands, just as he did in *Tabaco*. Josicú's mother is a poorly paid teacher whose home is the site of Theosophist meetings under the direction of Professor Ciro Jideputra.

Through these and other characters, the author presents scenes starring the corrupt policeman in collusion with the prostitutes, the lovesick university student, as well as specific Cuban literary and artistic personalities of the period: Nicolás Guillén, Félix Pita Rodríguez, Alejo Carpentier, Carlos Montenegro, and Carlos Enríquez. Cuban political history is sketched from the fall of Machado in 1933 through the elevation of sergeant-stenographer Batista to the presidency by Sumner Welles. Batista's promotion is the result of an absurd dialogue in which the sergeant replies "Yes" in English to eight very different questions posed in Spanish by the ambassador, ranging from "What do you think of democracy?" to "and how about the Salvation Army?"[162] The flavor of the mid-1930's is also captured by references to the movies, the first Joe Louis–Max Schmeling fight, Adolf Hitler, Edward VIII's abdication, British Prime Minister Neville Chamberlain, and, above all, the Spanish Civil War.

The two most constant topics of conversation, regardless of the social group, are sex and communism. Subjected to ridicule are Cheo, the boastful Don Juan who pursues or is pursued by a variety of women, all named Rosa; Fico, the homosexual with the Tarzan physique; prostitutes; teenagers of both sexes; and the still hopeful spinsters. The fact that the Communists are also targets of similar ridicule indicates the relative artistic freedom that existed in Cuba in 1967 when the novel was published. Almost all the members of the holdup gang are members of the Communist Youth Group called Jóvenes Martianos. However, the use of José Martí's name does not prevent the doctrinaire Communist Dámaso from criticizing Martí's limitations: "Well . . . I think that Martí has been inflated a little . . . his ideological limitations . . . Martí could have embraced the cause of proletarian internationalism. The time was ripe for it. Instead, he settled for a modest apostle-

[162] Ibid., p. 159.

ship . . . He was obsessed by the independence of Cuba, as if liberating Cuba were such a big deal. Wouldn't it have been much more glorious to liberate all mankind?"[163]

López-Nussa's ridicule of doctrinaire communism is even more poignant and timely in the argument about socialist realism:

Dámaso: I turn to Gorky in the Writers' Congress: "It is impossible to conceive of man outside reality, which is essentially political."

Josicú (waving a pamphlet): If that's the way you want it, I'll quote Fedor Panferov at the same Congress: "Socialist realism is the essential method of Soviet literature, art, and literary criticism; it demands of the artist an image that conforms to the truth, a concrete historical image of reality in its revolutionary development. This truth and this preciseness in the representation of reality should be linked to the problem of the ideological reeducation and education of the workers in the spirit of socialism."

Efrén: And why does it have to be "demanded?"

Cheo: That ruined the party. How about going for a ride?

Me: No, I'm staying.

Efrén: It seems to me that the artist needs complete freedom. When you start demanding that he stick to the truth, you wind up telling him what that truth consists of and what its range and limits are.

.   .   .   .

Dámaso: The great majority of Western writers don't feel anything, except the problems of technique. Therefore, in the future our epoch will be characterized by a return, brilliant but equally precarious, to *préciosité*. (Dámaso quotes Jean-Richard Bloch without saying so.)

.   .   .   .

Fernando: And does that hurt the masses? When the writers have grown tired of formal experimentation, they will have on hand a richer—precious—instrument to deal in depth with the problems of mankind.

Dámaso: Wait a minute, wait a minute. Let's go step by step. We can't stand by with our arms folded and watch the degradation of literature. We must point the finger at those who indulge in this game of mockery, which deep down reveals a reactionary attitude toward life and a profound contempt for the interests of the people . . . The creative process of life will destroy those indifferent observers locked up in their ivory towers, but, in

---

[163] Ibid., pp. 36–37.

the meantime, today's combatants can't stand idly by with their arms folded, for they have the obligation to participate actively in the roundup, to seize the bull by the horns if necessary, and to publicly denounce the traitors and cowards, the purists and the despicable advocates of art for art's sake. In "Art and Social Life" by Plekhanov . . .[164]

The discussion ends with Dámaso's borrowing three pesos and the narrator's sarcastically extolling his virtues: "Sir Dámaso López! . . . His only defect is being poor. But, from that condition, there has arisen another definite defect: when Dámaso doesn't have any money, he asks others for it. In short, he's a sponger."[165]

Most of the other conversations in the novel are not nearly so serious, and very often the reader gets the impression, as in *Tres tristes tigres*, that language itself is the main protagonist. The burlesque tone of the book is established by the sprightly repartee based on the Havana idiom of the 1930's. Unlike the *criollista* writers of the 1920's and 1930's, the author is not so much interested in phonetic transcriptions as in manipulating the more colorful slang expressions and inserting, in the appropriate spot, proverbs, puns, jokes, popular verses, and refrains from songs. The first-person narrative point of view predominates and shifts from character to character, including the author, who at times talks directly to his readers about the creative process in the manner of Julio Cortázar or J. D. Salinger. "Cheo left the gang. Josicú, Tembeleque, Nato, Efrén, and I were left. Menda has nothing at all to do with this. I write, I'm the chronicler. Sometimes I get mixed up with Josicú because I'm also a little Josicú. But I'm me. And now I'm sleepy and I don't give a damn what happens in the gang. Bye now!"[166]

The comments about three of Cuba's best-known authors, Félix Pita Rodríguez, Alejo Carpentier, and Carlos Montenegro, provide still another link with *Tres tristes tigres*. Pita Rodríguez, a long-time member of the Communist party, returns from Paris, where he attended a *congreso de intelectuales*, boasting of his amorous adventures. Carpentier's

[164] Ibid., pp. 32–34.
[165] Ibid., p. 35.
[166] Ibid., p. 14.

style is parodied in a full-page, enumerative, and excessively erudite description of the typical Spanish-Cuban grocery store, the *bodega*.[167] Carlos Montenegro, who was highly regarded in the 1930's, is strongly praised even though he abandoned literature in the following decade, left Cuba shortly after the triumph of the Revolution, and is rarely mentioned in Cuba today: "Carlos Montenegro greeted me; oh, envy and admiration! We liked his short stories and longer narratives; they had a virile, direct, and fiery passion that seemed fascinating to us. With his mussed-up lock of black hair, his constant growling, and his longing for the ten years of his life lost in prison. To write like him! It was too beautiful, a dream."[168]

Exorcism Continued

Although the 1961–1965 theme of exorcising the past was over-shadowed in the 1966–1970 period by the epic tableaux and the exuberant linguistic experimentation, it certainly did not disappear. Like *La búsqueda, Pequeñas maniobras, Los muertos andan solos, Los días de nuestra angustia,* and *Memorias del subdesarrollo,* the new "exorcising" novels create the mood of despair and anguish that pervaded pre-1959 Havana and depict the bourgeois obsession with material wealth and sex both before and after 1959. However, they do so by utilizing a variety of more experimental techniques in tune with the boom.

Whereas Cabrera Infante's vision of pre-1959 Havana nightlife is tinged with nostalgia, *Sonámbulo del sol* (1972) by Nivaria Tejera (b. 1933) presents the other side of the coin. After serving as cultural attaché in Paris and Rome, Nivaria Tejera, like Cabrera Infante, defected in 1965, but, unlike *Tres tristes tigres, Sonámbulo del sol* contains no trace of anticommunism or criticism of the revolutionary government. The fact that it was published in 1972, after winning the Seix Barral award for 1971, places it outside the chronological limits of the third period (1966–1970), which pertains more stringently to the novels published in Cuba.

The title refers to an unemployed mulatto who wanders around Ha-

167 Ibid., pp. 67–68.
168 Ibid., p. 41.

vana by daylight and never sees the glittering lights of *Tres tristes tigres*. In keeping with the protagonist's somnambulant state and the unrelenting bright tropical sun, the novel is comprised mainly of a series of highly poetic visual impressions, situated vaguely between 1953 (comments on the coronation of the queen, probably Elizabeth II of Great Britain) and 1958 (allusions to police brutality and to the general strike, probably the ill-fated one of April 1958). Although, like Severo Sarduy, Tejera is obviously influenced by the new French novels of Nathalie Sarraute and Alain Robbe-Grillet, her artistic techniques do not prevent the "exorcising" message from coming across very clearly. Plot and character development are reduced to the bare minimum, and people are dehumanized through the personification of inanimate objects, which are seen as a complex of geometrical figures: "Each one seemed to be equally distant, separated by the horizontal board that rested on the bench's green supports."[169] The abundant use of alliteration, similes, and metaphors at times gives the impression of art for art's sake: "The sun penetrated [penetrates] through the avid cracks like steps of silhouetted swordfishes scaling, dazzling, threatening the space of the room and scaling the walls with eyes as if it were drilling them, as if it were wrinkling them—broad brilliant brow."[170] Nonetheless, Tejera succeeds in penetrating below the surface in order to reveal a surprisingly broad panorama of the corrupt and decadent pre-1959 Cuban society.

Sidelfiro, the protagonist and the only named character in the whole novel, has been in Havana for three years. He recalls the bad conditions on the coffee plantation in Camajuaní, northeast of Santa Clara, but his inability to find a job in Havana leads him to find greater fault with the capital: ". . . and if they gave me a little chance, even if it were as a mailman, even on the docks, pal, for the twenty-five cents *café con leche* . . . the thing is that here in Havana everyone is corrupted . . ."[171] Cuban society is divided between whites and Negroes with the former on top and the latter on the bottom. The upper classes attend musical concerts, not because they appreciate the music but because they want

[169] Nivaria Tejera, *Sonámbulo del sol*, p. 91.
[170] Ibid., p. 221.
[171] Ibid., p. 13.

their names to appear in the society columns. The cultural elite are criticized for their "verborrea."[172] Politicians are bombastic and fraudulent. American tourists, marines, and diplomats all come in for their share of criticism, as well as the general American cultural influence as manifested in the Havana Hilton, the country clubs, and Coca-Cola.

A little past the midpoint of the novel, Sidelfiro obtains a job as messenger in a government ministry, which allows the author to contrast the incredibly superficial lives of the secretaries with the degradation of the countless number of unemployed who fill the waiting rooms day after day in response to a single announced vacancy. Although the author's attitude toward the world she presents is perfectly clear and is symbolized by the setting of Sidelfiro's age at thirty-three and an allusion to Easter, "Hoy lunes 22 pascuas resurrección de cristo,"[173] she does not sermonize. The secretaries' superficiality is recorded directly in their conversations while the author's views on Havana and Cuba are all conveyed through the eyes of the protagonist.

Although published in 1971, Gustavo Eguren's (b. 1925) short novel, *En la cal de las paredes*, like *Sonámbulo del sol*, has all the characteristics of the 1966–1970 novels. Furthermore, its ornate style, which is clearly reminiscent of Alejo Carpentier, is in marked contrast to the unadorned, more Spanish style of Eguren's own previous novel, *La Robla* (1967). The theme of *En la cal de las paredes* is the increasing isolation and gradual crumbling of the aristocratic world of the son of a hard-working Spanish immigrant. The central symbol of the book is the mansion's monumental marble staircase: ". . . thinking that within a few minutes he will have to go down that bare staircase, without handrails or banister, lighted by a single bulb swaying in the breeze, and walk through the likewise bare halls and vestibule, and cross the open doorway and go along the path through the overgrown lawn up to the pilasters that formerly held up the great iron gate."[174]

The theme as well as the poetic style and the touch of fantasy clearly identify this work with Antonio Benítez's short story "Estatuas

[172] Ibid., p. 14.
[173] Ibid., p. 107.
[174] Gustavo Eguren, *En la cal de las paredes*, p. 82.

sepultadas,"[175] although the element of fantasy is less predominant and the chronology is more complex. By moving back and forth from present to past, Eguren succeeds in presenting simultaneously the ascent and descent of Jorge Luis's family. The concern for architectural details, the enumerative style, and the many servants indicate the influence of Carpentier's "Viaje a la semilla" and "Los convidados de plata." Another similarity to "Viaje a la semilla" is its ambiguous genre. Too long and without the denouement of the usual short story, *En la cal de las paredes*, in spite of the novel label on the back cover, is too short (106 small pages) and too concentrated thematically to be considered a novel. Like Carlos Fuentes's *Aura* and Carpentier's *El acoso*, it belongs to that rather hybrid form of the short novel which has become increasingly popular in Latin America in recent years.

In *Mariana* (1970), David Buzzi (b. 1932) also creates a vague poetic atmosphere with Christian symbolism, but his purpose is to sound the final death knell for the remnants of the bourgeois society that had survived until the mid-1960's. Although *Mariana* is much more pretentious artistically, albeit no more successful, than Buzzi's soon-to-be-discussed first two novels, two things remain constant: the general theme of exorcism and the structural rather than linguistic experimentation. The number of characters as well as the number of novelistic threads are drastically reduced, the revolutionary message comes across with greater subtlety, and the prosaic uninspired view of reality is replaced by the highly poetized and mythified world of magic realism. However, the imprecise identification of characters and narrators as well as the confused chronology are too contrived, and outside literary influences are imperfectly absorbed. Furthermore, the recurring chapter headings UNO, MILAGRO, and NADA do not seem to follow any discernible pattern.

The theme of *Mariana* is the final exorcism of prerevolutionary sexual promiscuity, Catholicism, and bourgeois materialism. The title refers to the aged prostitute, whose six or seven former lovers have a mysterious pact to rendezvous on the day of her death. It is not until the last fourth of the novel that the identities of most of the lovers

[175] See pp. 185–186.

become relatively clear. Marcelo Toledo, "el poeta," Mariana's first lover, is now married to Aurora, a devout Catholic who spreads rumors about the revolutionary government and contributes heavily to the church. She constantly nags her husband to escape from Cuba and confides in the priest Cristo-Jesús, who is also one of Mariana's former lovers. Marcelo, who went to jail in 1950 for some unnamed crime and who was recently warned by the Comité de Defensa that he and his wife would have to stop selling sleeping pills, is portrayed as a negative character—"I've always been a crook."[176] Along with Lucio Arrieta, the former owner of a hardware store and also one of Mariana's lovers, he helps kill the Communist Severino. In marked contrast to Marcelo, mailman Pedro María, another of Mariana's former lovers, is the only one who is redeemed. His six-hundred-pound wife constantly plagues him with news of the material success of her exiled relatives in the United States and keeps pressing him to write a letter. When his patience finally runs out, he wreaks sweet revenge by resolutely telling the priest that he repents of having been such a coward and by confronting his elephantine wife with his newly purchased *miliciano* uniform. For the first time in his life, he dissociates himself from the world of Mariana's lovers: ". . . he thought that perhaps for the first time in his life, he was coming back from the other world."[177] Concentrating on his future devotion to the Revolution, he will no longer think of those "elephants" who cling to their prerevolutionary way of life: "—I'm never going to think of the elephants again."[178]

In addition to Marcelo, Cristo-Jesús, Lucio, and Pedro María, Mariana's other three lovers are the Negro Adrián, an anonymous hunchbacked circus performer, and, maybe, Moisés. While relatively little information is supplied about the first two, Moisés is a kind of eternal wandering Jew whose mysterious appearance seems to trigger Mariana's repentance shortly before her death.

If the identities of Mariana's six or seven lovers are difficult to decipher, the characterization of Mariana herself is even stranger. She was born in Havana in 1926, was initiated sexually in 1940, and now

[176] David Buzzi, *Mariana*, p. 125.
[177] Ibid., p. 161.
[178] Ibid.

lives alone wearing her black moth-eaten negligee. With the advent of the Revolution, she seems to have almost dissolved into a kind of Mary Magdalene spirit, which is reflected in the biblical tone that pervades the novel, a tone somewhat similar to that of Mariano Herrera's *Despues de la Z*. Into this "biblicized" environment, Buzzi inserts, unnaturally, several elements from *Cien años de soledad*. On the very first page, Mariana's impending death, like that of Ursula Buendía, is heralded by her shrinking and returning to infancy, the time before objects had names. In a manner reminiscent of the final fate of the last of the Buendías, ants crawl over Mariana and carry away her blonde locks. The periodic repetition of the phrase "it was a Tuesday" or "that Tuesday"[179] to designate the day of Mariana's death recalls the famous phrase José Arcadio Buendía used to indicate his withdrawal from the world of reality: "it's still Monday."[180] Remedios la Bella's ascent to heaven and Father Nicanor's levitation are combined in Moisés's casual disappearance: ". . . he disappeared with such a sudden levitation that nobody, except the children, realized what had happened."[181] Pedro María's vision of his future revolutionary heroism is couched in a grammatical form similar to that used very frequently by García Márquez to allude to Col. Aureliano Buendía's future execution: "He was not surprised to see two elephants floating loose in the air; nor did he offer them a couple of sausages; on the other hand, he felt confused when he thought that some day he might be able to stand up to a priest in a resolute manner, and that in his lifetime—still in the future—he might be able to look at himself in a mirror dressed as a soldier."[182]

In contrast to Buzzi's earlier novels, the specific references to the Revolution, particularly in the first three-fourths of the book, are minimal. The cries of "To the firing squad! To the firing squad!"[183] at a 1959 political rally and Fidel's words "We are a Socialist country"[184] on the occasion of the Bay of Pigs invasion are among the few intrusions of the Revolution into the dreamlike world of the past. In order

[179] Ibid., pp. 96, 110, 120, 130, 159.
[180] Gabriel García Márquez, *Cien años de soledad*, 3d ed., p. 73.
[181] Buzzi, *Mariana*, p. 159.
[182] Ibid., p. 24.
[183] Ibid., p. 17.
[184] Ibid., p. 77.

to forestall criticism of this predominantly fantastic novel, Buzzi chose three epigraphs that attest to the mythical as well as the epic quality of contemporary realism, to the mutual relationship between poetic language and the object it describes, and to the absence of a Marxist theory for the creation of art: "We have relied for some time on a theory for the historical process, but we need to come up with a Marxist theory for the creation of art."[185]

Buzzi's first two novels, *Los desnudos* (1967) and *La religión de los elefantes* (1969), deal with basically the same theme as *Mariana* but in a much more specific manner and through the use of other experimental techniques. Both works are highly critical of the prerevolutionary immoral bourgeoisie and the alienated intellectuals-artists who are incapable of adjusting to the new Cuba. Their attitudes are contrasted with revolutionary puritanism as exemplified by the rehabilitated prostitutes. In order to create complex mosaics of different levels of pre- and post-revolutionary society, Buzzi overindulges in "Faulknerism": varying point of view, alternating chronological planes, use of the same name for two related characters, and contrived parallelism between different plots. In *La religión de los elefantes*, Buzzi also borrows at least two techniques from Vargas Llosa's *La casa verde*:[186] the total fusion of narrative and dialogue, and the use of several different nicknames for the same character (Cecilio).

Los desnudos, more than *La religión de los elefantes*, has an excessively experimental structure for a relatively limited panoramic view of Cuba between roughly 1958 and 1964.[187] The title, *Los desnudos*, re-

[185] Ibid., p. 9.

[186] The second part of David Buzzi's novel has epigraphs from Louis Aragon, Cesare Pavese, and Vargas Llosa's *La casa verde*: "—No eran cristianos sino bandidos dijo Fushía" (*La religión de los elefantes*, p. 103).

[187] Julio E. Miranda is obviously exaggerating when he calls this novel "—in spite of its Manicheanism and some simplification in minor matters—the first great mosaic of the Revolution" (JEM, p. 24). Although Raúl Aparicio also bestows high praise on the novel for its narrative vigor and revolutionary viewpoint, he recognizes that it is basically "una obra de moral social," with an "excesiva acumulación de 'problemas.' " He also points out other defects: ". . . passages of naïve optimism (the rehabilitation camps) . . . , the weak grammar on page 21, the carelessness in the numbering of the chapters, the unsuccessful attempt to delve into Silvia's and her

fers to the Cubans' need to divest themselves of their prerevolutionary attitudes in order to be rehabilitated. How difficult this is for the artist was the sole theme of Desnoes's *Memorias del subdesarrollo* and is one of the main themes of *Los desnudos*. The writer Sergio explains to his former wife: "You, Silvia, if some day you read me, you'll understand that I am really not spiritually naked. No one ever is. It's only that the others corner you, and then they wind up deciphering you. Each one of us—not by chance—has lived while the historical events that cause us to be revealed do not stop; they continue, they advance, and a revolution continues to exercise its effect on men who, in magnificent eloquent silence, help it to survive for all the centuries to come."[188]

Silvia, the co-protagonist, is also a "rehabilitee" in spite of having participated actively in the urban underground fight against Batista and in the armed struggle in the Sierra Maestra. However, in order to become a true revolutionary, she has to sever ties with her bourgeois family and friends, study Marxism, teach in the literacy campaign, and, after failing as a factory manager, direct a rehabilitation camp for prostitutes. Only then does she become reunited with her former husband, Sergio, who has likewise proved his revolutionary mettle by working in a factory, denouncing an antirevolutionary friend, and directing a rehabilitation camp for criminals. This total rehabilitation of the two protagonists is planned by the Negro Eustaquio, the only character whose revolutionary credentials are exemplary from 1958 to the present. Most of the novel's pages are devoted to the situation in the factory, where the unionized workers resist the imposition of revolutionary sacrifices and where another "rehabilitee," Roberto, is killed by an antirevolutionary bomb.

This relatively simple plot is overextended and unduly confused by the use of several types of sections, which, unlike those of Otero's *En ciudad semejante*, are not consistently defined. Each of the eight chapters starts with Sergio's thoughts, recollections, and analyses of his relations with Silvia presented in normal roman type. Sergio's relations with Mirna, one of Silvia's former bourgeois friends, are narrated in

sister's infancy" ("Acotación a *Los desnudos,*" *Unión* 6, no. 3 [July–September 1967]: 124–131).
[188] David Buzzi, *Los desnudos*, p. 233.

italics, starting in the past but catching up with the present after they both go to work in the factory managed by Silvia. Silvia's thoughts about her past associations are presented in one or two sections per chapter printed in roman type and entitled NO QUIERE OLVIDAR. The entire first chapter, of less than two pages, and other untitled sections in roman type throughout the book present in first person the transformation of Leandro, the son of Leandro, the corrupt union leader, from a potential juvenile delinquent to a full-fledged revolutionary. Each of the eight chapters usually has one section entitled "Agnición," printed in small type, which concentrates on the sexual immorality and the profane language of Sergio and Silvia's former social group, several of whom also intervene in the other sections. The "Conteo" sections, also printed in small type, at first refer mostly to Panchito, a former Batista cabinet member who continually predicts the imminent fall of the revolutionary government, and Miguel, who talks only of sex. Later, other unknown characters appear and the chronology varies.

Equally complex and doctrinaire, *La religión de los elefantes* has greater unity than *Los desnudos* because the several different plot threads all emanate in one way or another from the bourgeois family of Virginia Troncoso. The enigmatic title refers to Virginia and her artist husband, Pablo, who are incapable of comprehending the Revolution and seek solace by going to church regularly. In other words, they are elephants who live in the past. Interwoven with the past sexual experiences of Alejandra and Virginia are Pablo's experiences on skid row during his estrangement from Virginia; the *noviazgo* between Virginia's Communist daughter, Grisel, and Alex, the poor university student, son of the later-to-be-rehabilitated prostitute Alejandra; the *noviazgo* between Renato and Virginia's sensual younger daughter, Cuqui; Renato's experiences as a member of an adolescent street gang; the adventures of the *chulo* Cecilio for whom Alejandra works as a prostitute and whose mistress is Virginia. These different threads are tied together by the military action in the Escambray Mountains. Alex is fighting with the government *milicianos* against his own brother, Carlos, Renato's father, and Cecilio, the leader of the *alzados*. The historical framework is strengthened by the periodic interjection of newspaper headlines and scenes involving Fidel Castro, referred to as "the big man with the thick beard."[189] A further exaltation of Fidel appears in the story of the mortally wounded soldier who desperately spells out FIDEL in his own blood before dying.[190]

Although Noel Navarro in *Los caminos de la noche* (1967) also resorts to the Faulknerian shifting point of view with delayed identification of the narrator and interior monologues, in both italics and bold-face type, he distinguishes himself from Buzzi, as well as from his more famous colleagues—Carpentier, Lezama Lima, Sarduy, Fernández, and Cabrera Infante—by adopting a simple, unadorned, almost comic-strip style of writing to complement the many comic-strip pop-art illustrations that are an integral part of the novel. The experiment is interesting and perhaps explains the fact that the characters are more stereotypes than real people, but the total product is disappointing.

The second volume of a trilogy, *Los caminos de la noche* is far less a continuation of the first volume, *Los días de nuestra angustia*, than was Lisandro Otero's *En ciudad semejante* a continuation of his *La situación*. Whereas *Los días de nuestra angustia* presents a panoramic picture of the gestation of the Revolution from July 26, 1953, to late 1958, *Los caminos de la noche* concentrates on the shorter but more vaguely defined period of the months preceding the April 1961 Bay of Pigs invasion. Furthermore, it is much less concerned with the historical theme of the counterrevolutionary plotting than it is with the personal sexual immorality of the wealthy protagonists. In fact, the greater concentration on a limited number of new characters from the same social class as well as protagonist Roberto Estévez's desire for revolutionary redemption liken this volume, thematically, more to Juan Arcocha's *Los muertos andan solos* than to Navarro's own *Los días de nuestra angustia*.

Just as the straightforward, simple language complements the comic-strip illustrations in *Los caminos de la noche*, a similar lack of linguistic adornment in Miguel Barnet's *Canción de Rachel* (1969) corresponds to a different concept of the novel as well as to a generational

[189] Buzzi, *La religión de los elefantes*, p. 11.
[190] Under the title "Tengo que hacerlo," this story appears in the Caballero Bonald and Ambrosio Fornet anthologies: *Narrativa cubana de la revolución* and *Cuentos de la Revolución cubana*.

revolt. Born in 1941, Barnet and his contemporaries, who were born in the late 1930's and early 1940's, were less traumatized by Batista's 1952 *golpe* than were their predecessors and were more unreservedly exhilarated by the revolutionary triumph of January 1959. Although their adolescence coincided with the Batista dictatorship, they reached maturity and began to write during the revolutionary process of the 1960's. Consequently, they differ from the generation of 1950 in that they no longer feel the need to exorcise the past, are not infected by the existentialist virus, and, with a few notable exceptions, tend to reject the structural and linguistic experimentation of their predecessors in favor of a more straightforward and at times documentary type of literature. This is particularly true of the short story as seen in *Los años duros* (1966) by Jesús Díaz (b. 1941), *La guerra tuvo seis nombres* (1968) by Eduardo Heras León (b. 1941), *Condenados de Condado* (1968) and *Cazabandido* (1970) by Norberto Fuentes (b. 1943), and Chilean Bernardo Subercaseaux's anthology, *Narrativa de la joven Cuba* (1971).

Nevertheless, Miguel Barnet's two works, the widely acclaimed *Biografía de un cimarrón* (1968) and *Canción de Rachel* (1969), are in a way just as innovative as *Paradiso*, *Tres tristes tigres*, *De donde son los cantantes*, and *Sonámbulo del sol*. By attempting a new kind of documented biographical work, Barnet is actually challenging the traditional concept of the novel along the lines of Truman Capote's *In Cold Blood* (1966) and Norman Mailer's *The Armies of the Night* (1968). Because the more famous *Biografía de un cimarrón* is based on a series of real tape-recorded interviews with the 108-year-old former slave Esteban Montejo, it is actually an autobiography and should not be considered a novel. On the other hand, *Canción de Rachel*, also the first-person narrative of a character out of the past, is clearly definable as a novel. The protagonist is not a real person but a fictitious *cupletera* probably born around 1892. During the Batista regime, she remembers her whole life in chronological order but particularly the period between 1902 and the late 1920's. Like the Sarita Montiel Spanish movie *El último cuplé* of the late 1950's, and Humberto Arenal's often anthologized short story "Mr. Charles" (1964), Rachel's memories re-create the make-believe world of the music halls

and the cabarets. However, whereas Arenal emphasizes the existentialist isolation and anguish of his protagonist in the present, Barnet is
much more concerned about reviewing the early years of Cuban independence through the eyes of his protagonist. The Negro uprising of
1912 is particularly singled out for detailed treatment. Although specific mention is made of the different presidents and other historical
figures, Rachel's various love affairs keep her in the spotlight at all
times and give her real human qualities. Other dimensions of her character are revealed by occasional newspaper clippings and comments
about her by other characters. Because Barnet is less obsessed than his
predecessors with structural and linguistic experimentation, *Canción
de Rachel* seems to be written almost effortlessly as a reflection of
Rachel's own singing style. Although Barnet certainly does not convey
the impression that he is longing for a return to the good old days of
the 1920's and earlier, he does not show the same compulsion to con-
demn the past as did Arcocha, Buzzi, Desnoes, Fernández, Navarro,
Otero, and Soler Puig. This new attitude may well signal the disappearance of the exorcism theme from future Cuban novels.

Batista Tyranny Revisited

Because of its more dynamic character and its revolutionary idealism, the theme of the 1957–1958 urban guerrilla warfare was revived
during the 1966–1970 boom and will most likely outlive the exorcism
theme. However, unlike the 1959–1960 novels, Severo Sarduy's *Gestos*
(1963) and the five other thematically similar novels published in
1967 and 1968 depict this thrill-packed period with varying degrees
of experimentation, in keeping with the literary fashions of the time.
Although all six novels allude to the pursuit and torture of anti-Batista
revolutionaries, they do so with varying degrees of intensity. Only two
of the novels limit themselves to the 1957–1958 period; the other four
play it off in a contrapuntal way against a variety of other time periods. Three of the six novels take place exclusively in Havana, one
almost exclusively in Havana, and the other two in provincial cities,
with some action in Havana. As in the 1959–1960 novels, the primary
goal is to overthrow Batista, and no mention is made of a socialist revolution. Probably the most significant thematic difference in the novel-

istic treatment of the 1957–1958 period between 1959–1960 and 1966–1970 is in the identity of the revolutionaries. In the latter novels, they are no longer primarily upper-middle-class university students. In only one of the six novels, *Ciudad rebelde*, by the older Luis Amado Blanco (b. 1903), do the revolutionaries have the same social and professional backgrounds as in the 1959–1960 novels, and, even in this case, the revolutionaries are helped by certain members of the working class. In three of the novels, the revolutionaries' social origins are not mentioned, while in the remaining two the urban proletariat, including Negroes, play prominent roles. Although the general characteristics of these six 1966–1970 novels invite comparison with those of the 1959–1960 group, their individual differences are more significant than those of the earlier novels.

The most important of these works is clearly Severo Sarduy's first novel, *Gestos* (1963). With the exception of Carpentier's *El siglo de las luces*, *Gestos* was the first of the new Cuban novels to reflect the high degree of experimentation that was to characterize the Latin American novelistic boom of the 1960's. It was also the first Cuban novel—Nivaria Tejera's *Sonámbulo del sol* (1972) was the second—and one of the few Latin American novels in general to be inspired by the new French novel of Sarraute and Robbe-Grillet. Like the latter's *La Jalousie* (1957), the characters of *Gestos* not only are nameless but also have no past. Only once, toward the end of the novel, is the protagonist's name, Dolores Rondón, mentioned.[191] Also in the Robbe-Grillet vein, certain objects assume the importance of characters, descriptions are often based on geometrical patterns, and a variety of motion picture photography techniques are skillfully used.

However, whereas *La Jalousie* is static and concentrates on one individual's personal jealousy, *Gestos* is a kind of modern folk epic of the urban guerrilla movement. Although the phrases "Today the bombs started . . . The war has started in Oriente"[192] refer to the December 1956 landing of the "Granma," the boldness of the revolutionaries

---

[191] Severo Sarduy, *Gestos*, p. 117. This is the same name used by Sarduy for the protagonist of the second part of his second novel, *De donde son los cantantes*.

[192] Ibid., p. 22.

and the dynamic rhythm of the whole novel give the impression that the action takes place during the last months of 1958 when the Batista dictatorship was crumbling rapidly. People are constantly moving in the streets, children are playing, and bombs are exploding. The revolutionary heroine, "ella," is identified with the July Twenty-sixth Movement only once, when the bartender asks her if she is "a little bearded."[193] "Ella" is a nightclub performer who washes clothes by day and sings and acts at night. She is always accompanied by her small satchel containing, among other things, aspirins for her persistent headaches and bombs. The only plot thread involves her planning and executing with her white *novio* the blowing up of Havana's electric power plant. The fact that she is unexpectedly aided by an older Chinese man gives the impression that all three racial components of the Cuban population were involved in the struggle against Batista. Although Batista is never mentioned by name, he is present as the typical bombastic, insincere candidate for reelection. The police are portrayed as bullies and cowards, but there are no torture scenes. Freedom of the press is derided and American influence is represented by the bottle-throwing sailors, the marching and shouting Jehovah's Witnesses, and the predominance of the English language in the Picasso Club.[194] The revolutionary goal is to overthrow Batista and, in the heroine's inimitable style, to turn things upside down: "We'll have to change everything, to turn life upside down, and then quickly go out into the street, to any corner, and surprise everyone who passes by, shaking him by the shoulders and shouting to him, listen look God damn it listen look we've got to turn life around."[195]

In addition to the "objectivity" of the new French novel, Sarduy employs the mythification process of magic realism. Reality is transformed into fantasy by the setting up of a series of parallel situations: the political rally and the carnival, the geometrical patterns of the wires in the power plant and the wires supporting the scenery in the nightclub, the Batista dictatorship, and the nightclub performance of the

[193] Ibid., p. 35.

[194] The author's choice of the name "Picasso" for the club may be a realistic detail, but it also reaffirms the geometric view of the world.

[195] Sarduy, *Gestos*, p. 139.

Greek tragedy about the besieged city of Thebes, which was also the subject of Antón Arrufat's later controversial play, *Los siete contra Tebas*. Since the "woods" refers to the revolutionaries' arsenal, the following lines illustrate how Sarduy envelops his epic in an air of make-believe: "We are in Thebes. We are in Havana. In the Havana Park [Woods]. In the Tale from the Vienna Woods."[196] The zooming and panning techniques are also particularly effective in sprinkling magic dust on Havana: the highly magnified close-up of the medallion around the watchman's neck, the description of "él" from toes to head, the concentration on the changing traffic lights, and the gradually amplified view of Havana as seen by the two protagonists going up a spiral staircase.

In keeping with the new Latin American novel, language itself is one of the novel's protagonists. Without resorting to the phonetic variants, lexical peculiarities, and puns that characterize *Tres tristes tigres*, Sarduy's short choppy sentences with frequently recurring leitmotifs succeed in capturing the simultaneous frivolity and tension of the revolutionary nightclub performer, whose name, Dolores Rondón, reflects her constant and simultaneous headaches and mobility. Even though she may be participating in the Revolution only as a service to her *novio*, her real heroism, presented in a concise, elliptical, and rhythmic style, plus the impression that she identifies with and represents the anonymous urban masses make *Gestos* a modern-day very Cuban *chanson de geste*, more effective than the much longer and more contrived "official" epics *Los niños se despiden* and *En ciudad semejante*.

At the opposite end of the experimental as well as generational spectrum from *Gestos* sits *Ciudad rebelde* (1967) by Luis Amado Blanco (b. 1903), a contemporary of Carpentier who published a volume of poetry as early as 1928.[197] Written in a straightforward, unpretentious style with a bare minimum of structural experimentation, *Ciudad rebelde* concentrates on the Havana conspiracies to overthrow

---

[196] Ibid., p. 117.

[197] Luis Amado Blanco was born and raised in Spain, went to Cuba for the first time in 1933, and emigrated definitely in 1936. His novel is dated October 31, 1966, in Rome, where he had been the Cuban ambassador to the Vatican for six years.

Batista in 1957–1958; police torture is decried, especially that of Captain Fortuna in the "novena estación"; the heroes are a dentist and a student; and Batista is called an "indio cobarde."[198] These similarities to the 1959–1960 novels in general outweigh the differences, which are nonetheless significant. The book's 433 pages make it almost twice as long as the earlier novels; several workers (garage mechanics, hotel bellboys, gardeners, etc.) collaborate with the revolutionary intellectuals; a few short modestly experimental sections depicting the action in the Sierra Maestra are interspersed throughout the book; concern is expressed over the future revolutionary struggle after Batista is overthrown; and Fidel is almost sanctified. The dedication reads, "To Dr. Fidel Castro, who one day resurrected us with the spring of an old hope."

Although the following four novels are also primarily concerned with urban guerrillas and police torture, they differ from *Gestos* and *Ciudad rebelde* as well as from the 1959–1960 novels in their varied use of the counterpoint technique. *Siempre la muerte, su paso breve* (1968) by Reynaldo González (b. 1940) is, in terms of the Latin American mainstream, the most conventionally experimental of these four novels. Like Carlos Fuentes's *La muerte de Artemio Cruz*, first-, second-, and third-person narrative points of view are alternated along with different chronological planes. Like Fuentes's *Cambio de piel* and Manuel Puig's *La traición de Rita Hayworth*, as well as the Cuban *Tres tristes tigres* and *Los niños se despiden*, numerous allusions to movie stars and comic-strip characters indicate United States cultural domination of Latin America from the 1930's through the 1950's, or from Shirley Temple to Rock Hudson. As in *Cien años de soledad*, characters from other novels are mentioned: Víctor Hugues from Carpentier's *El siglo de las luces* and Luis Dascal from Otero's *La situación*.[199] References to other Cuban novels are apparent in the homosexual writer Silvestre (Lezama Lima's *Paradiso*) and in popular singers Toña la Negra and Benny Moré (*Tres tristes tigres, De donde son los cantantes*).

Although *Siempre la muerte, su paso breve* resembles *Los niños se*

[198] Amado Blanco, *Ciudad rebelde*, p. 127.
[199] Reynaldo González, *Siempre la muerte, su paso breve*, pp. 19, 17.

despiden in its use of experimental techniques, it lost out to the latter in the 1968 Casa de las Américas competition, probably because of its more moderate experimentation and its reduced historical panorama. Although the protagonist's memories, with emphasis on his sexual experiences, re-create small-town life in the 1930's, 40's, and 50's, the absence of existentialist anguish and despair and the present role of the protagonist as a captured and tortured revolutionary identify the novel thematically more with the 1959–1960 group than with the 1961–1965 group. The setting is the city of Ciego de Avila in the province of Camagüey, thinly disguised as Ciego del Anima. The date is 1958, and the protagonist, guarded by two policemen, is attending his mother's wake. His personal memories, starting from childhood and alternating with impressions of the wake, gradually fuse with the gestation of the Revolution, particularly from 1956 on. Because the protagonist himself has recently been tortured by the police, the sense of exorcising the past is far outweighed by the positive commitment to the Revolution. In fact, the refusal of the protagonist's older brother to risk losing his job by becoming involved in the revolutionary movement contrasts with the greater revolutionary commitment of the new literary generation of the 1960's to which Reynaldo González (b. 1940) belongs.

Viento de enero (1968) by José Lorenzo Fuentes (b. 1928) resembles *Siempre la muerte, su paso breve* in that it could be identified thematically with both the 1961–1965 and the 1959–1960 novels. Like Soler Puig's *El derrumbe* (1964), it has only one antirevolutionary protagonist, a former army lieutenant under Batista whose roles as social and sexual oppressor are equated. Also as in *El derrumbe*, the protagonist's world crumbles with the triumph of the Revolution. Although Lt. Virgilio Mora's italicized thoughts and recollections of his childhood, occasionally expressed in the second person, provide glimpses of prerevolutionary rural Cuba, the chronological structure is based on the counterpoint between 1958 and 1959, when the roles of pursuer and pursued are reversed. Although Virgilio pursued the Santa Clara revolutionaries relentlessly for their terrorist bombings— in which the Communists did not participate—and although he even took part in their torturing, he is not by any means the sadistic torturer of the 1959–1960 novels. He is rather the typical lonely, insecure existentialist character who was unable to identify with his intelligent but unsuccessful father or with anyone else. He is estranged from his wealthy wife, rejected by his former mistress, and finally betrayed by his alcoholic cousin. Toward the end of 1958, Virgilio himself betrayed an old Santa Clara friend in order to prove himself to his superior officers in Havana Police Station Number 5. In spite of the protagonist's existentialist loneliness and despair, *Viento de enero* is closer to the 1959–1960 novels than *Siempre la muerte, su paso breve* because of the dynamic nature of the pursuits.

Reportaje de las vísperas (1967) by Gregorio Ortega (b. 1926), although far less experimental than *Siempre la muerte, su paso breve* and *Viento de enero*, presents one of the most vivid accounts of police torture under Batista to be found in any of the novels of the Revolution. These relatively brief sections, narrated in the present by the reporter-protagonist, alternate with the latter's memories of his experiences as a young crusading reporter during an unspecified two years of the Batista regime. In a very direct, unadorned style, similar to that of the 1959–1960 novels, the reporter exposes corruption and gangsterism at the highest level and particularly denounces the venal press, which protects the textile-smuggling business of an American magnate, probably the same Dayton Hedges who appears in Otero's *En ciudad semejante*. The immediate cause of the reporter's imprisonment is his involvement in an unsuccessful attack on the police barracks by the striking textile workers. The emphasis, as in the 1959–1960 novels, is on fast-moving action with very little attempt to delve into the protagonist's private life, even though we learn that he is married and has one child. Nonetheless, this novel represents a considerable improvement over Ortega's first novel, *Una de cal y otra de arena* (1957), which deals with the official venality and the gang warfare between the action groups of the 1940's.

The theme of Jaime Sarusky's (b. 1931) *Rebelión en la octava casa* (1967) is only apparently closer to that of the 1959–1960 novels. Two Havana revolutionaries leave their hideout at night to set off bombs and to send arms to the guerrillas in the Sierra Maestra in spite of the efforts of the police to locate them. Nonetheless, the whole revolutionary theme is overshadowed by Petronila, the mysterious woman astrolo-

gist in whose apartment they are hiding. She is a Dickensian-type character who constantly thinks of her 1933 revolutionary fiancé who fled
one day never to return. The contrapuntal interplay between 1933
and 1958 links the revolutionary movements against dictators Machado and Batista in a way that is somewhat reminiscent of Carpentier's cyclical interpretation of history in "El camino de Santiago." The
fact that the novel ends with the astrologist's expelling her revolutionary guests confers the role of protagonist on the apartment and the
world it contains. The title of the novel refers more to the conflict
within the apartment than to the struggle against Batista. In astrologi-
cal terminology, the eighth house is the house of death. Petronila becomes upset at the men's continuing their revolutionary activities and
at their incorporating her "niece" Clo into the group. The novel's in-
conclusive ending is totally in keeping with the mysterious, almost
supernatural, environment that pervades the apartment. The contrast
between Sarusky's first novel, *La búsqueda* (1961), with its epigraph
from Sartre, and *Rebelión en la octava casa*, in which a specific historical setting is combined with supernatural elements, reflects once again
the replacement of existentialism by magic realism in the 1960's as the
dominant literary current throughout Latin America.

*Escapism (?): Personal Problems, Rural and Foreign
Settings, Science Fiction*

Although the vast majority of the Cuban novels of the Revolution
have avoided controversial themes, roughly one-half of the works published between 1966 and 1970—and *Cobra* (1972)—are almost totally escapist in terms of their relationship to the Revolution. Like the
other 1966–1970 novels already discussed, many are highly experimental and fit comfortably into the mold of the new Latin American
novel.

César Leante's *Padres e hijos* (1967), Humberto Arenal's *Los animales sagrados* (1967), and Noel Navarro's *El plano inclinado*
(1968) are basically anachronistic examples of the 1961–1965 existentialist novels and, as such, bear a strong resemblance to Jaime Sarusky's *La búsqueda* and Virgilio Piñera's *Pequeñas maniobras*, without, however, the broader national implications of the latter two

novels. The protagonists are all introspective, lonely individuals who cannot communicate with their fellow human beings. Of the three, *Padres e hijos* is the closest to the 1961–1965 novels in its implied criticism of the prerevolutionary goal of most Cubans to be "successful": "Perhaps you want to be like the rest: make money, have fancy clothes, enjoy yourself, love."[200] Obviously related to Turgenev's 1861 novel of the same name, the generation gap is the source of the main conflict. Carlos and his older brother have no respect for their father, because he is an economic failure. The older brother, in spite of his ambition, cannot rise above the status of underpaid worker and, after his father's death, decides to leave Cuba for the United States. Carlos is equally frustrated and disoriented: ". . . the only thing that you know is that you're not happy and you're trying to find your way . . . You spin around in the gloomy whirlwind of your adolescence."[201] However, the belated recognition of their father's idealism and younger Carlos's decision to remain in Cuba may be interpreted as an optimistic ending, which implicitly heralds the forthcoming revolution. In this sense, there is some justification for the question mark after "escapism" in the title of this section, although, basically, *Padres e hijos* is more a psychological novel than a sociological one, and, in the words of reviewer Antonio Benítez Rojo, "it doesn't get to touch on the Revolution."[202]

More pessimistic, more existentialist, and less related to Cuban society, *Los animales sagrados* and *El plano inclinado* have protagonists who are every bit as lonely in spite of their apparent bourgeois success. *Los animales sagrados* takes place in Cuba, although references to the geographic and historical environment are minimal, while *El plano inclinado* is set in Paris. The protagonists of both novels search futilely for love, understanding, and a purpose for their lives. In *El plano inclinado*, the thirty-three–year–old protagonist is "crucified" because of his total lack of interest in what is happening in Cuba and because of his decision to view the world from a reclining position in his bed.

[200] Leante, *Padres e hijos*, p. 97.
[201] Ibid.
[202] Antonio Benítez Rojo, "Otros padres, otros hijos," *Casa de las Américas* 9, no. 50 (September–October 1968): 184.

In *Los animales sagrados*, no relationship at all is established between the protagonists' anguish and the situation in Cuba. Alberto, his wife Sara, and his mistress Susana suffer more because of their Sartrian models than because of their own situations. During the novel, mention is made of Sartre's *Los caminos de la libertad*, *El muro*, and *La edad de la razón*, while at the end Alberto vomits and then sits on the toilet and feels happy.

Although these three existentialist novels are really not so experimental as to warrant being classified among the new Latin American novels, they do reveal a greater interest in literary techniques than do their 1961–1965 predecessors. Like Carlos Fuentes's *Aura* and parts of *La muerte de Artemio Cruz*, *Padres e hijos* is narrated in the second person. *El plano inclinado* is narrated in the first person by the protagonist, Roberto, with occasional first-person sections narrated by one of his friends. Although chronological order is followed, at times the narrative is somewhat jumbled, apparently in order to reflect Roberto's confused state of mind. Arenal uses the Faulknerian techniques of interior monologues and the changing point of view with belated identification of the narrator, but his most experimental concern seems to be the development of the title, *Los animales sagrados*, which refers to the scavenging and predatory cat, sea gull, and shark, which in general terms symbolize the characters.

Lisandro Otero's *Pasión de Urbino* (1966), even more than *Los animales sagrados*, resembles an exercise in literary experimentation inspired by avant-garde films. Like the Japanese movie *Rashomon*, Otero presents three different versions of the death of his protagonist, Father Antonio Urbino—accident, murder, and suicide—and allows the reader to choose any or all of the three. Some of the scenes between Father Urbino and his mistress and adulteress sister-in-law, Fabiola, are reminiscent of Robbe-Grillet's *Last Year at Marienbad* and other experimental French films of the 1960's. The alternating paragraphs from the past and the present, very clearly defined, are the novel's least experimental item. Although the portrayal of a sensuous priest, upper-class sexual immorality, and an embezzlement is totally consistent with the revolutionary view of pre-1959 Cuba, the author makes absolutely no attempt to attach any historical significance to his short (eighty-eight pages) novel. Inferior to the two published volumes of Otero's epic trilogy, *La situación* and *En ciudad semejante*, *Pasión de Urbino* achieved a dubious degree of notoriety for its role in the Padilla case.[203]

In addition to those works that concentrate on personal problems, escapism is also manifested in a highly diversified and sophisticated group of novels with a variety of almost unreal rural settings. Paradoxically, the best known of these novels purports to ridicule the escapist attitude of an intellectual by transforming a very real town at the foot of the Sierra Maestra into a world of make-believe. Ezequiel Vieta's (b. 1922) *Vivir en Candonga*, which received the UNEAC prize for 1965, deals somewhat ambiguously with the relationship between the individual and reality. The protagonist is naturalist Waldo Utiello, who has been collecting butterflies in the Oriente town of Candonga since a little before Batista's March 1952 *golpe*. His lifelong ambition is to find the *Stella aequalis*, a specimen described by Christopher Columbus in his diary but which has not been seen since. Although Utiello is aware that Fidel Castro and his men are fighting in the nearby Sierra Maestra, he does not understand why that should deter him from his search. He actually discovers and captures the rare butterfly while talking to the unnamed but clearly identifiable Camilo Cienfuegos. The rebels have captured the town and ordered it evacuated in anticipation of the arrival of government bombers. Utiello, in the meantime, can think only of returning to his laboratory in order to photograph and study the *Stella* while it is still alive. He is delayed by an encounter with Fidel Castro himself (presented as Alejandro, his historical *nom de guerre*), who engages the "mad scientist" in a lively discussion. Totally exasperated, Fidel wonders how a man can be so totally divorced from reality:

—Where are we? Where are you standing? Do you know? Do you know what this is? Do you know what's happening? What's happening to us? Do you know? And tell me, now, what does the *Stella* have to do with all this, at this moment. (Even if you have it in your hand.) Humboldt and the very Admiral himself! It doesn't matter if Candonga is about to burn up. The universe . . . if a whole mountain comes down on top of you. The whole

Sierra. You wouldn't feel it, huh?! You already had a comfortable niche, your security! No? . . . Then what's the calendar for! In what world are you living![204]

The conversation is interrupted by the sound of rifle fire, which enables Utiello to make it back to his laboratory in the by-now abandoned town. Only his housekeeper, Lucía, still remains, feverishly packing and terribly bruised and half-crazed after a hilarious accidental collision with their neighbor Godofredo Pubillones, who had returned to urge her to leave Candonga. Like Don Quixote's housekeeper who participates in the burning of her master's books, Lucía destroys the *Stella* in order to liberate Utiello. Soon thereafter, Candonga is bombed for the second time by the B-26's, "los yanquimastodontes de la aviación batistiana,"[205] and Utiello is killed.

It is precisely the suggestion of Utiello's resemblance to Don Quixote and the absurd conduct of Batista's forces that make the ridicule of Utiello's escapism somewhat ambiguous. In spite of his obsession to photograph the *Stella*, Utiello's humanitarianism impels him to stop his mad dash and offer help to a boy who has become separated from his family. Previously he had aided a wounded government sergeant and agreed to deliver a packet of documents to one of Batista's *esbirros* in Candonga. The general atmosphere of Cervantes's novel is suggested by the literary convention of ascribing the Candonga manuscript to the unknown Manresa; by a pseudoerudite footnote involving Mateo Alemán's seventeenth-century *Ortografía*; and by occasional stylistic reminiscences. The fact that the second bombing raid on Candonga is ordered as atonement for the mistaken bombing of a baptism party for a wealthy senator's daughter causes the reader to wonder whether the realistic politicians and soldiers are any more sane than the idealistic and escapist Utiello. The author's own humorous footnotes and asides related to the creative process place Vieta in the tradition of Borges, Cortázar, Cabrera Infante, and Sarduy and undoubtedly contributed to the irritation of some revolutionary readers, commented on by José Antonio Portuondo in the award statement: "Its originality was in the

204 Vieta, *Vivir en Candonga*, p. 59.
205 Ibid., p. 84.

way it utilized techniques and language taken from the novel of the absurd for an absolutely realistic theme, which boils down to a sharp satire of the intellectual surprised by the Revolution. This satirical and absurd manner of expressing a fundamental problem besetting our present Cuban reality was destined to cause and will continue to cause irritation among many people. But, for some members of the jury, at least, this is precisely one of the cardinal virtues of the novel.''[206]

The question of the individual's responsibility to society is treated in a much more escapist manner in Vieta's previous novel *Pailock, el prestidigitador*, published in 1966 but allegedly completed in 1954. The earlier date of completion would seem to be confirmed by the prevailing Kafka-like atmosphere that appears in some of the stories of Vieta's *Libro de los epílogos*, also written in the 1950's. Fantastic and escapist as *Pailock, el prestidigitador* seems to be, the trial of the magician for having made his wife disintegrate on stage without being able to make her reappear may be related, as in *Vivir en Candonga*, to the role of the individual artist or intellectual in revolutionary Cuba. The trial is conducted by the magician's fellow performers in the variety show, who, after deliberating for hours, declare him innocent of any breach of discipline. However, upon the urging of the "Empresario," they later find him guilty, in a matter of seconds, of endangering the theatrical company. The novel ends with Pailock's expulsion.

Although Ezequiel Vieta (b. 1922) is ten years younger than Lezama Lima and only five years older than the majority of the generation of 1950, his works share with those of Lezama and his contemporary Virgilio Piñera (b. 1912) the reaction against *criollismo* and therefore the reluctance to portray realistically the contemporary Cuban scene. Although folklorist Samuel Feijóo (b. 1914) was not affected by the *anticriollismo* of his literary contemporaries Lezama, Piñera, and Vieta, his latest novel does reveal the influence of the new Latin American novel in its combination of the panoramic vision with elements of pure fantasy. The predominance of the latter tips the scales in favor of the escapist label. Whereas *Pancho Ruta y Gil Jocuma* (1968) resembles Feijóo's two 1964 novels in its blend of rural folklore and a

[206] Ibid., jacket flap.

dash of social protest, *Jira descomunal*, also published in 1968, is a much more ambitious undertaking. In spite of the subtitle, "Novela cubana, nativista, costumbrista, folklorista e indigenista," *Jira descomunal* transcends folklore both by interspersing fragments of a broad historical vision of prerevolutionary Cuba dating back to 1868 and by including a totally escapist, Jules Verne–like utopia, founded in Brazil by Ukrainians who escaped from nineteenth-century Czarist Russia and mated with the natives. The vehicle for this strange mixture of past, present, and future is the archetypal boatride, Cubanized into a hijacked bus on a hurricane-driven ferry. Most of the novel is taken up by each of the thirty-two passengers' narrating his prerevolutionary experiences in order to pass the time of day as the ferry drifts in the Caribbean. This Boccaccio-like technique allows the fisherman, the circus worker, the gravedigger, and other lower-class representatives to paint a picture of exploitation and injustice. One of the experimental features of the novel is the crude line drawings made by "El Mudo" to tell his particular story. After their visit to the Brazilian utopia, a magic ship returns them to the southern coast of Pinar del Río Province where the ex–bus passengers and survivors of the shipwreck will plunge into a variety of unnamed revolutionary tasks. As in Feijóo's other novels, one of the most delightful features of *Jira descomunal* is the reproduction and manipulation of the rural Cuban vernacular, which totally overshadows the almost lip service allusions to the Revolution.

Paradoxically, the most escapist of all the Cuban novels published since 1959, with or without a rural setting, is also one of the most authentically Cuban of all the novels, but only in a linguistic sense. It is also paradoxical that the author, Francisco Chofre (b. 1924), was born in Valencia, Spain, and did not emigrate to Cuba until he was twenty-five years old. His work, *La Odilea* (1968), like *Tres tristes tigres*, *De donde son los cantantes*, and *Los niños se despiden*, is obsessed with linguistic creativity, but to the point of excluding any possible reference to the Revolution. As the title suggests, *La Odilea* is a parody of the Greek epic in which the Greek characters are transformed into Cuban *guajiros*: Odileo, la Pena, Telesforo, Atenata,

Zeulorio, and others. All the episodes of the original epic are narrated in Cuban rural dialect, and the literary value of the book depends exclusively on the author's ingenious reproduction of the Cuban idiom.

Although the geographical setting of Reinaldo Arenas's (b. 1943) *Celestino antes del alba* (1967) is rural Cuba, there is absolutely no chronological reference, and, in general, the escapist label seems even more appropriate than in the case of *Jira descomunal*. In spite of its many thematic ingredients usually associated with the social protest novel, the dreamlike quality of *Celestino antes del alba* precludes it from being interpreted in any way as a revolutionary novel. Clearly influenced by William Faulkner and Miguel Angel Asturias, Arenas presents a highly poetic and fantastic vision of the sordid life of a poor rural family. A combination of Benjy in *The Sound and the Fury* and the protagonist of Asturias's *El alhajadito*, the narrator is a mentally retarded youngster, who does not distinguish between reality and fantasy. His only friend is his older cousin, Celestino, who writes poetry on tree trunks, which his grandfather promptly chops down. The hatred that exists among almost all the characters impels the narrator and Celestino to live and die in a world of witches, goblins, and talking birds and animals. The narrator mentally transforms his mother into a lizard and imagines that he eats his grandfather's ear to alleviate his hunger. The grandfather's denunciation of both boys as effeminate because of their love for poetry as well as the insertion of epigraphs and other quotes from such authors as Oscar Wilde, Jorge Luis Borges, Federico García Lorca, Arthur Rimbaud, and Tristan Corbière suggest that the novel is a plea for pure art and the spiritual instinct of man versus his material needs. This interpretation would indicate that the novel is actually not so escapist and is really a protest against official government policy, which is somewhat borne out by the author's own comment: "But what is sad about all this is that, when someone becomes concerned about expressing other aspects of reality, they are offended, or they label him as not being enough of a realist . . . which is the criterion followed by 99 percent of our critics."[207]

Arenas's nonconformist attitude is more clearly evident in his sec-

[207] Reinaldo Arenas, "Celestino y yo," *Unión* 6, no. 3 (July–September 1967): 119.

ond novel *El mundo alucinante* (1969), where "escapism" is historical as well as geographical. The quotation marks around "escapism" are justified by the fact that this novel has not yet been published in Cuba.[208] Along with *El siglo de las luces, Paradiso, Tres tristes tigres, Gestos,* and *De donde son los cantantes,* Arenas's novel is one of the better known, highly original Cuban examples of the new Latin American novel.

In addition to alternating boldly among first-, second-, and third-person narrative points of view, Reynaldo[209] Arenas often indulges in linguistic play. All of chapter 11 is written either in verse or in rhymed dialogue and narrative. In chapter 28, sentences are structured around different forms of the same word: "Entonces tú, oh, fraile, planeaste nuevos planes bien planificados."[210] As in the case of *Cien años de soledad,* only much more so, the most fantastic events are presented in a realistic, straight-faced manner. Arenas's protagonist is the amazing Mexican Fray Servando Teresa de Mier and the novel is based primarily on Fray Servando's own *Memorias*[211] and on Artemio de Valle-Arizpe's biography.[212] Arenas follows his hero from his childhood in Monterrey to his death in Mexico City to Buenos Aires, where his mummy was exhibited as a victim of the Inquisition, and, many decades later, to Belgium, where the mummy was displayed in a famous circus. During his lifetime, Fray Servando's odyssey began as a result of his 1794 sermon in which he eloquently attacked the official version of the legend of the Virgin of Guadalupe. According to Fray Servando's thesis, the Virgin of Guadalupe did not first appear on the "Indian John's dirty cape"[213] in the sixteenth century but rather on the cape of Quetzalcóatl, who was really the apostle Saint Thomas. This thesis not only was heretical in religious terms but also undermined one of the

208 A second edition of *Celestino antes del alba* was published in Buenos Aires in 1968, while the only edition in Spanish of *El mundo alucinante* was published in Mexico in 1969. An English translation under the title *Hallucinations* was published in 1971.

209 Arenas apparently changed the spelling of his first name from "Reinaldo" to "Reynaldo" between publication of his two novels.

210 Reynaldo Arenas, *El mundo alucinante,* p. 171.

211 José Servando Teresa de Mier, *Memorias.*

212 Artemio de Valle-Arizpe, *Fray Servando.*

213 Arenas, *El mundo alucinante,* p. 34.

supposed contributions of Spain to Mexico and, therefore, strengthened the movement for independence. In the novel, Fray Servando was imprisoned on the island of San Juan de Ulúa off the coast of Veracruz and escaped by eating his iron chains. From that moment on, he moves at a fantastic pace from country to country, from prison to prison: Spain, France, Italy, Portugal, England, the United States, Mexico, Cuba, and back to the United States and Mexico. He denounces the sexual immorality of the decadent court of Spanish King Carlos IV with Goya-like visions and, like Carpentier in *El siglo de las luces*, criticizes the excesses of the French Revolution: "I come from places where the most violent and radical changes have been applied. And I come fleeing. And I'm one who fought with my own hands to bring these changes into being."[214] He describes the horrible conditions on a slave ship in the Caribbean and on a premature train in the United States that runs on coal power and, later, on twenty-nine carloads of Negroes who are also fed into the furnace: " 'It's the closest thing to coal,' a lady explains to me."[215] In another deliberate example of anachronism, Fray Servando complains about the excessive number of taxes in the United States: "And once again I found myself in the country where for each breath of air you have to pay a tax."[216]

When he is not in jail, Fray Servando meets up with some of the leading political and literary figures of the period: Simón Rodríguez, Simón Bolívar, Napoleon, Alexander von Humboldt, Lady Hamilton, Chateaubriand, Madame de Staël, and José María Heredia. Arenas is not at all hesitant about inserting contemporary personalities in his late-eighteenth- and early-nineteenth-century tableau. Like Christine Jorgensen or Virginia Woolf's Orlando, Arenas's Orlando, whose name is always accompanied by the epithet "rara mujer,"[217] is sexually ambivalent. Asthmatic José Lezama Lima, who devotes six pages of his own *La expresión americana*[218] to Fray Servando and from whom Arenas quotes,[219] appears in the novel under the guise of the historical

[214] Ibid., p. 60.
[215] Ibid., p. 169.
[216] Ibid., p. 184.
[217] Ibid., chapter 27.
[218] José Lezama Lima, *La expresión americana*, pp. 61–66.
[219] Arenas, *El mundo alucinante*, p. 221.

Padre José de Lezamis, "preaching with his whimpering voice like that
of a hurt child."[220] Alejo Carpentier, although not mentioned by name,
is one of the many writers who, along with Fray Servando and Heredia,
reside in the presidential palace of Guadalupe Victoria, Mexico's first
president. The following passage is a direct allusion to Carpentier's
fondness for detailed descriptions of architecture and scenery in
general.

That man (already old), armed with compasses, set squares, rulers, and a
hundred other strange objects that Fray Servando could not identify, was re-
citing in the form of a litany the names of all the columns in the palace, the
details of each one, the number and the position of the pilasters and archi-
traves, the quantity of friezes, the texture of the cornices in relief, the composition of the plaster and the stonework that made up the walls, the variety
of trees that filled the garden, their exact number of leaves, and finally even
the different types of ants that thrived on their branches.[221]

As in Carpentier's *El siglo de las luces*, the question arises as to how
escapist *El mundo alucinante* really is. Since both authors cut across
chronological boundaries with the greatest of ease, the relationship of
the French Revolution and the Mexican War of Independence (which
was originally more of a social revolution than were the South American Wars of Independence) to the Cuban Revolution is not at all far-
fetched. In this respect, *El mundo alucinante* is much more intimately
tied to the Cuban experience than is *El siglo de las luces*. In the prologue, the author addresses himself to Fray Servando and identifies
with him completely: ". . . you and I are the same person."[222] He also
gives a possible explanation of why the novel has not yet been published in Cuba: "You are, dear Servando, what you are: one of the most
important (and unfortunately almost unknown) figures of the literary
and political history of America. An outstanding man. And that's sufficient grounds for some people to think that this novel should be cen-
sored."[223] While Fray Servando's condemnation of Napoleon and Iturbide for having betrayed the ideals for which their respective revolu-

220 Ibid., p. 201.
221 Ibid., p. 198.
222 Ibid., p. 9.
223 Ibid., p. 10.

tions were fought is historical and may be found in Fray Servando's writings, the portrayal of President Guadalupe Victoria in the relatively long penultimate chapter is not based on Fray Servando's *Memorias* and is apparently intended to suggest Fidel Castro:

Nevertheless, the enthusiasm of the people for serving their handsome president is so great that the line at the entrance is always longer than that of the corpses being taken out in back. The president enjoys almost unanimous support. Almost unanimous . . .[224]

But, occasionally, the delirium of his admirers, the applause, and the shouts of "Long live our Great Liberator!" "Long live the man who redeemed us from the empire!" along with the declaiming of the inevitable high-sounding poems, go beyond the usual limits (they set their goals too high). Then the president, no longer able to sleep, gets up rather irritated, goes out on the presidential balcony in his underwear and, with the utmost elegance, touches the tip of his mustache with his index finger.[225]

Now, with his eyes closed, he again gazes on the delirious crowd; the crowd that applauds with its very sore hands; the crowd that he silences by only raising one finger.[226]

[Fray Servando] "What are we in this palace but a bunch of useless objects, museum relics, rehabilitated prostitutes. What we have done counts for nothing if we don't dance to the sound of the latest tune. It counts for nothing. And if you try to correct mistakes, you're only a traitor, and if you try to tone down the bestiality, you're only a cynical revisionist, and, if you fight for real freedom, you're courting death itself."[227]

This constant hypocrisy, this constant repeating that we're in Paradise and that everything is perfect? And, really and truly, are we in Paradise?[228]

Shortly before Fray Servando's return to Mexico during the Iturbide reign, he finds himself in La Cabaña prison in Havana where the colors in his cell refer directly to the July Twenty-sixth Movement: "Summer. The walls of my cell are changing color, from pink to red, and from red to wine red, and from wine red to shiny black."[229]

[224] Ibid., p. 195.
[225] Ibid., p. 196.
[226] Ibid.
[227] Ibid., p. 207.
[228] Ibid.
[229] Ibid., p. 182.

The allusion in the final chapter to Iturbide's execution "on the scaffold in Padilla,"[230] although historically accurate—Padilla is a town in the state of Tamaulipas in Mexico—also serves to refer to Heberto Padilla, who has become the symbol of the repressed writer in Cuba today. The dedication of the novel to Camila Henríquez Ureña and Virgilio Piñera, "por la honradez intelectual de ambos," underlines the difficulties faced by Cuban writers in the late 1960's and further confirms the nonescapist interpretation of *El mundo alucinante*.

Alejo Carpentier, obviously aware that his style has been parodied by Reynaldo Arenas as well as by Cabrera Infante and López-Nussa, pokes fun at his own style in his most recently published novel, *El recurso del método* (April 1974), which is more genuinely escapist than *El mundo alucinante*.[231] Carpentier identifies himself stylistically with his protagonist, the almost anonymous dictator with the flowery speeches who is always referred to as the Primer Magistrado.

The Primer Magistrado was ridiculed for the affected and erudite expressions of his oratory. But . . . he did not use them out of mere verbal baroquism; he knew that with these linguistic devices he had created a style that displayed his original touch and that the use of unusual words, adjectives, epithets that his listeners hardly understood, far from hurting him, appealed to their atavistic cult of affectation and brilliant adornment. He had thus acquired the reputation of master of the language, and the tone of his speeches contrasted with that of the monotonous and poorly written barracks proclamations of his adversary.[232]

Carpentier, speaking vicariously again, confesses his disillusionment with his own style. "For the time being, those expressions (he was customarily his own severest critic) had acquired such a false-coin ring, like gold-plated lead, like a piastre that won't bounce up, that, tired of his verbal pirouettes, he would ask himself how he would fill the air waves and the printed page with unavoidable proclamations and admonitions while embarking on a military campaign, albeit a primitive one, like the one that was to begin shortly."[233]

---

230 Ibid., p. 218.

231 Like *Sonámbulo del sol* and Sarduy's *Cobra, El recurso del método* bears witness to the survival of the 1966–1970 tendencies in Cuban novels published outside Cuba.

232 Alejo Carpentier, *El recurso del método*, p. 48.

233 Ibid., p. 122.

However, the main purpose of *El recurso del método* is not a stylistic self-parody, nor a spoof of Descartes, as the title suggests, but rather a parody of the typical Latin American dictator. *El recurso del método* belongs to the novelistic genre of the composite Latin American republic, a genre with a rich seventy-year-old tradition that includes such outstanding works as Joseph Conrad's *Nostromo* (1904) and Valle-Inclán's *Tirano Banderas* (1926).

The nameless republic of *El recurso del método* is a Cuban-Mexican stew with a variety of other ingredients thrown in from Central and South America and the Caribbean. Like Mexico, Carpentier's republic produces silver and petroleum, oppresses the Indians who work on the sisal plantations, sings Mexican ballads, and has a Paricutín Volcano and a San Juan de Letrán Street. Rebel General Hoffmann meets the same death in a quagmire as revolutionary General Rodolfo Fierro, the subject of Rafael Muñoz's short story "Oro, caballo y hombre."

Like Cuba, the republic produces large quantities of sugar cane and tobacco; General Hoffmann's grandmother is a "back-patio Negress"; the new capitol is an imitation of the one in Washington; the Cantonese storeowners are the first to break the general strike; and the United States ambassador is Enoch Crowder, who really held that post from 1923 to 1927. The public acclaim for the Primer Magistrado is enhanced by the appearance of fluttering pigeons, which recalls one of Fidel Castro's early mass rallies.

Other countries represented include Peru and Argentina (the Universidad de San Lucas in the city of Nueva Córdoba), Colombia (coasts on the Atlantic and the Pacific), Bolivia (tin mines and the threat to hang the Primer Magistrado from a telegraph post), Nicaragua and El Salvador (the guardian volcano on postage stamps), and the entire Caribbean (banana plantations and the landing of United States marines).

Although the allusions to President Villarroel of Bolivia and to Fidel Castro give the impression that Carpentier is trying to create a chronological as well as geographical synthesis of Latin America, this novel, a few anachronisms notwithstanding, is limited precisely to the period between 1912 and 1927, which corresponds to part of Carpentier's childhood, his adolescence, and his youth. The combined nostalgic-picaresque tone that pervades the novel is surprisingly similar to that of Miguel Angel Asturias's last novel, *Viernes de Dolores* (1972), which deals with part of the same period. The chronology of *El recurso del método* is established by allusions to historical events and personalities as well as to American popular songs. The first chapter takes place between the fall of Mexican dictator Porfirio Díaz in 1911 and the sinking of the *Titanic* in 1912, while in New York they are playing "Alexander [*sic*] Ragtime Band." As the Primer Magistrado, now called El-Ex, is about to die, everyone is singing "Yes, We Have No Bananas," Benito Mussolini is the man of the hour, and in Brussels the First World Conference against Colonial Imperialism is held, with Barbusse presiding and Nehru and Cuban revolutionary student hero Julio Antonio Mella in attendance.

The sole protagonist of the novel is the Primer Magistrado, whose real name is mentioned only once when his enemies are stirred by the performance of the revolutionary opera *Tosca* to shout "Down with Valverde!"[234] Because of his cultural veneer and the period of his reign, the Primer Magistrado most resembles Guatemalan dictator Manuel Estrada Cabrero (1898–1920), who constructed replicas of the Greek temple to Minerva throughout the country and who served as the prototype for Miguel Angel Asturias's *El Señor Presidente*. However, the Primer Magistrado also has touches of Venezuelan dictators Antonio Guzmán Blanco (1870–1889) and Juan Vicente Gómez (1908–1935), Dominican Republic's infamous Trujillo (1930–1961), and other literary as well as historical tyrants. In spite of his notorious venality and the cruelty with which he suppresses revolts, the Primer Magistrado is characterized principally as a *pícaro*, and humor predominates over social protest. The book is framed by the dictator's immediate and distant memories of his sexual relations with a Saint Vincent of Paul nun. Shortly before he dies, the Primer Magistrado discovers that the secret of life is not the "pienso, luego soy" of Descartes but rather the "siento, luego soy"[235] of anti-Cartesian Latin America reflected in the dictator's personal fondness for music, food, and, especially, sex. The dictator's political activities also have a picaresque

234 Ibid., p. 199.
235 Ibid., p. 309.

flavor. During a period in which his popularity wanes, the dictator cancels the elections on the grounds that his country has not yet signed a peace treaty with Hungary after the end of World War I. Threatened later by a revolution of the masses, the Primer Magistrado confiscates all communist literature, including Stendhal's *The Red and the Black* and Hawthorne's *The Scarlet Letter.*

Although *El recurso del método* is only remotely related to the Cuban Revolution, its political message is clear. As in *El Señor Presidente*, the dictator cannot and should not be overthrown by a military revolt. Both General Galván's and General Hoffmann's uprisings are crushed with relative ease. Nor should we trust the revolutionary force and integrity of philosophy professor Dr. Luis Leoncio Martínez, who, because of his austere puritanical habits, resembles the octogenarian ex-president and dictator of Ecuador, José María Velasco Ibarra (1934–1935, 1944–1947, 1953–1957, 1968–1972). Dr. Martínez takes over the presidency after the Primer Magistrado's fall, thanks to active support from the United States. Carpentier's attitude toward a revolution of the masses is somewhat ambiguous. In contrast to Dr. Martínez, Miguel Estatua, a miner whose prototype may have been the Guanajuatan hero Pípila of the Mexican War of Independence, is a brave, uncorruptible, popular hero. Rather than surrender to the forces of the hated dictator, he blows himself up with dynamite. Much as he admires the popular *caudillo*, Carpentier seems to doubt the viability of an uprising of the masses. For Carpentier, as well as for Asturias, the hero is the anonymous university student. In *El recurso del método*, El Estudiante is a Marxist-Leninist who resists the dictator's threats and bribes in a dialogue constructed on alternating words and the speakers' italicized thoughts. El Estudiante also recognizes the need to continue fighting against Dr. Martínez: "We overthrew one dictator . . . but the same struggle continues, since the enemies are the same."[236]

In contrast to *El recurso del método*'s and *El mundo alucinante*'s historical escapism, the following two novels are truly escapist in geographical terms: they both take place in Europe. Beyond that, the only other similarity is the assonantal rhyme of their titles: *La Robla* (1967) and *Cobra* (1972). The former, by Gustavo Eguren (b.

[236] Ibid., p. 326.

1925), is probably the least experimental of all the 1966–1970 novels. A realistically narrated story about a Galsworthy-type strike against an individually owned factory and set in a Spanish town without any fixed date, its only link to the Cuban Revolution is the general theme of class conflict. Although the author is Cuban, he lived in Spain between 1928 and 1944, and his style seems much more Spanish than Cuban.

Cobra, on the other hand, exceeds even the experimentation of Severo Sarduy's first two novels, *Gestos* (1963) and *De donde son los cantantes* (1967). Although its publication date of 1972 falls outside the 1966–1970 confines of this chapter, separate parts of the novel were published as early as 1968 in Caracas, Buenos Aires, and Paris.[237] Furthermore, the fact that *Cobra* was published in Buenos Aires and Nivaria Tejera's *Sonámbulo del sol* (1972) in Barcelona indicates that the 1970 cut-off date does not apply to works published outside Cuba.

Although the first half of *Cobra* seems to take off from the Chinese cabaret-brothel world of the first third of *De donde son los cantantes*, the setting is not Havana, the characters are not Cubans, and there is not the slightest intention to create a panoramic epic of Cuba. In fact, the only allusions to Cuba are the chance encounter in Toledo, Spain, with the two stars of *De donde son los cantantes*, Auxilio and Socorro,[238] and the mention of Dolores Rondón.[239] The star of the show is Cobra, the "reina," who, together with the Señora, is reproduced in miniature. The Señora eliminates her double, the Señorita, but Cobra adores her own "square root" named La Poupée, and nicknamed Pup. These characters plus Cobra's rival, Cadillac, and the Indian tattoo artist with the enormous penis cavort in a world of fantasy conjured up by drugs, "anarquía yerbera."[240] Allusions to the Orient, linguistic games, and various definitions of writing—"the art of ellipsis," "the art of digressing," "the art of reproducing reality," "to take apart order

[237] *Les Lettres Nouvelles*, special issue, December 1967–January 1968, pp. 187–192; *Imagen*, October 1–15, 1968, with a brief introduction by Emir Rodríguez Monegal; *Sur*, nos. 316–317 (January–April 1969), pp. 24–37; *Papeles* (Caracas), no. 14 (August 1971), pp. 8–21.

[238] Severo Sarduy, *Cobra*, p. 91.

[239] Ibid., p. 61.

[240] Ibid., p. 34.

and to put together disorder"[241]—add to the anarchy. Toward the end of the first half, Cobra sings a mambo in Esperanto in a Tangiers nightclub before undergoing a weird operation together with Pup at the hands of the distinguished "condrólogo," Dr. Ktazob.[242]

Part two is even more fantastic, as Cobra, now identified as a transvestite, is initiated into an Amsterdam-based motorcycle club through a series of occult religious and sexual rites. The name "Cobra" also turns out to be a kind of acronym of Copenhagen, Brussels, and Amsterdam. The motorcyclists are named Tigre, Tundra, Escorpión, and Totem. Reflecting the total revolt against the novelistic tradition, *Cobra* flaunts its lack of plot and character development. Sarduy has even eliminated the human emotions that are evoked by one of his models, William Burroughs's *Naked Lunch* (1959). Like *Tres tristes tigres* and Sarduy's own previous two novels, *Cobra* is essentially a linguistic composition. However, in *Cobra*, Sarduy has eliminated all references to Cuba in order to dedicate his composition to the international drug culture with emphasis on the themes of sex and the oriental religions.

Further removed from revolutionary Cuba in time and space, but not necessarily in theme, are the science-fiction novels *Presiones y diamantes* (1967) by Virgilio Piñera and Miguel Collazo's *El libro fantástico de Oaj* (1966) and *El viaje* (1968). The popularity of science fiction in Cuba, in all of Latin America, and in the United States increased markedly during the 1960's because of space exploration by the United States and the Soviet Union. Although the fantastic short story was cultivated in Cuba in the 1930's by Arístides Fernández and Rubén Martínez Villena, it was not until the 1960's that Cubans turned their attention to science fiction. In 1969, Oscar Hurtado published a four-hundred-page international anthology, *Cuentos de ciencia-ficción*. Rogelio Llopis's *Cuentos cubanos de lo fantástico y lo extraordinario* (1968) contains a section on science fiction with stories by Angel Arango (b. 1926), Miguel Collazo (b. 1936), Juan Luis Herrero (b. 1939), Germán Piniella (b. 1935), and Manuel Herrera (b. 1943). Even Julio E. Miranda's *Antología del nuevo cuento cu-*

[241] Ibid., pp. 15, 16, 17, 20.
[242] Ibid., p. 97.

bano (1969), which thematically is more devoted to the Revolution, contains a science-fiction section with stories by Arango, Collazo, and Piniella. In the prologue to his anthology, Miranda attaches special importance to science fiction and singles out Collazo for special praise: "With Collazo, science fiction achieves a magnificent multiplicity of references from philosophical problems to political metaphors, always with a touch of very Cuban humor, sometimes subtle, other times hilarious, all of which combines to make him the best author of this genre . . ."[243]

Miranda's words are much more applicable to Collazo's first novel, *El libro fantástico de Oaj* (1966), than to *El viaje* (1968). The former cleverly alternates a Saturnian's account of Earth and an Earthman's account of Saturn. Spaceships whirl around in outer space and land in Havana. Saturnians arrive in flying saucers to spy on their enemies. Conflict builds up and terminates in a destructive war. The tone of the book is satirical and the extent to which the "metáfora política" could be applied to U.S.-Cuban relations is not always clear.

In *El viaje*, Collazo uses a much more serious tone to treat the broader problem of man's search for an ideal world. Several generations of people on the imaginary planet of Ambar reenact the basic patterns of human behavior with Old Testament overtones. The final voyage is launched to eliminate the causes of pain and sorrow, to establish a new relationship between mind and matter, and to create a new man. Although the latter is certainly one of the expressed goals of the Cuban Revolution, there are no other links between this novel and Cuban reality in general.

A more revolutionary attitude is expressed in Virgilio Piñera's latest novel, *Presiones y diamantes*. Whereas his existentialist novel *Pequeñas maniobras*, written in 1956–1957 and published in 1963, represents a deviation from his more characteristic short stories and plays in order to conform to prevailing literary currents, *Presiones y diamantes* fits neatly into both his own literary corpus and the new Latin American novel. In keeping with the absurdist formula, he employs a relatively simple and direct style to exaggerate to the extreme the flaws

243 JEM, p. 20.

of society.[244] The science-fiction milieu may seem escapist, but the sky-scrapers, the subway system, the Chiclets, the contraceptives, and the fact that the protagonist-narrator is a jewelry salesman all identify the disintegrating society as a kind of New York City, symbolizing the United States and the whole capitalist world. Although there is absolutely no mention of Cuba, the underlying implication is that the future belongs to the new revolutionary man of the socialist world. This broad vision of the world is characteristic of the new Latin American novel and the Cuban novel between 1966 and 1970, and it stands in marked contrast to both the existentialist microcosmic world of *Pequeñas maniobras* and the specific functionalism of the 1970 and 1971 Casa de las Américas prize winners, Miguel Cossío Woodward's *Sacchario* and Manuel Cofiño López's *La última mujer y el próximo combate.*

IV. The Ideological Novel: 1971–

Although there is no way of telling how long the newest period in the development of the Cuban novel will last, no doubt exists about its representing a distinct break with the 1966–1970 period. In contrast to the well over thirty boldly experimental novels published between 1966 and the end of 1970, six were published in Cuba in 1971 and then none in 1972 or 1973. The 1972 Casa de las Américas novel prize was awarded to Bolivian Fernando Medina Ferrada's *Los muertos están cada día más indóciles* with honorable mentions going to Argentinian Héctor Tizón and Colombian Manuel Mejía Vallejo. The 1974 award went to Peruvian Marcos Yauri Montero for *En otoño, después de mil años,* with honorable mentions for Argentinian Jorge Asis and Brazilian Paulo Carvalho Neto. The 1973 prize was declared *desierto.*

[244] According to Julio Miranda, "Piñera introduces the absurd in Cuba in 1942, with his play *Electra Garrigó* and continues in that trend immediately thereafter with several stories and a novel, *La carné de René,* most of which date from the same 1940's" (ibid., p. 8).

The 1972 and 1973 UNEAC novel prizes, for Cubans only, were also declared *desierto*, with honorable mention in 1972 going to three as yet unpublished "dawn" works by previously unknown authors: *Despertar 1959* by Marta Olga Manresa Lago, *Las barreras del alba* by Alfredo Reyes Trejo, and *Amanecer en silencio* by Armando Cristóbal Pérez. Five of the six 1971 novels and probably the 1972 UNEAC honorable mentions reflect directly the government's new policy characterized in 1969 by Uruguayan Mario Benedetti, a constant friend of the regime, as "a stronger social pressure on the intellectuals to be integrated into the Revolution."[245] More recently, Chilean poet Enrique Lihn, whose *Poesía de paso* was awarded the 1966 Casa de las Américas prize, pointed out that literature in Cuba is becoming ideology just as it has become in China: ". . . over there in China, in spite of all the brief and calm remarks to the contrary and in spite of the demands to raise the aesthetic level, literature is ideology, especially since the cultural revolution, just as literature is on the way to becoming ideology within the framework of the Cuban Revolution."[246]

The new policy was actually adopted at the October 1968 meeting of the UNEAC in Cienfuegos in response to the acute political and economic crisis that forced Cuba to seek a closer relationship with the Soviet Union: ". . . the writer must contribute to the Revolution through his work, and this involves conceiving of literature as a means of struggle, a weapon against weaknesses and problems that, directly or indirectly, could hinder this advance."[247] One of its clearest formulations was expressed over a year later, in a December 4, 1969, speech, by Juan Marinello, chancellor of the Universidad de La Habana. Literature must be committed and the style should be sufficiently clear so as to be accessible to the greatest number of readers. It should also be of the highest quality.

If literature is to be an important part of our revolution—and nobody

[245] Mario Benedetti, *Cuaderno cubano*, p. 112.

[246] Enrique Lihn, [Article on the Cuban government's new policy toward literature,] *Siempre*, December 8, 1971, p. iii.

[247] *Granma Weekly Review*, October 27, 1968, p. 8, quoted by Lourdes Casal in "Literature and Society" in *Revolutionary Change in Cuba*, ed. Carmelo Mesa-Lago, p. 460.

would dare to say otherwise—it should make an effort to incorporate in its trajectory, regardless of the style or the manner of presentation the authors may prefer, the powerful anxieties, the untiring efforts, and the energetic colors that are woven into today's heroic life of our people. In order to achieve this, the writer should wisely adopt a clarity accessible to everyone. It is by making his originality available to all that the author achieves the greatest feat. Let those authors who want to keep up with the times strive toward that goal. And let's not forget this cardinal truth: a committed historical period demands a committed literature; but the commitment must be fulfilled through an untiring effort to achieve the highest quality work, with a skill commensurate with the times that it serves.[248]

One of the frankest statements about the new direction being taken by the Cuban novel was made by Cuban critic Ambrosio Fornet in his review of Miguel Cossío Woodward's *Sacchario*, the Casa de las Américas prize winner for 1970: "The recent Cuban novel—which has never felt the temptation of objectivism [of the new French novel]—has been very careful to avoid pamphleteering. Today we strongly suspect that it has been too careful."[249]

Before launching into a fuller discussion of the role of literature in a revolutionary society, it would be appropriate at this point to analyze the fruits of this new policy. Although I have designated 1971 as the start of the fourth period, the October 1968 policy change was at least partially responsible for the sharp decline in novelistic production from 1969 on and in the awarding of the 1969 UNEAC prize to *Las cercas caminaban* (1970) by Alcides Iznaga (b. 1910). According to one of the judges, Iznaga's contemporary Félix Pita Rodríguez (b. 1909),[250] the principal merit of this novel appears to be its lack of experimentation: "Linear, direct, without time distortions or multidimensional points of view that convert the plot into an anagram."[251] Lacking in experimentation is actually an understatement. Indeed, this novel is so far out of the mainstream and off the beaten path that one is

[248] Juan Marinello, "Sobre nuestra crítica literaria," *Vida Universitaria* 21, no. 219 (May–June 1970): 48.
[249] Ambrosio Fornet, review of *Sacchario*, *Casa de las Américas* 11, no. 64 (January–February 1971): 183.
[250] The other two judges were Raúl Aparicio (b. 1913) and Agustín Pí (b. 1919).
[251] Alcides Iznaga, *Las cercas caminaban*, jacket flap.

almost tempted to comment snidely that the Cuban novel of the Revolution has come full circle from *Amalia—La novena estación* (1959)
to *María—Las cercas caminaban*. Like *María*, Iznaga's novel re-creates
the world of the large plantations from the point of view of the pater-
nalistic landowners. Although the title refers to the expansion of the
plantations, the situation of the dispossessed *guajiros* receives far less
emphasis than in *Tabaco* (1963). As in *Tierra inerme* (1961), the
archetypal exploiter is "devillainized." Ramiro Pertierra, colonel of
the Policía Nacional and friend of Batista, uses his political power to
acquire more land and to manipulate elections. However, the election
of Grau San Martín in 1944 and Batista's subsequent departure from
Cuba convince him that he, too, should leave.

Although some criticism of Cuban society between 1930 and 1944
is implied and even occasionally expressed, the author's attitude is
ambiguous. He seems much more interested in nostalgically portraying
the evolution of the Coltizo family with *costumbrista* scenes both on
the plantation and in the Cienmeros (an obvious and unnecessary disguise for Cienfuegos) high school. Some of these scenes were undoubtedly inspired by *María*, but they are far less charming than the
originals and also lack the picaresque quality of their Cuban counterparts in López-Nussa's *Tabaco* and Samuel Feijóo's *Juan Quinquín en
Pueblo Mocho*. However, the *costumbrista* tone is modified somewhat
toward the end of the novel. It almost seems as though Iznaga felt a
belated need to adopt a more critical attitude toward prerevolutionary
society. On the final page he even takes a ten-year leap in order to allude unexpectedly to the guerrillas in the Sierra. Two other major defects of the novel are the occasional change from the omniscient
third-person narrative point of view to the first person of a very minor
character and a pedestrian style that the author tries to embellish at
times with contrived elegance: "Doña Lupe's age is three score less
half a decade, her complexion is still fresh and her voice sweet and
young."[252]

Much more representative of the novels of the fourth period are the
1970 and 1971 Casa de las Américas prize winners, Miguel Cossío
Woodward's (b. 1938) *Sacchario* and Manuel Cofiño López's (b.

[252] Ibid., p. 28.

1936) *La última mujer y el próximo combate*. In contrast to the typical 1966–1970 novel, both these works are less boldly experimental, have primarily rural settings, and are more directly related to such current revolutionary topics as the sugar-cane harvest, the struggle against absenteeism, the development of a truly revolutionary conscience, and the new role of women in Cuba. The great reduction in the number of erudite images and references, as well as the elimination of dialect, derives from the leveling policy of the socialist state.

Although *Sacchario*'s one day in the life of a volunteer cane cutter takes place in April 1965, the novel was undoubtedly inspired by the supreme but unsuccessful effort to harvest ten million tons of sugar cane by 1970.[253] However, the sugar-cane harvest is only the structural framework for the real theme: the making of a revolutionary correlated with a revolutionary view of Cuban history from the 1930's to 1965. The protagonist is Darío whose recollections of his childhood and adolescence present the by-now stereotyped vision of the 1940's and particularly the 1950's: cabarets, the numbers game, parochial schools, and the all-pervasive American influence in the comic strips (Buck Rogers, Mandrake the Magician, Donald Duck), baseball (Joe DiMaggio and Minnie Miñoso), the movies, popular songs ("You Ain't Nothing but a Hound Dog"), and racism. The first step in the creation of the revolutionary man is taken when Darío helps the anti-Batista conspirators. After being pursued, jailed, beaten, and released without informing on his companions, he heads for the Sierra Maestra. Darío's coming of age (21) coincides with the triumph of the Revolution. Just as Cuba would have to change, Darío realized that he, too, would have to "change his skin."[254] His revolutionary ecstasis at the huge rallies in 1960 is falsely equated by him with his sexual climaxes at the seashore with his beloved María. The road to socialism, however, is long and difficult, and concern for love and sex is considered deviant. Darío recalls in chronological order the formation of the

---

[253] "To celebrate the ten-million-ton harvest, all the members of the UNEAC were sent during nine months to a sugar plantation and mill, not to work there with their hands, but to observe the activities in order to be able to talk about them, if they so desired" (René Dumont, *Cuba ¿es socialista?*, p. 191).

[254] Miguel Cossío Woodward, *Sacchario*, p. 114.

Comités de Defensa de la Revolución, the struggle against the Escambray counterrevolutionaries, and the Bay of Pigs invasion with the
heroism, previously narrated by David Buzzi, of the wounded militia
man who, before dying, wrote Fidel's name with his own blood.
Darío's socialist conscience grows with the combined fear and faith
provoked by the 1962 missile crisis. Totally in keeping with current
ideology, the author indicates that socialism will not come from the
bureaucrats seated in the Ministry of Industry or from the theoretical
books on communism but rather from the comradeship deeply felt
during the most critical challenges to the Revolution: the missile crisis,
the October 1963 Cyclone Flora, and the unprecedented sugar harvest.
One of the crucial moments in Darío's final conversion occurs when he
realizes that, in order to be a true revolutionary, he has to sacrifice
everything: ". . . it was necessary to break with everything, to rebel
against the mediocre lie of home and family."[255] Without any indication of personal problems, he abandons his wife, María, and goes off
to cut sugar cane: ". . . y empezó por marcharse a cortar caña."[256]

The novel thus ends where it began: in the sugar-cane field. All the
above memories are interspersed in the activities of a single day in
April 1965, divided into morning, afternoon, and night—which constitute the three parts of the novel. During this day, all the action is
narrated in the present tense, and the solidarity of the cane cutters is
reflected in an almost neoprimitive style that approximates a prose
poem: "The persistent whistling. They sleep like logs. Hunched up.
Curled in their hammocks. They snore. They saw logs."[257] The sacrifice of the individual for the group is also reflected stylistically in the
narrative point of view, which alternates among several characters and
varies from first-, to second-, to third-person narrative, but much less
boldly than in the 1966–1970 novels. Besides the protagonist, Darío,
the other most important character is his cane-cutting partner, the
older illiterate Negro Papaíto, whose experiences on a prerevolutionary
sugar plantation, on the docks, in a circus, and in the Tropicana Nightclub and his familiarity with Afro-Cuban superstitions broaden the

[255] Ibid., p. 245.
[256] Ibid., p. 247.
[257] Ibid., p. 19.

vision of Cuba's past. Among the other minor characters are the accountant incapable of coping with physical labor and the barber who was a counterrevolutionary but is now rehabilitated. Paralleling Darío's memories of his developing revolutionary conscience, a revolutionary conscience also develops during the day among the cane cutters. In the morning, emphasis is placed on each individual's reactions to the hard work of cutting cane. It isn't until lunch that the first conversation takes place, based on the latest news about the Soviet cosmonauts read in *Hoy* and heard on the radio. Darío's memories of the 1960 rallies are triggered by the cane cutters' cooperative effort to put out a fire in the canefield. That night, el Cantante atones for his obsession with sex by presenting a cultural program in a nearby school while Darío and Papaíto play dominoes. When some of the workers bring in the carcass of a cow run over by a train and prepare to devour it, Darío establishes his revolutionary superiority by telling them that they must first find out to whom it belongs. They assure him that they have already been granted permission, and the growing tension dissipates into a humorous scene of camaraderie.

Interspersed among the scenes from Darío's past and the cane cutters' present are nine one-page sections entitled "Sacchario," which constitute an informal history of the sugar-cane industry: paragraphs from a variety of historical books, parts of letters and speeches by Carlos Manuel Céspedes, Máximo Gómez, and Prío Socarrás's minister of agriculture, and a few lines from the song "Caña quemá—Qué le pasa al Buen Vecino."[258]

Although the "Sacchario" sections are reminiscent of John Dos Passos, the most direct antecedent of *Sacchario* is Pablo Armando Fernández's *Los niños se despiden*, which received the Casa de las Américas prize in 1968. Both novels reflect official government policy, but *Sacchario*'s message is much more explicit and its structural experimentation and language are far less complex and therefore accessible to a far greater number of readers than *Los niños se despiden*. This concept of writing for a wide reading public rather than for the literary élite—Lezama Lima's *Paradiso* is the prime example—is also reflected

[258] Ibid., p. 211.

in the contrast between Darío's study of his namesake's ivory-tower poetry and the urban squalor in which he lived:

> To be named Darío was not such an important thing, after all. There was, yes, that other Darío, Rubén. But his real name had been Félix Rubén and he was born in Nicaragua. Literature class, high school. Poems read in the dark shadows of the corridors in the tenement amidst the snores escaping through the blinds and children whimpering at midnight with a need to urinate and muttering about bills, that there's not enough, make it to the end of the month, and voluptuous moans from the couple in number eight, recently married behind the church, and the filthy language of men who couldn't sleep cooped up in their hot rooms and washing their armpits in washbowls, cat shit and gnashing of teeth and stomachs growling from hunger, and springs squeaking with the weight of the four Silvas, brothers and sisters, piled on top of each other and the whistling of the rusty plumbing and cats meowing, fighting on the rooftops, on the roof and the mythological alexandrines on the wings of Leda.[259]

The gap between author and average reader is further narrowed in the 1971 prizewinner, Manuel Cofiño López's *La última mujer y el próximo combate*. Although the structure is still somewhat experimental, the style is very simple. The vocabulary is quite limited, the sentences are short, and words are often repeated. Many of the oral traditions of the region are introduced by the phrase "dicen que" and are clearly set off from the main plot by indentation. Although the style has a distinctly Cuban flavor, as in *Sacchario*, no attempt is made at phonetic transcriptions as in *Tres tristes tigres* or at re-creating the rural dialect as in *La Odilea*.

Like *Sacchario*, *La última mujer y el próximo combate* is set in 1965 but is based on a current revolutionary problem: the elimination of abuses on a *plan* caused by the survival of prerevolutionary bourgeois attitudes among the rural population. However, unlike *Sacchario* and so many other Cuban novels of the Revolution, only a small part of the book is devoted to exorcising the past. Most of the pages present, almost step-by-step, the successful efforts of the new director, Bruno, to convert the *plan* into an efficient revolutionary operation. The former director, David, had permitted Milé to sell government lands

[259] Ibid., p. 48.

to the peasants and to charge them for visits to the doctor and for other free services. Bruno, little by little, gains the confidence of the peasants by introducing electricity into the *plan* and then providing movies. Absenteeism is gradually reduced. New houses are constructed for the peasants, who are then encouraged to return their falsely acquired lands to the *plan*. Bruno, who had been a captain in the revolutionary army, is aided in his mission by representatives of three revolutionary groups: his former Negro sergeant, a contingent of students from Havana, and the Women's Brigade led by the young, attractive, and hardworking Mercedes with whom Bruno falls in love at first sight.

The revolutionary attitude toward sex is reflected in the contrast between the hero, Bruno, and the villain, Siaco. Like the protagonist of *Sacchario*, Bruno sacrificed his marriage for the revolutionary cause. In 1959 his wife divorced him and left Cuba for the United States. He and Mercedes fall deeply in love, but in a strictly Platonic way. There isn't the slightest allusion to anything sensual about their feelings, and only as Bruno dies do they hold hands. Bruno is mortally wounded by Siaco and three counterrevolutionaries whom he had hidden after they landed on the nearby coast. Siaco no longer loves his wife, beats her, drinks constantly, and has an adulterous love affair with the sensuous Nati, who no longer loves her husband, Clemente. Nati recalls her initiation into a life of sexual promiscuity after being raped at the age of twelve by the typically cruel and licentious *hacendado* Alejandro de la O. The subordination of sex to the Revolution is summarized in the title and explained in one of the several short interspersed passages referring to the almost legendary hero Pedro el Buldocero. When Pedro was asked how he and the other revolutionaries were able to live without women, the reply was, ". . . here we think of the last woman we had and of the next encounter."[260]

In spite of Bruno's death, the novel's ending is optimistic. His counterrevolutionary assassins are killed, and his final words are, "I have faith in people. Everything will be possible."[261] The identification of *La última mujer y el próximo combate* as an ideological novel is obvious from both form and content and is confirmed by the author's

[260] Manuel Cofiño López, *La última mujer y el próximo combate*, p. 262.
[261] Ibid., p. 329.

own words: "*La última mujer y el próximo combate* had to be written with great ideological rigor. That helped me realize that content and form are one and the same thing. Because when you tighten the ideological rigor, mechanically you have to demand a more rigorous form."[262]

The official consecration of *La última mujer y el próximo combate* as a true revolutionary novel with a well-defined political goal is confirmed by official pundit José Antonio Portuondo: "*La última mujer y el próximo combate* is a fine realization of a revolutionary novel in the sense of that form of narrative in which the creative imagination is at the service of a clearly defined political goal: to demonstrate the dialectic process of the birth of a socialist conscience."[263]

Julio Travieso's *Para matar al lobo* (1971) also combines a clear political purpose with a relatively simple literary style. This "epic of urban guerrilla warfare in the struggle against Batista's police state"[264] is aimed at the youth of 1971 with the hope that they will emulate the revolutionary self-sacrifice of their heroic predecessors: "It's clear that Travieso aims his novel primarily at the younger generation. He wants them to seek examples among the heroes who died and who survived during the process [in order] to *feel* those years with their bomb explosions, murders, and torture devices."[265]

In marked contrast to many of the 1966–1970 works, language is no longer considered the protagonist of the novel but a tool for communicating with as large a reading public as possible: "As far as language goes, there is nothing remotely new: Travieso's only concern is to communicate with the large reading public, part of which is more used to the newspaper language than to the strictly literary language."[266]

Three of the four other novels published in Cuba in 1971 are also

[262] Manuel Cofiño López, interview, *La Gaceta de Cuba*, nos. 90–91 (March–April 1971).

[263] José Antonio Portuondo, review of *La última mujer y el próximo combate*, *Casa de las Américas* 12, no. 71 (March–April 1972): 105.

[264] Antonio Benítez Rojo, review of *Para matar al lobo*, *Casa de las Américas* 12, no. 71 (March–April 1972): 108.

[265] Ibid.

[266] Ibid.

politically motivated in spite of their relative escapism, while *En la cal de las paredes* by Gustavo Eguren is more appropriately discussed among the 1966–1970 group. Two of these 1971 works are first novels written by men born in the 1920's who were active members of the Communist party in the 1940's and 1950's. *Los negros ciegos* by Raúl Valdés Vivó[267] deals with American Negro soldiers in Vietnam, while *Enigma para un domingo* by Ignacio Cárdenas Acuña (b. 1924),[268] Cuba's first detective novel (according to the publisher's blurb), is framed by scenes depicting the efficiency, the fairness, and the courtesy of the revolutionary police in 1963 in contrast with the inefficient, venal, unjust, and brutal police of 1951. Over nine-tenths of the novel, however, is devoted to the solving of a murder mystery by private detective Júglar Ares. In addition to containing all the ingredients of the typical whodunit, *Enigma para un domingo* re-creates the by-now traditional view of prerevolutionary Cuba: corrupt politicians, a venal press, ties between businessmen and racketeers, prostitution, drug traffic, gambling, nightclubs, unemployment, and poverty. *Zona de silencio*, by the prolific Noel Navarro,[269] exalts poetically the revolutionary efforts of the Communists in Cuba and throughout Latin America in the 1930's and 1940's. Born around 1910 into a wealthy family, protagonist Mateo Ugarte becomes a revolutionary during the struggle against Machado. He later abandons his wife and child and turns up mysteriously in a variety of Latin American countries wherever he is needed by the Party. No allusions whatsoever are made to the

[267] Raúl Valdés Vivó was the secretary general of the "Juventud Socialista" in the Universidad de La Habana in the late 1950's and plays a relatively minor role in Guatemalan Carlos Manuel Pellecer's novel *Utiles después de muertos*, to be discussed in part five. More recently Valdés Vivó has served as Cuban ambassador to North Vietnam.

[268] Ignacio Cárdenas Acuña worked in a textile factory and studied electrical engineering before the Revolution. He entered the Communist party in 1945. After serving in the revolutionary militia, he completed his engineering degree in 1966 and now works in the Ministerio de la Industria Ligera.

[269] Navarro has published four novels (*Los días de nuestra angustia, Los caminos de la noche, El plano inclinado,* and *Zona de silencio*), has received honorable mention with two others still unpublished (*El principio y el fin* and *El sol sobre la piedra*), and has received prizes for the volume of short stories *Al final de la noche* (honorable mention, UNEAC, 1970), retitled *La huella del pulgar* (first prize, Casa de las Américas, 1972).

Cuban Revolution of Fidel Castro. Although the idealization of the older Communists is an acceptable theme under the new government policy toward the arts, the form of *Zona de silencio*, which received the UNEAC prize and was therefore written before 1970, would justify its classification with the 1966–1970 novels. In spite of its relatively simple language, *Zona de silencio* demands the active collaboration of the reader because of its chronological fragmentation, its frequently changing multiple points of view, its occasional omission of suffixes and elimination of spaces among a series of words, and, in general, its highly poetic tone.

Part Two. Literature and Revolution

I. Changing Government Attitude toward the Arts

The emergence of the ideological novel in 1970 and its predominance in 1971 call for a review of the general relations between the artist or intellectual and the Revolution since 1959. The tremendous notoriety given to the imprisonment and subsequent confessions of poet Heberto Padilla in the spring of 1971 has obscured the fact that conflicts between the artist and the revolutionary government go back almost to the very beginnings in 1959.

Lisandro Otero, one of the regime's spokesmen for cultural affairs, distinguishes five different stages in the development of Cuban revolutionary culture between 1959 and 1971. He summarizes briefly, as follows, the first four stages and then goes on to discuss at considerable length the fifth stage, 1969–1971.

First Stage (1959–1960): bewilderment, development of national conscience, emotional and fervent patriotism, works based on incidents that present journalistically the recent epic struggle, the spreading of bourgeois culture, united front of the intellectuals. Creation of the Cuban Institute of Movie Art and Industry.

Second Stage (1961–1962): the Revolution declares itself socialistic, intensification of the class struggle. Literacy campaign, Bay of Pigs, October missile crisis. Fears arise about the repetition in Cuba of dogmatic experiences: limitations on the freedom of artistic expression and bureaucratic pressures. Polemics over aesthetics. Meetings in the National Library between Fidel and the intellectuals. Creation of the National Council of Culture and the Union of Cuban Writers and Artists.

Third Stage (1963–1965): adoption of an international conscience. Greater attention is paid to the criteria and the activities of foreign intellectuals. Development of the Casa de las Américas. Emergence of a corpus of revolutionary poetry. Importance of the documentary film. Development of the graphic arts as a revolutionary vehicle with a high artistic quality. Che's *El socialismo y el hombre en Cuba* culminates and puts an end to the aesthetic polemic over socialist realism.

Fourth Stage (1966–1968): emergence of young intellectuals who have matured within the Revolution. Creation of the Cuban Institute of the Book. Development of the ideological polemic over the social role of the revolutionary intellectual. The Cultural Congress in Havana. Polemic over the literary prizes of UNEAC in 1968. Crystallization of the conscience of the role of the revolutionary intellectual as a contributor to the common cause and not as its critical conscience.[1]

The discrepancies between Otero's five stages and the four chronological groups into which I have divided the novels of the Revolution may be explained by the differences between government policy toward the arts and actual production. We both start with the same first stage, but Otero's second and third stages are indistinguishable in my 1961–1965 grouping. Although the end of 1968 is the dividing line between Otero's fourth and fifth stages, the newest government policy toward the arts was not fully implemented until 1971. Actually, the

[1] Lisandro Otero, "Notas sobre la funcionalidad de la cultura," *Casa de las Américas* 12, no. 68 (September–October 1971): 94.

relations between the artist and the revolutionary government since 1959 have depended much more on how policy was implemented than on policy itself. Therefore, some elaboration of Otero's concise summaries is necessary in order to put the present situation in the proper perspective. The following four headings are taken directly from Otero's article.

1959–1960: "... united front of the intellectuals"

Amid the euphoric atmosphere of the early days of the revolutionary government, Alejo Carpentier was appointed to the Dirección de Cultura and organized the Feria del Libro.

In 1960, the Casa de las Américas was founded to coordinate cultural relations with the rest of Latin America. Never before in the history of Cuba had the writer and the artist enjoyed such prominence. Alberto Baeza Flores (b. 1914), the Chilean poet and novelist, who had participated in the struggle against Batista but who left Cuba in March 1960 when the government closed down his journal, describes the situation in 1960 from his present anti-Castro point of view: "Never, in the history of Cuba, had writers and artists been so praised and offered so much as under the regime of Castro, who needed them. Never were so many books published. Never were they given such publicity, never was so much importance attached to them."[2]

Although the overwhelming majority of Cuban authors supported the Revolution during this period, there were a few significant defections. Lino Novás Calvo (b. 1903) took political asylum in the Colombian Embassy in August 1960 and went to New York, where he became assistant editor of *Bohemia Libre*. His contemporaries Carlos Montenegro (b. 1900) and Lydia Cabrera (b. 1900) also left. Ramón Ferreira (b. 1921), who worked for General Electric in Cuba before the triumph of the Revolution, left in October 1960 for Mexico and subsequently Puerto Rico. Also in 1960, Severo Sarduy (b. 1937) received an Instituto de Cultura scholarship to study art criticism in Paris and decided not to return to Cuba.

[2] Alberto Baeza Flores, "La cultura cubana en la encrucijada de su decenio conflictivo 1959–1969," in *Diez años de Revolución cubana*, by Carlos A. Montaner, p. 76.

1961–1962: "... limitations on the freedom of artistic expression ...
polemics over aesthetics"

The first serious conflict between the revolutionary government and
the literary community occurred shortly after the Bay of Pigs invasion
and Fidel Castro's speech about the socialist character of the Cuban
Revolution. The victim was *Lunes*, the cultural supplement of Carlos
Franqui's daily *Revolución*, and the immediate motive was film critic
Cabrera Infante's protest against censorship of the film *PM*. "Another
victim of these meetings was the film PM, which was not allowed to
be screened. Some said it was too sexy, others that it featured too many
Negroes, and yet others that it gave quite the wrong impression of
Cuban life and merely provided the enemy with ammunition. In fact,
when a copy of the film was discovered abroad, no counterrevolutionary organization rushed to buy it, and neither did American television, doubtless because PM does not lend itself to anti-Cuban propaganda."[3]

On June 16, 1961, Carlos Franqui and the editors of *Lunes*—
Cabrera Infante, Pablo Armando Fernández, and Heberto Padilla—
were called before a board of inquiry chaired by Edith García Buchacha and made up chiefly of other members of the Partido Socialista
Popular. Because of the importance of these authors in subsequent dis-
putes over intellectual freedom, the rather extensive account of the
episode by K. S. Karol is worth inserting at this point.

Needless to say, the Communists posed an even deadlier threat to intel-
lectual life. To them the Cuban situation was quite intolerable. How could a
country that called itself socialist and wished to form an integral part of the
Soviet bloc allow ordinary bookshops to display heretical works that were
bound to embarrass and offend all the comrades who had rushed over from
Eastern Europe to the aid of the Revolution? Quite apart from the works of
Trotsky, all the books banned in the Soviet Union—from *Doctor Zhivago* to
Kafka and Joyce—were spread out provocatively for all to see. The occasional blue-jacketed editions of the Moscow Foreign Publishing House
could barely make up for such outrages. And it was the same with the
cinema: people lined up to see trashy French and Italian films and obsti-

[3] K. S. Karol, *Guerrillas in Power*, p. 241.

nately stayed away from Russian masterpieces. And to crown it all, if a film from Eastern Europe happened to be a success, it was most often a Polish one or some other unorthodox production denouncing the evil side of socialism.

And so the Communists asked for a free hand to bring some sort of order into this cultural and ideological jungle. That this task proved inordinately difficult was due not simply to the bad habits of their Americanized fellow-countrymen, but also to the ideological crisis that was then gripping Russia herself. The "good old days" of Zhdanovism were a thing of the past. Edifying works in praise of Soviet heroes had become scarce even in Moscow, where the leading writers had begun to sail into the aberrations of the "personality cult" and, to get past the censors, were penning esoteric works full of allusions incomprehensible to such outsiders as the young Cubans. The other great achievements of "proletarian culture"—from genetics to socialist realism in painting—were faring no better. It was, of course, possible to dig up a few diehards of the old school in Moscow, but their works would have been poor examples to hold up to the new Cuban socialists.

The cultural leaders, foremost among them Mrs. García Buchacha, would have liked but were unable to supply their country with socialist culture imported from Russia in ready-made, easy-to-digest form. On the other hand, they were certain about what books Cubans must *not* be allowed to read. This explains the sad business of the *Lunes de Revolución* in the summer of 1961. *Lunes* was the cultural supplement of Carlos Franqui's daily, *Revolución*. It first came out in March 1959, and had always managed to combine revolutionary fervor with respect for cultural values. The paper was edited by young men: Guillermo Cabrera Infante, the editor-in-chief, was barely thirty. His second in command, Pablo Armando Fernández, was even younger, and so were Heberto Padilla and José Alvarez Baragaño, all of them poets and completely devoted to the cause of the Revolution.

The weekly supplement discussed such topics as avant-garde art and the aspirations of the modern Left. Trotsky's writings on art and revolution were deemed worthy of presentation to the Cuban public, and the space devoted to André Breton showed the group's attraction to surrealism. Yet they did not neglect the *Communist Manifesto* either, or the works of the great Bolshevik era, from John Reed and Mayakovsky to Isaac Babel. On January 18, 1960, on the sudden death of Albert Camus, they dedicated a whole issue to his writings; three weeks later, on the occasion of Anastas Mikoyan's visit, they published a special number on the Soviet Union, its films, theater, and literature. When Sartre came to Cuba a month later, they published his *Ideology and Revolution* together with a lengthy interview.

It would be unfair to say that *Lunes* followed no line: it was, in fact, a voice crying out against commercialized culture and a powerful means for the dissemination of neglected leftist classics. Moreover, it published fundamental studies of the history of the Cuban Revolution, and some of the most important works of Fidel Castro, Ernesto Che Guevara, and Camilo Cienfuegos. One possible objection was that *Lunes* did not express clear editorial views on the often contradictory articles it printed. But all the Cuban leaders acknowledged that it met a specific need for a new generation, eager for knowledge and quite capable of making up its own mind. According to Ernesto Che Guevara, *Lunes de Revolución* was a striking contribution to Cuban culture. And Fidel Castro described *Lunes* as "a worthy attempt to give expression to three similar things: revolution, the people, and culture."

To foreign visitors, the circulation of *Lunes* was a revelation. It had as many readers as the daily *Revolución*, and eventually sold 250,000 copies. Surveys showed that readers of the daily newspaper also read the cultural supplement carefully. Sartre and Simone de Beauvoir expressed their astonishment; conversations in all parts of the island had shown them that, thanks to *Lunes*, many ordinary Cubans knew more about Picasso and avant-garde art than did a good many Frenchmen.

But it was precisely these qualities that earned *Lunes* the stricture of the Communist old guard. Could a young and heterodox group be allowed to publish whatever works it chose—including even those banned in other socialist countries? And furthermore, could it be allowed to operate independently of the Party leadership? The sooner a stop was put to this scandalous state of affairs, the better.

On June 16, 1961, Carlos Franqui and his protégés were invited to a discussion at the National Library in Havana. They were told nothing about the purpose of the meeting and they expected a small, friendly gathering to discuss certain minor differences between them and their country's cultural leaders. Instead, they found themselves in a large hall, at a meeting attended by almost all the country's intellectuals, great and small. They had to face a board of inquiry chaired by Mrs. García Buchacha and made up chiefly of PSP leaders; and they were addressed in a manner far more suited to a court of law than to an intellectual debate. They were accused of splitting the ranks of the Revolution, a serious crime at a time when unity had become a matter of life and death. They were accused of lacking a proper socialist perspective, of hankering after Western culture, and, more generally, of upholding dubious cultural trends. A terrible indictment, all told.

However, the whiff of Zhdanovism their accusers exuded proved so offensive to a number of intellectuals not part of the *Lunes* group that they jumped to the defense of Carlos Franqui and Pablo Armando Fernández; Roberto Fernández Retamar and Lisandro Otero were but two who spoke up for them. They all declared that loyalty to the Revolution was perfectly compatible with the defense of avant-garde ideas and that they did not accept authoritarian definitions of socialist culture.

To be sure, a number of well-known intellectuals, including Alejo Carpentier who had previously supported and even praised *Lunes de Revolución*, were careful to take no part in the debate. Some others, such as the poet José Alvarez Baragaño, were even ready to indulge in self-criticism for their contributions, and confessed that their supposed errors had been due to their bourgeois origin. But on the whole this Communist attempt to bring the intellectuals to heel met with so much resistance that it could not be brought to a successful conclusion at that time.[4]

It was in this context that Fidel Castro met personally with the Cuban intellectuals and tried to reassure them with his three well-known speeches of June 16, 23, and 30, 1961, in which he categorically affirmed the artist's freedom to choose his own theme and his own style provided they were not antirevolutionary:

... within the Revolution, everything; against the Revolution, nothing ...
Does this mean that we are going to tell people here what they have to write? No. Let each one write what he wants to, and if what he writes is no good, that's his problem. We do not prohibit anyone from writing on his favorite theme. On the contrary. And let each one express himself in the manner that he deems appropriate and let him express freely the idea that he wants to express. We shall always judge his creative work through the prism of the revolutionary crystal. That, too, is a right of the revolutionary government, as respectable as everyone's right to express what he wants to express.[5]

In August 1961, the Unión de Escritores y Artistas Cubanos

[4] Ibid., pp. 236–241.
[5] Fidel Castro, *Palabras a los intelectuales*, pp. 11, 20–21.

(UNEAC) was founded to coordinate the activities of all creative artists under the presidency of poet Nicolás Guillén, a long-time member of the Communist party. Loló de la Torriente, in a 1963 article published in *Cuadernos Americanos*, describes the alarm of different groups of writers about their possible loss of creative freedom.

> In 1961—Year of Education—when we were carrying out the literacy campaign that mobilized thousands of teachers, technicians, and volunteers, the Union of Writers and Artists announced the convocation of the First National Congress of Writers and Artists in which it was understood that the "political line" for art and literature would be established.
>
> It is no secret for anyone that this decision caused alarm among the groups of different and even rival tendencies who feared the loss of their independence and creative freedom. It can be said that "fear" was the main theme of the Congress and of its preparations and that many artists had the sincerity to lay out in the open the "bewilderment," and others the "concern that this policy provoked in them."[6]

At this first meeting, President Osvaldo Dorticós reaffirmed the government policy of freedom of form: ". . . that the Revolutionary government would not 'limit or harm,' in the slightest degree, the exercise of freedom of form in art and literature . . ."[7]

Shortly thereafter, *Lunes* ceased publication and its three leading editors were sent abroad. Cabrera Infante became cultural attaché and then chargé d'affaires in Brussels. Pablo Armando Fernández's name appears as the "jefe de redacción" of numbers 11–12 (March–June 1962) of *Casa de las Américas*, but the following issue, 13–14 (July–October 1962), announces his appointment as cultural attaché in London. Heberto Padilla went as a journalist to Prague and Moscow. Juan Arcocha, Carlos Franqui's editorial assistant, was also assigned to Moscow as a correspondent. About a year later, Ambrosio Fornet, one of the government's literary spokesmen, recognized the vacuum created by the closing down of *Lunes*: "In fact, since the disappearance of

---

[6] Loló de la Torriente, "La política cultural y los escritores y artistas cubanos," *Cuadernos Americanos* 22, no. 5 (September–October 1963): 81.

[7] Ibid., p. 82.

Lunes, almost a year ago, no literary supplement circulates periodically and widely among the people."[8]

1963–1965: ". . . adoption of an international conscience . . . Che's *El socialismo y el hombre en Cuba* culminates and puts an end to the aesthetic polemic over socialist realism"

This period was marked by a kind of self-imposed censorship under which authors avoided controversial themes and were loath to violate the puritanical policy of the government. At the same time, dissatisfaction was expressed about the quality of the literature being produced and socialist realism was not considered helpful to the Revolution if it did not produce high-quality works.

In his laudatory prologue to Nicolás Guillén's book of revolutionary poems entitled *Tengo*, José Antonio Portuondo rejects two diametrically opposed attitudes: the creation of a popular propagandistic literature based on a limited vocabulary with a folkloric or traditional form and the "meaningless formalistic exercises destined to cover up the total lack or the weakness of the content with supposedly audacious formal innovations."[9] He proposes that authors should follow Guillén's example and search for new forms to express the new Cuban reality. "The artist, therefore, should make a great effort to search for and to discover new modes of expression that would correspond exactly to the newness of that content."[10]

The most categorical denunciation of socialist realism was made by Edmundo Desnoes in his 1964 review of Alexander Solzhenitsyn's *A Day in the Life of Ivan Denisovich*:

Any literature that does not examine deeply or enrich man's life is a swindle. Art as an instrument of propaganda or as a prophecy tends to devalue itself: it is an alienated art. Literature can only be at the service of the artist's vision.

The First Congress of Soviet Writers, held in 1934, defined the function of art in these terms: "Socialist realism is the fundamental method of Soviet

[8] Ambrosio Fornet, *En tres y dos*, p. 20.
[9] José Antonio Portuondo, Prologue to *Tengo*, by Nicolás Guillén, p. 16.
[10] Ibid., p. 17.

literature and literary criticism. It demands of the artist a true, historically precise representation of reality in its revolutionary development. And, besides, it must contribute to the ideological transformation and to the edücation of the workers within the spirit of socialism." By orienting artistic creativity, they imposed an idealistic dogma on reality. The writer was obliged in many cases to falsify reality in order to make it fit a theory. Thus, there also emerged the positive hero who was unaware of the existence of millions of ordinary men and workers, good and bad, who made up society. Likewise, by searching for "reality in its development," they overlooked the errors which for years impeded the development of socialism . . .

A Day in the Life of Ivan Denisovich is the novel of a mature society.[11]

Che Guevara's March 1965 letter to the Uruguayan magazine Marcha seems to have laid the debate over socialist realism to rest for at least the next four years. "Therefore, they look for simplification, what everyone understands, which is what the public officials understand. Authentic artistic research is stymied and the problem of general culture is reduced to an adaptation of the socialist present and the dead (and, therefore, safe) past . . . But, why pretend to search for the only valid formula in the frozen-stiff forms of socialist realism?"[12] By January 1966, José Rodríguez Feo was able to refer to socialist realism as belonging to the past: ". . . socialist realism does not seem to have appealed to the majority of our writers."[13]

In the January–April 1964 issue of Casa de las Américas, devoted to an appraisal of the first five years of revolutionary literature, Luis Agüero evaluated with the utmost candor the eight novels published in Cuba during this period by the generation of 1950. Although he singled out Desnoes and Otero for special praise, he criticized the total novelistic production for its amateurism and its lack of profundity: ". . . up to now, with notable and few exceptions, the present-day Cuban novel is in a state of amateurism . . . no young novelist has really succeeded in exploring in depth the themes that he tackles."[14]

[11] Edmundo Desnoes, review of Un día en la vida de Iván Denisovich, Casa de las Américas 4, no. 24 (January–April 1964): 100, 102.

[12] Ernesto Che Guevara, Obra revolucionaria, pp. 635–636.

[13] José Rodríguez Feo, Aquí 11 cubanos cuentan, p. 9.

[14] Luis Agüero, "La novela de la Revolución," Casa de las Américas 4, nos. 22–23 (January–April 1964): 67.

Agüero was particularly harsh on the 1962 Casa de las Américas prize-winning novel, Daura Olema García's *Maestra voluntaria*: ". . . her novel can in no way be called a novel—and that's what's bad about definitions: you wind up rejecting them—this is rather a long journalistic report on the literacy campaign. I confess that I couldn't finish it."[15] Agüero was later to be sentenced to a work battalion for wanting to leave Cuba.

The freedom of expression apparent in Luis Agüero's article is somewhat counterbalanced by a note in the same issue of *Casa de las Américas* alluding to the absence of contributions by three of the best-known revolutionary literati at that time: Cabrera Infante, Calvert Casey, and Heberto Padilla: "—for different reasons, writers like Cabrera Infante, Calvert Casey, and Heberto Padilla are not represented, because their contributions did not arrive on time."[16]

It was in the summer of 1965 that Cabrera Infante returned to Cuba to attend his mother's funeral. In October, he resigned his diplomatic post and went to live in England, although he did not comment publicly on his defection until 1968. An earlier defection during this period was that of Juan Arcocha in 1964. After a year in Moscow as a correspondent, Arcocha had returned to Havana in 1962, was reassigned to Paris as cultural attaché, and later returned to Havana to talk out his "problem" with Fidel Castro, who allowed him to go into exile in Paris.

It was also in 1965 that the government waged a campaign against homosexuals, which was responsible for the demise of the El Puente literary group in which the young short-story writer Ana María Simó (b. 1943) had distinguished herself. The involvement with this group of American beatnik poet Allen Ginsberg, who had been invited in early 1965 to be one of the Casa de las Américas poetry judges, caused the regime great embarrassment. Ginsberg was unceremoniously expelled from Cuba and put on a plane to Prague, where he was enthusiastically received at Charles University.[17] A short time later,

[15] Ibid., p. 62.
[16] *Casa de las Américas* 4, nos. 22–23 (January–April 1964): 2.
[17] For an eye-witness account of this episode, see José Mario, "Allen Ginsberg en La Habana," *Mundo Nuevo*, no. 34 (April 1969), pp. 48–54.

Calvert Casey (1924–1969), whose volume of short stories *El regreso* (1962) had won him widespread recognition as one of the best of the new revolutionary writers, escaped to Italy via Poland. He subsequently committed suicide in Rome.

The journal *Casa de las Américas* also made significant changes in 1965. Antón Arrufat, who had assumed the editorship in 1962, was replaced by Roberto Fernández Retamar, and the editorial board was expanded to include Cubans Desnoes, Otero, and Graziella Pogolotti, Peruvian Mario Vargas Llosa, Colombian Jorge Zalamea, Argentinian David Viñas, and Haitian René Depestre.[18]

1966–1968 and beyond: "Development of the ideological polemic over the social role of the revolutionary intellectual"

It is both paradoxical and natural that the ideological controversy over the role of the intellectual in a revolutionary society should have developed during the same period when the easing of moral restraints resulted in the novel's attaining its peak production while indulging in unbridled experimentation. At the same time that the authors took advantage of the greater artistic freedom to plunge headlong into the mainstream of Latin American literature, the government undoubtedly became concerned over this greater artistic freedom's leading to conflict with official policy in general. Consequently, from 1967 on, signs of government pressure on writers became increasingly evident. After serving as director of the Editorial Nacional since 1961, Alejo Carpentier was sent to Paris as cultural attaché. Although he undoubtedly welcomed the opportunity to return to Paris, it was reported by Havana radio on June 12, 1967, that Carpentier had been involved in controversies.[19] To my knowledge, this has not received any publicity and has not even been confirmed by any other sources. Quite the opposite is true of Heberto Padilla.

18 Other well-known Latin American writers who had previously been appointed to the editorial board for varying lengths of time were Argentinians Ezequiel Martínez Estrada and Julio Cortázar, Uruguayan Angel Rama, Paraguayan Elvio Romero, Peruvian Sebastián Salazar Bondy, Guatemalan Manuel Galich, and Mexicans Juan José Arreola and Emmanuel Carballo.

19 Reported by George Schanzer in "Carpentier Fallen from Grace," *Hispania* 51, no. 1 (March 1968): 188.

Although the Heberto Padilla case actually started in 1961 with the closing of *Lunes*, its latest and most dramatic phase began at the end of 1967 with a controversy over the relative merits of Lisandro Otero's novel *Pasión de Urbino* (1967), which had lost out to Cabrera Infante's *Tres tristes tigres* in the 1964 Seix Barral competition in Barcelona. Padilla was one of several writers invited by *El Caimán Barbudo*, the literary supplement of the newspaper *Juventud Rebelde*, to express his opinion about *Pasión de Urbino*. Since Otero was then vice-president of the Consejo Nacional de Cultura, Padilla was obviously courting danger when he severely denounced the novel and complained about *Tres tristes tigres'* not having been published in Cuba in spite of its artistic superiority. As a result of this controversy, Padilla lost his position with the newspaper *Granma*,[20] permission for a trip to Italy was revoked, and the editorial board of *El Caimán Barbudo* was totally changed.[21]

The following year, 1968, the controversy over Padilla was escalated by both sides. In the July 30–August 5 issue of the Argentine journal *Primera Plana*,[22] Cabrera Infante spoke out, in his inimitable style, for the first time, not only against intellectual repression in Cuba, but also against the physical deterioration of Havana and the lack of freedom in general.

Heberto Padilla praises *Tres tristes tigres* in writing, and, with a snap of the fingers that wouldn't do away with the czar, he starts the above-mentioned polemic. Within a week he is fired from that official newspaper whose name is too reminiscent of *Little Red Ridinghood*: "Granma, what great big teeth you have!" Now, after months of not being able to leave the country and with a different editorial board (the previous one was punished, I suppose, for having let the polemic out into the open), *El Caimán* publishes for Padilla his "Reply to the Editorial Board," end of the polemic, and, ready to travel to Italy to see the publication of his book of poetry by Feltrinelli, with

[20] According to Leopoldo Avila, Padilla never worked for *Granma* ("Las respuestas de Caín," *Verde Olivo*, November 3, 1968, p. 18, cited in Lourdes Casal, *El caso Padilla*, p. 24).

[21] Lourdes Casal, *El caso Padilla*, p. 6.

[22] Reprinted in *Letras Nacionales* (Bogotá), no. 20 (May–June 1968), pp. 61–70.

his tickets purchased in Milan, his permission to leave is abruptly withdrawn, his passport is taken away, and again he is fired.[23]

Socialism theoretically nationalizes wealth. In Cuba, through a strange perversion of the practice, poverty had been socialized.

I knew (and I told everyone who would listen to me), before returning, that you couldn't write in Cuba but I thought that you could live, vegetate, putting off death, postponing every day. Within a week after returning, I knew that not only couldn't I write in Cuba, but neither would I be able to live.[24]

Almost simultaneously, Cabrera Infante published in *Mundo Nuevo* (July 1968) "Delito por bailar el chachachá," a devastating satire of socialist censorship of the arts, which is announced by the author as the prologue of a thousand-page autobiographical and political novel to be called "Cuerpos divinos."

On November 3, 1968, in the first of a series of five articles published in *Verde Olivo*, the journal of the armed forces in Cuba, Leopoldo Avila (probably a pseudonym of José Antonio Portuondo, according to Lourdes Casal)[25] strongly denounced Cabrera Infante, all his literary works, and everyone associated with him, including Calvert Casey, Rodríguez Monegal (editor of *Mundo Nuevo*, "la revista de la CIA"),[26] and Padilla. Avila concludes the article by charging Cabrera Infante—his old pseudonym as a film critic was Caín—with responsibility for the government's current problems with a number of artists: "The fact is that microfaction and counterrevolution are the same thing. And, perhaps, Caín, in spite of his irrelevance, for a complex of reasons, has damaged our culture in such a way that many people have not yet recovered. It was this Mr. Kein who first opened the doors to individualism, variety, superficiality, and extravagance in art. He contaminated more than one of the climbers who are still causing trouble. But it is useful to analyze this case and to observe how atti-

23 Casal, *El caso Padilla*, p. 13.

24 Ibid., p. 15.

25 Ibid., p. 20.

26 Ibid., p. 23. For Rodríguez Monegal's reply to the charge, see *Mundo Nuevo*, no. 25 (July 1968), pp. 93–94.

tudes like his always end up in the garbage dump of the counterrevolution."[27]

On November 10, 1968, in a similar tone, Leopoldo Avila criticized Padilla's attitude toward the Revolution and his work as a poet. He refutes Padilla's remarks about "política stalinista" and Guanahacabibes: ". . . nor was Guanahacabibes so repressive (at any rate, in every society you have to sanction those who make mistakes or commit crimes)."[28] Padilla's poetry is not only counterrevolutionary, it is also bad poetry: "He describes himself as 'out of the game' and he plays into the hands of imperialism. His latest poems are strange, not only politically but also literary-wise."[29] According to Avila, *Fuera del juego* was awarded the UNEAC prize because of the friendship of the judges. "That's the way to win a prize, by having friends who are judges or fellow conspirators like César López."[30] Avila contends that what has led Padilla to his counterrevolutionary attitude is his artistic vanity, which is likened to that of the Czech writers in Prague before the August 1968 Soviet invasion:[31] "(As far as their contacts with foreigners are concerned, Padilla and other third- and fourth-rate writers like him take advantage of every opportunity to artificially inflate their reputations: they surround the visitors—writers, publishers, etc.—as eagerly as the Tuzex girls surround the tourists in liberalized Prague in search of a friendship that will guarantee them an edition, or at least a little corner or a mention in some off-beat international publication. They're the Tuzexers of our intellectual milieu.)"[32]

Even though Padilla, according to Avila, is an insignificant poet, he is being unmasked in order to alert the country to the danger of the rest of the "garbage" (one of Avila's favorite images) still afloat in Cuba: "It's not a question of Heberto's being more or less important, because he isn't; it's not a question of our ripping his beloved pages (beloved

[27] Casal, *El caso Padilla*, p. 24.
[28] Ibid., p. 27.
[29] Ibid.
[30] Ibid., p. 28.
[31] The 1968 *Encyclopedia Britannica Yearbook* states that intellectual life in Czechoslovakia was the liveliest of any Communist country in recent years.
[32] Casal, *El caso Padilla*, p. 28.

by imperialism), or breaking down any of his doors. It's a question of alerting others and alerting ourselves to a large quantity of garbage that is still floating in our country to the detriment of the people."[33]

The November 17, 1968, article, "Antón se va a la guerra," was directed against Antón Arrufat, author of the prize winning play for 1968, *Los siete contra Tebas*, which is obviously a thinly disguised criticism of the lack of freedom and the unfulfilled promises of the revolutionary government. In tracing Arrufat's previous literary activities, Avila criticizes the editors of the prerevolutionary journal *Ciclón*—Virgilio Piñera and José Rodríguez Feo—even though they occasionally published a serious study like Portuondo's essay on Villena. As in the case of Padilla, the awarding of the UNEAC prize is attributed to the identity of the theater judges: Cuban dramatist José Triana, whose *La noche de los asesinos* won the Casa de las Américas theater prize for 1965, and two foreigners.

On November 24, 1968, Avila called for a greater political awareness among certain artistic sectors and reviewed Fidel Castro's "Palabras a los intelectuales" of 1961 and Che Guevara's "El hombre y el socialismo en Cuba" of 1965. He deplores the lack of literature about some of the heroic moments of the Revolution, such as Cyclone Flora: ". . . it hurts to see the intense, heroic work that the people are carrying out day by day in each and every corner of this country, without any greater testimony to this epic feat than an occasional note in the newspapers."[34] After ten years, the revolutionary government is finally losing its patience with those artists whose defense of cultural freedom is used as a cover-up for an antirevolutionary attitude: "With these gentlemen the Revolution has been patient and tolerant, and, once again, they have been mistaken about the Revolution. The Revolution has not been nor is it interested in curbing artistic imagination or experimentation but rather in developing them; but it is not going to stop combatting those who plan to use that freedom which the people, absolutely by themselves, first won and now defend with their blood to stab the Revolution in the back and with the greatest impudence,

[33] Ibid., p. 29.
[34] Ibid., p. 35.

moreover, claim to be the defenders of our culture."[35] Personal criticism in this essay is directed only against exiles Lino Novás Calvo, Cabrera Infante, Severo Sarduy, and essayist Adrián García.

The final article, entitled "El pueblo es el forjador, defensor y sostén de la cultura" (December 1, 1968), points out that the pre-1959 American cultural imperialism—novels of pornography and violence, comics, movies, *Life*, *Selecciones*—was eliminated through the heroic struggle of the "pueblo." Therefore, in the future, the culture produced within the Revolution will be responsible to the "pueblo": "Furthermore, in the future, no filthy merchandise will be stamped with the seal of art without the people's giving their opinion in opposition or, at least, in defense of something that it cherishes and has defended at a high cost: the culture of the Nation."[36]

In apparent opposition to both the Casa de las Américas and the UNEAC, the Revolutionary Armed Forces organized their own literary contest for 1969. In the introduction to the prize-winning collection of short stories, Manuel Cofiño López's *Tiempo de cambio*, they make no bones about their goals to popularize literature, to seek out new authors, and to consider the political orientation of the works to be judged.

Art and culture definitely constitute today the patrimony of the people, and the revolutionary task in this sense consists of carrying to the largest number of the masses the creations of our artists and to interest them in those works that reflect their struggle and their history.

Art and culture reside in the people and it is precisely there that those creators whom we recognize today have emerged and where others will emerge whose names are still unknown but who, in the course of time, will occupy an outstanding place in the literature of our country.

It should also be pointed out that in this contest the political contents as well as the artistic quality of each work have been taken into consideration in the awarding of the prizes.[37]

In spite of the thinly veiled criticism of the Revolution in *Fuera del juego* and *Los siete contra Tebas*, the Executive Committee of the

[35] Ibid., p. 40.
[36] Ibid., p. 45.
[37] Manuel Cofiño López, *Tiempo de cambio*, pp. 7–8.

UNEAC decided to publish both works along with the judges' decisions and a dissenting note by the Executive Committee. The judges —José Z. Tallet, Manuel Díaz Martínez, César Calvo, J. M. Cohen, and José Lezama Lima—recognized the critical and polemical nature of *Fuera del juego*, but they claimed that it was also "essentially linked to the idea of the Revolution as the only possible solution to the problems that obsess its author, which are those of the times in which it has been our lot to live."[38] On the other hand, the Executive Committee statement points out that the 1968 UNEAC literary contest took place at a time when "certain phenomena typical of the ideological struggle, present in every profound social revolution, were reaching an unusual intensity in our country."[39] It goes on to say that several writers in the previous months had interpreted the decision to respect freedom of expression as the emergence of a climate of boundless liberalism in which they could express counterrevolutionary ideas and sentiments. *Fuera del juego* is specifically criticized for its exaltation of individualism as opposed to the collective needs of a developing society, for its unbalanced criticism of Stalinism in the Soviet Revolution, and for its equating the atmosphere in Cuba with that of the Stalin period in the Soviet Union. Padilla is personally criticized for his notorious absences from Cuba during the Revolution's most critical moments and for his defense of Cabrera Infante. *Los siete contra Tebas* is criticized more briefly for its imperialistically distorted interpretation of the attempted invasion of Cuba by the United States, in the guise of an adaptation of Aeschylus.

In December 1968, Heberto Padilla published in Madrid and in Buenos Aires a reply to Cabrera Infante's July 30 criticism of the Revolution.[40] He emphasizes that he is not in jail and that he is enjoying complete freedom and taking part in debates on problems confronting the Revolution. He contrasts Cabrera Infante's 1968 comments on Cuba with those he made in 1965, in the journal *Bohemia*, upon his return from a three-year stint in Belgium. Padilla ends his reply with a strong affirmation of his own revolutionary attitude: ". . . but I am

[38] Casal, *El caso Padilla*, p. 56.
[39] Ibid., p. 57.
[40] *Indice* (Madrid), December 1968, p. 9; *Primera Plana* (Buenos Aires), December 24, 1968, pp. 88–89. Reprinted in Casal, *El caso Padilla*, pp. 64–66.

here and I shall continue here, participating with my life and my work in the building of a more worthy and more just society. For a revolutionary writer, there can be no other alternative: either the Revolution or nothing."[41]

Three weeks later, on January 14, 1969, Cabrera Infante replied to Padilla in *Primera Plana*, pointing out that his 1965 statements were made in order to be allowed to leave Cuba. With many allusions to parallel situations in the Soviet Union, Cabrera Infante recounts the lack of artistic freedom in Cuba: the imprisonment of Virgilio Piñera, José Triana, and José Mario; the destruction of El Puente group; the exile of Calvert Casey; the sentencing to two years at forced labor of Walterio Carbonell for organizing a Cuban branch of Black Power; and the sentencing of Luis Agüero to work in the Havana Green Belt for applying for permission to leave Cuba. He also criticizes Haydée Santamaría's fanaticism, and Lisandro Otero and Roberto Fernández Retamar for their recently acquired orthodoxy. He quotes Otero's accusation of Padilla as a "disguised counterrevolutionary" who was trying to "provoke *Czechoslovakian problems* in our country . . ."[42] Cabrera Infante also explains Carlos Barral's decision to sever relations with him by quoting "what Alejo Carpentier expressed with esprit (and French accent): *'take refuge* in France? Idiot! As if I didn't know that the writer who fights with the left is ruined!' "[43]

During 1969 and 1970, the Padilla–Cabrera Infante controversy assumed international proportions. The March–April 1969 issue of *Casa de las Américas* published a declaration by the editorial board (Mario Benedetti, Emmanuel Carballo, Julio Cortázar, Roque Dalton, René Depestre, Edmundo Desnoes, Roberto Fernández Retamar, Ambrosio Fornet, Manuel Galich, Lisandro Otero, Graziella Pogolotti, Angel Rama), signed January 11, 1969, which in a very prorevolutionary way encourages criticism and ideological debate:

In the Cuban context, the intellectual's duty is to carry out a creative and critical work rooted in the revolutionary process and, above all, linked with

---

[41] Casal, *El caso Padilla*, p. 66.
[42] *Le Monde* (Paris), November 5, 1968, reprinted in ibid., p. 69.
[43] Ibid.

his dedication to tasks that support, orient, and stimulate the ascending march of the revolution.

In Cuba, where the intellectual has at his disposal the necessary freedom to use all forms of expression and where the mass media are at the service of the people, there has been formed a growing reading public, capable of demanding and sharing creative and thought-provoking works in a broad ideological debate. This opens new perspectives to cultural production and is one of the reasons why the world is paying attention to its experience.[44]

Shortly after the appearance of the French edition of *Fuera del juego* with the to-be-expected sensationalist advertising, Julio Cortázar became involved by attempting to write an objective account of the whole Padilla affair. However, according to Mario Benedetti, the newspaper *Le Nouvel Observateur* distorted the statement by entitling it "Defense of Padilla" and by omitting several important sections in which Cortázar was critical of Padilla and of the way in which he was being exploited by his French publishers.[45]

In spite of his objective intentions, Cortázar's position was interpreted as being critical of the Cuban Revolution. He had previously been embroiled in a polemic with Peruvian novelist José María Arguedas, who, in the spring of 1968, attacked him and his other European-based colleagues like Carlos Fuentes for not participating actively in their respective countries' revolutionary movements and for writing escapist works, such as *62 modelo para armar* (1968).[46] The criticism of this same novel was also the basis for a more ideological debate— on the role of literature in a revolution—in which the Colombian short-story writer Oscar Collazos took on both Cortázar and Mario Vargas Llosa. The original articles were published in *Marcha* in Montevideo between August 1969 and April 1970 and later republished as

[44] *Casa de las Américas* 9, no. 53 (March–April 1969): 5.

[45] Interview with Jorge Onetti, published in *Marcha* (Montevideo), May 23, 1969, and republished in Mario Benedetti, *Cuaderno cubano*, pp. 142–143.

[46] Arguedas's criticism is contained in the first chapter of his book *El zorro de arriba y el zorro de abajo*, which was published in the Peruvian journal *Amaru* 6 (April–June 1968). Cortázar replied in the April 7, 1969, issue of *Life en español*. A summary of the dispute appears in *Casa de las Américas* 10, no. 57 (November–December 1969): 136.

a small book in July 1970 by the Mexican publishing house Siglo XXI.[47]

In August 1969, an international literary "Encuentro" was held in Chile in which political issues predominated over literary ones. The August 26 Declaration of Viña del Mar comments on the role of the author in the exploited societies of Latin America, "con la sola excepción de Cuba."[48] The writer, both as a creator and as a man, should be in the forefront of the struggle for liberation: "In spite of such stigmas, Latin America has given birth in these times to a literature that has attained today a status of universal recognition. This is due to the fact that our continent has an important word to say in the struggle for its liberation. Writers must assume a leadership role in this movement. For ethical and intellectual reasons, they must carry it forward to its ultimate consequences, both as men and as artists."[49]

The September–October 1969 issue of Casa de las Américas published a tape-recorded round-table discussion entitled "El intelectual y la sociedad." The participants were Cubans Roberto Fernández Retamar, Edmundo Desnoes, Ambrosio Fornet, and three Latin Americans residing in Cuba: Haitian René Depestre, Salvadoran Roque Dalton, and Uruguayan Carlos María Gutiérrez. Shortly thereafter, the discussion was published as a small book in Mexico[50] and sparked another lively polemic between critics Gabriel Zaid and Federico Alvarez in the Mexican weekly Siempre. Zaid's critical review appeared in the December 10, 1969, issue and was answered by Alvarez in the February 4, 1970, issue, which also contained Zaid's counterrebuttal.

Against the backdrop of these theoretical discussions, José Lorenzo Fuentes, whose volume of fantastic short stories Después de la gaviota had been awarded an honorable mention in the 1968 Casa de las Américas competition, was expelled from the UNEAC in September 1969 and imprisoned for alleged involvement with a CIA agent work-

---

[47] Oscar Collazos, Julio Cortázar, Mario Vargas Llosa, Literatura en la revolución y revolución en la literatura.

[48] Wolfgang A. Luchting, "Los rabdomantes," Mundo Nuevo, no. 47 (March 1970), p. 65.

[49] Ibid., p. 66.

[50] "El intelectual y la sociedad," Casa de las Américas 10, no. 56 (September–October 1969), and Roque Dalton et al., El intelectual y la sociedad.

ing for the Mexican Embassy in Havana. Nicolás Guillén, on the occasion of the 1969 UNEAC award ceremony, served notice that writers could not expect to receive special treatment: "Cuban writers and artists have the same responsibilities as our soldiers with respect to the defense of the nation . . . He who does not [fulfill his duty], regardless of his position, will receive the most severe revolutionary punishment for his fault."[51]

The major event of 1970 related to the problem of intellectual freedom in Cuba was the publication in France of two historical appraisals of the Cuban Revolution written by Marxists: René Dumont's *Cuba Est-il Socialiste?* and K. S. Karol's *Les Guérrilleros au Pouvoir: L'Itinéraire Politique de la Révolution Cubaine.* The fact that both writers had previously been considered friends of the Revolution and had enjoyed the confidence of Fidel Castro caused the latter to bristle intensively at their critical attitudes:

> On April 22, 1970, Fidel Castro interrupted an oration in Havana marking the centenary of the birth of Lenin and delivered a scathing attack on certain leftist European intellectual critics of Cuba. "These days, as you know, there are super-revolutionary theoreticians, super-leftists, real 'supermen' you might say, who are capable of crushing imperialism in two seconds with their tongues." These "super-revolutionaries," Castro went on, "construct imaginary, hypothetical worlds from Paris and Rome," while they themselves live in comfort and "haven't the slightest notion of reality or the problems and difficulties of a revolution . . . they won't even forgive the Soviet Union for existing and this from positions on the left!"[52]

While Dumont's book was almost immediately published in Spanish by the leftist Venezuelan Editorial Tiempo Nuevo, the Mexican publishing house Siglo XXI refused to publish the Spanish version of Karol's book, and it was not published in Spanish until early 1973, by Seix Barral in Barcelona. Arnaldo Orfila Reynal, director of Siglo XXI, explained in a letter published in *Siempre* on June 9, 1971, that they had refused to publish the book because Karol had not lived up to

---

[51] *Granma Weekly Review*, December 7, 1969, p. 9, quoted by Lourdes Casal in "Literature and Society" in *Revolutionary Change in Cuba*, ed. Carmelo Mesa-Lago, p. 460.

[52] Lee Lockwood, review of English translation of Karol's book, *Guerrillas in Power*, *New York Times Book Review Section*, January 24, 1971, p. 3.

the terms of the contract signed in January 1968. According to Orfila, Karol had promised to use all the information that was made available to him for an objective study, and instead he used it to fabricate a distorted picture of the Revolution:

Indeed; the author was trusted to live up to his promise that his work would be based on an objective investigation of the Cuban process in order to produce a complete study of its development. We had direct information that in Cuba the doors of all the archives, of all the sources, even the most confidential, and of institutions, studies, and projects had been opened for him; we knew that the highest government officials had welcomed him as a faithful friend, providing him with information, opinions, news of progress and of setbacks, of successes and failures, of projects, calculations, and perspectives . . .

We soon noticed that the core of the work, and its essential purpose, was not to provide an objective examination of that process but rather to publicize conclusions already printed, not only in proclamations by declared enemies of the Revolution, but also in books and declarations of dozens of newspapermen and writers who were carrying out, and continue to carry out, a real information "invasion," spread to the four corners of the world, which is false and slanderous and which attempts to broadcast a distorted image of the Cuban process.[53]

The whole issue of intellectual freedom came to a head on March 20, 1971, with the arrest of Heberto Padilla and his subsequent release and confession on April 27. From March through the end of the year, the debate raged furiously and has left indelible scars on the intellectual Left all over Latin America and Europe. On March 22, Chilean author Jorge Edwards, Padilla's friend, had to leave Cuba after serving for four months as President Allende's *encargado de negocios*. Edwards's "nonfiction political novel," *Persona non grata* (December 1973), decries the police-state tactics used by the Cuban government to intimidate him and his literary friends. On April 2, 1971, the PEN Club of Mexico expressed its disapproval of the arrest of Padilla and deplored the declarations of Fidel Castro as reported by France Press. The signatories included artist José Luis Cuevas and writers Carlos Fuentes, Octavio Paz, Carlos Pellicer, José Revueltas, and Juan Rulfo. On April 9, 1971, *Le Monde* in Paris published a more respectful

[53] Arnaldo Orfila Reynal, letter to the editor, *Siempre*, June 9, 1971, pp. 8, 69.

petition to Fidel Castro, which reaffirmed solidarity with the Cuban Revolution but expressed concern over the as-yet-unexplained arrest of Padilla. The signatories included such outstanding figures as Jean-Paul Sartre and Simone de Beauvoir, Alberto Moravia and Italo Calvino, Julio Cortázar, Carlos Fuentes, Gabriel García Márquez, Juan Goytisolo, Octavio Paz, and Mario Vargas Llosa.

On the evening of his release from prison, Padilla appeared before a meeting of the Unión de Escritores y Artistas Cubanos and was introduced by Vice-President José Antonio Portuondo, in the absence of President Nicolás Guillén, who was ill at the time. According to Portuondo, Padilla had requested the opportunity to explain his situation. Padilla's speech was published in the March–June 1971 issue of *Casa de las Américas*, occupying twelve double-column pages. The tone of the whole speech is clearly "confessional":

I have committed many, many errors, errors that are really inexcusable, really worthy of censure, really reprehensible. And I feel truly relieved, truly happy, after all this experience that I have had, with the possibility of beginning my life over again with a new spirit.

I requested this meeting, and I'll never get tired of clarifying that it was I who requested it, because I know that, if anyone is suspect, it's an artist and a writer. And not only in Cuba but in many places of the world. And if I have come here to improvise my speech and not to write it out—and these few notes are always a crutch for the coward who thinks that he'll forget something—if I have come here to improvise it, it is precisely because of the confidence that the Revolution has, during all the conversations that we have had during the past few days, in my telling the truth. A truth that was really hard for me to accept—I must admit—because I always preferred my justifications, my excuses, because I would always find a justification for a series of positions that were really harmful to the Revolution.[54]

Padilla then proceeds to review his errors: his unjust attack on his "amigo verdadero"[55] Lisandro Otero and his defense of Cabrera Infante, "un agente de la CIA";[56] the writing of his antirevolutionary book, *Fuera del juego*, whose notoriety was due in part to the vote of

---

[54] Heberto Padilla, "Intervención en la Unión de Escritores y Artistas Cubanos," *Casa de las Américas* 11, nos. 65–66 (March–June 1971): 191.

[55] Ibid., p. 192.

[56] Ibid.

the British critic J. M. Cohen and the French publishing house Du Seuil; his friendship with foreign newspapermen; his having provided K. S. Karol and René Dumont with interpretations of Cuban reality, which they incorporated into their antirevolutionary books—"I exaggerated horribly with Dumont and with Karol, who wrote libelous books against the Revolution."[57] The basis for all of Padilla's errors was his vanity as a writer: "I wanted to become famous,"[58] was "dazzled by the great capitals, by international distribution, by foreign cultures."[59]

The fact that the Padilla case was not an isolated phenomenon is demonstrated by his denunciation of other intellectuals, first in general terms, and then specifically:

Nevertheless, I am convinced that many of those whom I see here before me while I have been speaking this whole time have felt consternation at how closely their attitudes resemble mine, at how closely my life, the life that I have led, resembles the life that they lead, that they have been leading all this time, at how closely my defects resemble theirs, my opinions theirs, my embarrassments theirs. I am sure that they must be very worried, that they were very worried, besides, over my fate during all this time, over what would happen to me. And, upon hearing my words now, they are probably thinking that by the same token the Revolution could not continue tolerating a situation in which all the little groups of disaffected intellectuals and artists were conspiring perniciously.[60]

He accuses his own wife, poetess Belkis Cuza Malé, of sharing his bitterness and resentment against the Revolution; his dear friend, poet and novelist Pablo Armando Fernández, has recently become "embittered, disaffected, sick and sad, and, therefore, counterrevolutionary";[61] his other dear friend César López, short-story writer and poet, has made with him negative analyses of the Revolution and has sent a manuscript of poetry, expressing his disaffections, to Spain for publication; poet José Yanes has recently followed the examples of Padilla

[57] Ibid., p. 196.
[58] Ibid., p. 193.
[59] Ibid., p. 197.
[60] Ibid., p. 198.
[61] Ibid., p. 199.

and César López in writing "defeatist poetry";[62] Norberto Fuentes's
personal attitude toward the Revolution differs considerably from the
warm affection for the revolutionary counterinsurgents expressed in his
short stories—"I remember that we were together exactly the day before I was arrested, talking continuously about subjects in which the
Security Force was pictured as people who were going to devour us";[63]
poet Manuel Díaz Martínez is similarly embittered; José Lezama Lima
has been unjustly critical of the Revolution, in spite of the fact that the
Revolution has published his works, which are based on political and
philosophical ideas other than those of Marxism-Leninism; David
Buzzi, who himself had spent some time in prison, had given Padilla a
distorted picture of the prison atmosphere—"I did not see that atmosphere that he described to me."[64] Padilla arrived at all these conclusions, not as the result of interrogations, not even as the result of
discussions, but rather as the result of conversations:

> The discussions I had with my comrades were incredible. Discussions!
> That's not the word. Conversations. They didn't even interrogate me, be-
> cause they used on me a long and intelligent, and brilliant, and fabulous
> form of intelligent, political persuasion. They have made me see clearly each
> one of my errors. And that's why I have seen how the Security Force was not
> the harsh, severe body that my feverish imagination many times, many many
> times imagined, and many many times defamed; but a group of most dili-
> gent comrades who work night and day to ensure moments like this one, to
> ensure generosity like this, to ensure almost undeserved comprehension like
> this: that to a man like myself who has fought against the Revolution they
> should give the opportunity to rectify his life radically, as I want to rec-
> tify it.[65]

A letter from Padilla to the Gobierno Revolucionario, dated April 5,
1971, was distributed by the Cuban news agency Prensa Latina on
April 26 and reprinted in the Mexican weekly *Siempre* on May 19,
1971. The text is quite similar to that of the speech before the
UNEAC, in spite of Padilla's assertion that the latter was improvised

[62] Ibid., p. 200.
[63] Ibid.
[64] Ibid., p. 201.
[65] Ibid., p. 202.

rather than written: "And if I have come here to improvise it and not to write it . . ."[66] The only major difference between the two documents is the omission in the letter of references to the other disaffected Cuban writers.

As might have been expected and, indeed, as Padilla himself might have expected, his speech was widely denounced by leftist writers all over Latin America and Europe as a Stalinist-type confession. The same May 19 issue of *Siempre* printed a series of strong denunciations by José Revueltas, Octavio Paz, Carlos Fuentes, and others, with a dissenting note by poet Juan Bañuelos. On May 20, 1971, the second letter from Paris was sent to Fidel Castro expressing "our shame and our anger"[67] at Padilla's confession. The signatories included almost all those who had signed the first letter, with two notable exceptions, Julio Cortázar and Gabriel García Márquez, and several additions, Nathalie Sarraute, Susan Sontag, José Revueltas, and Juan Rulfo.

The reaction of the Cuban government and its supporters to the criticism from the intellectual Left was virulent. The declaration of the Primer Congreso Nacional de Educación y Cultura, held in Havana from April 23 to 30, as well as Fidel Castro's speech closing the convention not only condemned "la maffia de intelectuales burgueses seudoizquierdistas,"[68] "Señores intelectuales burgueses y libelistas burgueses y agentes de la CIA,"[69] "ratas intelectuales,"[70] but also clearly defined the new government policy toward the arts, which obviously supplants Fidel Castro's oft-quoted 1961 "Palabras a los intelectuales." Under the new policy:

1. Art is an instrument of the Revolution: "El arte es una arma de la Revolución."[71]

2. Culture in a socialist society is not the exclusive property of an elite but rather the activity of the masses: "La cultura de una sociedad

---

[66] Ibid., p. 191.

[67] Casal, *El caso Padilla*, p. 123.

[68] "Declaración del Primer Congreso Nacional de Educación y Cultura," in ibid., p. 112.

[69] Fidel Castro, "Discurso de Clausura del Primer Congreso Nacional de Educación y Cultura," in ibid., p. 118.

[70] Ibid., p. 122.

[71] Casal, "Declaración," p. 110.

colectiva es una actividad de las masas, no el monopolio de una *élite.*"⁷²

3. The Revolution frees art and literature from the bourgeois law of supply and demand and provides the means for expression based on ideological rigor and high technical standards: "La Revolución libera el arte y la literatura de los férreos mecanismos de la oferta y la demanda imperantes en la sociedad burguesa. El arte y la literatura dejan de ser mercancías y se crean todas las posibilidades para la expresión y experimentación estética en sus más diversas manifestaciones sobre la base del rigor ideológico y la alta calificación técnica."⁷³

4. The ideological formation of young writers and artists in Marxism-Leninism is an important task for the Revolution: "La formación ideológica de los jóvenes escritores y artistas es una tarea de máxima importancia para la Revolución. Educarlos en el marxismo-leninismo, pertrecharlos de las ideas de la Revolución y capacitarlos técnicamente es nuestro deber."⁷⁴

5. Works of art will be judged politically according to their usefulness to man and society. A work without human content can have no aesthetic value: "Para nosotros, un pueblo revolucionario en un proceso revolucionario, valoramos las creaciones culturales y artísticas en función de la utilidad para el pueblo, en función de lo que aporten a la reivindicación del hombre, a la liberación del hombre, a la felicidad del hombre.

"Nuestra valoración es política. No puede haber valor estético sin contenido humano. No puede haber valor estético contra la justicia, contra el bienestar, contra la liberación, contra la felicidad del hombre. ¡No puede haberlo!"⁷⁵

6. Art and literature are valuable means of training youth within the revolutionary morality, which excludes selfishness and the typical aberrations of bourgeois culture: "Nuestro arte y nuestra literatura serán valiosos medios para la formación de la juventud dentro de la moral revolucionaria, que excluye el egoísmo y las aberraciones típicas de la cultura burguesa."⁷⁶

⁷² Ibid.
⁷³ Ibid., p. 111.
⁷⁴ Ibid.
⁷⁵ Castro, "Discurso," p. 119.
⁷⁶ Casal, "Declaración," p. 110.

7. A cultural movement should be promoted among the teachers, emphasizing children's literature and educational and cultural radio and television programs for children: "¿Es que acaso cien mil profesores y maestros, para señalar sólo un sector de nuestros trabajadores, no podrían promover un formidable movimiento cultural, un formidable movimiento artístico, un formidable movimiento literario? ¿Por qué no buscamos, por qué no promovemos, para que surjan nuevos valores, para que podamos atender esas necesidades, para que podamos tener literatura infantil, para que podamos tener muchos más programas de radio y de televisión educacionales, culturales, infantiles?"[77]

8. An apolitical attitude toward culture is despicable and reactionary: "El apoliticismo no es más que un punto de vista vergonzante y reaccionario en la concepción y expresión culturales."[78]

9. The rules governing national and international literary contests will have to be revised as well as the criteria for awarding prizes and the analysis of the revolutionary credentials of the judges: "Es insoslayable la revisión de las bases de los concursos nacionales e internacionales que nuestras instituciones culturales promueven, así como el análisis de las condiciones revolucionarias de los integrantes de esos jurados y el criterio mediante el cual se otorgan los premios."[79]

10. Great care must be exercised in order to avoid inviting foreign writers and intellectuals whose works and ideology are in conflict with the interests of the Revolution: "Al mismo tiempo, se precisa establecer un sistema riguroso para la invitación a los escritores e intelectuales extranjeros, que evite la presencia de personas cuya obra e ideología están en pugna con los intereses de la Revolución . . ."[80]

This new government policy toward the arts was immediately echoed by the editorial board of *El Caimán Barbudo* in its May 1971 issue in which it announced the dismissal of short-story writer Eduardo Heras León from the journal. Heras León was born in 1941, entered the armed forces at the age of twenty, served as an officer for more than six years, and then taught journalism at the Universidad de La Habana.

---

[77] Castro, "Discurso," p. 120.
[78] Casal, "Declaración," p. 107.
[79] Ibid., p. 106.
[80] Ibid.

His volume of stories *La guerra tuvo seis nombres* won the 1968 David award, and he received honorable mention in the 1970 Casa de las Américas competition for *Los pasos en la hierba*, the same volume that was responsible for his dismissal. In fact, one of the stories, "Jefe de pieza," was published by *El Caimán Barbudo*, only seven months before, in the same number 41 (October 1970) in which Heras was appointed to the editorial board. Perhaps because of the notoriety given to the Padilla case no publicity at all has been given to Heras's dismissal with the exception of the following from *El Caimán Barbudo*:

The Editorial Board of *El Caimán Barbudo*, motivated by the necessity to define an overall criterion in the face of the alternatives that were explicitly laid bare in the analysis of Eduardo Heras's book of short stories *Los pasos en la hierba*, decided in favor of the only position that it considers correct from the revolutionary point of view and in defense of the interests of the Revolution in this field: to relieve him of his responsibilities as a member of this Editorial Board because of the tendentious and critical connotations that, supposedly based on revolutionary positions, are apparent in his book. We believe it correct to take a stand not only in the specific case of Heras's book but also through this example—surprising because it involves a young man who ought to reflect a different type of contradictions and positions, but within the constructive desire to aid the Revolution, and not those contradictions and positions that are subservient to and in common with the enemies of the Revolution—we propose to define more precisely the limits of the term *revolutionary writer*.

It is not possible to continue using a phraseology that is the contradiction of the real effect of the literary works conceived by these self-named *writers of the Revolution*.

It is absolutely necessary to revise the values and judgments that up to now have been manipulated by *undefined* groups, in the strictest sense of the word, among our young artists and intellectuals.

El Caimán Barbudo considers that the greatest responsibility of its staff members and contributors is to think in terms of these examples, to compare these positions, to weigh the justice of the criteria debated, and to assume finally a profoundly revolutionary attitude with respect to issues that no longer fall into the category of complexity to be studied, but rather into diversionary positions to be combatted.

These tendencies will not be developed among us. We will follow the revolutionary road which we know exists in all forms of aesthetic richness, without cultural straitjackets, but without openings that are purposeless, confusing, and with imprecise boundaries. We support and hail the "Declaration of the First National Congress of Education and Culture, and the guiding words of our Commander in Chief, in the closing speech of the Congress."[81]

The international aspects of the Cuban government's counteroffensive against the "pseudorevolutionary leftist intellectuals" raged during the summer and fall of 1971. The main target seems to have been Peruvian novelist Mario Vargas Llosa, who originally antagonized the Cuban government by his September 1968 criticism of Fidel Castro's support, albeit qualified, for the Soviet invasion of Czechoslovakia. In response to Vargas Llosa's resignation from the editorial board of *Casa de las Américas*, Haydée Santamaría published a strongly worded reply in both the March–June and July–August 1971 issues of the journal, in which she takes him to task for his lack of revolutionary zeal dating back to 1967, when he refused to donate the money from the Rómulo Gallegos prize to the revolutionary struggle of Che Guevara. The June 1971 issue of *El Caimán Barbudo* and the July–August 1971 issue of *Casa de las Américas* published a declaration by a group of young Peruvian writers condemning Vargas Llosa's stance on Cuba and affirming their solidarity with the "really revolutionary cultural policy that is now developing in the First Free Territory of America, which is beginning to get rid of those who profited from its prestige."[82] Among the signatories were Winston Orrillo and Washington Delgado, who were members of the program committee of the convention of the Instituto Internacional de Literatura Iberoamericana held in Huampaní (outside Lima), Peru, in August 1971. At the same session in which Vargas Llosa was invited to comment on a paper by Benjamín Carrión, two other papers were presented that were highly critical of Vargas Llosa's novel *La casa verde*. José Miguel Oviedo, Vargas Llosa's friend, and the director of the Instituto Nacional de Cultura was not invited to participate in the convention. It was at this same

[81] *El Caimán Barbudo*, no. 46 (May 1971), p. 2.
[82] *Casa de las Américas* 12, no. 67 (July–August 1971): 145.

convention in Peru that José Antonio Portuondo declared that Padilla had not been castigated for his literary works but rather for his espionage and counterrevolutionary activities: "... el régimen de mi país juzgó a Padilla no por sus obras sino por su labor de espionaje y contrarrevolución."[83] A few weeks later at the theater festival in Manizales, Colombia, Vargas Llosa was received with hostility by a group of Colombian pro-Cuban leftists. Colombian essayist Carlos Rincón, professor at the University of Leipzig in East Germany, also in the July–August 1971 *Casa de las Américas*, severely criticized Vargas Llosa for his non-Marxist introduction to the 1969 edition of the sixteenth-century Catalán novel of chivalry *Tirant lo Blanc*.

At the same time, other pro-Cuban intellectuals followed the lead of the Peruvians and declared their solidarity with the Revolution. The Mexican letter appeared in the June 16, 1971, issue of *Siempre* and included the signatures of artist David Alfaro Siqueiros, critic Emmanuel Carballo, sociologist Ricardo Pozas, Brazilian politician-in-exile Francisco Julião, poets Efraín Huerta, Juan Bañuelos, and other lesser-known figures. This letter, along with similar ones from other Latin American countries, was also published in the July–August 1971 *Casa de las Américas*: Uruguay (Mario Benedetti, Juan Carlos Onetti, Francisco Espínola, Mario Arregui, Silvia Lago, Jorge Onetti, Hiber Conteris), Chile (Manuel Rojas, Francisco Coloane, Carlos Droguett, Antonio Skármeta), Colombia (León de Greiff), Ecuador (artist Oscar Guayasamín, Pedro Jorge Vera, Eugenia Viteri). This same issue contained what is probably the most significant defense of the Cuban position, a poem entitled "Policrítica en la hora de los chacales" by Julio Cortázar, one of the signatories of the first Paris letter protesting the imprisonment of Padilla. The poem is basically a denunciation of the news media for their distortions, and an acceptance of Fidel Castro's statements that only those who are actively involved in the Revolution have the right to criticize. At the same time, Cortázar asserts that he will continue to express himself freely and that he continues to feel himself an American regardless of where he lives:

[83] *Expreso* (Lima), August 13, 1971, p. 14; *La Prensa* (Lima), August 14, 1971, p. A 10.

You're right, Fidel: only in the battle exists the right to complain,
Only from within, should criticism come forth, the search for better formu-
    las,
Yes, but within is sometimes so outside,
And if today I dissociate myself forever from the fair-weather liberals, from
    those who sign the self-righteous texts
Be-cause-Cu-ba-is-not-what-their-of-fice-plans-de-mand-of-her,
I don't consider myself an exception, I am like them, what have I done for
    Cuba beyond offering my love,
What have I given for Cuba beyond a wish, a hope.
But now I dissociate myself from their ideal world, from their plans,
Precisely now when
I am asked to leave what I love, when I am prohibited from defending it,
It is *now* that I exercise my right to choose, to be once more and more than
    ever
With your Revolution, my Cuba, in my way. And my clumsy way, with arms
    flailing,
Is this, it is to repeat what I like or don't like,
Accepting your reproach for speaking from so far away
And at the same time insisting (how many times have my words been heard
    only by the wind)
That I am what I am, and I am nothing, and that nothing is my American
    land,
And however I can and wherever I am, I continue to be that land, and for
    its people
I write every letter of my books and I live every day of my life.[84]

And, finally, in this same July–August 1971 issue of *Casa de las
Américas*, the works of Cortázar and Vargas Llosa are gratuitously
criticized in Manuel Rojas's review of the 1971 prize-winning novel—
he was one of the judges—*La última mujer y el próximo combate*, an
example of the kind of novel likely to be produced as long as the April
1971 policy prevails:

One of the elements that makes up this novel is its savory, natural Cuban
flavor; next, its natural rhythm. It does not dazzle the reader with multiple

---

[84] Julio Cortázar, "Policrítica en la hora de los chacales," *Casa de las Américas*
12, no. 67 (July–August 1971): 159.

chronological and spatial planes or with multiple characters, à la Vargas Llosa, or with English or French words, allusions to New York or the docks along the Seine, à la Cortázar, no. Finally, neither is it decadent. It is a novel in which revolutionary workers and weak individuals have parts, in addition to thieves, traitors, and shirkers. Against them, the revolutionaries have no other course but to act as they do: to combat the antisocial characters.[85]

The April 1971 policy was further implemented and tightened three years later in the flyer announcing the new guidelines for the 1975 Casa de las Américas contest. Whereas individual awards were previously given in the novel, short story, poetry, and theater, for 1975 they were lumped together into one category for which eight prizes without distinction would be given, preferably two for each genre. The second category is for essays and *testimonios*, while the third category is specifically earmarked for children's literature, both fiction and didactic works. Manuscripts for categories two and three should deal with Latin American themes. All manuscripts must be signed by the author.

II. Literature and Revolution in Historical Perspective: France, Mexico, the Soviet Union, China, Vietnam

The new policy of the Cuban government toward the role of the arts in a revolutionary socialist society is not at all surprising considering the history of other revolutionary socialist societies. In fact, a historical survey of this problem might well start with the nonsocialist French Revolution.

Arnold Hauser's account of the role of art and the artist in the French Revolution bears a striking resemblance to the statements in the April 1971 Declaración del Primer Congreso Nacional de Educación y Cultura: "From now on the cultivation of art constituted an instrument of government and enjoyed the attention given only to important affairs of state. As long as the Republic was in danger and

---

[85] Manuel Rojas, review of *La última mujer y el próximo combate*, *Casa de las Américas* 12, no. 67 (July–August 1971): 172.

fighting for its very existence, the whole nation was called upon to serve it with all its combined strength. In an address given to the Convention by David, we find these words: 'Each one of us is responsible to the nation for the talents he has received from nature' (Jules David, *Le Peintre David*, 1880, p. 117)."[86]

As in Cuba, early artistic freedom gave way to greater regimentation as different organizations were formed in order to implement government policy:

The Academy was dissolved abruptly, but it was much more difficult to find a substitute for it. As early as 1793, David founded the *Commune des Arts*, a free and democratic artists' association without special groups, classes and privileged members. But owing to the subversive activities of the royalists in its midst, it had to be replaced in the very next year by the *Société populaire et républicaine des Arts*, the first truly revolutionary association whose duty it was to take over the functions of the suppressed Academy. It was, however, in no sense an Academy but a club of which anyone could become a member without regard to position and calling. In the same year, the *Club révolutionnaire des Arts* arose to which, among others, David, Prudhon, Gérard, and Isabey belonged and which, thanks to its famous members, enjoyed great prestige. All these associations were directly dependent on the "Committee for Public Instruction" and were under the aegis of the Convention, the Welfare Committee, and the Paris Commune. (Joseph Billiet: "The French Revolution and the Fine Arts" in *Essays on the French Revolution*, edited by T. A. Jackson, 1945, p. 203.)[87]

Although writers were less regimented under the Mexican Revolution of 1910, the government was quick to recognize the importance of literature, and the arts in general, as a social and political tool. As early as 1915, Carrancista Félix Palavicini called for the dedication of literature to the Revolution: "The vigorous impulse which has been stirring our country for five years cannot be understood nor will it ever be substantialized unless it is accorded literary consecration ... Modification, change, complete renovation are not understood, perceived or sensed until they have been profoundly impressed on people by literature."[88]

[86] Arnold Hauser, *The Social History of Art*, III, 148.
[87] Ibid., 161.
[88] Quoted in translation by John Rutherford, *Mexican Society during the Revolution*, p. 53.

It was, however, in the field of mural painting rather than literature that government policy bore fruit initially. Under Secretary of Education José Vasconcelos (1920–1924) and later, Diego Rivera, José Clemente Orozco, and David Alfaro Siqueiros were commissioned to cover the walls of many public buildings with panoramic murals that linked revolutionary heroes Madero, Carranza, and Zapata to their predecessors who fought for similar revolutionary ideals: Juárez, Morelos, Hidalgo, and Cuauhtémoc. This mythification process did not appear at first in the Mexican novel, because adequate techniques were not readily available. Vasconcelos's successor as secretary of education, José Manuel Puig Casauranc, promised to continue the former's policies and committed the government specifically to promote realistic literature: "The Secretariat of Education will publish and will assist the divulgation of any Mexican work in which the mannered decoration of a false understanding of life is replaced by the other kind of decoration, rough and severe and often gloomy, but always truthful, taken from life itself."[89] However, it was not until the 1930's that world literary currents combined with the government policy of providing employment for many writers to produce the well-known Mexican novel of the Revolution.[90]

The circumstances surrounding the evolution of the arts in Cuba seem to be following the pattern established by the Soviet Union and China of a decade of relative freedom, which then gives way to an absolute demand for the artist's positive incorporation into the Revolution. Between 1917 and 1929, tight Soviet censorship was employed "to prevent the appearance in print of openly 'counterrevolutionary' work."[91] Anatoli Lunacharsky, who was responsible for Party supervision of literary and artistic affairs during the 1920's, had written: "I have said dozens of times that the Commissariat of Enlightenment must be impartial in its attitude toward the various trends of artistic life. As regards questions of artistic form, the tastes of the People's Commissar and other persons in authority should not be taken into

[89] Ibid., pp. 57–58.
[90] Ibid., pp. 66–67.
[91] Max Hayward, Introduction to *Dissonant Voices in Soviet Literature*, p. xiii.

account. All individual artists and all groups of artists should be allowed to develop freely."[92]

Although Fidel Castro's 1961 "Palabras a los intelectuales" seemed to embody the same principle of "Dentro de la Revolución todo, contra la Revolución nada," Cuban writers in general tended to avoid writing about contemporary events, while "the Soviet prose of the period was, on the whole, remarkably objective in portraying the realities of the Revolution, the Civil War, and the period of N. E. P."[93] In 1929 came the final defeat of all political opposition to Stalin and the attack of the fanatical Association of Proletarian Writers (RAPP) on the All-Russian Union of Soviet Writers, which included most of the best authors with varying degrees of loyalty to the regime. The charges against Boris Pilnyak, chairman of the latter organization, and Evgeni Zamyatin, the author of *We* and chairman of the Leningrad branch of the Union, were "the first application to Soviet cultural life of the technique of the campaign against certain chosen scapegoats with the object of terrorizing a whole group into submission."[94] As in Cuba's Padilla case, the charges included contact with foreigners for the publication abroad of the authors' works, as well as the anti-Soviet nature of the works. The new Soviet policy also provoked serious divisions among the intellectual Left abroad, particularly in Paris: "Around 1930, when the aesthetic doctrine of socialist realism is being organized in an increasingly totalitarian form, the surrealist group breaks in two. Those who follow Breton will refuse to subscribe to all the aesthetic postulates from Moscow; on the other hand, Desnos will subscribe to them repeatedly."[95]

Except for the war years of 1941–1945, the remainder of Stalin's regime, between 1929 and 1953, was characterized by increasing pressure on the artists to adhere to the official policy within the All-Russian

---

[92] Quoted by Ilya Ehrenburg in his memoirs, *Novy Mir*, September 1960, and requoted by Hayward, Introduction to *Dissonant Voices in Soviet Literature*, pp. xiv–xv.

[93] Hayward, Introduction to *Dissonant Voices in Soviet Literature*, p. xiii.

[94] Ibid., p. xvi.

[95] Emir Rodríguez Monegal, "Lo real y lo maravilloso en *El reino de este mundo*," *Revista Iberoamericana* 37, nos. 76–77 (July–December 1971): 627.

Union of Soviet Writers established in April 1932. The new method elaborated between 1932 and the First Congress of Soviet Writers in 1934 was socialist realism,[96] promulgated officially by Zhdanov but devised and propagated by Maxim Gorky.[97] Some of its basic principles bear a striking resemblance to the "Declaración" and Fidel Castro's speech at the April 1971 Primer Congreso Nacional de Educación y Cultura and to the new ideological novel, *La última mujer y el próximo combate.*

—whereas the nineteenth-century Russian novelists used the realist method "to *negate* the society in which they lived, . . . the Soviet writer was required by the same method to *affirm* the new socialist order . . ."[98]

—"the rich 'ornamental style' . . . declared to have been an aberration in the development of Russian literature . . . henceforth denounced as 'formalism.' "[99]

—writers were supposed "to expose and hold up to scorn" the survivors of capitalism and "hasten the day when all would model themselves on the New Man."[100]

—"Soviet writers, in their anxiety to avoid being charged with 'naturalism' (a cardinal offense against 'realism'), began to use a sterilized language carefully shorn of all the expressive slang and dialect that had been characteristic of Russian writing in the twenties. Plots became more and more simple and their outcome more and more predictable. Optimism reigned supreme and all endings were happy—except, of course, in capitalist countries."[101]

Since Stalin's death in 1953 and Khrushchev's denunciation of him in 1956, Party control of literature and the arts has been exercised "with restraint and intelligence,"[102] although there have been periodic neo-Stalinist outbursts against "revisionism," especially in response to domestic and international crises, such as the Hungarian uprising of

[96] For a theoretical treatment of socialist realism presented sympathetically, see Georg Lukács, *Realism in Our Time.*
[97] Henry Gifford, *The Novel in Russia from Pushkin to Pasternak*, p. 133.
[98] Hayward, Introduction to *Dissonant Voices in Soviet Literature*, p. xxii.
[99] Ibid.
[100] Ibid., p. xxiii.
[101] Ibid., p. xxvi.
[102] Ibid., p. xxix.

1956, Khrushchev's attack on abstract art in 1962 after losing the confidence of his comrades at the October 1961 Party Congress, and the invasion of Czechoslovakia in 1968 followed by the 1969 expulsion of Alexander Solzhenitsyn from the Soviet Writers Union.

How long it will take before the Cuban government follows the Soviet example of relaxing its pressures for absolute conformity on the artist is a matter of guesswork, but for the moment, at least, the hardline attitude seems to be strengthened by the Chinese and Vietnamese models. Before they gained power in 1949, the Chinese Communists debated the role of literature and revolution for many years. In 1925, Guo Mo-ruo, the leader of the Creación group and, at the time, a recent convert to Marxism, stated that the only justification for literature was its use as a propaganda instrument: ". . . today, literature cannot justify its existence except for its capacity to hasten the attainment of the socialist revolution . . . We find ourselves in the propaganda era, and literature is the sharp weapon of propaganda."[103]

During the war against Japan, Mao Tse-tung reaffirmed the functional value of art. At the May 1942 Yenan Forum on Literature and Art, he stated that art cannot be isolated from political reality, that it must help the Revolution and be destined for the masses. Good revolutionary art is better than bad revolutionary art, but art must be revolutionary.[104]

At about the same time, Mao urged writers "to leave their desks and concentrate on the effort to gain a truly proletarian consciousness."[105] His words could well have been directed at the Cuban writers as they joined in the universal cutting of sugar cane: "Therefore I advise those of you who have only book knowledge and as yet no contact with reality, and those who have had few practical experiences, to realize their own shortcomings and make their attitudes a bit more humble."[106]

Since 1949 when the Chinese People's Republic was inaugurated, the role of literature and writers has fluctuated. In the "Hundred

[103] Lucien Blanco, *Los orígenes de la revolución china*, p. 69.

[104] Mao Tse-tung, *Speeches*, pp. 72–114.

[105] Jonathan Spence, "On Chinese Revolutionary Literature," in *Literature and Revolution*, ed. Jacques Ehrmann, p. 222.

[106] Ibid., quoted from Boyd Compton (trans.), *Mao's China, Party Reform Documents, 1942–44*, pp. 16–17.

Flowers Movement" of 1956–1957, Mao invited criticism of the regime by calling on the "hundred scholars" to contend. "The literary
monopoly of socialist realism was abrogated."[107] However, about ten
years later, as in the Soviet Union and Cuba, the period of relative freedom ended abruptly with the Great Proletarian Cultural Revolution of
1966.[108] "After years of bitter conflict with the writers, Mao appears to
have concluded that it is not only writers but literature itself that is
subversive."[109] The novel, the short story, and even poetry have given
way to the "true revolutionary literature: . . . an ultimate synthesis of
dance, music, and lyrics, drawn from the folk songs and folktales of
traditional China, blended with the true streams of a proletarian consciousness, girding itself for the final triumphant confrontation with
the world of imperialism."[110]

Although Cuba has allied itself in the course of its Revolution with
both the Soviet Union and China, it identifies much more with Vietnam because of its size and its being subjected to direct United States
aggression. Allusions to Vietnam abound throughout Che Guevara's
speeches culminating in his May 1967 "Mensaje a la tricontinental," in
which he hoped for more Vietnams: "How brilliant and immediate
our future would look if two, three, many Vietnams flourished on the
surface of the globe with their quotas of death and their enormous
tragedies, with their daily heroism, with their repeated blows against
imperialism, and the latter's need to disperse its forces against the
waves of increasing hatred of the peoples of the earth!"[111] The year
1967 was officially designated in Cuba as the "Año del Vietnam heroi-
co." The journal *Casa de las Américas* devoted its November–December 1969 and its November–December 1970 issues to eulogizing Ho
Chi Minh. In the latter issue, Roberto Fernández Retamar pointed out
the similarities between Ho and José Martí. However, it was in the

[107] *Encyclopedia Britannica*, 1968 ed., V, 596.

[108] For more details, see the articles by Felipe Pardinas, Lothar Knauth, and Ma
Sen in *Revista de la Universidad de México* 25, no. 1 (September 1971).

[109] Merle Goldman, "The Fall of Chou Yang," *China Quarterly*, no. 27 (July–
September 1966), p. 132, quoted by Spence, "On Chinese Revolutionary Literature,"
p. 223.

[110] Spence, "On Chinese Revolutionary Literature," p. 224.

[111] Guevara, *Obra revolucionaria*, p. 650.

September–December 1970 issue (published in 1971) of *Islas*, the journal of the Universidad de Las Villas, that the Vietnamese attitude toward the role of the artist was cited and developed as a model for Cuba. In his introduction to a selection of Vietnamese poetry, Cuban short-story writer Félix Pita Rodríguez (b. 1909) extols the Vietnamese concept of the function of literature as an instrument for the creation of a new man in a new society: "... la presencia de una concepción vietnamita de la obra literaria ... como fuerza combatiente ... teniendo como objetivo el logro de un hombre nuevo en una sociedad nueva."[112] In order to carry out this functional role of art, the artist must have a solid political and ideological base and must make contact with the masses. Pita Rodríguez quotes from a Ho Chi Minh statement of December 10, 1951: "In order to carry out their task faithfully, the soldiers of art must have a solid political position and a just ideology ... In order to create, the artists must put themselves in contact with the people and penetrate deeply into their lives in order to know them thoroughly. Undoubtedly someone will say: 'President Ho Chi Minh wants to tie art to politics.' And it is right for them to think so: culture and art, like all branches of human activity, cannot remain outside economics and politics, they must be among them."[113]

Pita Rodríguez, who from 1940 to 1943 directed the Sunday supplement of *Noticias de Hoy*, the official organ of the Partido Socialista Popular, and who is now president of the literature section of UNEAC, definitely proposes that Ho Chi Minh's words and the Vietnam experience in general serve as a model for Cuban writers. In an obvious reference to the cardinal sin of Padilla and his cohorts, Pita Rodríguez summarizes Ho's statement as service versus personal glory: "Servir como antítesis de brillar."[114] He then calls upon all writers in Cuba, and elsewhere, to make the effort to change themselves ("renovarse") in order to serve the Revolution and follow the example of Vietnam: "It's very hard to change, but it can be done if the decision to do so exists. And it would be wonderful, for the greater and better service to

[112] Félix Pita Rodríguez, "La poesía combatiente de Vietnam," *Islas*, no. 37 (September–December 1970), p. 61.

[113] Félix Pita Rodríguez, "Ho Chi Minh y la función del escritor," *Islas*, no. 37 (September–December 1970), p. 107.

[114] Ibid.

the Revolution, if all the writers of today, those of our island of freedom and those of all countries, adopted fully and without reservations that slogan in which our people have marvelously synthesized the striving for what is just, what is perfect, what cannot be surpassed: AS IN VIETNAM."[115]

At the beginning of his article "Ho Chi Minh y la función del escritor," Pita Rodríguez establishes the clear relationship between Ho and José Martí: ". . . el paralelismo extraordinariamente revelador entre nuestro Martí y nuestro Ho Chi Minh."[116] He concludes the article by reaffirming the strong bonds between Vietnam and Cuba in the persons of Martí and Ho, along with a salute to Fidel Castro: "And our people, united, firmly and strongly, sure of themselves, and therefore invincible in their revolution and guided without hesitation or compromise by their supreme leader Commander in Chief Fidel Castro, are drawing near to the real dream of Martí and Ho Chi Minh and showing all the peoples of the world that it can be attained."[117]

[115] Ibid., p. 108.
[116] Ibid., p. 106.
[117] Ibid., p. 114.

Part Three. The Cuban Short Story of the Revolution: An Anthological Survey and More

Since the triumph of the Revolution in January 1959, the rather astounding number of fourteen anthologies of the Cuban short story have been published, in addition to five other anthologies of revolutionary literature in which the short story predominates. Of the total of nineteen, eight appeared in Havana, two each in Santiago, Chile, and Lima, and one each in Mexico City, Caracas, Guayaquil, Montevideo, Buenos Aires, Madrid, and Baltimore.[1] At the same time, over one hundred volumes of stories of individual authors have been published, mostly in Cuba.

Unfortunately, the peculiarities of the short-story form as well as Cuban and Latin American literary trends constitute obstacles for applying the same chronological classification as that used for the novel.

[1] For an annotated bibliography of these anthologies with their respective abbreviations, see pp. 294–299.

Nevertheless, there is sufficient parallelism between the themes of the 1959–1960, 1961–1965, 1966–1970, and 1971–1972 novels and those of the corresponding short stories to warrant a modified use of the same scheme as a basis for comparison.

Before 1959, the short story clearly outstripped the novel in Cuba, in spite of a late start. Whereas the novel was well represented in the nineteenth century by Gertrudis Gómez de Avellaneda's *Sab* (1841) and Cirilo Villaverde's *Cecilia Valdés* (1882), the first important short-story writer is generally acknowledged to be Jesús Castellanos (1879–1912), who did not publish his collection *De tierra adentro* until 1906. However, from the early years of Cuban independence until the triumph of the Revolution, the novel was definitely surpassed by the short story. This is particularly noteworthy because of its contrast with the overall Latin American situation. While the 1920's witnessed the flourishing of the *novela criollista* with *Los de abajo*,[2] *La vorágine*, *Don Segundo Sombra*, and *Doña Bárbara*, as well as the highly poetic Chilean novels *Alsino* and *El hermano asno*, Cuba's best contributions were the naturalistic novels of Carlos Loveira, which were both anachronistic and relatively tedious. Likewise, in the 1930's and early 1940's, there were no Cuban equivalents of the social protest novels, such as Ecuador's *Huasipungo* and Peru's *El mundo es ancho y ajeno*, or of Argentina's national soul-searching novels *Bahía de silencio* and *Todo verdor perecerá*. It was only in the 1950's that Cuba's Alejo Carpentier gained continental stature. By contrast, the Cuban short story received a strong impetus from Alfonso Hernández-Catá (1885–1940) who was the "primer triunfador internacional de la literatura cubana."[3] His success undoubtedly influenced his contemporaries and successors to express the *criollista* search for national identity and the concurrent as well as ensuing social protest in the short story. Although Luis Felipe Rodríguez (1888–1947) is considered the "fundador de la cuentística nacional"[4] for having introduced rural themes,

---

[2] Although first published in 1915, *Los de abajo* was not "discovered" until the December 1924 polemic in *El Universal* between Julio Jiménez Rueda and Francisco Monterde.

[3] AF-1, p. 19.

[4] Ibid., p. 34.

his overly sociological stories were quickly surpassed by Carlos Montenegro (b. 1900) and the two Cuban short-story writers who are most
frequently represented in Latin American anthologies: Lydia Cabrera
(b. 1900) and Lino Novás Calvo (b. 1903). In the fantastic vein,
Virgilio Piñera (b. 1912) is among the first writers of the world to
cultivate the literature of the absurd. From 1942 on, the Hernández-
Catá national short-story prize provided a constant stimulus for aspiring young writers, and many stories were published in the 1950's in
the popular magazines *Bohemia* and *Carteles*, during the same decade
when all over Latin America the short story finally came into its own
with writers of the caliber of Jorge Luis Borges, Juan José Arreola,
Juan Rulfo, Juan Carlos Onetti, and Julio Cortázar.

A great many authors of the so-called first generation of the Cuban
Revolution began their literary careers in the 1950's, in the short story,
under the influence of the predominant literary mode of the decade:
existentialism. However, the tremendous and almost universal enthusiasm engendered by the triumph of the Revolution in 1959 and the
rapid development of a national consciousness coincided with a general Latin American swing back to the novel with a more sophisticated
treatment of national problems, beginning with Carlos Fuentes's *La
región más transparente* (1958) and Augusto Roa Bastos's *Hijo de
hombre* (1960) and culminating in 1967 with the success of Vargas
Llosa's *La casa verde* and García Márquez's *Cien años de soledad*.
Without abandoning the short story by any means, most Cuban authors could not resist the strong continental pull of the novel, and it
was not until the end of the 1960's that the short story appeared to re-
gain its traditional hegemony in Cuba.

A survey of the nineteen Cuban anthologies indicates the coexist-
ence of four distinct literary generations during the first decade of the
Revolution, although the vast majority of the stories have been written
by authors belonging to the two younger generations. Of the oldest
group, Alejo Carpentier (b. 1904) is clearly the dominant figure.
Much more a novelist than a short-story writer, he is nonetheless represented in several anthologies by his prerevolutionary stories "Viaje a
la semilla" (1944) (SCC, AF-1, RLL, CM) and "Los fugitivos"

(1946) (CB, JMO), or by a chapter from his new and as yet unpublished novel, *El año 59* (RW). In 1972, Carpentier published the first
edition in Spanish of *El derecho de asilo*, which had previously appeared in the French and American editions of *Guerra del tiempo*.[5]
A delightfully picaresque long short story, or novelette, situated in a
Nostromo-like composite Latin American republic, *El derecho de asilo*
undoubtedly sparked the writing of Carpentier's full-length novel *El
recurso del método* (1974). On the other hand, "The Chosen," which
also appears in the French and American editions of *Guerra del
tiempo*, is much more a vehicle for Carpentier's expression of the
Borgian concept of questioning the uniqueness of the biblical gospel.
In "The Chosen," it turns out that Noah was not the only man who
was forewarned about the great flood. Carpentier's contemporary Enrique Labrador Ruiz (b. 1902) is also represented in the anthologies
by an older story, "Conejito Ulán" (SCC, AF-1, RLL, CM), and has
not published any new stories in the past decade. A selection of his
short stories, prepared by Humberto Arenal, was published in 1970.
Of the well-known exiles Carlos Montenegro (b. 1900), Lydia Cabrera (b. 1900), and Lino Novás Calvo (b. 1903), the latter two have
recently published new collections: *Ayapá* (1971) and *Maneras de
contar* (1970).

From the following literary generation, Onelio Jorge Cardoso (b.
1914), Virgilio Piñera (b. 1912), and Félix Pita Rodríguez (b.
1909) are well represented in the revolutionary anthologies with a
wide variety of stories. Cardoso has been one of the most active of the
older writers and is generally acknowledged to be the best of the *crio-
llistas* writing today because of his poetic touch. Even though *criollismo* has fallen out of fashion, Cardoso has been anthologized with
seven different stories, of which there are only two repeaters: "El caballo de coral" (DA, RF) and "La otra muerte del gato" (JMC,
JMO). The latter, written in 1964, is one of the few instances in which
Cardoso takes cognizance of the Revolution: the new revolutionary
fisherman breaks the old habit of stealing fish from the other fisher-

[5] Alejo Carpentier, *El derecho de asilo*; "Right of Sanctuary," in *War of Time*,
trans. Frances Partridge, pp. 59–101; originally published in the French collection
Guerre du temps.

men. Between 1960 and 1969, four different editions of Cardoso's *Cuentos completos* (written between 1940 and 1962) were published, with two new collections, *Iba caminando* and *Abrir y cerrar los ojos* (GL), appearing in 1966 and 1969. In his review of the latter volume, Antonio Benítez stresses both the high quality of the stories and the departure they represent from Cardoso's previous works: "Because, in spite of the fact that their author has been offering us for thirty years the best short stories in Cuba, he has found out how to throw them overboard in order to launch another style, another continuation of his pioneering activity."[6] All ten stories present variations on the reality-versus-imagination theme. Imagined escape to adventures on the high seas, recollections of childhood, and the effects of superstition, hypnotism, and psychiatric consultations prevail over mundane reality, even in the one story involving a revolutionary captain in the Sierra, "Un tiempo para dos."

In contrast to Cardoso's work, all of Virgilio Piñera's stories belong to the more highly imaginative, fantastic, and absurd school of Borges, Arreola, and Cortázar. Furthermore, he has published very few new stories since 1959. Although his type of story is totally unrelated to the Revolution, his *Cuentos* (written between 1944 and 1962) was published in Havana in 1964, and he has also been anthologized, like Cardoso, with seven different stories, the repeaters being "El caramelo" (DA, RF, JMC), "Unas cuantas cervezas" (AF-1, JMO), and "El que vino a salvarme" (UN, CB, CM), the latter written in 1967. The publication of Piñera's complete stories in Buenos Aires in 1970, under the title *El que vino a salvarme*, and Julio Ortega's highly favorable comments[7] will undoubtedly give Piñera the boost toward the international recognition that he has long deserved.

Félix Pita Rodríguez's short stories reveal the conflict between his attraction to the fantastic literature of his contemporaries and his long-time political militancy in the Communist party. Although his *Cuentos completos* was published in 1963 and an anthology, *Poemas y cuentos*,

---

[6] Antonio Benítez Rojo, review of *Abrir y cerrar los ojos*, *Casa de las Américas* 11, no. 61 (July–August 1970): 173.

[7] Julio Ortega, "Sobre narrativa cubana actual," *Nueva Narrativa Hispanoamericana* 2, no. 1 (January 1972): 80–87.

in 1965, he seems to have abandoned the short story almost completely since 1959. Of his anthologized stories, "Cosme y Damián" (AF-1, CM), "Tobías" (SCC), and "Esta larga tarea de aprender a morir" (DA, CB) date from before the Revolution, while "The Seed" (SC), about Vietnam, is the only one related to the Revolution. In 1968, he published a volume of children's stories entitled *Niños de Vietnam*.

The most famous of this *orígenes* generation is poet and novelist José Lezama Lima (b. 1912). Internationally acclaimed for the novel *Paradiso* (1966), Lezama is represented in a small number of anthologies by two equally complex short stories, "Cangrejos, golondrinas" (JMO, CM) and "Juego de las decapitaciones" (RLL), and a selection entitled "Fronesis" (UN, CB) from a new unpublished novel.

Although a few other contemporaries of Lezama like Víctor Agostini (b. 1908), Dora Alonso (b. 1910), Raúl Aparicio (b. 1913), Samuel Feijóo (b. 1914), and Jorge Guerra (b. 1916) are also represented in the anthologies, the short story, even more than the novel, has been dominated by the generations of 1950 and 1960. In order to arrive at a meaningful classification of the anthologized stories as well as of the individual volumes published since 1959, the four groupings utilized for the novel will be applied to the short story and the outstanding practitioners of each group will be singled out for special attention.

I. The Struggle against Tyranny: Cabrera Infante

The large number of revolutionary stories that take place before January 1, 1959, fall into two groups that correspond to the 1959–1960 novels and to many of the 1961–1965 novels. In general, the short-story form is more suitable than the novel for the portrayal of the episodic pursuit and torture of young urban and, occasionally, small-town revolutionaries by the Batista police.

The most frequently anthologized stories of this type are some of the fifteen vignettes from *Así en la paz como en la guerra* (1960)

(RF, CB) by Guillermo Cabrera Infante (b. 1929), "Yo no vi na . . ." (RF, CB, JMO, GL) by Ambrosio Fornet (b. 1932), and "En el Ford azul" (RF, CB, JMO, CM, GL) by Lisandro Otero (b. 1932). Although it is difficult to ascertain the exact dates of composition, the above stories were probably written between 1958 and 1960. This theme, however, has continued to reappear in many stories written after 1960, even by the younger writers, such as the first four stories of *Tigres en el Vedado* (1967) by Juan Luis Herrero (b. 1939), the first five stories of *Días de guerra* (1967) by Julio Travieso (b. 1940), the first part of *Los años duros* (1966) by Jesús Díaz Rodríguez (b. 1941), and "Gracias Torcuatico" by Nicolás Pérez Delgado (b. 1944), the latter reprinted in Subercaseaux's 1971 *Narrativa de la joven Cuba*.

Nowhere is the official violence rampant in 1958 more vividly captured than in Cabrera Infante's fifteen untitled but numbered one-page vignettes. Written in February or March of 1958 in response to some of the senseless murders committed by the panic-stricken Batista government, these short compact scenes show young revolutionaries as well as nonrevolutionaries being beaten, tortured, or killed in a variety of ways.[8] Jeeps and machine guns abound. Except for the two vignettes that refer to specific historical events—the machine-gunning of Frank País on July 30, 1957, in the streets of Santiago and the September 1957 naval mutiny at Cienfuegos—Cabrera Infante emphasizes the anonymous unsung heroes. In the last of the vignettes, a variety of revolutionary writings on the prison walls is called "la verdadera literatura revolucionaria."[9] The hero of number 11 is "el muchacho gordo, pálido,"[10] while the brutally tortured protagonist of number 6 is referred to only as the son of a "vieja negra."[11] What makes most of the vignettes so effective is the Hemingway-like objective use of the third-person point of view. Sentences are relatively short, the preterite predominates, and there is no editorializing. In fact, the only vignette that clearly violates this last general principle, number 14, is undoubtedly

---

[8] Guillermo Cabrera Infante, *Así en la paz como en la guerra*, p. 9.
[9] Ibid., p. 201.
[10] Ibid., p. 157.
[11] Ibid., p. 84.

the weakest of all. In his only attempt to describe the military action in the countryside, Cabrera Infante makes a much too obvious claim for revolutionary brotherhood. After he leads the reader to believe that the two dying guerrillas whose bodies form a cross are really brothers, the final paragraph disproves the family relationship and stresses their identification as two racially different representatives of the Cuban common man: "The big mulatto's name was Juan Cáceres. The little blond peasant was Candito Plascencia. Neither one had stripes."[12] Although the narrative technique in most of the vignettes is quite similar, a proper amount of variety is provided: the lawyer's official complaint of number 2, the pure dialogue between the sadistic sergeant and the older prisoner of number 7, and the officer's telephone monologue about promotions resulting from the revolutionaries' being ambushed of number 10.

What makes the vignettes even more impressive is that they are interspersed among fourteen relatively long stories, written between 1949 and 1958, which reveal various aspects of the violence that characterized interpersonal relations in prerevolutionary Cuba. "En el gran ecbó" is considered by Cabrera Infante to be the best of these stories,[13] although the existentialist lack of communication and comprehension between two lovers is not captured quite as effectively as in some of the works of Eduardo Mallea and Juan Carlos Onetti. "Un rato de tenmeallá" (1950) and "El día que terminó mi niñez" (1956) were inspired by the author's own childhood poverty—"an environment of misery, promiscuity, and neglect in which the author lived with his family of five: the single twelve–by–twenty-four room, the common toilets, the days with breakfast, lunch, and supper consisting only of *café con leche*"[14]—and are among the few Cuban stories that portray the conditions of the urban poor. "Resaca" (1951) stands out in the volume because of its anticipation of the Revolution: two peasants set fire to a sugar-cane field and are then pursued in the Sierra Maestra. When one cannot continue fleeing because of a wounded leg, he is reassured by his companion: "When the Revolution comes, you and I

[12] Ibid., p. 185.
[13] Ibid., p. 13.
[14] Ibid., p. 10.

... will be the government ... and all the workers of the sugar mill, those of Sao, those from all over Cuba: all the workers of the world will seize power and we'll govern and we'll make just laws, and there'll be work for everyone, and money."[15] At the same time, they harbor resentment against their labor union, the Federación Nacional de Trabajadores Azucareros, for having given them such a dangerous assignment. Although some of the stories are based on the interior monologue and other experimental techniques, and although the themes of sex, gangsterism, jazz, marijuana, and American tourists are present, albeit not dominant, the stories of *Así en la paz como en la guerra* could hardly be considered harbingers of the boldly experimental vision of Havana nightlife expressed in Cabrera Infante's novel *Tres tristes tigres.*

As in the novel, the urban aspects of the struggle against Batista are depicted in the short story much more than is the fighting in the Sierra Maestra. In fact, except for Samuel Feijóo's "El soldado Eloy" (DA, SC) and possibly one or two others, the only pre-1966 story that really concentrates on the guerrilla warfare in the Sierra Maestra is Argentinian Julio Cortázar's "Reunión," an artistic account of the December 1956 "Granma" landing, narrated "asthmatically" by Che Guevara.[16] Although the two-year epic struggle of Fidel Castro and his companions in the Sierra Maestra has still not been adequately treated in Cuban prose fiction—Che Guevara's hard-to-surpass autobiographical *Pasajas de la guerra revolucionaria* (1963) could hardly be considered as fiction—three of the outstanding younger writers have found inspiration in the events of those heroic days, at least in individual stories: "La tierra y el cielo" (JEM, AF-2, GL) by Antonio Benítez Rojo (b. 1931), "Con la punta de una piedra" (BS) from *Los años duros* by Jesús Díaz (b. 1941), and "Mi primer desfile" (AF-2) by Reinaldo Arenas (b. 1943).

[15] Ibid., p. 65.
[16] For a detailed analysis, see pp. 255–258.

II. Exorcism and Existentialism: Calvert Casey and Humberto Arenal

The very strong 1961–1965 tendency in the Cuban novel to justify the socialization of the Cuban Revolution—portraying pre-1959 Cuba as the country plagued by corruption, devoid of ideals, and populated by alienated anguish-laden individuals—is equally strong in the short story during those same years. However, the fact that several of the short stories as well as the novels were undoubtedly written before 1959 indicates that this existentialist vision was not basically contrived ex post facto in response to political needs. The first of the revolutionary anthologies, *Nuevos cuentistas cubanos* (1961) by Antón Arrufat and Fausto Masó, which contains stories written between 1954 and 1958 by twenty-nine authors born between 1908 and 1943, reveals a distinct preference for existentialism. This is less marked in the 1964 anthology, *Nuevos cuentos cubanos*, compiled by Dora Alonso, Salvador Bueno, Calvert Casey, José Lorenzo, and José Rodríguez Feo. The selection of authors and stories in both anthologies is quite different, and only two of the almost thirty stories in each volume are duplicated: Oscar Hurtado's *costumbrista*-fantastic "Carta de un juez" (1955) and Antón Arrufat's existentialist "El viejo" (1957). The single most anthologized of the existentialist stories is "El caballero Charles" (DA, RF, JMC, SC, JEM) by Humberto Arenal (b. 1926), while the more highly regarded Calvert Casey (1924–1969) is represented in even more anthologies but with different stories, five of which—"El paseo" (AF-1, JEM), "En el Potosí" (AM), "El regreso" (RF), "El sol" (CB), and "Los visitantes" (DA, JEM)—were published along with "Mi tía Leocadia, el amor y el paleolítico inferior" and "El amorcito" in the 1962 volume *El regreso*. The two stories selected by J. M. Cohen for his anthology in translation, "The Execution" and "The Lucky Chance," are taken from the 1967 Seix Barral edition of *El regreso*, which contains a total of eleven stories.

Although the themes and techniques vary from story to story, Casey is distinguished from his existentialist contemporaries by the extremely personal and sincere alienation of most of his protagonists. Despite the admitted influence of Hemingway and Moravia,[17] and the Kafka epigraph for "The Execution," Casey's stories never give the appearance of being literary exercises. The title story, "El regreso," considered by Vicente Molina-Foix the best and the most representative,[18] is similar in theme to Edmundo Desnoes's novel *No hay problema*. However, the alienation of Casey's protagonist is more convincing emotionally, both as a real Cuban and as a symbol of humanity. Introduced with an epigraph from Sartre's *Les jeux sont faits*—"But try, always try"[19]—the story begins with a somewhat excessively intellectual analysis of the life of the nameless forty-year-old protagonist, but the reader is gradually made to feel the loneliness of this man in New York City, his loneliness as an inhabitant, any inhabitant, of a large modern city. After a short visit to Cuba, he decides to move there permanently. On his second day in Cuba, he is picked up—obviously by mistake—by the Batista police and brutally tortured without ever knowing why. He is finally released, half-crazed, on the rocky coast and stumbles to his death. The succinct ending, devoid of any literary image but replete with verbs, is in marked contrast to the philosophical-literary beginning and gives the story a distinctly nightmarish quality: "Then he began to walk, shouting harshly with his mouth wide open, singing, trying to talk, howling, staggering on his unsteady legs, balancing himself miraculously on the jagged reef.

"It was in his near-sighted eyes that the swarm of crabs first stuck their claws. Then between his soft lips."[20]

The story attains a transcendent level because the torture scenes are presented in all their gruesome detail, while allusions to the Cuban political situation in 1958 are minimal. In this way, Casey not only effectively denounces the Batista police brutality against an innocent

---

[17] AF-1, p. 203.

[18] Vicente Molina-Foix, "En la muerte de Calvert Casey," *Insula*, nos. 272–273 (July–August 1969), p. 40.

[19] Calvert Casey, *El regreso*, p. 107.

[20] Ibid., p. 124.

Cuban but also symbolizes the senseless tortures to which the individual human being is submitted in the hostile world of the atomic age, and perhaps in all ages. Can the injunction of Sartre's epigraph to keep on trying be taken seriously, or did Casey intend it to underscore the irony of his protagonist's death upon returning home to the promised land?

The other six stories in the volume indicate a far greater concern for personal problems projected on a universal plane than for the immediate political problems of Cuba. Paradoxically, only one of the stories, "El sol," is not specifically set in Havana. Its six independent scenes involving different characters succeed each other without any typographical separation. This device plus the complete absence of any home, personal or geographic, emphasize how meaningless are the lives of all men in the few minutes remaining before the destruction of the world by atomic bombs.

Even though the other stories take place in Havana and refer specifically to the Ten-Cén, the various cemeteries, and the Parque de los Filósofos in the old city, the author always gives the impression that his protagonist's inner world is much more important than his surroundings. Whether the story is narrated in first or third person, the protagonist's actions are subordinated to a feeling of alienation, which Casey, unlike most of the other existentialist writers, does not explicitly express. In fact, one of Casey's most distinguished characteristics is his ability to vaguely suggest his characters' inner drama without resorting to the psychoanalytical probe. "Mi tía Leocadia, el amor y el paleolítico inferior" presents in counterpoint technique the aunt's unfortunate experiences with men as remembered by the protagonist while he sits at the luncheonette counter of the Ten-Cén and sips his coffee. The aunt's anxieties and despair are transmitted through the narrator's own neurotic reactions to the hustle-bustle around him and through his identifying with the lonely tragic figure of his aunt. His recollection of her death at the end of the story adds a personal touch of poignancy to his philosophical musings at the beginning of the story about the living being so tremendously outnumbered by the dead.

The obsession with death is combined with a strange hostility toward the mother in "En el Potosí." "Potosí" refers not to the fabulous Bolivian mining town but to a Havana cemetery the protagonist visits on All Soul's Day. However, the outer reality of the cemetery, as in the case of the Ten-Cén, is not of primary importance but rather complements the main theme of the protagonist's identification with his aunt and his hatred for his mother, expressed by his alluding to her only with the pronoun "ella." It is not until the final word of the story that "ella" is identified as "mamá."

The protagonist's attitudes toward his aunt and mother determine his attitude toward younger women in two other stories, "El amorcito" and "El paseo." The former is a diarylike account of the narrator's very commonplace chance meeting with Esther in the park and their growing affection for one another. However, one day, after he responds to *her* advances by kissing her on the neck, she suddenly jumps up and starts shouting that she doesn't want to see him again. The transformation of the typical erotic conquest into Kafkaesque despair is brusque and is never explained. The only surety is that the protagonist suffers and finds it unbearable to stay at home with his sick mother.

"El paseo" differs from most of Casey's stories in that the protagonist's alienation is not so overwhelming. This may be explained by the fact that he is a youngster about to try on his first pair of long pants. The lonely sensitive adolescent is taken to a brothel by his worldly bachelor uncle but is unable to perform sexually in spite of the very understanding attitude of the young prostitute. There are no recriminations and no feelings of guilt or frustration expressed. The story ends with a poetic note that expresses the protagonist's bewilderment rather than despair at the immense, mysterious world that surrounds him. "After dinner, Ciro sat down on the bench that always occupied a spot at the end of the balcony. The street was deserted. Only the breeze murmured at the corners. Ciro looked at the summer sky and the immense world that surrounded him, so mysterious for him, and then again at the street where the noises that were heard were now very few and far between."[21]

Calvert Casey left Cuba in mid-1965 and committed suicide in Rome in May 1969. In his second volume of stories, *Notas de un simulador* (1969), his personal Kafkaesque anxieties are exacerbated not by the pre-1959 bourgeois, Americanized, materialistic Cuban environment

[21] Ibid., p. 25.

but rather by the post-1959 socialist society of both Cuba and the Eastern European countries. This work will therefore be discussed with the other antirevolutionary works.

Calvert Casey's contemporary Humberto Arenal (b. 1926) is the author of two volumes of short stories, *La vuelta en redondo* (1962) and *El tiempo ha descendido* (1964), in which three of the better stories also exorcise the pre-1959 Cuban past within the existentialist mode. The protagonists of both title stories are old men at the point of death who feel terribly alone. In "La vuelta en redondo," the old man is taken in a bus to the hospital in Havana by his wife and daughter whom he hates intensely. His only son, whom he loved dearly, died a number of years ago. The interior monologue technique does not prevent the ending from appearing to be somewhat contrived in the existentialist manner. He asks his wife to take him to the men's room, where he feels intense pain, has a blood vessel burst, falls down, and dies cursing his wife.

"El tiempo ha descendido" is equally tragic but more convincing in spite of the somewhat contrived frame. The story begins with the protagonist's having already committed suicide by hanging and with his corpse dangling at the end of the rope in the cold damp night air. As the third-person narrator makes time retreat and reconstructs the events leading up to the hanging, the protagonist recalls events from different moments of his life. The fact that he had been happily married with two children whom he loved indicates a much less pessimistic view of the world than that of Calvert Casey, Eduardo Mallea, Juan Carlos Onetti, Sartre, and other more typical existentialist writers. Arenal is much more interested in presenting the tragic situation of an older man, which is made more tragic and more human by the contrast with his former happiness. His present loneliness and anguish stem from his wife's death and his children's being far away. Without his loved ones, life is reduced to a daily routine of insignificant acts, which convinces him that it is futile to continue living.

This less dogmatically existentialist view of the world is also present in the frequently anthologized "El caballero Charles," the one Arenal story in which the concern for re-creating the Cuban environment is at least of equal importance to the presentation of individual problems.

The title character, Mr. Charles, never appears in the story, but he symbolizes Cuba's "belle époque" during World War I. Through his name, his wealth, his trips abroad, his contacts with the lawyers and owners of the sugar plantations, he represents the upper-class xenophile Cuban exploiter of his compatriots who were enthralled with music (his mistress, Doña Clarita) and baseball (his Negro chauffeur, Jacinto). That way of life has now ended: Mr. Charles is dead, Doña Clarita suffers from rheumatism and is totally alienated from the surrounding world, while Jacinto continues to live in the past. The dramatic tension of the story is based on the counterpoint between Jacinto's memories and those of Doña Clarita. While the latter retains no illusions about Mr. Charles's true character, she prefers not to destroy Jacinto's false image of his former master.

The present loneliness of both of Mr. Charles's survivors is underlined by the lack of real dialogue between the two. By using a very simple, unadorned, and undramatic style, along with the typically existentialist use of pronouns—"él" and "ella"—and the symbolic cat, Arenal succeeds in creating a world completely devoid of hope. The characters merely exist. Nevertheless, the somewhat ambiguous ending is not quite as bleak as in Casey's stories. When Doña Clarita tells Jacinto not to return, she may be preparing to commit suicide, but she may also have decided to close the door on her past life.

Of the other ten stories in Arenal's two volumes, six present cases of unhappy marriages, or liaisons, involving Americans and Latins, but the other four delve into the world of children with an intensification of the dreamlike quality, also present in "El caballero Charles." In three of these four stories, the action is narrated by a child in a poetically simple style. In "En lo alto de un hilo," a boy plays with his kite and imagines himself dancing in air at the end of a string. Although he is brought down to earth by his father's announcement that he has no money for Epiphany presents, the effect is not unduly tragic. In "La pérdida de un amigo," the boy's separation from his favorite tree is attenuated by the doubt over whether the neighbor ever told his mother that once, from the tree, he accidentally saw her naked in her apartment. Even in "El periquito era de todos," where the little boy chases and almost mindlessly kills the little escaped parrot that had

brought domestic peace to his family, the emphasis is more on capturing the child's emotions and his view of the world than on making a
statement about man's tragic destiny. In "Chichi," the ending is un-
usually happy, for any short story. The narrator finds a little dog in the
street and is allowed to keep it in spite of the protestations of his aunt,
in whose house he, his widowed mother, and his older brother live.

The magic, unreal element in these stories about children makes
Arenal a transitional author between his existentialist contemporaries
who began writing in the early 1950's and dominated the early 1960's
and the Cuban exponent of magic realism, Antonio Benítez Rojo
(b. 1931), who, although a contemporary of Cabrera Infante, Calvert
Casey, and Humberto Arenal, did not make his literary debut until
the late 1960's.

III. Epos, Experimentation, and Escapism: Antonio Benítez Rojo

Whereas novelistic production soared to its all-time high between 1966
and 1970, the number of volumes of short stories decreased somewhat
from the previous period of 1961–1965. After three insignificant
volumes in 1961, the second period picks up steam in 1962 and 1963
with eleven and thirteen volumes, respectively, reaches its peak of nineteen in 1964, and falls to nine in 1965 for a total of fifty-five over the
five-year span. For the five-year period from 1966 through 1970, the
total is forty-five: seven, twelve, seven, eight, and eleven respectively.[22] At the same time, the general boom in Latin American literature
for this period probably accounts for the publication of eleven of the
sixteen short-story anthologies between 1967 and 1969.

The very nature of the short-story form precluded it from following
the example of the 1966–1970 novel in creating broad tableaux of the
Cuban nation as in *Paradiso*, *Los niños se despiden*, *De donde son los
cantantes*, and many others. The only real exceptions are José Miguel

22 See the chronological list.

Garófalo's (b. 1936) *Se dice fácil* (1968) and Manuel Granados's (b. 1931) *El viento en la casa sol*, neither of which is represented in any of the anthologies. The six stories of Garófalo's volume depict different moments in Cuban history from the 1895–1898 War of Independence to the Bay of Pigs invasion. Also representing the author's panoramic intentions is his use of a range of narrators including an eighty-year-old Negro, a Batista military officer, and a businessman. The influence of Dos Passos is obvious in the intercalation of newspaper headlines, radio announcements, and anonymous dialogues. However, this volume resembles some of the 1961–1965 novels, such as Lisandro Otero's *La situación* (1963), more than it does the more boldly experimental 1966–1970 novels.

The thirteen stories of *El viento en la casa sol*, on the other hand, are more highly experimental, but with a reduced panoramic scope. With a clearly perceptible effort to make a positive revolutionary contribution, Granados runs the gamut from the existentialist anguish of the mid-1950's and the urban terrorism and guerrilla warfare of the late 1950's to the 1960's with the emergence of the new revolutionary man as opposed to the few surviving members of the bourgeoisie. An anti-Catholic as well as anti-American attitude is quite prevalent, and some of the stories reflect the Negro's identification with the Revolution.

Just as the short-story form was ill-suited for the boldly experimental, capsule portrait of the nation, conversely the relatively long-time Cuban preference for science fiction and other fantastic short stories combined with the experimentation and the escapism of the period to produce the dominant type of short story, particularly in 1966 and 1967, culminating in the publication of Rogelio Llopis's *Cuentos cubanos de lo fantástico y lo extraordinario* (1968) and Oscar Hurtado's *Cuentos de ciencia-ficción* (1969). Actually, the fantastic story, like the existentialist story, was a heritage of the 1950's. Whereas the theme of personal alienation has its literary roots in the works of Sartre and Camus and the contemporary Latin American works of Eduardo Mallea and Juan Carlos Onetti, the escapism of science fiction, the fable, the absurd, and other fantastic stories stems from the Latin American models of Jorge Luis Borges and Juan José Arreola and from

Cuba's own Virgilio Piñera. Although in many if not most of Borges's and Arreola's stories the escapism is only apparent, it tends to be much more authentic in the works of their Cuban epigones who held a dominant position in the mid-1960's, until the new government policy of October 1968 demanded a greater revolutionary commitment on the part of the artist.

1962: Rogelio Llopis, *La guerra y los basiliscos*
1963: Oscar Hurtado, *Cartas de un juez*
      Rogelio Llopis, *El fabulista*
      César López, *Circulando el cuadrado*
      Julio Matas, *Catálogo de imprevistos*
1964: Angel Arango, *¿A dónde van los cefalomos?*
      Carlos Cabada, Juan Luis Herrero, and Agenor Martí, *Cuentos de ciencia ficción*
      Oscar Hurtado, *La ciudad muerta de Korad*
      Nelson Rodríguez, *El regalo*
      Evora Tamayo, *Cuentos para abuelas enfermas*
1965: María Elena Llana, *La reja*
      Angela Martínez, *Memorias de un decapitado*
      Evora Tamayo, *La vieja y la mar*
1966: Angel Arango, *El planeta Negro*
      Arnaldo Correa, *Asesinato por anticipado*
      Esther Díaz Llanillo, *El castigo*
      Marinés Medero, *Cuentos y anticuentos de Juan Dolcines*

(The only other volumes of short stories published in 1966 were Dora Alonso's two volumes of children's literature, *Ponolani* and *Las aventuras de Guille*, Onelio Jorge Cardoso's *Iba caminando*, and prize-winning Jesús Díaz's *Los años duros*.)

1967: Angel Arango, *Robotomaquia*
      Arnaldo Correa, *El primer hombre a Marte*
      Germán Piniella, *Polífagos*
1968: José Lorenzo Fuentes, *Después de la gaviota*

Although Antonio Benítez Rojo's (b. 1931) two prize-winning collections, *Tute de reyes* (1967) and *El escudo de hojas secas* (1969), do not really fit into the realm of the fantastic short story, they do qualify for the title of magic realism and reveal clearly the influence of Julio Cortázar, who replaced Jorge Luis Borges in the 1960's as the most important short-story writer in Latin America. In spite of Benítez's being a contemporary of the existentialists who made their literary debuts in the 1950's and dominated the early 1960's (Agüero, Arenal, Arrufat, Cabrera Infante, Casey, Desnoes, Fornet, Lorenzo Fuentes, Otero), he is not represented in any of the anthologies published before December 1967. Nonetheless, his two published volumes and a third collection, "Gran arena," which received honorable mention in the 1970 UNEAC contest, make Benítez probably the best short-story writer produced by the Revolution. Mario Benedetti, in his December 1968 survey of Cuban culture, singles out Benítez for special praise: "In the short story, the most pleasant and at the same time the most profound continues to be Antonio Benítez (two first prizes in less than two years: one in Casa de las Américas and the other in UNEAC), the author of a story that is a must in every anthology, 'Estatuas sepultadas' (included in *Tute de reyes*), and endowed with the creative tools that place him, with only one book published and another about to appear, at the head of the short-story writers of his generation."[23]

Thematically, Antonio Benítez's twelve published stories resemble to a certain extent Garófalo's *Se dice fácil* and many of the 1966–1970 novels in their panoramic portrayal of different moments in Cuban history with representatives of different sectors of the population. "La tijera rota" (UN, CB, JMO) and "La tierra y el cielo" (JEM, AF-2, GL) both deal with Negro or mulatto Haitian immigrants, and the former presents a picture of Havana in 1854. Seven of the stories portray critically different aspects of prerevolutionary life, covering a wide range from exploitation of the rural poor in "La tierra y el cielo" to the excessive luxuries and prejudices of the wealthy in "El escudo de hojas secas," "Tute de reyes" (CM), and "Salto atrás." The existentialist hero of "Puesta de sol," the scenes of Havana night life in "A la gente le gusta el azul," the obsession with American jazz in "Recuerdos de

[23] Mario Benedetti, "Situación actual de la cultura cubana," dated Havana, December 7, 1968, published in *Marcha* (Montevideo), December 27, 1968, and in *Cuaderno cubano*, by Mario Benedetti, p. 104.

una piel" (JEM), and the allusions to police torture under Batista in
"Evaristo" all link Benítez to his contemporaries who dominated the
1961–1965 period. Five of the stories take place after 1959, all involving people who, for a variety of reasons, have been unable to adapt to
the revolutionary changes: the wealthy aristocratic family in "Estatuas
sepultadas" (RLL), the exiled jazz enthusiast abandoned by his Negro
mistress in "Recuerdos de una piel," the mulatto folklorist who lives
in the past in "La tijera rota," and the unsavory counterrevolutionaries
in "Peligro en La Rampa" and "A la gente le gusta el azul."

However, the singling out of these representative historical periods
and people gives a very incomplete and even misleading impression of
Benítez Rojo's stories. Thematically, a much more accurate statement
would be that eleven of the twelve stories, all but "La tierra y el cielo,"
fit into the category of exorcising the past. Criticism is leveled at pre-
1959 society as well as the inability of its survivors to adapt to the revolutionary changes. Even this statement, however, hardly explains Benítez's success.

The stories of *Tute de reyes* and *El escudo de hojas secas* are distinguished from those of Benítez's contemporaries by their complexity.
Like Cortázar's "La noche boca arriba," "Continuidad de los parques,"
and so many other stories, Benítez's "Primer balcón," "Estatuas sepultadas," and "La tijera rota" erase the traditional boundaries between
reality and fantasy. In "Primer balcón," the heroine of a radio soap
opera is identified by the twelve-year-old narrator, Lidia Rosa, with the
young blind medium, Marcela, who moves into the house across the
street. As the trials and tribulations of the soap-opera heroine parallel
those of the real Marcela, the narrator identifies her boy friend, Lauro,
with a corresponding figure on the radio program. When the real Marcela dies, the narrator realizes that Lauro had fallen in love with her.
In a further elaboration of the reality-fantasy theme, the narrator disguises herself as Marcela and plans to appear to Lauro as her ghost during the night in order to ask him to forget her. However, the planned
dream sequence turns into a nightmare when the narrator unexpectedly
encounters her own mother in bed with Lauro. The shock is somewhat
attenuated by the narrator's fainting, the "espléndidas aclaraciones de

mamá,''[24] and Aunt Julia's assurances that she was imagining things. Although the reader is convinced that Mother was indeed not innocent, the fact that the narrator is a twelve-year-old girl with a previously demonstrated high degree of imagination does leave some doubt at the end about what actually happened. In addition to the manipulation of the reality-fantasy theme, the story contains another of Cortázar's traits, the convincing portrayal of the sentiments experienced by a child or an adolescent in love, as in "Los venenos" and "Final del juego."

A similar fantastic environment involving adolescent love is created in "Estatuas sepultadas" without recourse to dreams or the confusion between·fiction and reality. The air of fantasy stems from the creation of a real but very unlikely, and at times magic, situation laden with symbolism: the survival of an aristocratic family within the walls of its Vedado estate in 1968. The description of the estate is reminiscent of Carpentier's chapter "Los convidados de plata" from his unpublished novel "El año 59": Greek statues in the garden, French blinds in the music room, a Japanese birdhouse, and lessons for the three cousins on the German poetry of Goethe, Hölderlin, Novalis, and Heine. The family has been living in a state of siege for nine years, almost totally isolated from the outside world: the servants are gone, electricity has been cut off, the radio and telephone are not functioning, no newspapers are received, and letters remain unopened. Only at night does Uncle Jorge, a former undersecretary of education, trade for food through the rusty iron fence.

Clear as the allusions to the Revolution may be, an air of magic prevails because of the subordination of outside reality to the interpersonal family relationships and the symbolism of the statues and the butterflies. The title "estatuas sepultadas" symbolizes the death of a way of life. The sixteen-year-old narrator, Lucila, compares herself to the statue of Venus that has been knocked off its pedestal, as she lies in the grass, a moment before her cousin Aurelio happens on the scene and overcomes her resistance to his sexual desires. As the scene is repeated in the following days, Lucila does not enjoy the encounters but rather uses her sex in a statuesque way in order to exercise control over Aure-

[24] Antonio Benítez Rojo, *El escudo de hojas secas*, p. 74.

lio: "Day by day I perfected a rigid style, which aroused his desires and made him dependent on me."[25] Aurelio also exercises a decadent, incestuous, and somewhat magic fascination over the other women in the family: Lucila's alcoholic mother, her devoutly religious aunt, and her crippled cousin. The only other man of the house is Uncle Jorge, whose impotence is indicated by his indecisiveness—"Don Jorge never reached a decision"[26]—and by his crying at the edge of the sofa after the disappearance of his son Aurelio.

The symbolic role of Aurelio as a kind of golden sun god signifying life is clarified at the end of the story with the appearance of the "mysterious stranger" Cecilia.[27] She is allowed into the estate by a family vote of three to two, Jorge abstaining, along with the appropriately and somewhat absurdly named tubercular Mohicano, who has supplied the family with food during the long years of the siege. The following morning the Mohicano is found dead, and a day later Cecilia is transformed into a gold-colored butterfly—the same one that had terrified Lucila earlier—and apparently leads Aurelio across the river into the world of the living. Thus, Lucila's earlier fear that the butterflies were a secret weapon of the enemy, in apparent complicity with the invading wild grass, is substantiated by the prophetic nature, albeit altered, of the picture in Aurelio's room. "We spent that summer hunting butterflies. They came from the river flying over the grass and the flowers . . . it bothered me that they should come from outside and—like mother— I thought that it was a secret weapon that we still didn't understand; perhaps that is why I enjoyed hunting them. Although at times they would startle me by moving the grass aside and fleeing, making me think that they would take me by my hair, by my skirt—like the picture that was hanging in Aurelio's room—and would carry me off over the fence across the river."[28] The story ends with the abandoned family plunged into eternal darkness: "Then someone fell on the candelabrum and everything turned dark."[29]

[25] Antonio Benítez Rojo, *Tute de reyes*, p. 91.
[26] Ibid., p. 80.
[27] Cf. Truman Capote's "Miriam," in *A Tree of Night and Other Stories*, and Uslar Pietri's "La lluvia," in *Red, cuentos*.
[28] Benítez Rojo, *Tute de reyes*, pp. 82–83.
[29] Ibid., p. 98.

The failure to accept the reality of the Revolution is also the theme of "La tijera rota," in which the fusion of reality and fantasy is made even more complex by the intermingling of different chronological planes and the use of the double, reminiscent of Cortázar's "Todos los fuegos el fuego" and "El otro cielo." The structural complexity of "La tijera rota," or "La tijera" as it is called in the anthologies, is balanced by the concentration on only one protagonist, a mulatto librarian and folklorist who in 1965 would like to emigrate to the United States. Imagining himself at the Library of Congress being consulted by Harvard sociologists, Jorge Emilio Lacoste envelops himself in a world of fantasy with successive retreats in time from the future in the United States to the present in the Havana of 1965, and from there back to the *belle époque cubaine* of 1854 in Havana and a few years earlier in Haiti. The principal vehicle for this backward trip in time is the presentation of Donizetti's opera *Don Pasquale*. While performing his present job of clipping old newspapers, Lacoste happens upon an 1854 number of the *Diario de la Marina*, which advertises the première of *Don Pasquale* along with carnival dances. Since, as chance would have it, he was planning to see a revival of *Don Pasquale* that very evening, he cuts out the note but, in doing so, drops the scissors, which jab him in the thigh and break as they fall to the floor. Upon returning home, he takes a nap and begins to dream. When Lacoste awakens and rushes off to the opera, the author purposely makes it ambiguous—as in Borges's "El sur"—as to whether Lacoste really woke up or whether everything that follows is a dream.

Once in the theater, Lacoste observes its state of disrepair, which he converts into a criticism of the Revolution: "There was an arm missing on the seat and, as if that weren't enough, he could see only half of the drop curtain. And to think that they had just remodeled the building, a real disaster, sloppy work, they don't know how to do anything, one look at this was enough . . ."[30] In what is perhaps a dream within a dream, Lacoste imagines himself at the 1854 performance of the same opera. He goes outside the theater and steps into the Havana of 1854 with its "pretty colonial boulevard,"[31] instead of the present Prado,

[30] Benítez Rojo, *El escudo de hojas secas*, p. 105.
[31] Ibid., p. 107.

and its Isabel II Alameda dimly lit by "un farol que apenas alumbraba."[32] In this strange atmosphere, Lacoste meets two carnival-bedecked mulattoes, Encarnación and Rosa. When he tells them that he was born in Port-au-Prince (Haiti) and had come to Havana to sell his large grocery store, they entice him into a dark alley, where an accomplice knocks him unconscious. They are naturally disappointed to find only a broken pair of scissors in his pocket. As Lacoste comes to and is pursued nightmarishly by the figure of Death, his dream becomes further complicated by the association of the bump on his head with one caused by his fall from a hammock when he was still living in Haiti. Ultimately, his dream takes him back to Haiti where he had been an escaped slave who killed a storekeeper and stole his money.

In addition to playing with the concept of reality by inserting one possible dream after another into the unreal world of the newspaper-clipping librarian, Benítez also criticizes the future exile's racial attitude, which explains the contents of his dream. If Lacoste himself, or one of his ancestors, was an escaped mulatto slave, a thief, and a murderer, his sense of guilt and inferiority is expressed in self-hatred, projected onto his fellow worker Legón, who seems proud of his Negro heritage and is an appointee of the Revolution. Lacoste, on the other hand, denies his Negro roots, which emerge in the dream, and boasts of having been able to pass for white before the Revolution: ". . . and Legón wiping the table with his snotty handkerchief, a real pig, and listen to him tell that the Revolution has liberated *us* Negroes, to tell that to him who always passed for white and Romualdo used to take him to the Tropicana and play golf in the Country Club, let Legón boast about being an old slave, conceited ape, and all because he graduated from a crash course to train librarians, in short he didn't learn anything, only to do things upside down . . ."[33]

The identification of Jorge Emilio Lacoste with his double, the escaped slave, is reinforced by the fact that the latter's description was published in the newspaper. In like manner, the two mulattoes who deceived Lacoste are identified with the two whites, Fred and Romualdo, who may also be planning to deceive him, as is suggested by their

32 Ibid.
33 Ibid., p. 102.

confused juxtaposition in his dream, a moment after he is struck on the head. In other words, Lacoste the mulatto is the marginal man between the Negro world that he rejects and the white world to which he aspires but which will undoubtedly reject him. In the following paragraph, Lacoste dreams that the two mulattoes are beating him with the tulips and squirrel tails previously alluded to in a description of springtime Washington, D.C. The presence in the dream of his Negro co-worker Legón, of the opera singer Steffenone from an earlier epoch, and of Port-au-Prince completes the typically jumbled chronology of Lacoste's dream world.

Lacoste was able to get to the opening of a large doorway. For the moment, the dream had changed into another one where Fred and Romualdo, holding colossal fans, were waiting for him in the underground airport of the Washington Monument. Although it was Fred and not Romualdo who, bowing politely, gave him the newspaper in the yellow elevator on the way to Port-au-Prince before the trap fell. Immediately Legón gave the signal, clapping his hands, and Doña Rosa and Doña Encarnación pulled the tulips and squirrel tails out of their bosoms, and, ignoring the shrieks of Steffenone, who was chained to the theater seat, they beat him sadistically all over until they removed him limp and face down into the dark doorway, the doorway of the first dream.[34]

A less complex use of the double is employed by Benítez in the presentation of another antirevolutionary—but less typical for him—character, the former Batista official in "Evaristo." In his anxiety to escape, the narrator accepts a job, offered by a wealthy woman, of aiding her with her idiot son, who is confined to a wheelchair. However, little by little he identifies the idiot with Luisa, whose neck he broke by pushing her down a flight of stairs while his sergeant was killing her brother. Pursued relentlessly by the vision of Luisa in a wheelchair, he finally tries to kill the idiot boy with a dirty hypodermic needle but confesses everything when the doctor and nurses arrive. He is now in prison and narrates the story under the influence of sedatives.

More similar to "La tijera rota" because of their chronological complexities, "A la gente le gusta el azul" and "La tierra y el cielo" are also more explicitly related to the Revolution than are the previously

[34] Ibid., p. 110.

discussed stories. "A la gente le gusta el azul" is a portrait of the stereo-typed immoral counterrevolutionary from four different chronological angles. The present is 1966 and finds Julio Salcedo transmitting incon-sequential economic data to the enemy on bits of microfilm concealed under postage stamps pasted on postcards. He has relations with two women: Seida, his counterrevolutionary contact, and Inés, his former young mistress who is now a revolutionary teacher and would like to rehabilitate him. As Julio rests in his hotel room, his specific memories of New Year's Eve 1958 are blended with earlier memories of the past and with an imagined scene from the future. Like the counterrevolu-tionary characters in Benítez's less complex "Peligro en La Rampa," Julio is a totally immoral character who in 1958 was a crooked real-estate salesman after having worked for years as a photographer in the depraved atmosphere of Greenwich Village, New York. The first word of the story that defines Julio's attitude toward life is "engañao" (deceived), repeated five times on the first page. He spent New Year's Eve of 1958 in a typical Havana nightclub getting the fifteen-year-old Inés drunk. After initiating her sexually, he drives her around Havana in his Studebaker taking note of the public reactions to the news of Batista's flight. In the future, he imagines himself in a revolu-tionary court confessing his crime and talking his way out of a severe sentence. The leitmotifs that unite the different scenes and further de-fine Julio's character are all variations on the theme of the United States consumer society: André Kostelanetz, contraceptives, porno-graphic magazines, radio commercials, chewing gum, Coney Island. The Americanized Havana of the 1950's as well as the excitement gen-erated by Batista's fall are also reflected in the rapid-fire dialogue and in the choppy style, which is quite different from that employed by Benítez in his more fantastic stories, "Las estatuas sepultadas" and "La tijera rota." Nonetheless, "A la gente le gusta el azul" also has its deft touches of fantasy: the philatelic comments (possibly inspired by Cor-tázar's "Cartas de mamá"), Seida's mysterious breasts, and the ending of the story when Julio wonders whether his economic espionage isn't all a big joke: "Sometimes I've thought that [Seida] is pulling my leg, that the negatives that I cleverly slip into the Obispo St. mailbox every Friday are the little pieces of an enormous joke."[35] He even wonders whether Inés and the old man who sells him the stamps are also in on the joke. However, he comes to no decision, and Benítez ends the story by having his deceitful protagonist symbolize himself with the crocodile, as a reflection of the initial repetition of "engañar": "It's all the same, old crocodile. Now that we're surfacing, let's take a deep breath, put our head under water, and continue diving."[36]

"La tierra y el cielo" combines elements of both "A la gente le gusta el azul" and "La tijera rota," but the end result is more an accumulation than a fusion. The variety of characters, plots, and chronological planes seems more suitable for a novel than a short story. As in "La tijera rota," the main characters are Haitian immigrants, which immediately lends a touch of magic to the atmosphere, as in Carpentier's novel *El reino de este mundo*. The main plot revolves around Aristón's absolute faith in the prophecy of the *houngan* Tiguá that he would not be harmed as long as he remained together with the narrator Pedro Limón. The setting, most unusual for Benítez, is the Sierra Maestra, where both men have joined the guerrillas in 1958. After escaping from an encounter with a government patrol, Aristón kills one of the revolutionaries from the plains for accusing him of being a cowardly Negro. The revolutionary captain reluctantly sentences Aristón to be executed. Confident that Tiguá's prophecy will hold true, Aristón asks that Pedro Limón form part of the firing squad. As the bullets ring out, Aristón falls dead and a snake (his nahual?) emerges from the smoke and slithers off into the woods.

The concision and concentration of this part of the story, however, are weakened by the development of the narrator's character in three different chronological planes, somewhat reminiscent of "A la gente le gusta el azul." Rogelio Llopis points out that the two characters complement each other but criticizes Benítez for not having given to Aristón more space in the story: ". . . Aristón, a herculean and bewitched Haitian . . . Pedro Limón, another Haitian who is like the other side of the coin from Aristón because he's too human . . . It's a

---

[35] Ibid., p. 100.
[36] Ibid.

pity that Benítez did not give more space to Aristón, that he didn't
portray him better. If he had, the contrast would have come out much
more sharply defined . . ."[37] In each of the three chronological planes,
there is sufficient material for independent stories. In the present, 1965,
Pedro Limón walks along the railroad tracks on his way to his home-
town of Guanamaca, where he will begin teaching for the first time.
After an absence of seven years, many changes have taken place, but
Pedro Limón is especially preoccupied about the plastic surgery performed on his own face after he had been hit by mortar fire at Playa
Girón (1961) and about the news that his former girl friend, Leonie,
now lives with his friend Pascasio and that they have a six-year-old
child. The veteran's memories take him back to 1958 when he slept
with his "brothers," Pascasio and Aristón, in the hut next to that of the
houngan Tiguá, after escaping from Batista's *rurales*. Ultimately, he
recalls his childhood with his own family, their being robbed by the
taxi driver, their hunger, the death of his sister, and the deportation of
his parents to Haiti. Although the narrator's memories are realistic
and he does not project himself magically into another time zone as
does the protagonist of "La tijera rota," the feeling for his Haitian
roots is heightened by Tiguá's allusions to President Dessalines, Ma-
kendal, and Toussaint L'Ouverture. In spite of this rather full biographical development of Pedro Limón and his assuming the role of
first-person narrator, after his initial encounter with Pascasio is presented in the third person—with a brief transitional use of the second
person—his role as protagonist is usurped by Aristón because of the
build-up of the latter's execution, which occurs at the very end of the
story.

Although Antonio Benítez has not written any novels, the abundance of novelistic material in "La tierra y el cielo" as well as in the
unique title story "El escudo de hojas secas" may indicate the direction
of his future literary efforts. "El escudo de hojas secas," in spite of its
enigmatic title, is actually unique because of its relative simplicity, its
chronological order, and its absurd humor—all of which distinguish it
from the majority of the magic-realism, Cortázar-inspired stories.

[37] Rogelio Llopis, review of *El escudo de hojas secas, Casa de las Américas* 11, no.
62 (September–October 1970): 199.

Whereas the multiplicity of chronological planes in the previously discussed stories serves to develop in-depth portraits of the protagonists, the swiftly moving, chronologically ordered episodes of "El escudo de hojas secas" reflect the superficiality and the ephemeral quality of prerevolutionary Cuban bourgeois society between roughly the late 1930's and 1959. The chronology, although occasionally anachronistic, is established by off-hand allusions to Hollywood stars Dorothy Lamour and Stewart Granger; baseball players Johnny Vandermeer ("no hit no run"), Ted Williams, and Mickey Mantle; World War II; Batista's *golpe*; and the very precise 1958 Christmas–New Year's card. The linear story, narrated solely in the omniscient third person, follows the adventures of a railroad worker and his wife who became millionaires after receiving a lucky dog from a *santero*. The appropriately named Lucky helps them locate a hidden treasure in an old piece of furniture and selects winning lottery tickets. The appropriately named Miyares not only accumulates money and luxury items but also subsequently aspires to the presidency: "—todavía me falta ser Presidente de la República."[38] The only condition imposed by the *santero* is that they should never forget to give charity. The Havana *nouveaux riches* of the 1940's and 1950's are lampooned because of their crass ostentatiousness, their identification with American culture exemplified by baseball, the movies, and commercial products, as well as their syncretic "religion" made up of Afro-Cuban occultism, astrology, and Catholicism. The Spanish element in this frivolous society is indicated by the title of the story. On the literal level, it refers to a title of nobility purchased in Spain. However, it also symbolizes the absurdly weak cultural protection afforded to Cubans by the Spanish shield and the decadent crumbling nature of Cuban bourgeois society doomed to be swept away, like dry leaves, by the Revolution.

However, the seriousness of this interpretation belies the farcical tone of the story. Miyares's wife, Isolina, a devout member of the Hijas de María, gives birth to a twenty-nine–pound girl, named Isolinita, who is raped at the age of eight because she was able to pass for twenty-three. Her name is used for Miyares's sandal company, Isolinite Rubber, S.A. Miyares unexpectedly surprises his wife naked in bed with

---

[38] Benítez Rojo, *El escudo de hojas secas*, p. 47.

his business partner, dressed in elegant riding garb. An eccentric tea-drinking beggar, dressed as an explorer, is delighted to receive the exquisite food that the dog Lucky leaves. However, with each succeeding encounter, the beggar deteriorates physically. In his final appearance, he is on crutches and his face is marred by "that scraggly beard and swollen eyes and a nose half eaten away by an ugly sore."[39] Miyares forgets his Catholic charity and has the beggar thrown against the bougain-villaea vine, which causes all hell to break loose: Lucky growls and attacks Miyares's henchman, Miyares kicks Lucky, Lucky bites Miyares, shots ring out, and, at that very moment, the by-now fifteen-year-old Isolinita is stuck accidentally with a pin by her seamstress ("Sleeping Beauty"?) and goes insane, and Lucky escapes.

The story ends on a pensive note. Miyares and his wife kneel down in Lucky's kennel before the statue of Babalú-Ayé attended by two dogs. Miyares recognizes the similarity between one of the dogs and Lucky, as well as that between the eccentric beggar and Babalú-Ayé, the Yoruba equivalent of San Lázaro, earlier described as "the ragged, bearded, pustulant, desperate man with a crutch and knapsack."[40] When Isolina suggests that they leave the kennel door open, Miyares does not reply, but he knows that Lucky will not return and that his good fortune has ended: "Miyares, pensativo, tampoco contestó."[41] This suggestive ending, with its equating of reality and sculpture and its symbolic representation of the end of an era, rounds out Benítez's conversion into a world of fantasy and the absurdity of the different aspects of Cuban society that became antiquated by the Revolution: "Estatuas sepultadas," "La tijera rota," "A la gente le gusta el azul," and "El escudo de hojas secas."

A somewhat similar fantastic view of the remnants of prerevolutionary bourgeois society is presented in the often anthologized "Casa sitiada" (UN, CB, JMO, AF-2, CM, GL) by César Leante (b. 1928) and "Cerdos o perros adiestrados para encontrar trufas" (JMO, AF-2, CM) by Humberto Arenal (b. 1926). On the other hand, Gustavo Eguren's (b. 1925) "Uno de esos viajes" (CB, AF-2) is based almost

[39] Ibid., pp. 48–49.
[40] Ibid., p. 34.
[41] Ibid., p. 58.

exclusively on a direct, unadorned dialogue and emphasizes the personal emotions involved in a young man's decision to leave Cuba in spite of his mother.

IV. The Generation of 1960: Jesús Díaz Rodríguez, Norberto Fuentes, et al.

Although magic realism characterizes many of the best stories of the 1966–1970 period, particularly those of Benítez, quantitatively it was only one of three currents, the other two being science fiction and other fantastic themes, on the one hand, and a more definitely committed revolutionary literature, on the other. As far as the latter is concerned, the importance of *Los años duros* (1966) by Jesús Díaz Rodríguez cannot be overestimated. The publication of this volume has been heralded for sparking the Cuban novelistic boom of 1966–1970. Paradoxically, however, Díaz's short volume represents a distinct reaction against the highly experimental, highly ornate, and at times somewhat escapist works, written for the most part by authors of the so-called first revolutionary generation, those born in the late 1920's and early 1930's. Díaz also signals the emergence of the second literary generation, writers born in the late 1930's and early 1940's who no longer feel compelled to exorcise the pre-1959 past and who, to a certain extent, anticipate the new revolutionary attitude toward literature and the arts, officially proclaimed in October 1968.

Of eighteen short-story writers born between 1938 and 1944, only six made their literary debuts before 1966. Of the latter's seven published works, six may be classified as escapist: science fiction in *Cuentos de ciencia ficción* (1964) by Juan Luis Herrero (b. 1939); literature of the absurd in *El regalo* (1964) by Nelson Rodríguez (b. 1943); and a variety of other nonrevolutionary themes in the works of three women: *Las fábulas* (1962) by Ana María Simó (b. 1943), *Cuentos para abuelas enfermas* (1964) and *La vieja y la mar* (1965) by Evora Tamayo (b. 1940), and *Memorias de un decapitado* (1965) by Angela Martínez (b. 1938). Only Reynaldo González's (b. 1940) *Miel para hojuelas* (1963) describes life in Havana under Batista and the effects of the Revolution on the decadent bourgeois society as do the works of the previous generation of writers. On the other hand, of the twelve writers born between 1938 and 1944 who made their debuts between 1966 and 1972, only Reynaldo Arenas (b. 1943) and, to a much lesser extent, Sergio Chaplé (b. 1938) published stories that resemble thematically and stylistically those of the previous generation. Although Arenas's volume of short stories *Con los ojos cerrados* was not published until the fall of 1972 (in Uruguay), two of his three previously anthologized stories, "Con los ojos cerrados" (RLL, JMO) and "El hijo y la madre" (UN, CB, JEM, CM), reflect the same high degree of formal experimentation and delicate sensitivity as does his novel *Celestino antes del alba*. "Mi primer desfile" (AF-2), on the other hand, is far less esoteric and deals specifically with the 1959 revolutionary triumph. The five other stories of *Con los ojos cerrados* are all variations on the theme of the mean, domineering mother and the weak, sensitive, and dreamy son.[42] The most atypical of these variations is "La Vieja Rosa," which fuses scenes and characters from *Cien años de soledad* and sets them down in the midst of the Cuban Revolution. Sergio Chaplé's "Camarioca la bella" (BS), from his volume *Ud. sí puede tener un Buick* (1969), resembles thematically the stories of Antonio Benítez that deal with those elements of Cuban society that have been unable to adapt to the Revolution. However, there is no attempt to transform reality into fantasy and there is only a bare minimum of stylistic embellishment. Benítez's influence, both thematic and structural, is more apparent in five of the six stories of Julio Travieso's (b. 1940) *Los corderos beben vino* (1970).

One of the three main currents, then, in the 1966–1970 Cuban short story is comprised of the following works written by members of the generation of 1960, most of whom are represented in Bernardo Subercaseaux's 1971 anthology:[43]

---

[42] Besides those stories mentioned, the volume includes "A la sombra de la mata de almendras," "Los heridos," "El reino de Alipio," and "Bestial entre las flores."

[43] Bernardo Subercaseaux, *Narrativa de la joven Cuba*.

Jesús Díaz (b. 1941), *Los años duros* (1966)
Juan Luis Herrero (b. 1939), *Tigres en el Vedado* (1967)
Norberto Fuentes (b. 1943), *Condenados de Condado* (1968)
Cazabandido (1970)
Eduardo Heras León (b. 1941), *La guerra tuvo seis nombres* (1968)
Los pasos en la hierba (1970)
Luis Manuel Sáez (b. 1942), *El iniciado* (1967)
Julio Travieso Serrano (b. 1940), *Días de guerra* (1967)
Nicolás Pérez Delgado (b. 1944), "Los cuerdos nunca hacen nada," Honorable Mention, Premio Casa de las Américas (1970), unpublished
Sergio Chaplé (b. 1938), *Ud. sí puede tener un Buick* (1969)
Hugo Chinea (b. 194?), *Escambray 60* (1970)
Víctor Casáus (b. 1944), "Girón en la memoria," Honorable Mention, Premio Casa de las Américas (1970), unpublished
Bernardo Callejas (b. 1941), *¿Qué vas a cantar ahora?* (1971), written between 1966 and 1970
Julio A. Chacón (b. 194?), *Canción militante a tres tiempos* (1972)

The characteristics of all these works distinguish them most clearly from those of their predecessors Calvert Casey, Humberto Arenal, and Antonio Benítez Rojo. The emphasis is on violent action narrated objectively in an unadorned style, direct, to the point, fragmentary, elliptical, and including much dialogue. Language is equally violent and is no longer the protagonist, because these more committed authors, who participated in the events they describe, are more concerned with communicating directly their personal impressions of the most heroic moments of the Revolution: the struggle against Batista, the repulsion of the Playa Girón invasion, and the elimination of the counterrevolutionary guerrillas in the Escambray Mountains and elsewhere. As in the longer works of their contemporary Miguel Barnet (b. 1941), *Biografía de un cimarrón* (1968) and *Canción de Rachel* (1969), the boundary line between fiction and nonfiction is at times hardly discernible in Norberto Fuentes's *Cazabandido* and Víctor Casáus's "Girón en la memoria." The foreign counterpart of this type of literature is certainly not the magic realism or absurdism of Julio Cortázar but rather the neorealism and concision of Hemingway and Juan Rulfo.

The influence of Rulfo's *El llano en llamas* is particularly evident in

Jesús Díaz's *Los años duros*, the first and only book on the above list to be published in 1966 and, because of its enthusiastic reception, the inspiration for the subsequent works. Like Rulfo, Díaz uses simple, unadorned, "stark naked" language to capture the sincere emotions of his characters. Monologues alternate with dialogues, the point of view shifts from one character to another, and at times different chronological planes are presented simultaneously—without, however, impeding comprehension or diminishing the violent impact. The fact that this volume is not a collection of unrelated stories is indicated by the tripartite division of the first and last selections. Whereas the first story, "Muy al principio," presents three different views of a student strike against Batista, the final story, "No matarás," presents an episode from the struggle against the counterrevolutionaries from the point of view of both victors and vanquished. The violent emotions aroused by Batista's torture methods are similar to those caused by the counterrevolutionaries. Of the two three-part stories, "El cojo" (AF-1, JMC, CM, GL) stands out because of its expert fusion of suspense, personal tragedy, and historical background. In a scant seven pages, the author brings together three tense situations. As the crippled narrator, armed with crutch and knife, is about to take revenge on Salas, his effeminate former high-school teacher, the suspense is intensified by the re-creation in the present tense of the scene in which Salas denounced him to the Batista police as leader of the revolutionary students after another teacher had attempted to protect him. This scene, in turn, is fused with a previous one, in the preterite but also charged with suspense, in which the narrator stood up in class and publicly disclaimed any relationship with Salas: "—For anyone who's interested:—I said in the middle of the class—I hereby declare that our official teacher and alleged homosexual ('fruit' someone shouted), Salas, has nothing to do with Carlos Fuentes Chang, alias El Chino, that is, with me."[44]

In addition to the violence and the suspense, "El cojo" captures the personal tragedy of the narrator, who, in the very first few lines of the story, indicates that he plans to commit suicide after eliminating the last of the Batista informers: "He's coming right away. He definitely has to come by here to get his car. There are few of them left. Only

44 Jesús Díaz Rodríguez, *Los años duros*, pp. 14–15.

this rotten little teacher tonight and one other squealer. Then I'll be all by myself and I know exactly what I have to do with myself now that I'm not even a man."[45] The fact that the protagonist's almost pathological obsession with revenge is at odds with revolutionary justice is expressed in an excellent example of Díaz's appropriately brusque elliptical style: "But first I have to finish, and fast. If not, these people with their trials and their laws will screw me."[46]

The torturing of the rebels by the Batista forces assumes more importance in the even more concise and equally violent "Con la punta de una piedra" (JEM, BS). In a two–and–one-half–page monologue, the narrator, a Batista soldier, talks to his companion Mauro, whom he has just killed with a sharp rock for having drunk more than his share of the water remaining in their canteens. With one brief allusion to the "rebels who are almost on the plain,"[47] the author informs the reader that the action is taking place in mid-1958. Mauro's treachery is linked to his previous sadistic torture of the rebels: "You were the king with the electric wire in their ears and on their balls, the king, the truth."[48] The narrator's continuing conversation with the dead Mauro—"I never thought that you had such a hard head, I had to hit you over and over again"[49]—adds a touch of Rulfian magic to this otherwise brutally cruel story. The final words of the story leave no doubt that the narrator himself will soon die of thirst: "This canteen was open, dripping. When I realized it and grabbed it, there was only a little trickle left, three fingers worth. The rest had been spilled and I couldn't drink it because it fell on the shit."[50]

The element of magic assumes greater importance in the one–and–one-half–page "El polvo a la mitad," which combines elements from Juan Rulfo's "Luvina" and Juan José Arreola's "El guardagujas." As in the former story, an abandoned, desolate town is described in the bleakest "colors": "Outlines of faded shacks, dusty shelves in dusty

[45] Ibid., p. 9.
[46] Ibid.
[47] Ibid., p. 29.
[48] Ibid.
[49] Ibid., p. 31.
[50] Ibid.

stores, stray dogs, a school. That used to be, or probably was, or must have been, a town.''[51] As in Arreola's story, the "mysterious stranger," a man picked up on the road by the narrator and his wife, gets out in the town and disappears in a cloud of dust. When the wife indicates that she was unaware of the stranger's existence, the reader wonders whether the stranger was a product of the narrator's imagination. Although the town and the whole dust-covered landscape may symbolize prerevolutionary Cuba—"Look—he pointed out a tottering church— that's where they baptized Batista, nothing's left, not even I—he said"[52] —this story seems very much a contrived literary composition and lacks the impact of Díaz's best stories.

The two longest stories of the volume, "No hay Dios que resista esto" (SC) and "Diosito" (JEM), deal with more contemporary situations. "No hay Dios que resista esto" may be considered the younger generation's version of Edmundo Desnoes's "Aquí me pongo" (RF, AF-2) and the source of Miguel Cossío Woodward's prize-winning novel *Sacchario*. Whereas Desnoes presents the opposition of the bourgeois intellectual to cutting sugar cane with his continued obsession with sex and skepticism about revolutionary idealism, Jesús Díaz focuses on similar attitudes in a lower-class mulatto. In both cases, the doubting protagonists are converted to the revolutionary cause. The principal differences are that Desnoes dwells at greater length on his protagonist's cultural background and his thoughts and comments en route to the plantation, while Jesús Díaz concentrates on the actual cane-cutting experience with a unifying plot line. In the Díaz story, the protagonist's thoughts alternate with dialogues involving him and the other cane cutters. The story's tension depends on his anxiously awaiting a telegram from his wife, which would give him an excuse to return to Havana. When the telegram finally arrives, the protagonist refuses to leave because he is shamed or converted by Jorge, the revolutionary leader, who has also just received a telegram informing him of his mother's death. The simultaneous arrival of the two telegrams, the rather abrupt conversion of the protagonist, and the final revelation of his identity—he is referred to as Fresneda, Caballo, and mulatto—

[51] Ibid., p. 36.
[52] Ibid.

decidedly detract from the story's literary merits. As in Desnoes's "Aquí me pongo," the abrupt and relatively unexpected final conversion lends greater credence to the protagonist's previous griping.

By contrast, the absence of a final revolutionary conversion in "Diosito" (JEM) actually presents the Revolution in a more favorable light and is one of the story's positive aspects. Nonetheless, the almost equal attention given to the three characters—the timid immature sixteen-year-old Catholic recruit nicknamed "Diosito," his rough-and-tumble sergeant, and his surprisingly understanding lieutenant—the relative lack of tension, and the excessive changes in the narrative point of view make this story less concentrated, less forceful, and less impressive than many of the others.

The sentimental note in the lieutenant's attitude, which is unique in the six stories of *Los años duros*, becomes predominant in Jesús Díaz's most anthologized story, "Amor la Plata Alta" (CB, JMO, AF-2), which belongs to his second, still unpublished volume. Although the consummation of sexual intercourse between two volunteer rural schoolteachers who are looking for their mountain village on a dark rainy night may appear at first sight to be an example of socialist realism, the author's analysis of the timidity of both the narrator and his companion as well as the latter's final feelings of guilt is a much more personal and more successful treatment of love within the revolutionary context than that in Cofiño's novel *La última mujer y el próximo combate*.

The final story of *Los años duros*, "No matarás," introduces the theme of the struggle against the counterrevolutionaries, which has attracted the attention of several of the younger writers. With the same violent action and language that characterized "El cojo" and the two other parts of "Muy al principio," "No matarás" presents three moments in a dramatic episode of the government campaign against the counterrevolutionaries. Scene one, "Los bandidos," concentrates on the interpersonal conflicts among the three fleeing counterrevolutionaries: the undaunted Niño, who refuses to surrender; the wounded and cowardly Lolo; and the kicked and beaten treacherous guide Jabao, on whom the other two depend. Scene two, "Erasmo," also involves a trio of different types, but among the government troops: the young, impetuous recruit Carmenati; the clear-thinking, understanding officer Méndez; and Erasmo, the implacable, obsessed hero, who is determined to atone for his having previously allowed the counterrevolutionaries to escape. In the third and final scene, "La negativa," both groups meet as Carmenati stands guard duty outside the cell where Jabao and Lolo await execution. Through the prisoners' arguing and insulting each other, the reader is apprised of their previous atrocities and of Jabao's shooting Niño in the back. On the other side, the drama is based on Carmenati's participation in his first firing squad and the impending trial of Erasmo for his earlier "irresponsibility."

Even more starkly violent themes and language characterize Julio Travieso's (b. 1940) *Días de guerra* (1967). Four of the eight stories present different points of view of the brutal police torturing of an urban revolutionary in 1958. Equally violent is the discord in "Todos juntos" among a varied group of disaffected Cubans fleeing by boat to Miami. In "Negro, sí," an upper-class counterrevolutionary invader is captured by his former Negro chauffeur, who recalls his pent-up anger during the years of subservience.

This same parallelism between the violent action of 1958 and 1961–1962, which Jesús Díaz as well as Julio Travieso use to begin and end their respective volumes, forms the basis for all nine stories in Juan Luis Herrero's (b. 1939) *Tigres en el Vedado* (1967). After making his debut in 1964 with a series of science-fiction stories, Herrero rejected escapism and joined his contemporaries in capturing, with a brusque, direct, unadorned Rulfian style and structure, some of the more dramatic scenes from the periods of armed conflict.

Tigres en el Vedado (1967) is comprised of four stories related to the urban terrorism of 1958 and five about the 1962 rural LCB, "Lucha contra Bandidos," the government's counterrevolutionary campaign in the Escambray Mountains. Although police torture and jeeps are as prominent as in Cabrera Infante's vignettes, Jesús Díaz's "El cojo," and the other anthologized stories about 1958, Herrero's stories, because they were probably written later, are somewhat more complex. In "El Chota" and "El juicio," as in Gregorio Ortega's novel *Reportaje de las vísperas* (1967), Herrero is less concerned about denouncing police torture tactics than he is with exploring the psychological processes of the revolutionary's response to torture, the limits of human endurance, and the consequences of not being able to withstand the torture. The other two stories, "Acuérdate de Ramón Rodríguez" and "Tigres en el Vedado," present Batista's soldiers and police at the mercy of the revolutionaries and, therefore, like the narrator of Jesús Díaz's "Con la punta de una piedra," these villains are more humanized. The best of the four stories is "Acuérdate de Ramón Rodríguez" because of the tension based on the revolutionaries' indecision about what to do with the captured jeep full of soldiers. Although their human instincts impel them to pardon the soldiers, the narrator's recollection of his friend Ramón Rodríguez, who died precisely because he had not killed a policeman in a similar situation, spells death for the soldiers. They die precisely at the moment they think that they have been saved.

The title story refers to Senator Masferrer's private police force, a few of whom are surprised and killed by the triumphant revolutionaries in the early days of January 1959. The dramatic tension, however, which depends on the group's waiting for other companions before trying to escape from Havana, is sacrificed by the author for the sake of historical background: the ability of the Masferrer group to collaborate with any and all of the prerevolutionary governments dating back to 1933.

The last five stories of Herrero's *Tigres en el Vedado*, interrelated with one another, differ from Jesús Díaz's "No matarás," just as the first four differ from "El cojo": less emphasis on violence per se and a greater interest in the enemy as a human being. In fact, of the five LCB stories, four deal almost exclusively with a variety of *alzados*. Only the first one, "M-3," focuses on a member of the government's antiguerrilla unit and his relations with his father. The latter, an old peasant, was angry at his son for becoming a Communist, but, after the *alzados* kill his lifelong friend, the old man becomes reconciled with his son. When the *alzados*, armed with American M-3 rifles and accompanied by an American, surround his son, the old man goes to his rescue, with his own M-3. Although this confirms the son's previous suspicion that "the old man was involved in something,"[53] he

[53] Juan Luis Herrero, *Tigres en el Vedado*, p. 44.

accepts his father's help, and the story ends on this note, without any indication of whether they'll both survive or die: "He recognized an M-3 and didn't ask him where he had gotten it."[54]

In the other four stories, the tables are turned and individual *alzados* are fleeing, besieged, killed, or taken prisoner. "No has vuelto a ladrar, Canelo" is the most Rulfian of the stories because of the similarity of its title to "No oyes ladrar los perros," the terrible suffering of the fugitive as in "El hombre," and the eeriness created by the man's monologue with both his long-dead dog and the silent peasant who gives him some food. After five years without any human contact, the protagonist no longer remembers why he joined the *alzados*. The protagonist of "Uno," also a fugitive, appears to be even less committed to the *alzados*. Fearful and unenthusiastic about their anti-Communist cause, he was repelled by the senseless murder of the old man Nacho in "M-3." Nevertheless, even though he is surrounded and wounded in the leg, he continues firing his gun—not heroically but almost automatically—until he is killed: "You don't want to do it, but you fire. You feel the lead response penetrating your body."[55]

Aldo Pérez, the protagonist of "Isla de Pinos," joined the *alzados* only because he seems predestined to be on the wrong side: "It's always been the same, I'm always on the losing side. I joined up as a soldier when I could have gone into the Sierra. I became a counterrevolutionary when I could have been a revolutionary. Then I joined the guerrilla forces in the Escambray Mountains when I could have been a member of the government militia."[56] Although he is now in a rehabilitation camp with over thirty thousand other prisoners,[57] Aldo, like Herrero's other Rulfian characters, creates his own isolation chamber by revealing both past and present through a monologue. Torn between his reluctance to betray and his lack of identification with the counterrevolutionary leaders—"If it were possible to be neither square nor round!"[58]—Aldo finally decides to change his attitude, if for no

[54] Ibid., p. 47.
[55] Ibid., p. 54.
[56] Ibid., p. 79.
[57] Ibid., p. 77.
[58] Ibid., p. 79.

other reason than to try to change his luck: "Square or round. I've got
to. Turn my life around completely. I've got to. Even if it's just to try
my luck. I've got to."⁵⁹ The story ends with his release from the rehabilitation camp, but on a much more ambiguous note than in David
Buzzi's novel *Los desnudos*, from which Herrero chose this story's
epigraph about the effects of the Revolution on every man: ". . . the
historical events that cause us to reveal ourselves do not stop, they continue, they advance, and a revolution continues to exercise its effects on
people."⁶⁰

The longest and most complex story of *Tigres en el Vedado* is "La
Niña de Aguadilla," which could actually serve as the basis for a novel.
The leader and only survivor of a band of thirty-five Escambray *alzados*, the besieged "Niña de Aguadilla" is a kind of Doña Bárbara
whose past sexual experiences explain both her violence and her political position. After four Batista soldiers hanged her parents and
raped her, she joined the revolutionary forces in the Sierra. Felipe, a
revolutionary companion and medical student, teaches her how to read,
as did Asdrúbal in *Doña Bárbara*. Later, however, Felipe's refusal to
make love to her and his subsequent marriage in Havana alienate her
from the Revolution. In the meantime, she encourages Nico to make
love to her in order to prove her femininity and has a child by him.
Ultimately, it is Nico who convinces her to surrender. The scenes of
the past are inserted into those of the present, but whatever is gained
in psychological complexity and historical background is lost in dramatic tension, as in the case of "Tigres en el Vedado."

The influence of *Doña Bárbara* on "La Niña de Aguadilla" and the
better absorbed influence of Rulfo's *El llano en llamas* on many of the
other stories indicate a conscious preoccupation with literary creativity,
which is much less apparent in Norberto Fuentes Cobas's (b. 1943)
two volumes, *Condenados de Condado* (1968) and *Cazabandido*
(1970), both devoted exclusively to the LCB.⁶¹ The twenty-five stories

---

⁵⁹ Ibid., p. 80.
⁶⁰ Ibid., p. 75.
⁶¹ The relationship between fiction and nonfiction exemplified in these two volumes
is carefully studied in Julio Ortega's review in *Libre* (Paris), no. 2 (December–February 1971–1972), pp. 146–151.

of the former and the thirty-nine *crónicas* of the latter give a rather detailed account of the government's counterinsurgency campaign, which lasted from 1960 to 1966, "la más larga campaña militar de este siglo en Cuba,"[62] and, although concentrated in the Escambray Mountains, stretched from one end of Cuba to the other, as indicated by the "mapa de operaciones" in *Cazabandido*. This volume also includes photographs of some of the insurgents and counterinsurgents whose exploits are narrated in the *crónicas*. Although Fuentes mentions in the introduction to *Cazabandido* the influence of Beck, Babel, Hemingway, Ehrenberg, Rulfo, and the Cuban Pablo de la Torriente Brau, the main inspiration for these stories and *crónicas* stems from his own experiences as a newspaperman who at times doubled as interrogator: ". . . it's only right to point out that [the influences] are suitably assimilated, that they appear as genuine reminiscences, which at no time tarnish the authenticity of *Condenados de Condado*."[63] It is precisely his lack of dependence on previous literary models that recently prompted Uruguayan critic Angel Rama to call him the most original writer of prose fiction produced by the Revolution: ". . . Norberto Fuentes que es para mí el narrador más original producido en el período revolucionario cubano."[64]

In a complete rebellion against the previous literary generation, Fuentes eschews the multiple chronological planes, the changing narrative point of view, the interior monologue, and all elements of fantasy. He writes in a direct, unadorned, and at times elliptical style. The short sentences are made up primarily of verbs and nouns. Adjectives are conspicuous by their scarcity. The following paragraph from one of Fuentes's best stories, "El capitán Descalzo" (BS),[65] describes in the starkest terms how the revolutionary hero kills the fleeing insurgent: "Descalzo struck unerringly, and the machete sliced into the butt of the Garand rifle that the man was holding on his thighs. His hand fell to

---

[62] Norberto Fuentes Cobas, *Cazabandido*, p. 7.

[63] Antonio Benítez Rojo, review of *Condenados de Condado*, *Casa de las Américas* 9, no. 49 (July–August 1968): 159.

[64] Angel Rama, interview in *Imagen*, May 9–16, 1972, section 2, p. 4.

[65] Also included with "Para la noche" and "Orden número 13" in the recent anthology of Spanish American literature in translation: Hortense Carpentier and Janet Brof, *Doors and Mirrors*.

the ground, holding the piece of bread. The man tried to pick up his hand, but another blow with the machete, this time on the back of his neck, made the man's shout drown in spurts of blood that coagulated in his mouth."[66] However, the story does not end at this point, because, unlike Jesús Díaz Rodríguez and despite this paragraph, Norberto Fuentes is not primarily concerned with violence and cruelty. He is more interested in pointing out that the men on both sides are basically human beings. In this story, Captain Descalzo's revolutionary devotion and heroism are complemented by his personal life and his sense of humor. Saddened by his wife's death, Descalzo is a kind of *zapatista* who, when not fighting, works hard on his land to support his dozen children. His picturesqueness derives from his refusal to live in Havana as a revolutionary hero, because he will not wear boots or shoes. The tension of the story does not depend so much on the encounter between Descalzo and the fugitive as it does on the relaxed conversation between Descalzo and Bunder Pacheco, the officer in charge of the counterinsurgents, who is looking for the fugitive. It is only after sipping a cup of coffee that Descalzo reveals to Pacheco in the final words of the story that he doesn't have to hurry off, because the fugitive is already dead: "—There's no rush, there's no rush—repeated Descalzo—. I tell you that there's no rush because it seems to me that Magua Tondike must be rotting away in the sun, in my field."[67]

In addition to Captain Descalzo and his victim, Magua Tondike, *Condenados de Condado* presents an interesting array of characters on both sides of the struggle, without dividing them into heroes and villains. Actually Captain Descalzo is the only heroic, epic figure of the whole collection. Commander Bunder Pacheco appears in several of the stories without ever assuming a primary role. Fuentes prefers to single out for attention those soldiers who have personal problems: the young, fearful, and constantly griping recruit of "La Llorona," whose untimely death deeply affects his companions; the tongue-tied victim of the town's youngsters, who gains revenge on his tormentors with his newly acquired gun in "Belisario el aura"; the homosexual topogra-

---

[66] Norberto Fuentes Cobas, *Condenados de Condado*, p. 15.
[67] Ibid., p. 17.

pher in "La yegua," who commits suicide after being denounced; the soldier, who also commits suicide after his theft is discovered in "Melo"; the ingenuous old peasant Abuelo Bueno in "Santa Juana," who offers to be shot after Bunder Pacheco gently scolds him for allowing his platoon to wear necklaces of peony seeds and other decorations. Not all the *cazadores*, however, are such devout revolutionaries. Lieutenant Bombillo in "La vanguardia" quickly moves ahead of his men in the search for the *alzados* in order to help the latter escape. The fact that he has been chosen as "combatiente de vanguardia para la construcción del Partido en su unidad de cazadores"[68] is a momentary but nonetheless significant criticism of the Communist party's role in the counterinsurgency campaign. This criticism is more fully developed in "Visita," which describes the well-furnished, air-conditioned office of the regional secretary of the Communist party with its large pictures of Fidel Castro and Walter Ulbricht, "in his youth when he used to participate in sports dressed in athletic gear."[69]

Although the large majority of the stories deal with life among the revolutionary government forces, a few focus on some of the individual insurgents. Without condoning their past conduct, the author concentrates on their present reactions as human beings. When the interrogated prisoner Claudio in "El marcado" finally confesses to having murdered one of the militiamen, the author's emphasis on his present humility and fear does not imply forgiveness of his crime. On the contrary, Claudio's cringing attitude serves to make the crime that much more heinous. How a man can appear to be so different in different circumstances seems to interest Fuentes most. This same theme is developed in the rather irregular military trial of the portly landowner, Don Margarito Abejón, in "La ley." Although the author seems at first to be faulting revolutionary justice for the arbitrary way in which the sentence is meted out, Don Margarito's subsequent activities prove that he was indeed guilty of collaborating with the insurgents. In two other stories, "Guantanamera" and "Bebeson," plot development is almost completely eliminated for the sake of two tragic portraits: the old farmer who stops Bunder Pacheco's convoy in order

[68] Ibid., p. 141.
[69] Ibid., p. 64.

to plead for the lives of his nine sons, who have joined the insurgents, and the former insurgent captain seated in an improvised wheelchair because his legs were shot off by the same militiaman who is drinking beer with him. By deploring the tragedy of war in general, Norberto Fuentes bestows a certain degree of transcendency on these stories that belies their very specific time and place. In no way does he attempt to glorify the campaign nor does he sympathize with the insurgents. His attitude is spelled out most explicitly in the title story, "Los condenados," which does not refer exclusively to the condemned insurgents but rather to the soldiers of both opposing forces who are condemned to die in a struggle symbolized by the mortal combat between a serpent and a rat. Antonio Benítez recognizes this in his comments on the whole volume: "Because actually the *condemned* are all of them: some to death and prison, others to the nightmare of a violent and strange form of life."[70]

Like *Condenados de Condado, La guerra tuvo seis nombres* (1968) by Eduardo Heras León (b. 1940) has one unifying theme, the victorious battle against the Playa Girón invaders. Although there is absolutely no ambiguity about the identification of the heroes and the villains, this, too, is more of a book about man at war than it is a fictionalized account of the actual invasion. The volume contains only six stories and has a greater unity than *Condenados de Condado* because of the reappearing characters and the restricted locale. The main themes are the relations between the young recruits and their officers and the individual's fear of death coupled with his anger at the enemy. As in the works of his contemporaries, action and dialogue prevail over description, the elliptical style reflects the intense drama of the moment, and the first- or second-person point of view conveys the impression of actual immediate involvement. Although Heras León's second volume of stories, *Los pasos en la hierba,* received honorable mention in the 1970 Casa de las Américas competition, he was dismissed from the editorial board of *El Caimán Barbudo* because of the book's "connotaciones de criticismo tendencioso."[71] As in *La guerra tuvo seis nombres,* all six stories of *Los pasos en la hierba* present different moments in the

---

[70] Benítez Rojo, review of *Condenados de Condado,* p. 159.
[71] *El Caimán Barbudo,* no. 46 (May 1971), p. 2.

conversion of a small group of individualistic *milicianos* into a tightly knit artillery unit. Although the book's artistic value depends on the individualization of the characters, it was probably this same trait that caused it to be considered suspect. During the military training process, the excessively harsh disciplinary measures of a certain lieutenant are questioned, and the assertion of individual personalities is defended.

V. The Ideological Story: Noel Navarro

Whereas the new government policy toward the arts is exemplified in the 1970 and 1971 Casa de las Américas prize-winning novels *Sacchario* and *La última mujer y el próximo combate*, it was not until 1972 that an equivalent volume of short stories received similar Casa de las Américas recognition, *La huella del pulgar* by well-known novelist Noel Navarro (b. 1931).[72] However, in December 1969, the Dirección Política de las Fuerzas Armadas Revolucionarias published *Tiempo de cambio* by Manuel Cofiño López (b. 1936) as the prize-winning volume of its first literary contest. The prologue emphasizes the fact that the recognized writers of the present and the future must emerge from the *pueblo* and that the political contents as well as the artistic quality were taken into account in the awarding of the prizes. The book itself is a collection of seven stories that, with one exception,

---

[72] The 1970 Casa de las Américas short-story prize was given to Venezuelan Luis Britto García for *Rajatabla*. No prize was awarded in 1971. The 1970 UNEAC prize winner was *La sonrisa y la otra cabeza* by Imeldo Alvarez García (b. 1928), whose structural complexities make it inaccessible to the masses. The 1971 UNEAC prize in the Colección David for young writers was awarded to Julio A. Chacón, an active member of the Communist party, for *Canción militante a tres tiempos*. Three of its nine mediocre stories portray the violence of the anti-Batista struggle. In 1972, the UNEAC prize was declared *desierto* and honorable mentions were given to Bernardo Callejas's *El pulso de lo real* and Rafael Garriga's *El pueblo de los cien problemas*. The 1973 Casa de las Américas prize was given to Chilean Poli Délano for *Cambio de máscara*. The 1973 UNEAC prize was awarded to Hugo Chinea for *Contra bandidos*, while an honorable mention was given to Bernardo Callejas for *De las armas y letras*. The 1974 prize went to Uruguayan Alfredo Gravina's *Despegues* with an honorable mention for *Una cierta ventana enloquecida* by Chilean Miguel Cabezas.

contrast the revolutionary present with the distant past of the 1950's. The former prostitute of the title story is now a self-respecting waitress in an ice-cream parlor; a former boy friend becomes the statue of a fallen hero in "Los besos duermen en la piedra"; an ex-Batista police captain is a pitiful crazed figure dressed in rags who runs wildly through the streets until he is taken to the hospital in "Donde ahora crece un framboyán." The one rural story, "La noche baja," deals with an episode in the Escambray campaign against the antirevolutionary guerrillas and could easily have been written by either Juan Luis Herrero or Norberto Fuentes. Even more than the stories of these two writers, *Tiempo de cambio* in general reveals the influence of Juan Rulfo's *El llano en llamas*. Like "Luvina," five of Cofiño's seven stories are monologues or almost monologues addressed to other characters who are only gradually identified and who do nothing but listen. The simple unadorned prose, the lack of phonetically transcribed dialect, and a touch of fantasy are also clearly Rulfian characteristics. The air of fantasy in the stories comes from the silent listeners as well as from the fact that the prerevolutionary era is made to appear so remote in time. The last story in the volume, ". . . y por última vez," is the only one narrated completely in the second person and is less effective because it sacrifices dramatic tension for panoramic coverage of the life of a prerevolutionary poor family in Havana.

The winner of the 1970 F.A.R. prize was journalist and humorist Juan Angel Cardi for his first volume, *Relatos de Pueblo Viejo*. As the title suggests, the eleven stories are written in the nineteenth-century *costumbrista* vein and reveal the inequities and miserable conditions in a prerevolutionary small town. The volume ends with the triumph of the Revolution and the changing of the town's name to Pueblo Libre.

Noel Navarro's *La huella del pulgar*, unlike *Tiempo de cambio*, was conceived more as an artistic unit. The volume's eight stories are divided into three more or less equal groups entitled "AHORA," "AYER," and "ANTES." The first of the "now" stories, "Donde cae la luna," appears to be a combination of the prize-winning novels *Sacchario* and *La última mujer y el próximo combate*. As in the former, the narrator is a volunteer cane cutter in a brigade that has to struggle to achieve group solidarity and whose most effective worker is an older (eighty!) Negro. The one-word sentences, and the choppy, elliptical style in general, differ from the style of Navarro's earlier works and seem to be an imitation of Cossío Woodward: "Cut. Pile up. Raise. Only me."[73] As in *La última mujer y el próximo combate*, the appointment of a new official leader puts the group back on the revolutionary track. Following his example, the brigade now fares better in competition (socialist emulation) with the other groups. The tension of the story derives from the new leader's revolutionary devotion and his inability to forget that in this same area his counterrevolutionary brother had participated in the murder of a peasant family before being captured. The gradual emergence of the new leader as the protagonist of the story is somewhat unexpected because of the earlier importance bestowed on the old Negro.

The other "now" story, "Delfín," is also strongly reminiscent of *La última mujer y el próximo combate*. In a meeting of the cane cutters, the expulsion of Delfín is discussed democratically while the narrator struggles to overcome his reluctance to testify against his former mentor.

The first two of the three "yesterday" stories are more officially revolutionary versions of Norberto Fuentes's *Condenados de Condado*. "Al final de la noche" and "Soplo" describe, in different ways, attempts on the part of two counterrevolutionary leaders to escape. The former resembles some of Norberto Fuentes's stories in its stark violence, narrated unemphatically. When the militiamen surround Segundo Barcino's house, they are unexpectedly invited by his wife to come in out of the rain and spend the night there. While they are asleep, she tries to escape and is caught. It is then revealed that, before allowing the militiamen to enter the house, she had decapitated her own husband to prevent him from surrendering and had hid the corpse under the fireplace. Her fanatic opposition to the revolutionary government is attributed to her being a fervent Catholic.

"Soplo" is more reminiscent of some of Juan Rulfo's stories. The narrator is a peasant who engages in an unanswered monologue in a rainy, foggy atmosphere pierced by a dog's barking. The counterrevo-

---

[73] Noel Navarro, *La huella del pulgar*, p. 13.

lutionary Confesor Fuentenegra, who apparently escaped by jumping into a well that had a tunnel leading to the nearby thicket, repeats his exploit with a touch of the fantastic.

In both stories, the author makes sure that the reader does not sympathize with the pursued and defeated counterrevolutionaries by forcefully recalling their barbaric crimes against the rural population. This is also true of "No hay quien me pare," which gives an expanded vision of the counterrevolutionary movement. The three unsavory characters who participate in the infiltration landing were recruited in Miami by an American. Their mutual distrust, which breaks out into the open once they are detected and subsequently captured, recalls a similar episode in *La última mujer y el próximo combate*, as well as Jesús Díaz Rodríguez's story "No matarás." On the other hand, the identification of the narrator as a former Batista police officer who enjoyed torturing his victims is a more authentic, integral element of the story that serves as the bridge to the "before" section.

Because of the broader time period covered by the first two of the three "before" stories, their dramatic tension is sacrificed for the sake of giving to the volume a more complete coverage of revolutionary topics. "La superficie" (CM) dwells on the pre-1959 existentialist intellectual who, like the characters in so many of the 1961–1965 exorcising novels, is fond of American cowboy movies, Al Jolson, Joyce, Faulkner, and Sartre, but who is incapable of revolutionary action. Although Rubén joins a cell of the July Twenty-sixth Movement, he is responsible for his friends' death at the hands of the police. Ever the indecisive intellectual, he cannot quite get himself to eliminate the growing memories of his treachery by committing suicide. "Diciéndote" contrasts the persistence of antirevolutionary attitudes in a family of "gusanos" with the revolutionary conversion of a former illiterate chauffeur. The final story of the volume, "Pepón," concentrates on the emotions and recollections of a castrated and blinded victim of a Batista police officer as he walks up the steps to attend the latter's trial.

Since seven of the volume's eight stories are narrated as monologues in the first person by nonintellectuals ("La superficie" is the only exception), the language is clear, straightforward, and conversational in

tone. Although the initial situation in each story is somewhat enigmatic, it becomes readily comprehensible through the piecemeal revelation of past events. Far less complex than the stories of Antonio
Benítez and lacking the psychological depth of those of Calvert Casey
and Humberto Arenal, Navarro's *La huella del pulgar* more closely
resembles the works of Jesús Díaz Rodríguez, Juan Luis Herrero,
Norberto Fuentes, and Eduardo Heras León than those of his own
contemporaries. However, because his stories seem to be following an
imposed (self- or otherwise) formula, they lack the sincerity and the
fresh impact of the ones written by the generation of 1960.

Part Four. Antirevolutionary Prose Fiction

I. The Novel

Anticommunism, Vilification of Fidel, and Miami

Although some well-known Cuban novelists like Guillermo Cabrera Infante, Severo Sarduy, Nivaria Tejera, and Juan Arcocha have defected and are now living in exile, only Arcocha has published, in English, what could be termed an antirevolutionary novel. The majority of the novels to be discussed in this chapter are the first literary works of lawyers, teachers, and newspapermen, several of whom were born at the turn of the century and hold doctorates from the Universidad de La Habana, mainly in civil law. Most of the books have been published in the United States (Miami and New York) and Spain (Barcelona, Madrid, and Oviedo), with a few in Mexico and Puerto

Rico, and single volumes in Medellín, Colombia, and San José, Costa Rica. As might be expected, the number of antirevolutionary novels gradually increased through the 1960's in response to the growing number of exiles and spurted in the early 1970's, due possibly to their adaptation to the new environment and to the greater availability of antirevolutionary publishing enterprises. Between 1959 and 1963, inclusive, only three antirevolutionary novels were published, while the best years have been 1965, 1967, 1969, and 1971 with three each, and 1972 with six. Unlike the revolutionary novels, the twenty-seven antirevolutionary works do not lend themselves to chronological groupings, because they reveal no clear-cut evolution between 1959 and the present either by theme or by literary technique.

About the only characteristics that almost all twenty-seven novels share are anticommunism and vilification of Fidel Castro, which are expressed with varying degrees of intensity. The extreme right-wing, Catholic position is articulated most passionately, if not most effectively, by Salvador Díaz-Versón (b. 1905) in . . . *Ya el mundo oscurece* (1961).[1] Communism is criticized as a world-wide atheistic conspiracy, and specific denunciations are made of its role in the Spanish Civil War and in the Guatemalan Revolution of 1944–1954. Even though the novel is dated March 1960, only one month after the signing of the first commercial treaty between Cuba and the Soviet Union, Fidel Castro is denounced as a communist dictator. The Cuban *ortodoxos* are blamed for having paved the way for communism by urging too many changes. In spite of its defects, the Batista regime is said to have had many positive aspects and is by far preferable to communism: "The Batista regime had certain deficiencies and defects, but it was a regime that respected private property, international treaties, freedom, religion, and, although some of its members got out of hand, their behavior may be attributed to the heat of battle."[2]

Similar undisguised preaching about the evils of communism is also

---

[1] Salvador Díaz-Versón is listed in Fermín Peraza's *Personalidades cubanas* as a professional newspaperman. He was, however, also chief of the Havana police in 1933 and head of the counterespionage section of the army between 1949 and 1952. He has been president of the Organización Interamericana de Periodistas Anticomunistas and resides in Miami.

[2] Salvador Díaz-Versón, . . . *Ya el mundo oscurece*, p. 225.

found in four more recent novels. In *De buena cepa* (1967), René G. Landa traces briefly the history of the Cuban Communist party, to which he links, before 1959, Raúl Castro, Che Guevara, and Camilo Cienfuegos, but not Fidel Castro.[3] The Spanish Civil War is singled out as the first step taken by the Communists to achieve world domination, and Pope John XXIII is criticized for having granted an audience to a Russian official. Raoul A. Fowler's (b. 1903) *En las garras de la paloma* (1967), which is written from the point of view of a wealthy landowner, criticizes Batista for his alliance with the Communists, but Castro is denounced as being worse than both Machado and Batista.[4] The revolutionary agrarian reform is presented as part of the communist plan to stir up class warfare in Cuba. The author's attitude toward communism may be summed up by his statement: ". . . nature detests equality."[5] As late as 1972, the same tone prevails in *El gallo cantó* by Miguel Márquez y de la Cerra (b. 1905):[6] "Cuba, the beautiful land trampled by the ferocious red beast."[7] Undoubtedly influenced by the Latin American boom novels, José Sánchez-Boudy (b. 1928) gives this theme a new twist in *Los cruzados de la aurora* (1972) by equating the communist dictatorship of Fidel Castro with that of John Calvin in sixteenth-century Geneva.[8]

---

[3] René G. Landa has a prerevolutionary doctorate in civil law and another one in social sciences from the Universidad de La Habana.

[4] Raoul A. Fowler y Cabrera holds a doctorate in civil law from the Universidad de La Habana and was co-owner of sugar plantations and *centrales* between 1929 and 1950. He went into exile in November 1960 and resides in Coral Gables, Florida.

[5] Raoul A. Fowler, *En las garras de la paloma*, p. 39.

[6] Miguel F. Márquez y de la Cerra was professor of philosophy of law at the Universidad de La Habana and supreme court justice until he resigned in early 1960 to go into exile in Miami. He had previously written for the *Diario de la Marina* and *Bohemia*.

[7] Miguel F. Márquez y de la Cerra, *El gallo cantó*, p. 10.

[8] José Sánchez-Boudy received his law degree from the Universidad de La Habana in 1952 and did postgraduate work at the universities of Madrid and Puerto Rico. He later studied in the Spanish Department at the University of Miami and has been teaching at the University of North Carolina at Greensboro for the past few years. He is probably the most prolific of the authors in exile with volumes of poetry (*Ritmo de Solá* [1967]), short stories (*Cuentos grises* [1966], *Cuentos del hombre* [1969], *Cuentos a luna llena* [1971]), plays, and literary criticism (*Las novelas de César Andreu Iglesias y la problemática puertorriqueña actual* [1968], *La temática nove-*

218 ANTIREVOLUTIONARY PROSE FICTION

Although all the antirevolutionary novels are anticommunist, only in some of the later ones do Communists actually appear as characters. The two best known of the antirevolutionary novelists, Luis Ricardo Alonso (b. 1929)[9] and Juan Arcocha (b. 1927),[10] both deal rather objectively with the inefficiency of the communist operation of factories in *Territorio libre* (1966) and *A Candle in the Wind* (1967). As in David Buzzi's revolutionary *Los desnudos* (1967), *Territorio libre* presents the reluctance of the factory workers to sacrifice their gains achieved through active unionism for the sake of the Revolution. The protagonist, Santiago, comments that the workers would be willing to "accept the hardships with better grace if they could at least enjoy the freedom they were provided. The hardest thing is putting up with the march toward Marx-cum-trujilloism . . . all the characteristics of an old-fashioned *caudillo* decked out with a Marxist fig leaf."[11] *Territorio*

219

lística de Alejo Carpentier [1969], *La nueva novela hispanoamericana y tres tristes tigres* [1971]), in addition to his two published novels (*Lilayando* [1971] and *Los cruzados de la aurora* [1972]) and others completed.

[9] Luis Ricardo Alonso was born in Asturias, Spain. He received a doctorate in civil law from the Universidad de La Habana and worked as a newspaperman before the Revolution. He was a member of the Partido del Pueblo Cubano, an *ortodoxo*. In the early years of the revolutionary government, he served as Cuban ambassador in Lima, Scandinavia, and London. He resigned in August 1965 and went into exile in the United States. He taught at the University of Miami and is now teaching at the Boston campus of the University of Massachusetts. He has published two other novels, *El candidato* (1970) and *Los dioses ajenos* (1972). *El candidato* is the account in diary form of an alienated Puerto Rican's plot to assassinate a presidential candidate who resembles Robert Kennedy.

[10] Juan Arcocha worked as a staff writer and assistant to Carlos Franqui during the latter's editorship of the newspaper *Revolución*. As a result of the June 1961 controversy over government censorship of *Lunes de Revolución*, Arcocha was sent to Moscow as a correspondent and married a Russian. His experiences there are narrated in *Por cuenta propia* (1970). Upon returning to Havana, he published a prorevolutionary, procommunist novel, *Los muertos andan solos* (1962). Reassigned to the Cuban Embassy in Paris, he later defected. Those 1962–1963 experiences form the basis of *La bala perdida* (1973), which, like *Por cuenta propia*, may be considered a nonfiction novel. Since 1965, Arcocha has been working in Paris for UNESCO and other UN agencies. A chapter of *A Candle in the Wind* entitled "La confusión," which was not overtly antirevolutionary, appeared in Nos. 22–23 (January–April 1964) of *Casa de las Américas*.

[11] Luis Ricardo Alonso, *Territorio libre*, p. 120. The English translation was published one year before the Spanish version.

libre and *A Candle in the Wind* also focus on the conflict between the communist administrators' demands for greater productivity and the technicians' criticism of the defective machinery sent by the Eastern European countries and the lack of spare parts.

Probably the least critical of the antirevolutionary novels is the most recently published, *El sitio de nadie* (December 1972) by Hilda Perera, author of the previously discussed *Mañana es 26* (1960). The title refers to the recognition by one of the upper-class protagonists, Teresa, of the positive aspects of the revolutionary changes even though they are threatening her own privileged position in society. Rather than criticize the Revolution, Hilda Perera seems to criticize the inability of the neurotic and unhappily married wealthy protagonists to adjust to the badly needed Revolution. Although the human dramas are poignantly presented, the novel is marred by an excessive number of main characters whose identities are further confused by the duplication of names and the shifting points of view.

With a worker rather than an intellectual as protagonist, *Un obrero de vanguardia* (1972) by Francisco Chao Hermida (b. 1925) is a more extensive account of the relationship between the urban proletariat and the governments of Batista and Fidel Castro, from April 1958 through the missile crisis of October 1962.[12] Although no more sophisticated than the other antirevolutionary novels, this work has a few distinct advantages: there is only one protagonist; the fictitious characters interact naturally with such historical figures as Fidel Castro, Blas Roca, and Aníbal Escalante; the author creates a good series of dramatic situations, and he subordinates the expression of his own political beliefs to the narration of the plot. The protagonist, the forty-year-old baker Mariano "Chano" Febles, is happily married and has

---

[12] Francisco Chao Hermida, the son of Spanish immigrants, spent part of his childhood in Galicia but attended school in Havana. After a brief stint as a university law student, he switched to journalism and was graduated from the Escuela Manuel Márquez Sterling. In addition to writing for *Bohemia* and *Diario Nacional*, Chao was director of public relations for the Confederación de Trabajadores de Cuba and general manager of Unión Radio. He broke with Fidel in early 1959 and went into exile in Mexico. Later, in the United States, he worked as an editorial writer for Radio Swan and Voz de los Estados Unidos. In 1965, he resigned his position and moved to Caracas in protest against the tribute paid to Che Guevara.

two children. As the book opens, he is involved in the urban guerrilla movement to overthrow Batista. When the April 1958 strike fails because of the opposition of the Eusebio Mujal-led Confederación de Trabajadores de Cuba, Chano and his fellow conspirators are arrested. While his colleagues are tortured, Chano is released thanks to the intervention of his neighbor, a mulatto police sergeant. After the triumph of the Revolution, Chano rises rapidly as a labor leader who enthusiastically endorses and at times even anticipates Fidel Castro's changing attitudes toward the Communists. A former Communist himself, Chano founds the first rehabilitation center for the Bay of Pigs invaders and later sends his children to school in the Soviet Union. After devising a successful plan to infiltrate the counterrevolutionary organization, Chano ultimately falls from grace when a revolutionary deserter fails to include him among the counterespionage agents he denounces. As in Guatemalan Carlos Manuel Pellecer's *Utiles después de muertos* (1966) (see part five), the protagonist is forced to sign a confession. Although Chano is sentenced to only two years, the author implies that he is killed shortly after arriving in the prison camp.

Three other novels, although not primarily devoted to communism, present other aspects of the problem. Alvaro de Villa's relatively dispassionate *El olor de la muerte que viene* (1968) presents the disenchantment with communism of Teresa, a Havana counterespionage agent.[13] Her brother returns from a trip to the Soviet Union, where he came into contact with young Russian dissidents, and convinces Teresa of the dehumanizing and totalitarian features of communism. In Celedonio González's (b. 1923) *Los primos* (1971), an opportunistic rabble-rousing local communist leader is put in his place, at least temporarily, by a veteran *guerrillero*, in a town near Santa Clara.[14] In *Refugiados* (1969) by Angel A. Castro (b. 1930), two university stu-

---

13 Alvaro de Villa is a newspaperman, humorist, and scriptwriter for radio and television who has been writing for *Bohemia Libre* since 1961 while residing in Miami. He has also written two unpublished novels, "Los olvidados" and "Los pobrecitos pobres."

14 Celedonio González was born in the province of Las Villas in 1923, and now resides in Miami. He has published a volume of short stories, *La soledad es una amiga que vendrá* (1971), and has written a second novel, "Los cuatro embajadores," still unpublished.

dents who are jailed in 1961 for demanding elections discover upon their release in 1963 that the university has been taken over by the Communists.[15]

One of the most frequently criticized aspects of the Communist regime is that loyalty to the state is placed before loyalty to one's own family. In . . . *Ya el mundo oscurece*, a twelve-year-old boy denounces his parents. The main conflict in *Territorio libre* is between Karelia's love for her husband and her devotion to communism, on which she had been raised by her father, a labor leader who was murdered before the Revolution. In Fowler's *En las garras de la paloma*, Inés informs against her own brother, who is subsequently executed. In Jorge Pérez's *Los Buenos*, a revolutionary major is responsible for the death of his two brothers, and he in turn is stabbed to death by his own mother. The fraternal conflict is treated with much greater complexity and subtlety in *El olor de la muerte que viene* and *A Candle in the Wind*. In the former, Julio Martín, who was raised almost as a twin brother of Jesús, rejected the whole family when his "father," Carlos, belatedly revealed to him that he was really the illegitimate child of Carlos's sister. When the rest of the family fled to Miami, Julio remained in Cuba and joined the counterespionage bureau. However, upon discovering that he was responsible for the death of his counterrevolutionary "brother," Jesús, he almost goes out of his mind and tries desperately to leave Cuba. In *A Candle in the Wind*, Luis, a member of the militia, argues with his engineer brother, Esteban, about the latter's role in the Revolution, even though he himself has his own doubts. Luis ultimately finds security as a revolutionary when he is mortally wounded at the Bay of Pigs, while Esteban and his family leave for Miami.

In most of the more impassioned antirevolutionary novels, not only the active counterrevolutionaries but also relatively innocent dissenters are punished by being sent to prison. Although sanitary conditions in the prisons are abominable and various techniques of mental torture

---

[15] Angel A. Castro received his law degree from the Universidad de La Habana in 1960, one year before migrating to the United States, where he has taught Spanish language and literature in several colleges. He has published two volumes of short stories: *Cuentos del exilio cubano* (1970) and *Cuentos yanquis* (1972).

are applied, there is no description of physical torture comparable to that of the 1959–1960 anti-Batista novels. Márquez y de la Cerra's *El gallo cantó* is perhaps the only exception: a woman prisoner is flogged by women officers before being shot.

Beyond their unanimous opposition to communism and Fidel Castro, the authors of these antirevolutionary novels reveal different points of view on a variety of issues. A racist attitude prevails in four and possibly five of the works, while the opposite stance is taken in *El grito*. In Díaz-Versón's . . . *Ya el mundo oscurece*, a young woman is imprisoned for refusing to "go out on a date with a revolutionary soldier of a race different from hers."[16] A Negro revolutionary officer is portrayed as having a large, red mouth: "The Negro who had formulated the question, also opened his large reddish mouth just as you open a slice of mammee, and made a kind of grin in approval of the olive-green-clad soldier's disgusting joke . . ."[17] In Angel Castro's *Refugiados*, Fidel Castro is criticized for fomenting revolution in other Latin American countries and among the Negroes in Cuba: ". . . mira los líos que ha formado en Guatemala, Argentina, República Dominicana, Haití, Venezuela, Perú, Bolivia, y aquí la rebelión de los negros."[18] Elections in Cuba are opposed by a mulatto, for whom the author expresses his disdain by using the diminutive -*ico*: "—¿Elecciones . . . ? ¿Para qué . . . ? preguntó un mulatico con uniforme de conductor o chófer de ómnibus."[19] In Raoul Fowler's *En las garras de la paloma*, a mulatto soldier tries to beat the sick protagonist with his rifle butt, and, after the latter is arrested, he is turned over to a jailer "of oriental features."[20] In *El gallo cantó*, Fernando, the director of a state farm, falls under suspicion when his wife flees Cuba, and he is interrogated by "un mulato gigantesco, con aspecto de gorila o de Drácula."[21] Juan Arcocha, whose revolutionary *Los muertos andan solos* celebrates the end of racial discrimination in Cuba, has the antirevolutionary wife

[16] Díaz-Versón, . . . *Ya el mundo oscurece*, p. 94.
[17] Ibid., p. 26.
[18] Angel A. Castro, *Refugiados*, p. 60.
[19] Ibid., p. 33.
[20] Fowler, *En las garras de la paloma*, p. 107.
[21] Márquez y de la Cerra, *El gallo cantó*, p. 47.

of his co-protagonist, Esteban, in *A Candle in the Wind* express fear of the Negroes along with fear of the Committees for the Defense of the Revolution.

It is ironic that the racism expressed in the above novels is similar to that found in some of the 1959–1960 revolutionary novels in which the Negroes are portrayed as having supported Batista. Although the revolutionary government has undoubtedly made great strides in overcoming racism in Cuba, some vestiges still remain.[22] One of the antirevolutionary novels, *El grito* (1966) by Orlando Núñez Pérez,[23] makes a point of identifying an anticommunist as a "strong, husky Negress"[24] and Antonio, the counterrevolutionary who has been in jail, as a mulatto.

In contrast to the 1959–1960 revolutionary novels, the protagonists of the antirevolutionary novels are not young, unmarried bourgeois activist university students, except in *Refugiados*, but, rather, they represent a broad spectrum of society. The only social type to appear in more than one novel is the public schoolteacher in . . . *Ya el mundo oscurece*, *El grito*, and *Territorio libre*. The former Batista officer in hiding, who is one of the minor characters in the revolutionary *En el año de enero* (1963) by José Soler Puig, is the hero of the very first antirevolutionary novel, Andrés Rivero Collado's *Enterrado vivo* (1960). Other antirevolutionary heroes range from the factory workers and bureaucrat in *Territorio libre* to the wealthy sugar plantation owner and lawyer in Fowler's *En las garras de la paloma* and the bank president's son and cabinet minister's daughter in *Los desposeídos* (1972) by Ramiro Gómez Kemp (b. 1914).[25]

---

[22] See Nelson Amaro and Carmelo Mesa-Lago, "Inequality and Classes," in *Revolutionary Change in Cuba*, ed. Carmelo Mesa-Lago, pp. 346–353.

[23] Orlando Núñez Pérez, a newspaperman, migrated to San José, Costa Rica, where he became President Figueres's press secretary and editor of *La República*.

[24] Orlando Núñez Pérez, *El grito*, p. 12.

[25] Ramiro Gómez Kemp published his first book, a volume of Afro-Cuban poetry, in 1934. He was active in the motion picture industry in Mexico between 1942 and 1946. In the years preceding the Revolution, he became one of the leading television producers in Cuba. Since leaving Cuba in 1960, he has worked in television in San Juan, Puerto Rico, and Caracas. He moved to Miami in 1965, where he is now teaching at Miami-Dade Junior College. In 1973, he published two other novels, *El Turpial* and

In three of the more ardent antirevolutionary works, the author's goal is to show that prerevolutionary rural conditions were not so bad as is generally claimed. By dint of hard work, virtuous conduct, and economizing, the families in Manuel Linares's *Los Ferrández* (1965), Pablo A. López's *Ayer sin mañana* (1969),[26] and Jorge T. Pérez's *Los Buenos* (1970) all improve their positions until the Revolution turns things topsy-turvy. *Los Ferrández* traces in idyllic *costumbrista* fashion three generations of the title family and then focuses on their demise with the advent of atheistic communism. Widespread discontent because of food shortages, confiscations, injustices, and the rule of the incompetent finally results in a popular uprising. The Bueno family in Jorge Pérez's novelette faces greater hardships in the prerevolutionary period but finally succeeds in buying its own parcel of land. After the Revolution, the father dies defending his land against the agrarian reform. In the still shorter novelette *Ayer sin mañana*, Pedro Ruiz, the son of a poor farmer, becomes a university professor and marries the wealthy landowner's daughter. His father-in-law's estate is intervened by the Revolution, and Pedro is arrested and subjected to mental torture until he dies in a prison hospital.

Of the four novels that deal primarily with counterrevolutionary plots and invasions, Manuel Cobo Sausa's *El cielo será nuestro* (1965), René G. Landa's *De buena cepa* (1967), Pedro Entenza's *No hay acera* (1969), and Alvaro de Villa's *El olor de la muerte que viene* (1968), only the latter identifies the social class of his protagonists. Jesús Martín, who was captured in the Bay of Pigs invasion, was later freed thanks to the efforts of his father, a self-made wealthy and honorable man who moved his family to Miami because of the Revolution. Whether seen from Miami or Havana, the Bay of Pigs invasion and the subsequent missile crisis play prominent roles in several of the novels, but particularly in *El cielo será nuestro* and *El olor de la muerte que viene*. In the former, the CIA is blamed for refusing to trust the Cuban exiles, and President Kennedy is criticized for not providing the in-

---

La garra y la carne, in both of which revolutionary politics and personal love affairs are intertwined dramatically in unidentifiable Latin American countries, with no specific references to the Cuban Revolution.

[26] Pablo A. López is professor of Spanish at Saint Leo College in Florida.

vaders with an air cover. The scene shifts back and forth from the counterrevolutionaries in Havana and the Escambray Mountains to the conspirators in Miami, the training camp near Retalhuleu in Guatemala, and the embarkation point of Puerto Cabezas in Nicaragua. In *El olor de la muerte que viene*, each chapter is preceded by a short day-to-day nonfiction chronicle of the missile crisis between October 20 and November 2, 1962. In a variation on the Bay of Pigs theme, *El gallo cantó* (1972) foresees the success of a future invasion due to the widespread unrest and sabotage among a variety of rural and urban sectors in Cuba, as well as to a new united exile organization "El Hombre Nuevo," pledged to a kind of Christian democracy.

The experiences of the Cuban refugees in Miami and other parts of the United States in *Refugiados, El cielo será nuestro, Los primos, El gallo cantó*, and *Los desposeídos* provide the opportunity for criticism of the consumer society with its dehumanized life, drug addiction, and sexual immorality. In fact, the protagonist of *Los primos* becomes so thoroughly disenchanted with the American capitalistic system that, after almost ten years in Miami, he decides to return to Cuba with his family even though he has no illusions about what awaits him. Likewise, the protagonist of *Los desposeídos*, after enjoying academic success at the University of Miami and brief financial success as the young vice-president of a large corporation, decides to abandon the land of heartless capitalism and immorality and begin life anew in Spain. A rather odd presentation of life outside Cuba distinguishes Emilio Fernández Camus's (b. 1897) *Caminos llenos de borrascas* (1962).[27] The story of an Italian immigrant family in New York, only a relatively small part of this work deals with the Cuban Revolution. Mario, the son of the restaurant-manager protagonist, meets a Communist in New York who converts him to the revolutionary cause. He goes to Mexico and participates in the struggle against Batista. With the triumph of the Revolution, he becomes a captain but dies fighting against the Bay of Pigs invaders. The narrator is opposed to all revolutions and expresses a pro-Batista, pro-Catholic point of view. He denies that there was social injustice in Cuba before the Revolution and deplores the

[27] Emilio Fernández Camus was professor of Roman law and philosophy of law and dean of the law school at the Universidad de La Habana.

fact that the Catholics were duped by the revolutionaries' wearing of medallions.

The dramatic escape from Cuba by boat is the exclusive theme of Eugenio Sánchez Torrentó's strongly Catholic *Francisco Manduley, la historia de un pescador de ranas* (1965),[28] while other equally dramatic escapes by boat or by plane to Miami constitute important episodes in *Los primos, Los desposeídos,* and *El grito.*

Into the Mainstream (?)

Although the above novels are interesting documents of the refugees' view of events in Cuba, the overwhelming majority of them cannot be considered serious works of literature. A reversal of this trend and the incorporation of the antirevolutionary novel into the Latin American mainstream may develop from the recent publication of Luis Ricardo Alonso's third novel, *Los dioses ajenos* (1971), Sánchez-Boudy's two recent works, *Lilayando* (1971) and *Los cruzados de la aurora* (1972), and Carlos Alberto Montaner's first novel, *Perromundo* (1972).

Although Alonso's novel has its flaws, it shares with many of the 1966–1970 revolutionary novels a panoramic scope and the use of experimental techniques, while, even more importantly, it differs from most of the antirevolutionary novels in its dispassionate tone and lack of sermonizing. Alonso is most successful in his presentation of the social panorama, the interaction of the many different types of Cuban refugees in Miami. Of the three university students who conspired against Batista, Carlos Gálvez is the most authentic human being. After the fall of Batista, he came to occupy an important position in the revolutionary government, but by 1967 he became disaffected because of the lack of democracy and escaped to Miami in a small boat. Once settled there, he conspires against the Castro government without compromising his political ideals with the former Batista supporters. The main novelistic conflict is between Carlos's love for Linda Howard

[28] Eugenio M. Sánchez Torrentó (b. 1926), newspaperman, radio announcer, and teacher, received a doctorate in education from the Universidad de La Habana and a doctorate in psychology from the Universidad de Camagüey. He also has an M.A. and an M.E. from the University of Miami. He has written six children's plays.

Ramos, who helped him outwit the Batista police in the first chapter, and his sense of obligation to his wife and two children. The conflict is further complicated by the fact that Linda's husband, a Protestant minister, is unjustly interned in a work camp for homosexuals in Cuba. Carlos's sense of duty prevails until the Reverend Ramos escapes to Miami. At that point, Carlos follows his true feelings and for a brief period enjoys an ecstatic love affair. Ultimately, Linda's sense of guilt, usually expressed in second-person monologues, overwhelms her, and she rejoins her husband even though it leads inevitably to her suicide.

Carlos's two companions lead equally tortured existences. Ernesto Salcedo is forced by the Communists in Cuba to become a counterespionage agent operating out of Miami. While he pretends to resume his friendship with Carlos, he sends information to Cuba about the counterrevolutionary raids, which causes the death of some of his own companions. Panchito Díaz, who lived a martyr's existence at the university in the late 1950's because of his father's high position in the police force, is arrested in the late 1960's by the Florida police for planning, together with Carlos and Ernesto, a raid against Cuba. As a result, he is sent to Vietnam, where, in an interior monologue, he muses over the tragedy of the absurd war.

Among a trio of older-generation representatives, only one adjusts successfully to the American way of life. Don Francisco Aspilicueta y Salsmendi, who inherited a thriving hardware business from his Basque grandfather, had no compunctions about changing his political affiliations from Prío Socarrás to Batista, and then to Fidel Castro. After arriving in Miami, he changes his name to Mr. Aspill and becomes a wealthy manufacturer of speedboats who refuses to aid the antirevolutionary conspirators.

More sympathetic treatment is accorded by the Asturias-born author to Anselmo León, the hardworking successful Spanish haberdasher who sincerely tries to adjust to the Revolution even after his store is confiscated. However, the hostility of the government bureaucrats to his integrity finally forces him to leave for Miami with his twin daughters. Unable to adjust to his new surroundings, he prefers to return to his native village in Asturias, where he anxiously awaits news from his daughters: one, a reformed prostitute turned factory worker; the other, a nun who leaves the Order when church officials adopt a conciliatory attitude toward the Revolution.

One of the more tragic figures in the novel is Col. Clotilde Díaz, in spite of his previous responsibility for the torturing of revolutionary heroes Carlos and Ernesto. Through a series of interior monologues, the author shows Díaz's indebtedness to Batista for having raised him from his poor rural background to a position of power and wealth in Havana. Because of his age, he is unable to find work in Miami and resorts to selling birds and stealing mangoes. He feels so humiliated that he decides to return to Cuba even though it will mean almost certain death. When this endeavor also fails and he is "rescued" by the United States Coast Guard, all hope for him disappears and he soon dies in the hospital.

The gallery of refugee types in *Los dioses ajenos* also includes the professional politician, the mother who refuses to believe that her son has been executed, and the eight-year-old singer-beggar who lives in the bars while his mother remains in Cuba hoping in vain for her husband's release from prison. The lives of all the above characters are interwoven, some better than others, and most of the novel's forty-four chapters consist of short alternating scenes based to a large extent on dialogue. The most notable exception is chapter 10, an independent short story about an anonymous and alienated Cuban's absurd but tragic search for a nonexistent subway station in the Boston area. The story is somewhat reminiscent of Juan José Arreola's famous "El guardagujas."

In addition to the scenes that take place in Miami and Cuba between roughly 1958 and 1968, the author attempts to expand the geographical and chronological scope of the novel by the displacement of certain characters already mentioned and by the interpolation of interior-monologue childhood scenes. Col. Clotilde Díaz recalls the heroic death of his father in the War of Independence against Spain, while Carlos remembers his childhood protest against police brutality under dictator Machado. Although the muralistic Dos Passos–like approach at times leads the author to include extraneous material and the experimental techniques occasionally appear forced, the total effect of *Los dioses ajenos* is that of a serious novel aimed at recording the human

dramas triggered by revolutionary events in Cuba as well as by political, economic, social, and cultural conditions in the United States in
the late 1960's.

Far less pretentious than *Los dioses ajenos*, Sánchez-Boudy's *Lilayando* is a very shortened Miami version of *Tres tristes tigres*. With
no plot and even less character development than in Cabrera Infante's
novel, Sánchez-Boudy has strung together a delightful series of loosely
related anonymous dialogues in the picturesque vernacular of the
Cuban exiles in Miami. Although language is definitely the protagonist, with the emphasis on puns, the contents of the dialogues—social
gossip and problems of acculturation—do provide sociological insight
into the character of the speakers and the society in which they live.
There are relatively few allusions to the political situation in Cuba,
although one of the notable exceptions is the poem "Las toxinas y la
dieta balanceada," a satire of the Cuban government's justification of
the food shortages. As in *Tres tristes tigres*, remarks are made about
the author's colleagues—Sánchez-Boudy puts in a plug for Celedonio
González's *Los primos*—and the antinovel ends on a note of self-
appraisal:

> —Negra, shall I pick you up to go to the dressmaker?
> —O.K., sure. I've just finished that novel that Salvat is selling,
> *Lilayando*.
> —What did you think of it?
> —Me? You could add thousands of pages to it and make an
> infinite novel, one that never ends.
> —Then it's like this life of ours here in the U.S.: it never
> ends.[29]

Sánchez-Boudy's second novel, *Los cruzados de la aurora*, also inspired by the new Latin American novel, has greater literary pretensions, which, however, fall short of the mark. As in Carpentier's story
"Semajante a la noche," Sánchez-Boudy presents chronological variations of one basic situation. However, unlike Carpentier, Sánchez-
Boudy does not give equal time to each of the chronological periods.
Most of the novel takes place during the puritanical dictatorship of

[29] José Sánchez-Boudy, *Lilayando*, p. 80.

John Calvin in sixteenth-century Geneva, Switzerland.[30] The hero is the Spanish Catholic physician and theologian Michael Servetus (1511–1553), who dies for the cause of truth and freedom. The roles of oppressor and freedom fighter recur in all societies, and Servetus recognizes himself as being centuries old: "I feel very old, really very old, as if I had lived for many generations. As if I had been in Greece at the time of the tyrants."[31] However, the brief scenes that actually take place in Greek, biblical, and Roman times are insufficiently developed to the point of seeming very contrived. Likewise, Calvin's Comandante Fadel, his "policía roja,"[32] his campaign against homosexuals, and the blockade by imperialistic France are such obvious allusions to the Cuban situation of the 1960's that the picture of the Geneva dictatorship never comes into real focus. The novel is further marred by the gratuitous references to Don Quixote, Negro slaves in the United States, IBM centers, and the dates 1890 and 1970.

A much more successful attempt to universalize the Cuban experience is Carlos Alberto Montaner's (b. 1943) *Perromundo* (1972), the single best novel produced by the antirevolutionary exiles.[33] Utilizing a variety of experimental techniques, Montaner concentrates on the brutality of prison life in the tradition of Dostoevsky's *House of the Dead*, Federico Gamboa's *La llaga*, José Revueltas's *Los muros de agua*, Miguel Angel Asturias's *El Señor Presidente*, José María Arguedas's *El Sexto*, Solzhenitsyn's *A Day in the Life of Ivan Denisovich*, and José León Sánchez's *La isla de los hombres solos*. Although the setting is obviously the Cuba of Fidel Castro, Montaner denationalizes his novel by not mentioning the names of any Cuban historical figures and by avoiding the use of Cuban dialect. The novel is further decubanized by a discreet number of references to other historical examples of

[30] For some inexplicable reason, the author consistently uses "Génova" (Genoa, Italy) instead of "Ginebra" (Geneva, Switzerland).

[31] José Sánchez-Boudy, *Los cruzados de la aurora*, p. 24.

[32] Ibid., p. 33.

[33] Carlos Alberto Montaner studied and taught at the University of Miami before moving to Puerto Rico and, in 1970, to Madrid, where he writes a newspaper column and is the literary director of a publishing house. He has published two volumes of short stories, *Póker de brujas* (1968) and *Instantáneas al borde del abismo* (1970), and edited a collection of essays on the Revolution, *Diez años de revolución cubana* (1970).

man's brutality toward his fellow man from the times of Hammurabi and the ancient Greeks up through Nazi Germany. Rather than comment politically on the Cuban situation, Montaner prefers to examine the reactions of different human beings to the infernolike violence of prison life.

By judiciously alternating first-, second-, and third-person narrative, Montaner achieves excellent balance between his individual protagonist, Ernesto Carrillo, and the other inhabitants of the inferno. Carrillo is both a real human being and the vehicle for expressing the book's moral dilemma: the validity of violent opposition to injustice and oppression. Montaner proposes a somewhat ambiguous solution. Although Carrillo has many of the characteristics of other prison-novel heroes, his resistance to all attempts by the prison officials to "rehabilitate" him leads only to his ultimate execution and the prolonged suffering of his followers. Just as Carrillo's heroics are attributed to his *luzbelismo*, the argument for resisting to the bitter end is also responsible for destroying his idyllic love affair with Marcia, who later defends her right to continue searching for happiness. During the terroristic campaign against the previous government of Batista, Carrillo's shooting of Police Captain Azcárate at close range in a movie theater is comparable to his own death at the hands of Lieutenant Wong, who forces his victims to look into the cannon of his revolver before firing. On the other hand, Carrillo's final statement that "all that remains of me as a man is my resistance"[34] and his being compared to Jesus— only twelve others of the original twelve hundred have survived the ordeal—tend to tip the scales in favor of a positive interpretation of his stance.

Although none of the supporting cast threatens Carrillo's role as protagonist, several are sufficiently individualized to stand out as characters in their own right. Moleón, the silent, impenetrable, rocklike peasant, is Carrillo's Saint Peter. It is, significantly, his wife who makes possible Vilar's tragicomic escape disguised as the fourteen-year-old son of one of the prisoners on visitors' day. Dr. Taboada is psychologically crucified by his fellow prisoners when they discover his latent

---

[34] Carlos Alberto Montaner, *Perromundo*, p. 206.

homosexualism. In one of the novel's most dramatic scenes, Taboada is dissuaded from blowing up the whole prison block by the quixotic Quijano, only to be shot seconds later, along with Quijano, by the prison guards. The cowardly student Llorente actually does commit suicide rather than betray his friends by accepting the rehabilitation offer. On the other hand, Musiú, the old one-armed Haitian witch doctor, has his face smashed in with a paving stone while he is asleep for having deserted his companions. Among the prison officials, the sadistic Lieutenant Wong and Horacio Barniol, the new director who institutes the rehabilitation plan, are sufficiently delineated to allow them to take their places alongside the several individualized victims.

The contrast between Lieutenant Wong and Director Barniol and between Carrillo's *luzbelismo* and his "crucifixion" in the beginning and final pages of the novel—". . . the Judas phase . . . Thirteen of us are left"[35]—is also reflected in the contrast between the moments of human compassion and the prevailing tone of violence. In addition to those instances of violence already mentioned, the following scenes, all experienced directly by Carrillo, are equally unforgettable: standing for three consecutive days in the tiny solitary-confinement cell, cleaning out the rat-infested muddy prison basement, and suffocating in the sealed truck that transports the remaining fifty holdouts to the sugar-cane fields. Whereas many of the violent scenes are reminiscent of Cela's *tremendismo* and Buñuel's surrealism, some of the stylistic techniques are derived from Asturias's *El Señor Presidente*, particularly the repetition of words, syllables, and letters in order to create the impression of terror:

—It's uuseless . . . God has diied on my chessst.
—Lieutenant, it's 5 A.M. already, let's put the wooden suit on that son of a bitch.
CUT!
They heard, pity for Mario. Pity, yes. Pity, damn it. Mario, no. Pity. I heard it. I tell you I heard it. God was shouting. He had died on him. Me lying down. God lying down. God shouting lying down. Me there. There lying down. There God. Mario there. Pity, damn it. Pity. Twenty-five. And then fear. Mario fear. God fear. Fear lying down, shots. One big one, then a

[35] Ibid., p. 13.

little one. Coup de grâce. Thanks death. Thanks night. God cold. God of mine. My eyes. My red frightened eyes. Who brought those eyes? Who brought them red? Who brought them, eyes? No, Mario, pity, damn it, pity. Six, a big shot. A little one. Thanks shot. Grace of lead. Grace of blood. Grace of death. Mario, of death. Of God who is dying. Pity. Ha. Pity. Ha. Pity. Pity. Pitiha. Pitihaha. Pitihahaha. Mario. Twenty-five. No, my eyes. Red. Frightened.[36]

The filming instructions—CUT!—printed in large capitals indicates not only the occasional use of motion-picture techniques in the novel but also an example of how the violent tone of the novel is intensified by the use of alternating kinds of type: roman for first- and third-person narrative, boldface for second-person narrative, italics for recollections of the past, and large capitals for stage directions. The final moments preceding Carrillo's death are made more dramatic by alternating fragments of first- and second-person narrative placed respectively on the right- and left-hand sides of the page with the words of Director Barniol in large capitals normally across the whole page. The impression of violence is not achieved by the use of any single technique but rather by the abrupt and unexpected changes in style. Although *Perromundo* differs from *El Señor Presidente* in that the characters are predominantly real human beings rather than infernally grotesque puppets, Montaner occasionally surprises his reader by introducing some Asturias-like monsters: ". . . A flattened face appeared with a gigantic half-moon scar under his nose. He was followed by a long, filthy, blackish, hairy figure belonging to the spider family. A little fat fairy with a big nose and reddish cheeks. An Aztec god, mysterious, priestlike. A lewd face, with a hand in his pocket. A smell of whiskey enclosed in a big-bellied semidwarf. Another one with heretical baldness (Leninesque baldness, Nazarene glow). A small Negro bongo player fallen on hard times . . ."[37]

In keeping with Cortázar, Cabrera Infante, Sarduy, and other new novelists, Montaner comments on the creative process of his own novel —but infrequently:

[36] Ibid., pp. 34–35.
[37] Ibid., p. 135.

... Both of us, you think, have to play at old-time literature, have to play at the old-time novel with its hero, its villain, its plot, its deadly conflict, and its denouement. Except that the point of view produces two separate novels. You, the hero of yours; Barniol, the hero of his. He, your villain in your fiction. You, his villain in his. His novel is about the efficiency with which an intelligent official handles a dangerous group of antisocial rebels until he reincorporates them into society ... Your plot is different. It's about a man who has been half-dead for many years, who only feels alive when he is rebelling, refusing, clenching his fists ... You're Lucifer, Ernesto, you're an incorrigible Lucifer.[38]

The judicious adaptation of the above new literary techniques as well as the avoidance of strident anticommunism give *Perromundo* a literary stature unequalled by its antirevolutionary predecessors and one that cannot be ignored by critics of Latin American literature.

II. The Short Story

A Mirror of the Antirevolutionary Novel

An analysis of the twenty or more volumes of antirevolutionary short stories reveals the same characteristics as those of the majority of the antirevolutionary novels. Such titles as *Cuatro cuentos cristianos* (1964), *Rojo y negro, cuentos sobre la tragedia cubana* (1964), *Castro quedó atrás* (1970), and *Cuentos del exilio cubano* (1970) by nonprofessional authors Pedro Ernesto Díaz, Andrés Rivero Collado, José Saínz de la Peña, and Angel A. Castro discourage serious consideration of these works. The one exception is the unpretentious little volume *Los unos, los otros ... y el seibo* (1971) by Beltrán de Quirós. Its twelve two-page stories describe conditions in a UMAP (Unidades Militares de Ayuda a la Producción) camp between 1965 and 1968 in Camagüey Province. The protest against the loss of freedom, the hard work in the canefields, and the ineffective revolutionary methods is convincingly expressed in a direct, sincere, unimpassioned low-key style

[38] Ibid., pp. 92–93.

and by means of nonviolent plots. Another thin volume that deserves special mention at this point is Carlos Ripoll's (b. 1922) *Julián Pérez por Benjamín Castillo* (1970), a delightful spoof of literary censorship based on the Padilla-Arrufat incident.[39] The story involves a confrontation between the spirit of José Martí, in the person of Julián Pérez, and Fidel Castro, ending in the latter's violent death at the hands of his own men. However, the most noteworthy feature of the volume is not its story but its physical format, which is exactly the same as that of the Casa de las Américas prize-winning volumes.

Three Professionals: Novás, Ferreira, Casey

Whereas Juan Arcocha is the only one of the relatively well known novelists in exile to have published an antirevolutionary novel—and only in English—three distinguished short-story writers have published several antirevolutionary stories that are worthy of comment.

Lino Novás Calvo (b. 1903), whose volume *La luna nona y otros cuentos* (1942) was called by Cuban critic Ambrosio Fornet in 1967 "el libro más importante de nuestra cuentística,"[40] published nine antirevolutionary stories in *Bohemia Libre*,[41] *Revista de Occidente*,[42] and *Exilio*[43] between December 1961 and 1968, and republished them in the volume *Maneras de contar* in 1970 along with some of his more

---

[39] Carlos Ripoll received a degree in agronomy from the Universidad de La Habana, an M.A. from the University of Miami, and a Ph.D. from New York University. For several years he has been teaching Spanish American literature at Queens College in New York. He has published a study of the *Revista de Avance*, an edition of Carlos Loveira's novel *Juan Criollo*, and two anthologies: *Conciencia intelectual de América, antología del ensayo hispanoamericano* (1966) and, in collaboration with Andrés Valdespino, *Teatro hispanoamericano* (1972).

[40] AF-1, p. 38. After leaving Cuba in September 1960, Novás Calvo became one of the assistant directors of *Bohemia Libre* in New York. Since 1967, he has been teaching Latin American literature at Syracuse University.

[41] "Un buchito de café" (December 13, 1961), "El milagro" (April 29, 1962), "Fernández al paredón" (May 27, 1962), "La abuela Reina y el sobrino Delfín" (July 8, 1962), "El hombre-araña" (May 12, 1963), and "Nadie a quien matar" (May 12, 1963).

[42] "La noche en que Juan tumbó a Pedro" (3 [September 1965]).

[43] "Un 'bum'" (Winter 1965) and "Una cita en Mayanima" (Summer 1968). A tenth story, "La vaca en la azotea," was published in *Papeles de Son Armadans* (March 1973).

famous earlier stories. Although these new stories fall below the literary quality of "La noche de Ramón Yendía," "La luna nona," "Long Island," and "Aquella noche salieron los muertos," Novás is still a skilled craftsman who is able to create suspense and maintain the reader's interest until the very end of the story. The most frequent themes are the death of innocent people at the hands of the revolutionaries in 1959, and even earlier, and the subsequent revenge sought and often consummated by counterrevolutionaries against those who had betrayed them. Two of the first stories not only criticize the revolutionaries' wanton violence but also actually defend three consecrated villainous types. "Un buchito de café" is unique in its criticism of the way Fidel Castro's guerrillas treated a family of peasants on the road leading to the Sierra Maestra. Food and animals are taken arbitrarily, and the whole family is machine-gunned by a nervous revolutionary officer who wrongly suspects the mother of having served him and his men poisoned coffee. By contrast, the narrator, who is the lone survivor, is saved by the rural police and a few years later escapes to the United States with the aid of the benign neighboring landowner. In "Fernández al paredón," an innocent Batista policeman is executed by a revolutionary firing squad directed by his own illegitimate son, whom he had previously saved from the police.

Although the following two stories are equally critical of revolutionary violence, their literary value is somewhat enhanced by a touch of the same magic realism characteristic of "La noche de Ramón Yendía." In "El milagro," the protagonist, a professor, anticipates that he will be executed unjustly by the triumphant revolutionaries. His imminent death occurs ironically at the same time that his crippled wife overcomes her psychological block and walks again after hearing Fidel Castro say on television: "Now you'll see how I walk unarmed through the people."[44]

"La abuela Reina y el sobrino Delfín" is the broadest in scope of Novás's antirevolutionary stories and probably would have been better as a novel. Rather than concentrating on one individual, which he does

---

[44] *Bohemia Libre*, April 29, 1962, p. 83. In the new version of the story, Fidel's words are reduced to "Voy a avanzar entre el pueblo . . ." (Lino Novás Calvo, *Maneras de contar*, p. 242).

in most of his better stories, Novás presents the disintegration of an entire family during the first three years of the revolutionary government. In a letter written to her sister in New York, María tells how Uncle Martín died in a foolhardy defense of his hardware store against the government confiscation order. Teresita burned herself alive after discovering that her fiancé, a government spy, informed against all their friends. The servants took over the house, civil service employees were dismissed, bank accounts were confiscated, religious instruction was prohibited, there is a shortage of everything, and counterrevolutionary activities have increased in the mountains, on the sugar plantations, and in the city. Although the entire narrative is in the form of a letter, reality is transformed into fantasy by the constant presence of the half-crazed grandmother, who swears to get revenge when her nephew comes down from the mountains. Both narrator and reader are left in a state of disbelief when he actually appears.

Revenge, in an increasingly concentrated form, is a dominant theme in the five other stories. "El hombre-araña," published in 1963 but written in 1960, resembles "La abuela Reina y el sobrino Delfín" in its relatively broad scope and its magic realism. The title refers to the long-limbed revolutionary leader of a group of scholarship students who is shot by the narrator for having an affair with his wife. Since the narrator was subjected to two or three mock executions before being led to Miami in a small boat by the very same members of the execution squad, part or all of the episode of the "spider man" might have been a hallucination. This interpretation is further encouraged by the author's reserving for the final page the information that the narrator is telling the story from a Miami hospital. Although the tension builds as the narrator plots his revenge against the "spider man," the first few pages, which contrast the idyllic life of the narrator in the 1950's with the cataclysmic effects of the Revolution, detract from the story's unity.

In the next four stories, the author seems to assume that the Revolution is evil, and, therefore, he no longer includes gratuitous political comments. In "Nadie a quien matar" (1963), from the first to the last line, attention is focused on how Dr. Lauro Aranguren died. The replacement of the linear chronology of the earlier stories by a more "circular" chronology—the gradual filling in of details to explain how the protagonist arrived at his present situation—also heightens the concentration. The title refers to the doctor's frustration at not being able to kill the three informers who were responsible for his having spent two years in the Isla de los Pinos prison, during which time his wife died and his father-in-law took his children to Spain. He cannot kill them, because they have escaped to the United States. Knowing that he has only weeks or months to live, the half-crazed doctor decides to wreak revenge on the unknown family that occupies his former home. However, before Dr. Aranguren can fire his gun, he is shot by the present homeowner, who, in a surprise ending, turns out to be his apolitical step-brother, Romilio, a mechanic who had been his only friend and who had given him a place to sleep in his shop. That this is the true version of Dr. Aranguren's death is confirmed by the final, and not totally credible, revelation of the narrator's identity: Romilio.

"Una cita en Mayanima," less pretentious artistically, also depends heavily on a surprise ending. Ricardo Pallares, a counterrevolutionary who had fought in the Sierra Maestra against Batista, is pursued through the streets of Havana as he impatiently waits out the hours before the rendezvous that his wife has arranged in order for both of them to escape to the United States. As the appointed time approaches, Ricardo is irresistibly drawn to the home of his sister and brother-in-law, whom he hates with a vengeance because of their self-seeking violent revolutionary posture. With great satisfaction, he shoots his brother-in-law and then proceeds to the rendezvous. He is dumbfounded to find his sister there. In the last line of the story, Ricardo's wife tells him that they are waiting for his brother-in-law who had made the arrangements for the escape.

Revenge is the even more exclusive theme of the two stories that take place in New York City: "La noche en que Juan tumbó a Pedro" (1965) and "Un 'bum' " (1965). The former is based on the revenge taken by a *guajiro* on an ex-revolutionary sergeant within a detective-story framework, but, as the author himself recognizes, "it brings together incongruent elements artificially."[45] "Un 'bum,' " on the other hand, involves only two characters and is clearly inspired by Edgar Allan Poe's "The Cask of Amontillado," a volume that the victim's

[45] Novás Calvo, *Maneras de contar*, p. 263.

eyes happen to light on in the protagonist's office. From a chance meeting on the subway on a cold Sunday morning, Jorge Pallares takes sweet revenge on the unscrupulous Lucio Corbeta for having stolen his life's savings, sent his books and pictures to the museum, and turned his home over to another family. Pallares walks Corbeta through the snow-covered streets of lower Manhattan, pointing out some of the sights and conversing about mutual Cuban acquaintances in an apparently friendly manner. The tension builds as the author presents Pallares's thoughts, simultaneously, in italics. Although Corbeta's thoughts are not presented, his growing mistrust is clearly conveyed. In a well-executed ending, Pallares finally kills Corbeta in a lonely construction site, returns home pleased, and three or four days later reads in the newspaper about the discovery of the corpse, one of four that have been found in the snow in the last few days. The concentration on one single episode is enhanced by the use of the third-person omniscient narrator, a linear structure, and a relatively terse style in which the preterite tense predominates. Because of the New York setting and the concentration on the one act of revenge, the author's critical attitude toward revolutionary Cuba comes across in a lower key than in the other stories but is equally if not more effective. In fact, the many different ways in which the revenge theme is handled in these nine antirevolutionary stories complement the varied techniques of Novás's nine other stories in *Maneras de contar* and bear witness to his professional virtuosity expressed in the volume's title.

Ten years after Novás published his *La luna nona y otros cuentos* (1942), his younger fellow Galician Ramón Ferreira (b. 1921) published *Tiburón y otros cuentos* (1952), which, together with Ezequiel Vieta's *Aquelarre* (1954), is considered by Ambrosio Fornet one of the two best volumes of Cuban short stories of the decade.[46] In October 1960, Ferreira left his position as advertising manager for General Electric and went into exile in Mexico and, subsequently, Puerto Rico. His story "Sueño sin nombre," which was written in 1958, received honorable mention in the competition sponsored by *Life en español* and was published in *Ceremonia secreta y otros cuentos de América*

---

[46] AF-1, p. 43.

Latina (1961). It is probably the only Cuban work that expresses a somewhat ambiguous attitude toward the urban terrorism directed against Batista. Although the usual critical view of Havana in 1958 is presented replete with policemen, prostitutes, and American tourists, the revolutionaries also are apparently criticized for inveigling an innocent twelve-year-old boy to place a bomb in front of a department store. The story is based less on the conflict between the two opposing political forces than on the symbolic death of the boy's idealized woman and its possible traumatic effects on his future life.

"Sueño sin nombre" is one of nine stories that comprise Ferreira's 1969 volume *Los malos olores de este mundo*. Published by the Fondo de Cultura Económica in Mexico City and sporting a brief preface by John Dos Passos, this volume does not enhance Ferreira's reputation. With the exception of the title story, the selections were written during the last years of the Batista regime and could be considered prorevolutionary. The most common theme is man's moral degradation, particularly in sexual matters. The nightmarish quality and the possible influence of Kafka, Hemingway, and Poe to which Dos Passos alludes place them in the same category as some of the 1961–1965 existentialist novels and short stories, except that Ferreira shows less concern for identifying the situations of his characters with the Cuban political background.

"Los malos olores de este mundo," which is more a novella—it has eighty pages—than a short story, reflects the author's lack of confidence in the Revolution's ability to change human nature and to alleviate the tragic conditions of the urban poor. The anonymous protagonist is an illiterate gravedigger during the Batista dictatorship whose wife, Eneida, gives birth to daughters only. After suffering an injury, he loses his job to a friend of the bishop. His brother, a revolutionary, finds work for him as a garbage collector. The second part starts in 1959 with boundless enthusiasm for the Revolution. Food is distributed to the poor, and better housing and jobs are promised. The protagonist, now tubercular, attempts to enter the hospital, but he is turned away because of the shortage of beds. He is then taken by his brother, now a sergeant in the revolutionary army, to bury dead dogs in the patio of a veterinarian whose house has been confiscated. For this work, he receives only half of what his brother had promised him. Thoroughly disgusted with life, he returns home determined to commit suicide by igniting a can of gasoline with the candle from a religious image. In a totally unexpected and unjustified "happy" ending, the breeze blows out the candle, and Eneida still hopes that they will be able to produce a baby boy.

Among the short-story writers who came into prominence in the early 1960's with the Revolution, Calvert Casey (1924–1969) was undoubtedly the most esteemed, on the basis of his one previously discussed volume, *El regreso* (1962). In mid-1965, he left Cuba convinced that his presence there was no longer desirable: "He often repeated to me that if he left the island he did so because of unbearable pressures directed especially against his intellectual activity, in a drive to make him understand, he thought, that his presence on the island was no longer necessary or desirable. This, feeling alienated from a great movement of moral transformation with whose ideology he obviously agreed, made him feel even more lonely than ever."[47] The pretext for his leaving was a trip to Poland on the occasion of the publication in Polish of *El regreso*. From there, he made his way to Paris, Madrid, and Rome, where he committed suicide in May 1969.

The Kafka-like anguish that prevails in many of Casey's early stories is also present in *Notas de un simulador*, published in Barcelona in January 1969. The volume consists of the eighty-page title story, divided into nineteen chapters, and four average-size stories. Only two of the latter may be considered as antirevolutionary, "In partenza" and "Polacca brillante."[48] The former describes the strange farewell séance prepared for the narrator by his cook, Angela. The guests are her friends, rather than his, and include a portly *mulata* and her black son, a blonde and her young daughter, and an elderly Negress. The fresh-smelling flowers, incense, soft lights, and hermetically closed balcony doors create the proper atmosphere for a religious ceremony, from

---

[47] Vicente Molina-Foix, "En la muerte de Calvert Casey," *Insula*, nos. 272–273 (July–August 1969), p. 40.

[48] As an indication of the relative freedom that existed in Cuba in 1966, "In partenza" was published in *Casa de las Américas* 6, no. 34 (January–February 1966): 109–110.

which the narrator's clearest recollection is the young Negro's accusing
his mother of being a man. She finally admits that this is true and friv-
olously declares that she hates the narrator. The vagueness of this
homosexual incident reflects the vagueness of the insinuated motives
for the author's overseas departure from what is presumably, but not
explicitly, Havana: "Wonderful Angela, how you were worried about
this short sentimental trip for which you saw me get ready without
enthusiasm, rather with a certain sadness, afraid of the real reasons
that were impelling me to cross the ocean."[49] The final paragraph
breaks the tension of the séance and returns to the feigned casual tone
with which the narrator began the story. From the burning of a large
cross dipped in alcohol, the narrator, without any transition, recalls
how in the stormy Bay of Biscay he forgot the magic song that Angela
had taught him to use in just such moments.

A very different and much more complex and effective treatment of
the departure scene characterizes "Polacca brillante." In only four and
one-half pages, Casey succeeds in creating a truly Kafkaesque mood
based on the narrator's preparations to leave Poland. When the unidentified persons who are supposed to escort him out of the country fail to
appear, his mental anguish causes his language to become distorted to
the point of combining self-contradictory verbal forms and temporal
adverbs: "the children were running tomorrow,"[50] "the aristocratic
brothers who will take me to dinner last night."[51] These examples of
oxymoron heighten the reader's awareness of the other less obtrusive
examples. The cold night in May of the first paragraph establishes the
general setting, but reality is transformed into nightmare with the appearance in the fourteenth paragraph of the blinding sun. The intensification of the narrator's despair is reflected in the seasons' being out
of joint, as well as the time of day: "Huge yellow leaves fall from the
trees and a warm smell of smoldering leaves arrives from the other
side of the river. Exhausted by the summer, the people abandon the
city. The heat is overwhelming. A snowflake rolls down my neck, I feel
the first shiver: from the crust of ice rises an icy draft. A yellowish

49 Calvert Casey, *Notas de un simulador*, p. 117.
50 Ibid., p. 98.
51 Ibid., p. 99.

moon shines weakly. In full sunshine, the blackbird repeats its call. Its eyes stare at me through the acacias."[52] This paragraph is framed by the two-word self-contradictory phrase in Polish "Meski Damski," meaning "masculine feminine."

The individual's loneliness is emphasized by the deserted streets and sidewalks and by references to the ancient wall with its niche containing two images of the Virgin Mary and one dying candle. The only remaining inhabitants of the city are the hotel porter, who offers silently to watch the narrator's one piece of luggage, and the barber, who, before going home, sweeps up the blond, brown, and white hairs.

The nightmarish polonaise, or polacca, ends with a rousing crescendolike description of the ball at the Sala Leopoldina, which is abruptly doused by the final oxymoron "dazzling ashes": ". . . of the ticket for the ball, the ball, of the Leopoldina Ballroom, ah, of the splendid of the splendid Leopoldina Ballroom (I'm sure) of the splendid Leopoldina Ballroom only dazzling ashes remain."[53]

Escapism

Among the Cuban exiles, as well as among the writers living in Cuba, the short story is apparently better suited for escapist themes than the novel. The six authors to be discussed briefly in this section represent three of the four literary generations that have been active in the 1959–1972 period, and their stories cover a broad range of non-revolutionary themes. Conspicuous by its absence is science fiction, which was one of the favorite escapist genres in Cuba during the mid-1960's.

The most famous of these writers is clearly Lydia Cabrera (b. 1900), whose *Cuentos negros de Cuba* (1940) and *Por qué . . .* (1948) constitute, along with Nicolás Guillén's poetry, the finest examples of Afro-Cuban literature. After a silence of over twenty years, she published in 1971, in Miami, *Ayapá: Cuentos de Jicotea*. Somewhat more diverse than her previous collections, this group of nineteen stories combines elements of Afro-Cuban folklore with universal-type fables and *costumbrista* scenes from nineteenth-century Cuba. The constant

[52] Ibid., p. 98.
[53] Ibid., p. 99.

ANTIREVOLUTIONARY PROSE FICTION

heroine is Jicotea, a weak ugly turtle with whom the Negroes identified because she consistently outwitted her more powerful neighbors like the lion, the tiger, and the elephant.

Julio Matas (b. 1931), professor of literature at the University of Pittsburgh, appears to be equally escapist whether writing in Cuba or the United States.[54] His 1971 volume *Erinia* consists of the ten stories of *Catálogo de imprevistos*, published in 1963 in Havana, plus nine new stories. All nineteen stories fall into one of two categories: the short story of the cruel-absurd variety of Virgilio Piñera and the longer stories involving the abnormal psychology of impotent men and frigid women with a dash of the fantastic. Only "Carambola del 57," one of the newer stories, is related to the Revolution by its implied criticism of the Batista police.

A much more impassioned antirevolutionary (cf. his novel *Los cruzados de la aurora*) than Julio Matas, José Sánchez-Boudy (b. 1928) has nevertheless published three volumes of short stories, *Cuentos grises* (1966), *Cuentos del hombre* (1969), and *Cuentos a luna llena* (1971), which have nothing at all to do with the Revolution. The total of seventy-four stories are all relatively short (three to five short pages) and for the most part depend on unexpected endings, which are not always convincing. The majority of the *Cuentos grises* are based on *criollista* themes but without an authentic *criollista* setting. *Cuentos del hombre* deals with a greater variety of themes and locales, with a few stories taking place in Spain and the United States respectively. *Cuentos a luna llena* reveals a predilection for the Poe terror story, episodes from unidentified wars, and abnormal psychology. Even in the very few stories that obviously take place in Cuba, there is no attempt to create either the geographical or the historical setting.

In the volumes by Asela Gutiérrez Kann and Matías Montes Huidobro (b. 1931), a few antirevolutionary stories are appended to the

---

[54] Julio Matas studied law at the Universidad de La Habana and was active in the Cuban theater movement as actor, director, and author. In 1956, he staged Ionesco's *The Bald Soprano*. After beginning his doctoral studies at Harvard, Matas returned to Cuba in 1959 as director of the National Cuban Theater. He worked in both theater and television until 1965, when he went into exile and completed his Ph.D. at Harvard.

escapist majority.[55] The former's *Las pirañas y otros cuentos cubanos* is a collection of fourteen stories, twelve of which are nostalgic sketches of the tender and humorous aspects of prerevolutionary life, mainly in the Casalba district across the bay from Havana. A variety of racial types are depicted, with some of the more colorful characters being Spanish and Greek immigrants. The time span is from 1926 to the early years of the Revolution. In the twelfth story, "La isla de acíbar," the execution of one of the Greek's sons in the Cabaña is the motive for recalling a 1958 party in which the characters from all the previous stories reappear. The last two selections, however, have nothing to do with Casalba and resemble the other antirevolutionary stories discussed briefly at the beginning of this chapter. In "El refugiadito," a poor fisherman is forced to kill his *miliciano* friend when the latter tries to prevent him and his wife from escaping by boat to the United States. The title refers to their gorgeous child born in Los Angeles. The volume's title story, "Las pirañas," refers to the unprincipled and opportunistic young revolutionaries who put on a show for their gullible European and American hippie and liberal devotees. The protagonist is a *miliciana* who gradually becomes disenchanted with the Revolution by reading the Bible.

In Montes Huidobro's *La anunciación y otros cuentos cubanos* (1967), the first six stories deal with the unhappy-marriage theme in a broad variety of literary styles, including *criollismo*, existentialism, and "garcialorquism." The relatively long title story and three others are highly critical of Fidel Castro and the Revolution.

The youngest of the exiled writers is Carlos Alberto Montaner (b. 1943), whose previously discussed novel *Perromundo* is a distinct improvement over his two earlier collections of escapist short stories, *Póker de brujas y otros cuentos* (1968) and *Instantáneas al borde del abismo (con un epílogo desde el fondo)* (1970). The abyss in the second title refers to insanity, and both volumes reveal a predominant interest in abnormal psychology, sexual frustrations and aberrations,

---

[55] Matías Montes Huidobro is mainly a playwright whose works, based on universal rather than Cuban themes, were performed in Cuba from 1949 to 1961. He is currently teaching languages and literature at the University of Hawaii.

and violence in a variety of social settings with occasional literary allusions, as in "La Odisea de Homero" and "La cólera de Otelo." The
evolution from these two volumes to the novel *Perromundo* indicates
that Montaner may represent a new trend among the younger exiles by
rejecting both rabid anticommunism and escapism and by applying
some of the techniques of the new Latin American novel and a short
story to themes that are relevant for Cubans and, at the same time, have
universal appeal.

Part Five. Foreign Prose Fiction
of the Cuban Revolution

Of all the Latin American revolutions, the Cuban one has had the greatest international repercussions. The organization and preliminary training of the future guerrillas took place in Mexico from the summer of 1955 to November 1956. Once they had established themselves in the Sierra Maestra, Fidel Castro and his men began to receive clandestine arms shipments from Miami. Venezuela and Costa Rica also supplied aid. Herbert Matthews's interviews published in the *New York Times* in February 1957 belied Batista's announcement that the rebels had been killed and helped arouse international enthusiasm for the Revolution. Shortly after the triumphant entry of the revolutionary army into Havana, the first problems with the United States arose, and, as the two countries continued on their collision course, Cuba became a symbol of antiimperialism for all of Latin America. The arrival in Havana of Anastas Mikoyan in February 1960 led to the establishment of commercial ties with the Soviet Union, which paved the way for Cuba's entry into the socialist bloc. The April 1961 Bay of Pigs invasion and the October 1962 missile crisis attracted world-wide attention, and since that time the fate of Cuba has been intimately related to the ups and downs of international politics, including the conflicts between the capitalist and socialist nations as well as the conflicts within the socialist bloc.

Realizing the difficulties involved in carrying out a socialist revolution in a country so closely situated to the United States and in a hemisphere dominated in so many ways by the United States, the revolutionary government of Fidel Castro has made a supreme effort to establish close cultural ties with the rest of Latin America. Capitalizing on the tremendous sympathy and enthusiasm aroused by its struggle against the Colossus of the North, Cuba has made a conscious attempt to become the cultural center of Latin America. In one of Che Guevara's August 1961 speeches in Punta del Este, Uruguay, he included among the many positive achievements of the Revolution the "exaltación del patrimonio cultural de toda nuestra América Latina, que se manifiesta en premios anuales dados a literatos de todas las latitudes de América, y cuyo premio de poesía, señor Presidente, ganó el laureado Roberto Ibáñez [Uruguayan], en la última confrontación!"[1] Large editions have been made of many Latin American "classics" while younger, lesser-known writers have also seen their works rewarded and published: Mexican Jorge Ibargüengoitia (b. 1928) for *El atentado* (1963) and *Los relámpagos de agosto* (1964), Chilean Antonio Skármeta (b. 1940) for *Desnudo en el tejado* (1969), and Bolivians Renato Prada Ozores (b. 1937) and Fernando Medina Ferrada for *Los fundadores del alba* (1969) and *Los muertos están cada día más indóciles* (1972), respectively. These annual literary contests in poetry, novel, short story, theater, and essay have been sponsored by the Casa de las Américas, which has also published since 1960 one of the best literary journals of all of Latin America. The list of contributors and members of the editorial board at one time or another reads like a who's who of Latin American literature: Argentinian Julio Cortázar, Uruguayans Mario Benedetti and Carlos Martínez

[1] Ernesto Che Guevara, *Obra revolucionaria*, p. 423.

Moreno, Chilean José Donoso, Paraguayan Augusto Roa Bastos, and Mexicans Juan José Arreola, Rosario Castellanos, Carlos Fuentes, and José Revueltas. A much greater number of Latin American authors have been invited to Cuba to serve as judges in the annual literary contests or to deliver lectures and participate in round-table discussions.[2] Several issues of *Casa de las Américas* have been devoted to the new literature of Colombia, Venezuela, Chile, Uruguay, El Salvador, Panama, Peru, and Puerto Rico.

In view of all this, it is not surprising that between 1959 and the present a variety of non-Cubans have published twenty-two novels, one volume of short stories, and one outstanding short story, Julio Cortázar's "Reunión," about the Cuban Revolution.[3] Although all these works do not fall neatly into the four chronological categories used for the Cuban novels, almost all the prorevolutionary ones parallel the 1959–1960 and the 1961–1965 groups.

I. The Struggle against Tyranny

Four of the foreign novels published between 1959 and 1960 plus *Flush Times* (1962), *Los padrenuestros y el fusil* (1964), and *The Yoke and the Star* (1966) resemble their 1959–1960 Cuban counterparts in that they are primarily concerned with the struggle to overthrow the tyrant Batista. Surprisingly enough, four of the seven volumes were written by Americans, while a fifth one, *The Yoke and the Star*, in spite of having been written by a Spaniard, was first published in English. Another interesting phenomenon is the presence of the

[2] The purpose of these visits is clearly stated by the young Uruguayan Carlos María Gutiérrez in Roque Dalton et al., *El intelectual y la sociedad*: ". . . the comrades [were] welcome up to now in Cuba, because they represented a valuable channel for revolutionary publicity abroad" (p. 41).

[3] Argentinian Marta Lynch (b. 1929) published a short story "El cruce del río" in *Cuentos de colores* (1970), which was inspired by Che Guevara's campaign in Bolivia, as was Uruguayan Sylvia Lago's "Antes del silencio," published in *Marcha*, April 2, 1971. There may also be other individual stories written by non-Cubans about the Revolution but certainly none as well known as "Reunión."

armed struggle in the Sierra Maestra as the main theme of two of the novels, and, in a third work, as an alternating theme with the revolutionary activities in Havana. This is in marked contrast to the almost total absence of the revolutionary guerrillas from the Cuban novels. Like their 1959–1960 Cuban counterparts, the relatively low literary value of these works does not eliminate their significance as complements of the historical documentation of the period.

Of the seven volumes, the only one written by a Spanish American is *Una cruz en la Sierra Maestra* (1960), published in Buenos Aires, by one of Ecuador's best known writers, Demetrio Aguilera Malta (b. 1909). Throughout his long literary career, Aguilera Malta's best works have been those that deal with the rural coast of his native Ecuador: his stories in *Los que se van* (1930) and the novels *Don Goyo* (1933), *La isla virgen* (1942), and *Siete lunas y siete serpientes* (1970). On the other hand, his works dealing with foreign revolutionary situations—*Canal Zone* (1935), *Madrid* (1939), and *Una cruz en la Sierra Maestra* (1960)—seem to have been written hastily without the intimate knowledge and feeling for the subject matter that characterize his Ecuadorian works.[4] Aguilera Malta actually wrote his Cuban novel while living in Mexico and without having visited Cuba during the revolutionary period.

Una cruz en la Sierra Maestra is reminiscent of Hemingway's *For Whom the Bell Tolls* in its attempt to portray the whole guerrilla campaign against Batista by concentrating on one single episode, albeit a fictitious one. Aguilera Malta was also undoubtedly thinking of the Spanish Civil War in the selection of a line from Lincoln's Gettysburg Address as the novel's epigraph (the Abraham Lincoln Brigade) and in the international composition of the guerrilla squad. Of the six men, only two are Cubans, and they are less important in the novel than their foreign comrades. Emilio Mondragón, the Mexican newspaperman descended from Cuauhtémoc and Cortez, provides the artistic frame for the novel by recalling the details of the episode as he watches the triumphant entry of Fidel Castro into Havana on January

[4] Aguilera Malta has also published a series of historical novels called "Episodios americanos"—*La caballeresa del sol* (1964), *El Quijote de El Dorado* (1964), and *Un nuevo mar para el rey* (1965)—with the primary purpose of popularizing history.

8, 1959. The only other survivor of the squad is the Spanish teacher, one of the few relatively older revolutionaries in all the novels of the Cuban Revolution. The other two members of the group are the Argentinian Che Cavalcanti and the Texan Bob. After a skirmish, the wounded Mexican and the Spanish teacher make their way to a small village, where they are welcomed as heroes and hidden by a family. Although the psychopathic sergeant of the government troops tortures the members of the family, they do not reveal the whereabouts of the revolutionaries. Like the 1959–1960 Cuban novels, Aguilera Malta's work is a suspense-packed thriller, so much so, however, that the action often becomes melodramatic. This is apparent from a glance at some of the chapter titles: "Suicide Patrol," "Death Wears Boots," and "The Shark Shows His Fin." Like their Cuban counterparts, the only purpose of Aguilera Malta's revolutionaries is to overthrow Batista in order to put an end to police and army brutality. Absolutely no mention is made of the need for social reforms, and the revolutionaries are not identified with the July Twenty-sixth Movement.

Even more reminiscent of *For Whom the Bell Tolls*, *Kings Will Be Tyrants* (1959) by the American Ward Hawkins (b. 1912) also narrates the adventures of a small group of revolutionaries who belong to Fidel Castro's July Twenty-sixth Movement.[5] Although the author's attitude appears to be anti-Batista, it is far from being prorevolutionary. In fact, this is probably the first novel of all to express any criticism of Fidel Castro. The hero is the Gary Cooper–like O'Brien, the son of a New England businessman and a Cuban sugar plantation owner. O'Brien's only reason for joining the guerrilla forces is that he saw his cousin killed by the Batista police for having printed subversive propaganda. However, O'Brien's enemy and rival is not any Batista officer but Tomás Vilar, the leader of the guerrilla group, a brave young Cuban who is also vain, boastful, and ambitious to the point of secretly planning to assassinate Fidel Castro in order to replace him as head of

---

[5] First published in the *Saturday Evening Post* in serial form, under the title "Island of Hate." The last installment appeared in the July 4, 1959, issue. Judging from his letter of July 5, 1971, sent to me, Hawkins seems to be primarily a popular magazine writer. He also published a detective novel *Death Watch* in collaboration with his brother John.

the revolutionary movement. Unlike almost all the Cuban novels, the love story assumes at least equal if not greater importance than the Revolution. Tourist Jill Corby succeeds in overcoming her puritanical upbringing and wins O'Brien's love, while the young Cuban widow, Angela Díaz, who had preferred O'Brien to Tomás Vilar, dies in battle. Both Jill and O'Brien view Fidel Castro as an impractical visionary, a "feather-headed fanatic"[6] whose plans change from day to day.

In *Journey Not to End* (1959) by Paul Herr (b. 1920), the Cuban Revolution is only a relatively insignificant episode in the life of a Hungarian underground fighter.[7] It begins with his release from a displaced-persons camp in Europe at the end of World War II. From the United States and Mexico, he participates in the smuggling of arms to the Cuban revolutionaries without ever coming to grips with the issues involved. During the protagonist's brief stay in Cuba, the Batista government is criticized only for its corruption and inefficiency.

The other four volumes that correspond to the first Cuban group of 1959–1960 also resemble some of the later Cuban novels like *Tres tristes tigres, Gestos,* and *De donde son los cantantes* in their emphasis on the frivolous and immoral aspects of life in Havana before the Revolution. In contrast to *Kings Will Be Tyrants* and *Journey Not to End,* Andrew Tully's *A Race of Rebels* (1960), Warren Miller's *Flush Times* (1962), and Tana de Gámez's *The Yoke and the Star* (1966) are all more historically oriented and are clearly sympathetic to the Revolution. In *A Race of Rebels,* Andrew Tully (b. 1914) captures the emotion and the rhythm of the Revolution from the end of 1958 to mid-1959 through the eyes of an American newspaperman.[8] The latter covers the military action near Santa Clara and subsequently watches the triumphal entry of Fidel Castro into Havana on January 8.

[6] Ward Hawkins, *Kings Will Be Tyrants,* p. 205.

[7] Paul Herr, *Journey Not to End.* The author is a Chicagoan, and this is his first novel. Beyond that, I have been unable to discover any information about him.

[8] Andrew Tully was born in Massachusetts and is a journalist-author. He covered Patton's Third Army during World War II and since 1948 has been assigned to Washington, where he writes the popular column "National Whirligig" for the Bell-McClure Syndicate. He has written three other novels: *The Time of the Hawk, Supreme Court,* and *Capitol Hill,* and several nonfiction works.

He also interviews Che Guevara in La Cabaña Fortress and attends the trials of some of Batista's officers. By locating his protagonist within the frivolous atmosphere of the Havana tourist hotels and night clubs, the author implicitly justifies the Revolution. Nevertheless, the historical transcendency of the Revolution is overshadowed by the Hollywood-type love affair between the hero and his American secretary.

By contrast, Warren Miller's *Flush Times* (1962) comes closer to fusing the novelistic plot and history.[9] The love affair between American tourist Jonathan Weller and Cuban mestiza Celia Chang comes to an abrupt end when she realizes the tremendous disparity between the hedonism of the wealthy tourists and the misery of the Cuban masses. By identifying with the Revolution, Celia puts herself on the road to personal redemption. Batista's tyranny and corruption as well as the revolutionary activities of the university students and the poverty of the lower classes are presented through the first-hand experiences of the characters. Because *Flush Times* was published in 1962, references are made to some of the revolutionary reforms: casinos and brothels are closed down and the landowners become concerned about the plans for an agrarian reform.

The best of these first six foreign novels is *The Yoke and the Star* (1966) by Tana de Gámez (b. 1920), a Spaniard who resides in New York.[10] Although it is not by any means an outstanding literary work of art, it was considered sufficiently significant to merit publication in Spanish by the prestigious Mexican publisher Joaquín Mortiz as *El yugo y la estrella* (1968). Dedicated to Arturo Barea, the chronicler of the Spanish Civil War, *The Yoke and the Star* attempts to capture the epic proportions of the Revolution. Historically, the novel is struc-

[9] Warren Miller is the author of *90 Miles from Home*, a diary account of his experiences in Cuba in December 1960–January 1961. He has also published stories in *The New Yorker, Saturday Evening Post*, and *Harper's Bazaar*, and five novels in addition to *Flush Times: The Way We Live Now, The Cool World, The Sleep of Reason, Looking for the General*, and *The Siege of Harlem*.

[10] Tana de Gámez, author-journalist, is a native of southern Spain and a sometime resident of Cuba who has been living in New York since the Spanish Civil War, which is the theme of her novel *Like a River of Lions*. She contributes to New York art and dance publications and speaks on foreign affairs over the Riverside Church radio station WRVR-FM. In 1971, she published *Alicia Alonso at Home and Abroad*, a pictorial biography of the outstanding Cuban ballerina.

tured on the genesis of the July Twenty-sixth Movement. The novelistic present is December 1956, date of the almost completely disastrous invasion by Fidel Castro and his men from the "Granma." Among the recollections of the past, the July 26, 1953, attack on the Moncada Barracks is presented more completely than in any other novel, from the initial planning to the torturing of the prisoners. In keeping with its epic pretensions, the major part of the novel takes place in Havana, where the love triangle is formed by three individualized but nonetheless representative figures. Frank, the Cuban artist who rebels against his decadent aristocratic family, wins the love of Mari, a lower-middle-class Cuban secretary who lives with her grandmother, in competition with John Hannan, the American correspondent who goes to the Sierra Maestra, in spite of his boss's opposition, in order to inform the world that the rebels really do exist. Throughout the novel, the bravery of the rebels is contrasted with the corruption and brutality of the Batista regime, but very little mention is made of the social goals of the Revolution.

In the only volume of short stories written about the Revolution by a non-Cuban, Spaniard José Antonio Mases (b. 1929) presents a cross-section of Cuban society in 1957 and 1958. The long title story of *Los padrenuestros y el fusil* (1964) as well as the fourteen shorter stories paint a picture of government corruption, American cultural and business influence, social injustice, and hope in the future based on the revolutionaries in the Sierra. A Cuban senator and his American friend traffic in drugs; sugar-cane cutters are overworked and summarily dismissed by the American plantation owner; large-scale unemployment forces decent human beings into theft and prostitution; revolutionaries set fire to canefields and place bombs in air-conditioned movies and department stores, blow up an electric generating station, and are pursued by the trigger-happy and sadistic police. The emphasis, however, is not on the dramatic action but rather on the presentation of *cuadros* involving the run-of-the-mill Cuban citizens, including Negroes and Spanish immigrants. Sociologically and historically interesting, the stories are of limited literary value because of the lack of dramatic tension and the particularly weak endings.

Mases, who was born in Asturias, lived in Cuba in the late 1950's and returned to Spain in the early 1960's where he is now co-director of the Gran Enciclopedia Asturiana. In 1965, he published the novel *La invasión*, which is somewhat ambiguous in its attitude toward the Revolution. Continuing with his favorite protagonists, Mases intertwines different stages in the lives of a *gallego* night club owner and a mulatto prostitute and popular singer with five different sociohistorical panoramas: rural Galicia in the 1930's; rural Cuba in the 1940's; the corrupt Havana of the 1950's; the revolutionary Cuba of the early 1960's; and the plight of the Cuban exiles in Madrid and Gijón, Spain, in the mid-1960's. Although Mases deals most extensively with the latter period, during which the exiles refer incessantly to the forthcoming invasion that will overthrow Fidel, his choice of protagonists indicates that his sympathies are not 100 percent with the exiles. As in *Los padrenuestros y el fusil*, the sociohistorical value of the book outweighs its literary value. Although the novel is interesting and well structured, its spatial and temporal fragmentation prevents the characters from developing any real depth.

II. Binational Contrasts

During the 1961–1965 period, the majority of the Cuban novels published justified the socialization of the Revolution by describing in existentialist tones the decadent bourgeois society of prerevolutionary Cuba. In a somewhat similar fashion, three outstanding Latin American authors published works between 1963 and 1965, a fourth one in 1969, and a fifth one in 1972, which contrast in varying degrees the decadent bourgeois societies of their own countries with the euphoric enthusiasm generated in different moments of the Cuban Revolution. A sixth "binational novel," published in December 1973, is the only one of this group that is critical of the revolutionary government.

Of all the foreign works discussed in this chapter, the most successful artistically is ironically the short story, "Reunión," by Julio Cortázar (b. 1914). First published in the May 1964 issue of the

Revista de la Universidad de México and then in the volume *Crónicas de América*, it was not until 1966, when "Reunión" was published in Cortázar's own collection, *Todos los fuegos el fuego*, that it circulated widely. Although the theme is unique among Cortázar's many stories, the techniques of magic realism, musical structure, and the double are quite characteristic. In fact, what is so impressive about "Reunión" is Cortázar's ability to single out the most absurd elements of perhaps the most dramatic episode of the Revolution—the landing from the "Granma" and the ascent to the Sierra Maestra—in order to mythify the rebel leaders. At the end of the story, the Argentine narrator, who is obviously Che Guevara, sees "a star in the center of the picture,"[11] which represents the apotheosis of Luis, who is obviously Fidel Castro. The implicit comparison of Fidel Castro to Jesus, which is almost a commonplace in the Cuban novels of the Revolution,[12] is reinforced by the contrast with the "diabolical" Argentine narrator: "devilish asthma,"[13] "my evil way of looking at the world,"[14] "everything went to the devil with the Diadochi,"[15] "infernal path,"[16] "the darkness of the cave."[17] However, the religious symbolism is saved from degenerat-

[11] Julio Cortázar, *Todos los fuegos el fuego*, 10th ed., p. 86.

[12] See the discussion of *Los niños se despiden* on pp. 63–64. In Eduardo Manet's *Un cri sur le rivage*, one of the characters comments on Fidel's resemblance to Jesus: "Haven't you heard how Fidel is sometimes praised: he resembles Christ" (p. 123). In Che Guevara's *Pasajes de la guerra revolucionaria* (1963), the number of survivors of the "Granma" landing is fixed at twelve plus Fidel (cf. Jesus and his twelve disciples), although Guevara actually names fourteen besides himself (*Obra revolucionaria*, p. 121): "That's our Cuban experience, where once twelve men were able to create the nucleus of the army that was formed because all these conditions were met and because the man who led them was Fidel Castro" (*Obra revolucionaria*, p. 96). Carlos Franqui published a collection of eye-witness accounts of the "Granma" landing and the guerrilla activities in the Sierra Maestra, first in French, *Le livre des douze*, and then in Spanish, *El libro de los doce*. In the early days of the Russian Revolution, Christian symbolism was also used to exalt the Revolution: "In Blok's 'Twelve' (1918), Jesus Christ in a white crown leads the triumphal march of the Red Guards, and in Bely's 'Christ is Risen' (1918), Russia's ordeal by revolution is compared to Calvary: the martyrdom of the Cross will be followed by Resurrection" (Max Hayward, *Dissonant Voices in Soviet Literature*, p. ix).

[13] Cortázar, *Todos los fuegos el fuego*, p. 67.

[14] Ibid., p. 69.

[15] Ibid., p. 71.

[16] Ibid., p. 77.

[17] Ibid., p. 78.

ing into trite propaganda by the atmosphere of magic realism with which Cortázar effectively envelops his characters. In spite of the historical details of the landing, the fact that the narrator is a feverish asthmatic intellectual who recognizes the absurdity of his own situation —"Me like an idiot with my adrenaline sprayer"[18]—transforms reality into fantasy. The absurd nature of the landing is further underlined by the use of circus imagery. The landing launch reels and staggers "like a drunken turtle,"[19] while the invaders wander around in the marshes "like stupefied fools in a completely broken-down circus of mud for the amusement of the baboon in his Palace."[20] The use of Mozart's quartet "The Hunt" to symbolize the Revolution in its three movements: charge (*halalí*), rest (*adagio*), and victory (*allegro final*) adds still another touch of fantasy.

The fusion of reality and fantasy is also reflected in the ultimate encounter on top of the mountain. The humor of the following dialogue, in which the Jesus-like Cuban leader and the demonic Argentine doctor imitate each other's national dialects, not only makes the religious exaltation more acceptable but also reinforces Cortázar's concept, derived from Borges, that one man is the double of the other, that each man is both hero and coward capable of both good and evil.

—So you arrived, Che—said Luis. Naturally he pronounced "Che" very badly.

—And what you think?—I answered him just as badly. And we doubled over again laughing like idiots, and everyone laughed with us without knowing why.[21]

By his conscious choice of the Cuban leader as his double, the narrator rejects his other double, the Argentine friend who chose to remain in Argentina and who continues to absurdly defend the false values of the decadent bourgeois society of his poor lost country, "through fear, through dread of change, through skepticism and distrust, which were the only living gods in his poor lost country."[22]

[18] Ibid., p. 68.
[19] Ibid., p. 67.
[20] Ibid., p. 68.
[21] Ibid., p. 85.
[22] Ibid., p. 81.

Although the narrator's vision of Argentine life occupies only one and one-half pages of the story's nineteen, its importance is underscored by its role in the mythification process. The fact that the vision appears to the narrator in the darkness of the cave after he has received the false news of Luis's death identifies the episode with the archetypal descent into the underworld, as in Don Quixote's descent into the cave of Montesinos. Endowed with a greater and truer knowledge of the world, the demonic hero sallies forth and begins his ascent to the summit. At the same time, by restricting the vision of Argentina to the confines of the cave, Cortázar makes his point without violating one of the short story's principal canons, concentration.

By contrast, the following three "binational novels" give more or less equal time to Cuba and the authors' native countries. In *El paredón* (1963) by Uruguayan Carlos Martínez Moreno (b. 1917), whose fame as a novelist and short-story writer transcends his country's boundaries, the very dynamic Cuban experience of a Uruguayan newspaperman constitutes the second and central part of the novel and is preceded and followed by a pessimistic vision of the Montevideo bourgeoisie. The triumph of the Blanco political party in 1958 marked the failure of the Colorados in their fifty-year attempt to transform Uruguay into a Scandinavian-type socialist democracy without altering the basic economic structures of the country. Protagonist Julio Calodoro (anagram for Colorado) disagrees with his father's opinion that the victory of the Blancos signifies disaster for the country. By recalling the widespread official corruption and the smugness of the intellectuals, Julio feels the stagnancy of the whole country, a condition that cannot be remedied by mere elections. After Julio returns from Cuba, the imminent death of his father from cancer and his ambiguous attitude toward his bourgeois fiancée symbolize the profound effects of the Cuban Revolution on the rest of Latin America.

In that respect, Cuba's Operación Verdad was successful. Julio was one of many foreign newspapermen invited by the Cuban government in January 1959 to prove to the world that the executions of the war criminals were justified and carried out fairly. In contrast to Julio's boring life in Montevideo, the days spent in Cuba whirl at break-neck speed on two axes: the Sosa Blanco trial in the Sports Palace and the love affair with Raquel, a rabid revolutionary divorcee. Martínez Moreno does not attempt to openly defend the acts of the revolutionary government as much as he tries to capture Julio's amazement at the ingenuous exuberance and faith of the Cuban people, which is such a refreshing change from the Uruguayan situation. Events and conditions in Cuba often evoke memories of his days spent covering the 1952 Bolivian Revolution. In his previous novella *Los aborígenes* (1960), Martínez Moreno converted the Bolivian situation into a prototype of all Latin America. Although the oligarchy is bitterly denounced, little faith is placed in the so-called revolutionary coups. In *El paredón*, Martínez Moreno is less cynical about the Cuban Revolution, but he has not completely overcome his skepticism. Julio cannot quite make the decision to reject his previous life and remain in Cuba. He leaves Raquel and returns to his fiancée in Montevideo. However, by refusing to marry her, Julio indicates his preference to remain on the margin of society.

Much greater enthusiasm for the Cuban Revolution is found in *La primera batalla* (1965) by the well-known Mexican dramatist and novelist Luisa Josefina Hernández (b. 1928). Like "Reunión" and *El paredón*, *La primera batalla* differs from most of the author's other works. In her more famous plays and novels, Hernández prefers psychological and *costumbrista* themes to political ones.[23] However, in *La primera batalla*, as in *El paredón*, the Cuban Revolution is used to underscore a pessimistic vision of the author's own society, but with a totally different structure. Whereas, in *El paredón*, the two contrasting worlds are drawn together by the single protagonist, parallel situations, and mutual recollections, Luisa Josefina Hernández alternates from chapter to chapter two completely independent narratives. The Mexican part of the novel, which is actually a complete unit in itself, develops chronologically in the even-numbered chapters. The realistic unexperimental techniques reflect the stagnation of the Revolution.

---

[23] The first part of her 1970 novel, *Nostalgia de Troya*, also takes place in Havana in 1963, but hardly any references are made to the Revolution. The novel is much more concerned with exploring the psychology of the divorced French film maker René and a Colombian widow. The other five parts of the novel present scenes from previous periods in René's life in other countries.

The protagonist, Lorenzo, is an idealistic version of Carlos Fuentes's Artemio Cruz. His "primera batalla" was his revolutionary struggle to aid the Indians in southeastern Mexico in the waning years of the Porfirio Díaz dictatorship. After the Revolution, he moves to Mexico City, watches the parade of presidents from Alvaro Obregón to Miguel Alemán, and gradually sacrifices his revolutionary ideals to concern over his personal problems. His death at the end of the novel, like that of Julio Calodoro's father in *El paredón*, symbolizes the failure of the early twentieth-century revolution.

By contrast, the odd-numbered chapters of *La primera batalla* present in experimental form the new, dynamic Latin American revolution as exemplified by Cuba. There are no plot lines or characters in the traditional manner. Each chapter is a poetic essay that praises a different aspect of Cuba—"Paradisíaca es esta isla"[24]—or that criticizes those Latin Americans who travel to the island without realizing the great hope that Cuba represents for the whole continent. Several of these chapters are written in the innovative second-person narrative point of view. However, too many of them are devoted either to a touristy treatment of typical folklore themes or to an undisguised political exaltation of the Revolution: Afro-Cuban religion, conversations on the bus and over the telephone, cutting sugar cane, the tropical sun, the bloody martyrs, the "gusanos," the children with scholarships, and, finally, Fidel Castro. In short, the realistic interpretation of the failure of the Mexican Revolution is relatively effective by itself, but it is not at all enhanced by the contrast with the overly superficial vision of the Cuban Revolution.

El francotirador (1969) by Puerto Rican Pedro Juan Soto (b. 1928) is the most technically complex of the "binational novels." At the same time, the contrast between the stagnation of Puerto Rican life and the enthusiasm for the Cuban Revolution is less clearly defined. It is not that Soto views conditions in his own country any more optimistically. Actually, the reverse is true. Unlike Cortázar, Martínez Moreno, and Luisa Josefina Hernández, all his work—a volume of short stories, *Spiks* (1957), and three novels, *Usmaíl* (1959), *Ardiente suelo, fría*

---

[24] Luisa Josefina Hernández, *La primera batalla*, p. 86.

estación (1961), *Temporada de duendes* (1970)—is devoted to the portrayal of the anguish-laden Puerto Rican alienated by the cultural and political conflicts stemming from the ambiguous relationship with the United States. Where Soto differs from his predecessors is that the Cuban Revolution is no longer presented with the same, almost unqualified, enthusiastic support. Nonetheless, the basic contrast is quite similar. Soto establishes a clear parallelism between the moral and intellectual bankruptcy of the Puerto Rican government, especially the university, with the lack of ideals among the counterrevolutionary conspirators in Cuba. As in *El paredón*, one protagonist unites the two worlds, but in *El francotirador* he is the first-person narrator, and time is divided between the present and the future. Tomás Saldivia, a Cuban novelist and professor of Latin American literature, suffers from the same anguish that characterizes the Puerto Rican protagonists of Soto's other novels. In spite of his cynicism, Saldivia is desperately looking for some ideal. He tries to adapt to university life in Puerto Rico but feels constrained and uncomfortable in the anticommunist environment. The struggle between the governor (obviously Muñoz Marín) and the chancellor (Jaime Benítez) contributes to his complete disillusionment. He subsequently volunteers for a United States–sponsored counterrevolutionary expedition to Cuba but without any real conviction. Once in Cuba, he will discover—the predominant use of the future in this part of the novel adds a certain dreamlike quality— that the Cuban counterrevolutionaries are as lacking in ideals as his Puerto Rican colleagues and that the Cuban people will, by and large, remain faithful to the Revolution. Finally, Saldivia will be betrayed by his friend and imprisoned. Convinced that he will be shot, he will seize the gun of one of his guards and shoot himself. As in *La primera batalla*, the even-numbered chapters devoted to Puerto Rico alternate with the odd-numbered ones in Cuba. However, *El francotirador* differs from *La primera batalla* as well as from *El paredón* and "Reunión" in that the protagonist's personal problem predominates over the sociopolitical problems of the two countries. Another unique characteristic of *El francotirador* is the contrast between the very specific characters and events on which the Puerto Rican part of the novel is

FOREIGN PROSE FICTION OF THE CUBAN REVOLUTION

based and the vagueness of the Cuban part, undoubtedly attributable to the author's not having had first-hand contact with revolutionary Cuba.

Don Juan's Bar (1971) by Brazilian Antônio Callado (b. 1917) deals, in part, with the plans of Cuban revolutionaries to coordinate guerrilla movements in other Latin American countries.[25] Although roughly 85 percent of *Don Juan's Bar* deals with the lives of a group of Brazilian revolutionaries in Rio and Mato Grosso, the weight of the Cuban experience is constantly felt through the presence of Che Guevara in neighboring Bolivia and the efforts of the Cuban Eustaquio to enlist aid for Che among the Argentine and Brazilian guerrillas. Interspersed among the ten pages devoted to the capture and subsequent murder of Che Guevara in Bolivia are memories of the more important moments in the Sierra Maestra odyssey. Che's recollections of his experiences in the Peruvian leprosarium also serve, not only to mythify Che, but also to clarify the author's skepticism about middle-class Brazilian revolutionaries who spend much of their time in Don Juan's Bar in Rio: "—The fate of this continent depends on us, and here we are sopping up the booze."[26] It's not that Callado's sympathies are not with the revolutionaries. The theme of police torture is featured in the very first chapter, and the need for a revolution seems to be taken for granted. However, Callado's Brazilian revolutionaries are still too concerned over drinking, fornicating, and writing to make good Guevara-type revolutionaries. Their bourgeois backgrounds are implicitly contrasted with the dark-skinned Eustaquio's recollections of his childhood poverty and adolescent frustrations on a banana plantation in Oriente Province, Cuba, before he joined the guerrillas in the Sierra Maestra. It is significant that one of the few survivors of the Brazilian group is Aniceto, the nonintellectual *pistoleiro* from the poverty-stricken northeastern state of Alagoas, who, toward the end of the

[25] Antônio Callado is a well-known journalist who since 1963 has been an editor of *O Jornal do Brasil*. He has written two other novels, *Assunção de Salviano* (1956) and *Quarup* (1967), two plays, and three nonfiction works, one of which is a collection of his 1968 interviews with American prisoners of war in North Vietnam. *Don Juan's Bar* was originally published in Portuguese as *Bar Don Juan* by the Editôra Civilização Brasileira in Rio de Janeiro.

[26] Antônio Callado, *Don Juan's Bar*, p. 48.

novel, hijacks a plane to Cuba armed only with an Indian spear. Revolutions are not made by Don Juans like Mansinho, who playfully robs banks for the guerrilla movement until he is shot in a moment of carelessness by a bank clerk in Corumbá. In fact, Callado gives the impression that even austere and experienced guerrillas like Che Guevara, regardless of their noble aims, may fail in the struggle against insurmountable odds.

The most recent of the "binational novels," *Persona non grata* (1973) by Chilean Jorge Edwards (b. 1931), like Juan Arcocha's *Por cuenta propia* (1970) and *La bala perdida* (1973), is among the first Latin American manifestations of the new nonfictional novel genre made famous in the United States by Truman Capote and Norman Mailer.[27] Edwards's vivid recollections of his experiences in Cuba as President Allende's *encargado de negocios* from December 1970 to March 1971 are enhanced by occasional italicized notations from his diary as well as by comments based on subsequent information. Although *Persona non grata* is no more a novel than is *The Armies of the Night*, a somewhat novelistic flavor is achieved by Edwards's interspersing a judicious number of past experiences and by his skillful recreation of key dramatic scenes, particularly his final confrontation with Fidel Castro. Although the book's main theme is the Cuban government's new hostile policy toward "dissident" writers, such as Heberto Padilla, David Buzzi, Pablo Armando Fernández, José Norberto Fuentes, and José Lezama Lima, the overall structure is based on the inevitable comparison between Cuban and Chilean socialism. In spite of the historical examples, Edwards refuses to believe that freedom of expression must be curtailed in a socialist state. At the same time, as Allende's attitude toward the Chilean middle class becomes more and more intransigent, Edwards fears that Chile's democratic traditions may be threatened by a Cuban-type rationalization for the suppression of individual freedom. When the right-wing military coup finally occurs in September 1973, Edwards bitterly denounces the

---

[27] Jorge Edwards served in his country's diplomatic corps from 1957 to September 1973. He has published one novel, *El peso de la noche* (1964), and four collections of short stories: *El patio* (1952), *Gente de la ciudad* (1961), *Las máscaras* (1967), and *Temas y variaciones* (1969).

complicity of the United States and of former President Frei although he does not condone the distortions of leftist European newspapers. In addition to the parallelisms between Cuba and Chile, Edwards points out the similarities between Presidents Allende and Balmaceda (1886–1891), both of whom espoused nationalistic policies and were opposed by more conservative legislatures.

As a novel, *Persona non grata* has an interesting plot, a fascinating historical setting, and a cohesive structure. It is less successful, however, in character development. Although Fidel Castro and Pablo Neruda become real characters in certain scenes, Edwards was undoubtedly reluctant to give more prominence to his "dissident" Cuban friends. Only Heberto Padilla's personality is clearly defined. The protagonist of the novel is the author himself, Jorge Edwards, whose initial candor is gradually transformed into a realistic and even somewhat paranoiac attitude toward his enemies, without wavering in his loyalty to his principles. In the book's climactic scene, Edwards's calm and forceful statement of his position actually succeeds in changing Fidel's hostile and contemptuous attitude to one of respect.

III. Antirevolutionary Novels

Since the publication of Andrés Rivero Collado's *Enterrado vivo* in 1960, Cuban exiles have denounced the revolutionary government of Fidel Castro with different degrees of passion in more than twenty novels. The seven non-Cuban works that fall into this category were published between 1962 and 1970 in Mexico, Argentina, Spain, the United States, and Puerto Rico and share the same characteristics with their Cuban counterparts. Artistically all seven are clearly inferior to the "binational" works. The main theme is that Fidel Castro has betrayed the Revolution by converting Cuba into a totalitarian communist state.

Adiós al cañaveral: Diario de una mujer en Cuba (1962) by the Chilean poetess Matilde Ladrón de Guevara (b. 1908) recounts in diary form the great disillusionment suffered by the protagonist, a Chilean utopian socialist on her second trip to Cuba between April 3 and September 10, 1961.[28] When she first went to Cuba in 1960, she was greatly impressed and enthusiastic over the joy and freedom that she observed. Dissatisfied with her life in Chile, she decides to settle in Cuba with her husband and teen-age son. During her five-month stay, she still thrills to the revolutionary fervor generated by Fidel Castro in his outdoor rallies—"it's just that the revolution attracts me"[29]—but little by little she becomes concerned over the executions in La Cabaña; the bureaucratic confusion; the scarcity of food, clothing, and medicine; and the exodus of many of her friends. She identifies completely with the Revolution during the Bay of Pigs invasion and maintains her faith in Fidel, but she comes to believe that he is being manipulated by the Communists. When she herself is unexpectedly taken prisoner on July 27 without charges, her life becomes a nightmare. After going through an apparently endless amount of red tape, she and her family are finally allowed to depart for Mexico. Her experience is Kafkaesque and this work has a much greater air of authenticity than do most of the other antirevolutionary novels because of the protagonist's sincere faith in the Revolution and her personal conversations with the leaders of the regime: Fidel Castro, Che Guevara, Carlos Rafael Rodríguez, and Nicolás Guillén. When she first hears criticism of the Revolution from a taxi driver—"We were all in agreement with Fidel. But that was some time ago. Now things are happening that smack of the Batista days. You can't talk any more or you have to talk the way those in command tell you to"[30]—she is loath to believe it. However, by the time the writers' convention takes place in the summer of 1961, she is convinced that the Revolution has been subverted.

La muerte en el paraíso (1965) by Ladrón de Guevara's compatriot

[28] Matilde Ladrón de Guevara is the author of five volumes of poetry, *Amarras de luz* (1948), *Pórtico de Iberia* (1951), *Desnuda* (1960), *Celada 13* (1960), and *Che* (1968); three other novels, *Mi patria fue mi música* (1953), *Madre soltera* (1966), and *Muchachos de siempre* (1969); and a study of Chile's first Nobel Prize–winning poet, *Gabriela Mistral rebelde magnífica* (1957, 1962).

[29] Matilde Ladrón de Guevara, *Adiós al cañaveral*, 3d ed., p. 121.

[30] Ibid., p. 51.

Alberto Baeza Flores (b. 1914) resembles *Adiós al cañaveral* but includes a wider range of characters, a broader time period, and a more clearly antirevolutionary posture.[31] The protagonist is Antonio Baena (a rather thin disguise for Alberto Baeza), an author who returns to Cuba in the euphoric early days of 1959.

When he tries to help a friend take refuge in a foreign embassy, he is denounced to the police by his mistress and is taken prisoner. Later, during the Bay of Pigs invasion, his wife, Diana, is also taken prisoner. Many pages are devoted to the unsanitary conditions of the prisons, but, significantly, there is no mention of physical torture.

Both Antonio and Diana become upset when their daughter, Elisa, decides to volunteer for the literacy campaign. Baeza Flores seems to be criticizing the Revolution for family crises, but he presents a relatively weak case in view of the fact that both Diana and Antonio have extramarital love affairs. The contrast between two soldiers in the revolutionary army is also mishandled. Mario Peláez, an officer who fought in the Sierra Maestra, is assigned to command the firing squads that are executing the Batista officials. He becomes unhappy at the arbitrary way in which justice is meted out and goes into exile. At the same time, Aníbal, his assistant, is a simple peasant who by following orders winds up as a captain. Although Baeza Flores obviously sympathizes with Mario Peláez as opposed to Aníbal, Peláez's participation in the Bay of Pigs invasion and Aníbal's commanding a group of soldiers who repel the invaders seem to be at odds with the author's intent. However, this is not really surprising in view of the overall subordination of both plot and character development to the political message, namely that Cuba was transformed step-by-step into a totalitarian state between January 1959 and April 1961.

[31] Alberto Baeza Flores fought with the Loyalists in the Spanish Civil War and later founded the journal *La Poesía Sorprendida* (1943–1947) in the Dominican Republic during the Trujillo dictatorship. He participated in the struggle against Batista and founded the journal *Acento* in 1959. When the Cuban government closed down his journal, Baeza left Cuba and has since lived in Paris, Madrid, and, recently, Costa Rica. He has published *Antología de la poesía hispanoamericana* (1959) and studies of two prominent anticommunist reform-minded politicians: *Haya de la Torre y la Revolución constructiva de las Américas* (1962) and *La lucha sin fin* (on Costa Rican José Figueres) (1969). *Las cadenas vienen de lejos* (1960) is a denunciation of Soviet imperialism.

Baeza Flores's recent book, *La frontera del adiós, novela del exilio* (1970), has relatively few references to Cuba even though the main characters are a family of Cuban refugees. The emphasis is on the difficulties encountered by the family from the long wait in the Havana airport *"pecera"* to the search for a means of livelihood and cultural adjustment in Mexico City, Paris, and finally Madrid. While they are in Mexico, the protagonist cannot avoid becoming involved with his fellow exiles, but he quickly notes the mutual distrust that pervades the group. His son joins a group of would-be invaders and dies without the author's supplying any information about the circumstances.

Cuando la caña es amarga (1966) by the Mexican Francisco Castellanos Velasco (b. 1926) resembles *La muerte en el paraíso* in its panoramic approach, which includes initial support of the Revolution and subsequent disillusionment, the suppression of individual freedom, the unsanitary prison conditions, and impressions of the Bay of Pigs invasion.[32] This work is distinguished from those already discussed by its emphasis on the struggle for freedom of the press under both Batista and Castro and its somewhat melodramatic tone. The protagonist, Rodrigo Alonso, is a very wealthy and honorable newspaper publisher who never loses faith in individual civil liberties. From 1957 on, he criticizes the Batista government for its corruption and, even more, for its attempts to control the press. He participates in the clandestine revolutionary movement in Havana and establishes contact with the guerrillas in the Sierra Maestra. However, soon after the Revolution triumphs, freedom is restricted, and Alonso resumes his idealistic struggle, but with less successful results. His daughter's fiancé is sent to prison on the Isla de Pinos and dies in the hospital. Alonso manages to send his wife and two children to Miami before taking refuge in the Venezuelan and, later, the Mexican Embassy. A considerable part of the novel actually takes place in the embassies, where Alonso's adulterous love affair with Raquel is intertwined with news of the Bay of Pigs invasion. Although the novel is full of interesting allusions to historical events, including newspaper documentation,

---

[32] Francisco Castellanos Velasco is a professional accountant who has been associated for many years with the Asociación Nacional de Artistas. His second novel, *Piel de angustia* (1971), is about racial discrimination against the blacks in the United States.

and novelistic suspense is maintained throughout, the happy Hollywood ending detracts from the novel's seriousness. Alonso's son, who was captured during the Bay of Pigs invasion, is released in the December 1962 exchange of prisoners for equipment and pharmaceutical products. Alonso himself, after spending over a year in the embassies, finally receives a safe-conduct to travel to the United States. Sincerely repentant of his marital infidelity, he is determined to effect a reconciliation with his wife and to continue to struggle for freedom. Although Alonso's political idealism seems genuine, his faith in the Organization of American States is extremely naïve.

With far fewer novelistic elements than the previous antirevolutionary novels but with much greater thematic concentration, *Utiles después de muertos* (1966) by Guatemalan ex-Communist Carlos Manuel Pellecer (b. 1920) is a Cuban version of Arthur Koestler's *Darkness at Noon* (1940).[33] Through the 1964 trial of Marcos Rodríguez, Pellecer denounces the intrigues of the Communist party in Cuba between 1952 and 1964. All the important characters are historical, with the hero's role bestowed on Joaquín Ordoqui and the villain's role shared by Carlos Rafael Rodríguez and Blas Roca. Although the trial revolves around the specific ill-fated March 1957 attempt to assassinate Batista, the novel reaches out to Mexico, Costa Rica, and Czechoslovakia in order to broadly trace the gradual infiltration of the Communists into the revolutionary government. In spite of the author's anticommunist stance, the tone of the novel is remarkably dispassionate.

After the four more or less anti-Batista novels of 1959–1962, the only other American novel dealing with revolutionary Cuba has been Leon M. Uris's (b. 1924) best seller *Topaz* (1967). Like Uris's earlier novels *Battle Cry* (1953), *Exodus* (1958), and *Armageddon* (1964), *Topaz* has been a big commercial success in the bookstores and on the

---

[33] Carlos Manuel Pellecer participated in the revolutionary governments of Juan José Arévalo (1945–1951) and Jacobo Arbenz (1951–1954). He has published a short social protest novel, *Llamarada en la montaña* (1947), *Renuncia al comunismo* (1963), *Agua quebrada y otros cuentos* (1966), and the autobiographical *Memoria en dos geografías* (1964), which recounts his childhood and adolescence in Antigua, his conflicts with the Ubico dictatorship in the 1930's, and his experiences as a rural schoolteacher in Sonora, Mexico, in the early 1940's.

screen. Actually the Cuban Revolution is not the main theme. It is far overshadowed by the international intrigues of the French, Russians, and Americans. De Gaulle, rather than Fidel Castro, is the chief villain, while the real hero is the French diplomat André Devereaux. The personal conflicts of both Devereaux and the Soviet defector and the international intrigue behind the 1962 missile crisis make for quick fascinating reading. As for the portrayal of Cuba, Uris's attitude can be compared to that of the "Ugly American." The Cuban revolutionaries are stereotyped as lustful cowards. Devereaux is able to escape from Cuba because the Cuban officials cannot locate Fidel Castro, who is assumed to be with one of his mistresses. The anti-Castro heroine is the wealthy and passionate aristocrat, Juanita de Córdoba, who submits to the advances of the sinister Rico Parra in order to permit the escape of her favorite lover, Devereaux. She is later arrested, but, before the Cubans get around to torturing her, she commits suicide by taking poison supplied by an American agent. Thanks to the agrarian reform, the peasants are no longer exploited by the plantation owners but rather by the bureaucrats who drive them off the land in order to build the Soviet missile bases.

The weakest of the antirevolutionary foreign novels is *En La Habana ha muerto un turista* (Guipúzcoa, Spain, 1963) by X. Aramayo, who, from the wording of the prologue, appears to be a Spaniard. The novel, written in the form of travel notes by American tourist William Brampton, denounces the Communist dictatorship of Fidel Castro from a Catholic point of view. The almost mystically religious passages, however, predominate over the political commentary.

IV. Prorevolutionary Miscellany

The final three works to be discussed in this chapter do not fit into any of the previous three classifications. They are prorevolutionary, but they are not based on a binational contrast nor are they concerned with the heroic struggle against Batista.

"El majá" o el pérfido Julián (1963) by Peruvian Juan Aguilar Derpich (b. 1921) is actually more similar to some of the Cuban novels written between 1961 and 1965 than it is to the foreign works.[34] Like Soler Puig's *En el año de enero* (1963), Edmundo Desnoes's *El cataclismo* (1965) and *Memorias del subdesarrollo* (1965), and Eduardo Manet's *Un cri sur le rivage* (1963), Aguilar Derpich's novel presents the difficulties experienced by many Cubans in exchanging their bourgeois values for revolutionary ones. However, unlike Desnoes's protagonists, there is absolutely no internal conflict within the "serpentlike" Julián. Aguilar Derpich condemns in doctrinaire fashion this fifty-year-old opportunistic accountant, who attempts to use the Revolution to satisfy his lust for money, women, and power. This Uris-like stereotype is so lazy and inept that he soon antagonizes almost all of his subordinates and is destined to follow his cousin to the disciplinary internment camp at Guanahacabibes.

In 1969, besides Pedro Juan Soto's *El francotirador*, two other foreign works were published about the Cuban Revolution that are unique thematically: *Nadie escribe la historia de la próxima aurora* and *A 90 millas, solamente*. The former, by Manuel Grimalt,[35] was published in Andorra and presents with a minimum of novelistic plot a panorama of Cuban revolutionary life in 1966–1967 from a Pan-Hispanic and anti-American viewpoint. The protagonist, a nonsocialist Spanish newspaperman who had fought on the side of the Hungarian rebels against the Soviet Union in 1956, volunteers to fight against an imminent American invasion. The purpose of the invasion will be to put an end not only to the Cuban Revolution but also to revolutionary

[34] Juan Aguilar Derpich has published two other novels. *Se alquilan cuartos amueblados* (Havana, 1962), republished in Lima under the title *Mil vidas en el fango* (1965), portrays the mainly Negro and Latin inhabitants of a cheap New York City hotel as sexual deviates, drug addicts, and alcoholics victimized by heartless capitalism. *¿Oficio? Guerrillero* (1970) is a revolutionary novel about Peru. The humanitarian communist redeemer from Lima is captured and tortured by the Huancayo police in 1965 while trying to contact the guerrillas. Alternate chapters depict the tragic life of juvenile delinquents in Lima and prostitutes in Huancayo. Other volumes published by Aguilar Derpich are *Al cantío de un gallo (estampas cubanas)* (Havana, 1962), *Cantos de bronce (poemas)* (Havana, 1963), essays on the Mexican and Bolivian revolutions (Milan, 1969), and short biographies of Nehru and Perón (Milan, 1971).

[35] I have been unable to obtain any information whatsoever about Grimalt.

movements throughout Latin America. Spanish solidarity with Latin American revolutionary movements is also exemplified by the Spanish priest who identifies with the Colombian revolutionary priest Camilo Torres.

A 90 millas, solamente by Ecuadorean short-story writer Eugenia Viteri (b. 1932) shares with *El francotirador* an anti-antirevolutionary character, but with a Miami setting.[36] The theme is the disillusionment and disintegration of a bourgeois Cuban family in Miami. The father comes to realize that many of his fellow exiles are scoundrels, but he is unable to dissociate himself from them and he is killed in the Bay of Pigs invasion. The mother, a stereotype of the bourgeois Cuban woman, depends so much on her husband that without him she dies, apparently without any medical cause. The younger son becomes involved in a gang of teen-age hoodlums and winds up in jail without a trace of shame. The only one who is saved is the older daughter, the heroine Elisa. After allowing herself to follow the pattern of her American companions—drunken sprees, sexual promiscuity, pregnancy, abortion—she struggles to redeem herself after her parents' death. She works hard as a seamstress, raises her younger sister, and helps a maiden aunt. After meeting and falling in love with the Argentinian Ricardo, she studies Marxism with him and, at the end of the novel, they both leave for Cuba. The influence of the new Latin American novel is somewhat visible in the interspersion of scenes from prerevolutionary Cuba that emphasize social class differences, but, in general, the novel suffers from the same idealized and sentimental Marxism that mars the end of Juan Arcocha's *Los muertos andan solos.*

Since 1969, only three foreign novels have been published about the Cuban Revolution: *La frontera del adiós, Don Juan's Bar,* and *Persona non grata.*[37] This decline in the past three years may be attributed to a

[36] Eugenia Viteri, wife of novelist Pedro Jorge Vera, has published two volumes of short stories, *El anillo* (1955) and *12 cuentos* (1963).

[37] Chilean Antonio Undurraga wrote "Los dioses no dan la cara," an antirevolutionary work commented on by Leonardo Fernández-Marcané in "Tres novelas de la Revolución cubana" in *Diez años de Revolución cubana,* by Carlos Alberto Montaner, pp. 103–119. However, Fernández-Marcané informed me in a letter dated July 1, 1972, that the novel had not yet been published.

waning enthusiasm for the Cuban Revolution among Latin American intellectuals because of the controversial Padilla case. However, another factor may be the normal decrease of interest in a given historical event that occurred fourteen years ago. Also to be considered is that in the past three years Cuba has had to share the Latin American spotlight with Peru and Chile.[38]

[38] In an interview in the first issue of *Hispamérica* (University of Maryland, 1972, p. 65), Argentine novelist David Viñas (b. 1927) revealed that he is working on a new novel tentatively entitled "Mutación," which uses Cuba as the revolutionary hub of Latin America:

About five characters who get together in Havana to draw up a political document. With all the difficulties caused by the different shades of meaning in the Spanish spoken in Latin America from Mexico to Argentina: language as a concrete problem, troublesome and precise. That's the first level. The second, what is happening in Havana at that moment, after the departure and death of Ernesto Guevara. The third level, the messages that these men send to their respective points of origin and their daily lives. And the fourth component, the history of those reciprocal points of origin: from the Mexican Revolution crystallized in the bureaucracy of the PRI to the Chilean government's reformism challenged by the MIR, by the adolescents and tourists in Paris, to a Buenos Aires plagued by leftist intellectuals who have fallen into a devout and screaming "Ultraperonism."

Twelve Conclusions

1. The first fifteen years of the Cuban Revolution have witnessed the publication of an unprecedented number of novels and volumes of short stories due to three factors: the enthusiasm generated by the momentous historical event, official government encouragement, and the influence of the Latin American literary boom of the 1960's.

2. In comparison with prerevolutionary Cuban literary traditions, the expansion of novelistic production is more noteworthy than that of the short story and may be attributed to the growing national consciousness as well as to the preeminence of the novel in the Latin American literary boom.

3. With all due respect to the dangers of rigid classification, the Cuban novels of the Revolution fall into four clearly discernible chronological periods: 1959–1960, 1961–1965, 1966–1970, and 1971–. These four

divisions have been determined by specific changes in the government's attitude toward literature and the arts in general.

4. The role of literature and the arts in a revolutionary society has been widely debated in Cuba, with international repercussions. Cuba has not deviated significantly in this respect from the model established by other socialist countries.

5. The novelists and short-story writers of the Revolution include representatives of four distinct literary generations—those born at the turn of the century like Alejo Carpentier (b. 1904), between 1910 and 1920 like José Lezama Lima (b. 1912), between 1920 and 1937 like Guillermo Cabrera Infante (b. 1929) and Edmundo Desnoes (b. 1930), and in the late 1930's and early 1940's like Jesús Díaz Rodríguez (b. 1941). The large majority of the works have come from the two younger generations.

6. The most prolific of the novelists with three or four titles, but not necessarily the best, are Noel Navarro, Samuel Feijóo, Edmundo Desnoes, José Soler Puig, David Buzzi, Lisandro Otero, and Severo Sarduy. The most prolific short-story writers are Angel Arango, Antonio Benítez Rojo, and José Lorenzo Fuentes. Those who have published both significant novels and volumes of short stories are Humberto Arenal, Reynaldo Arenas, and Noel Navarro.

7. The best known of the Cuban novels published between 1959 and 1972 are artistically innovative and are related only indirectly in varying degrees to the Revolution: Alejo Carpentier's *El siglo de las luces*, José Lezama Lima's *Paradiso*, Guillermo Cabrera Infante's *Tres tristes tigres*, and Severo Sarduy's *De donde son los cantantes*.

8. Among the novels that deal more directly with the Revolution, the best are Lisandro Otero's two volumes of a planned trilogy, *La situación* and *En ciudad semejante*, Severo Sarduy's *Gestos*, and Edmundo Desnoes's *Memorias del subdesarrollo*.

9. The best of the short-story writers are Calvert Casey, Humberto Arenal, Antonio Benítez Rojo, Jesús Díaz Rodríguez, and Norberto Fuentes Cobas.

10. A rather large majority of the Cuban novels and short stories published between 1959 and 1973 are concerned with the portrayal of prerevolutionary Cuba, and particularly prerevolutionary Havana. The clandestine urban movement against Batista receives much more attention than do the guerrilla exploits of Fidel Castro in the Sierra Maestra. Among the works that take place in Cuba after 1959, the most frequently treated themes are the reluctance of the bourgeoisie to accept the revolutionary changes and the counterinsurgency campaign of the early 1960's. In general, authors have avoided controversial aspects of the Revolution. Some criticism of the regime appears in books published outside Cuba: Guillermo Cabrera Infante's *Tres tristes tigres*, Reynaldo Arenas's *El mundo alucinante*, Eduardo Manet's *Un cri sur le rivage*, and, possibly, Alejo Carpentier's *El siglo de las luces*. Of the works published in Cuba, the following are somewhat ambiguous in their revolutionary zeal: Edmundo Desnoes's *Memorias del subdesarrollo*, Ezequiel Vieta's *Vivir en Candonga* and *Pailock, el prestidigitador*, Leonel López-Nussa's *Recuerdos del 36*, and Norberto Fuentes Cobas's *Condenados de Condado*.

11. A growing number of novels and volumes of short stories have been published by Cuban exiles. Most of them are anticommunist diatribes with scarce literary merit. However, a few novels by Juan Arcocha, Luis Ricardo Alonso, and Carlos Alberto Montaner and individual short stories by Calvert Casey, Lino Novás Calvo, and Beltrán de Quirós are serious literary efforts to portray conditions in Cuba, in Miami, and elsewhere from the exiles' point of view. A few of the exiles, like Lydia Cabrera and Julio Matas, have continued to publish the same kind of escapist stories that they published in Cuba.

12. The Cuban Revolution is the principal or partial theme of twenty-two pro- as well as antirevolutionary novels, one volume of short stories, and one other short story written by a variety of Americans and Latin Americans. Of these, the best are clearly Carlos Martínez Moreno's *El paredón*, Julio Cortázar's "Reunión," and Antônio Callado's *Don Juan's Bar*.

CHRONOLOGY OF NOVELS AND SHORT STORIES

Cuban Novels of the Revolution

1959   Arenal, Humberto, *El sol a plomo*
       Becerra Ortega, José, *La novena estación*
1960   Perera Soto, Hilda, *Mañana es 26*
       Soler Puig, José, *Bertillón 166*
1961   Alonso, Dora, *Tierra inerme*
       Aparicio Nogales, Raúl, *Frutos del azote*
       Desnoes, Edmundo, *No hay problema*
       Pogolotti, Marcelo, *El caserón del Cerro*
       Sarusky, Jaime, *La búsqueda*
1962   Arcocha, Juan, *Los muertos andan solos*
       Carpentier, Alejo, *El siglo de las luces*
       Lorenzo Fuentes, José, *El sol ese enemigo*
       Navarro, Noel, *Los días de nuestra angustia*
       Olema García, Daura, *Maestra voluntaria*
       Piñeiro, Abelardo, *El descanso*
1963   Aguililla, Araceli C. de, *Primeros recuerdos*
       López-Nussa, Leonel, *Tabaco*
       Manet, Eduardo, *Un cri sur le rivage*
       Otero, Lisandro, *La situación*
       Piñera, Virgilio, *Pequeñas maniobras*
       Sarduy, Severo, *Gestos*
       Soler Puig, José, *En el año de enero*
1964   Feijóo, Samuel, *Juan Quinquín en Pueblo Mocho*
       ———, *Tumbaga*
       González de Cascorro, Raúl, *Concentración pública*

Herrera, Mariano Rodríguez, *Después de la Z*
Leante, César, *El perseguido*
Soldevilla, Loló, *El farol*
Soler Puig, José, *El derrumbe*
1965 Agostini, Víctor, *Dos viajes*
Desnoes, Edmundo, *El cataclismo*
———, *Memorias del subdesarrollo*
1966 Collazo, Miguel, *El libro fantástico de Oaj*
Lezama Lima, José, *Paradiso*
Otero, Lisandro, *Pasión de Urbino*
Vieta, Ezequiel, *Pailock, el prestidigitador*
———, *Vivir en Candonga*
1967 Agüero, Luis, *La vida en dos*
Amado Blanco, Luis, *Ciudad rebelde*
Arenal, Humberto, *Los animales sagrados*
Arenas, Reinaldo, *Celestino antes del alba*
Buzzi, David, *Los desnudos*
Cabrera Infante, Guillermo, *Tres tristes tigres*
Eguren, Gustavo, *La Robla*
Granados, Manuel, *Adire y el tiempo roto*
Leante, César, *Padres e hijos*
López-Nussa, Leonel, *Recuerdos del 36*
Navarro, Noel, *Los caminos de la noche*
Ortega, Gregorio, *Reportaje de las vísperas*
Piñera, Virgilio, *Presiones y diamantes*
Sarduy, Severo, *De donde son los cantantes*
Sarusky, Jaime, *Rebelión en la octava casa*
1968 Collazo, Miguel, *El viaje*
Chofre, Francisco, *La Odilea*
Feijóo, Samuel, *Jira descomunal*
———, *Pancho Ruta y Gil Jocuma*
Fernández, Pablo Armando, *Los niños se despiden*
González, Reynaldo, *Siempre la muerte, su paso breve*
Lorenzo Fuentes, José, *Viento de enero*
Navarro, Noel, *El plano inclinado*
1969 Arenas, Reynaldo, *El mundo alucinante*
Barnet, Miguel, *Canción de Rachel*
Buzzi, David, *La religión de los elefantes*

1970 Buzzi, David, *Mariana*
    Cossío Woodward, Miguel, *Sacchario*
    Iznaga, Alcides, *Las cercas caminaban*
    Otero, Lisandro, *En ciudad semejante*
1971 Cárdenas Acuña, Ignacio, *Enigma para un domingo*
    Cofiño López, Manuel, *La última mujer y el próximo combate*
    Eguren, Gustavo, *En la cal de las paredes*
    Navarro, Noel, *Zona de silencio*
    Travieso, Julio, *Para matar al lobo*
    Valdés Vivó, Raúl, *Los negros ciegos*
1972 Carpentier, Alejo, *Los convidados de plata* (3 chapters)
    Sarduy, Severo, *Cobra*
    Tejera, Nivaria, *Sonámbulo del sol*
1974 Carpentier, Alejo, *El recurso del método*

Cuban Short Stories of the Revolution

1959 Gómez, José Jorge, *La corteza y la savia: Cuentos por Baltasar Enero*
    Guerra, Jorge, *Nueve cuentos por un peso*
    Ortega, Antonio, *Yemas de cocos y otros cuentos*
1960 Amado Blanco, Luis, *Doña Velorio y otros cuentos*
    Cabrera Infante, Guillermo, *Así en la paz como en la guerra*
    Cardoso, Onelio Jorge, *El caballo de coral*
    ————, *Cuentos completos* (other editions 1962, 1966, 1969)
    ————, *La lechuza ambiciosa*
    García Vega, Lorenzo, *Cetrería del títere*
    Henríquez, Enrique C., *Sin freno ni silla: 7 cuasirelatos y 9 temas
        humanos abreviados*
    Perera Soto, Hilda, *Cuentos de Adli y Luas*
    Pita Rodríguez, Félix, *Esta larga tarea de aprender a morir y otros
        cuentos*
1961 Díaz Chávez, Luis, *Pescador sin fortuna*
    Ferrer, Surama, *Cuatro cuentos*
    Sergio, Gil Blas, *Dos hombres*
1962 Agüero, Luis, *De aquí para allá*
    Arenal, Humberto, *La vuelta en redondo*
    Cardoso, Onelio Jorge, *Gente de pueblo*
    Casey, Calvert, *El regreso*
    Cuevas, Guillermo, *Ni un sí, ni un no: Cuentos y cosas*

González de Cascorro, Raúl, *Gente de Playa Girón*
Herrera, Mariano R., *La mutación*
Juárez Fernández, Bel, *En las lomas de El Purial*
Llopis, Rogelio, *La guerra y los basiliscos*
Simó, Ana María, *Las fábulas*
Suárez Solís, Rafael, *Un pueblo donde no pasaba nada*

1963   Abascal, Jesús, *Soroche y otros cuentos*
Agostini, Víctor, *Bibijaguas*
Arrufat, Antón, *Mi antagonista y otras observaciones*
González, Reynaldo, *Miel sobre hojuelas*
Hurtado, Oscar, *Cartas de un juez*
Llopis, Rogelio, *El fabulista*
López, César, *Circulando el cuadrado*
Lorenzo Fuentes, José, *Maguaraya arriba*
Matas, Julio, *Catálogo de imprevistos*
Otero, José Manuel, *El paisaje nunca es el mismo: 10 cuentos*
Pita Rodríguez, Félix, *Cuentos completos*
Pogolotti, Marcelo, *Detrás del muro*
Vieta, Ezequiel, *Libro de los epílogos*

1964   Abdo, Ada, *Mateo y las sirenas*
Alvarez, Antonio, *Noneto*
Aparicio, Raúl, *Hijos del tiempo*
Arango, Angel, *¿A dónde van los cefalomos?*
Arenal, Humberto, *El tiempo ha descendido*
Cabada, Carlos, Juan Luis Herrero, and Agenor Martí, *Cuentos de
    ciencia ficción*
Camps, David, *Balance*
Cardoso, Onelio Jorge, *La otra muerte del gato*
————, *El perro*
Cruz Díaz, Rigoberto, *Postales de mi pueblo*
Feijóo, Samuel, *Tumbaga* (short novel and 7 stories)
Fernández, Angel Luis, *La nueva noche*
Fernández, José Manuel, *Todo ángel es terrible*
————, *El tren de las 11:30*
Gómez, José Jorge, *Los hijos de Abel*
Hurtado, Oscar, *La ciudad muerta de Korad*
Piñera, Virgilio, *Cuentos*
Rodríguez Leyva, Nelson, *El regalo*

Tamayo, Evora, *Cuentos para abuelas enfermas*
1965 Gallegos Mancera, Eduardo, *Cartas de la prisión, Héctor Mujica: Cuentos de lucha*
González de Cascorro, Raúl, *La semilla*
Llana, María Elena, *La reja*
Martínez, Angela, *Memorias de un decapitado*
Miranda, Anisia, *Becados*
Otero, José Manuel, *4 cuentos*
Pita Rodríguez, Félix, *Poemas y cuentos*
Solís, José, and Sixto Quintela, Víctor Casaus, and Carlos Quintela, *Voluntario*
Tamayo, Evora, *La vieja y la mar*
1966 Alonso, Dora, *Ponolani*
Arango, Angel, *El planeta Negro*
Cardoso, Onelio Jorge, *Iba caminando*
Correa, Arnaldo, *Asesinato por anticipado*
Díaz Llanillo, Esther, *El castigo*
Díaz Rodríguez, Jesús, *Los años duros*
Medero, Marinés, *Cuentos y anticuentos de Juan Dolcines*
1967 Abascal, Jesús, *Staccato*
Acosta, Leonardo, *Paisajes del hombre*
Arango, Angel, *Robotomaquia*
Benítez Rojo, Antonio, *Tute de reyes*
Correa, Arnaldo, *El primer hombre a Marte*
Daranas, Manuel A., *Tres cuentos*
Herrero, Juan Luis, *Tigres en el Vedado*
Lorenzo Fuentes, José, *El vendedor de días*
Piniella, Germán, *Polífagos*
Sáez, Luis Manuel, *El iniciado*
Travieso, Julio, *Días de guerra*
Valle, Gerardo del, *1/4 fambá y 19 cuentos más*
1968 Agüero, Luis, *Primer día del año en la casa de los muertos*
Aparicio, Raúl, *Espejos de alinde*
Desnoes, Edmundo, *Memorias del subdesarrollo* (This edition includes four stories: "Jack y el guagüero," "¡Créalo o no lo crea!" "Yodor," "What Can I Do?")
Fuentes Cobas, Norberto, *Condenados de Condado*
Garófalo, José Miguel, *Se dice fácil*

Heras León, Eduardo, *La guerra tuvo seis nombres*
Lorenzo Fuentes, José, *Después de la gaviota*
1969 Benítez Rojo, Antonio, *El escudo de hojas secas*
Cardoso, Onelio Jorge, *Abrir y cerrar los ojos*
Casey, Calvert, *Notas de un simulador*
Catorce cuentistas
Chaplé, Sergio, *Ud. sí puede tener un Buick*
Cofiño López, Manuel, *Tiempo de cambio*
Eguren, Gustavo, *Algo para la palidez y una ventana sobre el regreso*
Leante, César, *La rueda y la serpiente*
1970 Alonso, Dora, *Once caballos*
Cardi, Juan Angel, *Relatos de Pueblo Viejo*
Chinea, Hugo, *Escambray 60*
Collazo, Miguel, *Cuentos*
Fuentes Cobas, Norberto, *Cazabandido*
Granados, Manuel, *El viento en la casa sol*
Heras León, Eduardo, *Los pasos en la hierba*
Labrador Ruiz, Enrique, *Cuentos*
Nueve cuentistas
Piñera, Virgilio, *El que vino a salvarme*
Travieso, Julio, *Los corderos beben vino*
1971 Alvarez García, Imeldo, *La sonrisa y la otra cabeza*
Arango, Angel, *El fin del caos llega quietamente*
Callejas Ros, Bernardo, *¿Qué vas a cantar ahora?*
Cirules, Enrique, *Los perseguidos*
Llopis, Rogelio, *El buscador de tesoros*
Piniella, Germán, *Otra vez al camino*
Quiñones, Serafín, *Al final del terraplén el sol*
1972 Arenas, Reynaldo, *Con los ojos cerrados*
Callejas Ros, Bernardo, *Para aprender a manejar la pistola*
Carpentier, Alejo, *El derecho de asilo*
Chacón, Julio A., *Canción militante a tres tiempos*
Eguren, Gustavo, *Al borde del agua*
Navarro, Noel, *La huella del pulgar*

Antirevolutionary Cuban Novels

1960 Rivero Collado, Andrés, *Enterrado vivo*

1961 Díaz-Versón, Salvador, . . . *Ya el mundo oscurece*
1962 Fernández Camus, Emilio, *Caminos llenos de borrascas*
1965 Cobo Sausa, Manuel, *El cielo será nuestro*
    Linares, Manuel, *Los Ferrández*
    Sánchez Torrentó, Eugenio, *Francisco Manduley: La historia de un pescador de ranas*
1966 Alonso, Luis Ricardo, *Territorio libre*
    Núñez Pérez, Orlando, *El grito*
1967 Arcocha, Juan, *A Candle in the Wind*
    Fowler, Raoul A., *En las garras de la paloma*
    Landa, René G., *De buena cepa*
1968 Villa, Alvaro de, *El olor de la muerte que viene*
1969 Castro, Angel A., *Refugiados*
    Entenza, Pedro, *No hay aceras*
    López, Pablo A., *Ayer sin mañana*
1970 Arcocha, Juan, *Por cuenta propia*
    Pérez, Jorge T., "Los Buenos"
1971 Alonso, Luis Ricardo, *Los dioses ajenos*
    González, Celedonio, *Los primos*
    Sánchez-Boudy, José, *Lilayando*
1972 Chao Hermida, Francisco, *Un obrero de vanguardia*
    Gómez-Kemp, Ramiro, *Los desposeídos*
    Márquez y de la Cerra, Miguel F., *El gallo cantó*
    Montaner, Carlos Alberto, *Perromundo*
    Perera, Hilda, *El sitio de nadie*
    Sánchez-Boudy, José, *Los cruzados de la aurora*
1973 Arcocha, Juan, *La bala perdida*

Short Stories by Cubans in Exile

1961 Viana, Roberto, *Los que por ti murieron*
1963 Brenes, María, *Diez cuentos para un libro*
1964 Díaz, Pedro Ernesto, *Cuatro cuentos cristianos*
    Martínez Solanas, Gerardo E., *Dos cuentos y dos leyendas*
    Rivero Collado, Andrés, *Rojo y negro: Cuentos sobre la tragedia cubana*
    Viera Trejo, Bernardo, *Militantes del odio y otros relatos de la revolución cubana*

1965   Alcover Herrera, Wilfredo, *Cuentos cortos*
1966   Sánchez-Boudy, José, *Cuentos grises*
1967   Montes Huidobro, Matías, *La anunciación y otros cuentos cubanos*
1968   Alcover Herrera, Wilfredo, *Recopilación de cuentos cortos*
        Andino Porro, Alberto, *Polvos y lodos: Cuentos de Cuba*
        Montaner, Carlos Alberto, *Póker de brujas y otros cuentos*
1969   Casey, Calvert, *Notas de un simulador*
        Ferreira, Ramón, *Los malos olores de este mundo*
        Sánchez-Boudy, José, *Cuentos del hombre*
1970   Abella, Lorenzo, *Más allá del espejo*
        Alvarez Fuentes, Germán, *Ficciones y realidades*
        Castro, Angel A., *Cuentos del exilio cubano*
        León, Joaquín de, *Sin reproche y otros cuentos*
        Montaner, Carlos Alberto, *Instantáneas al borde del abismo*
        Novás Calvo, Lino, *Maneras de contar*
        Ripoll, Carlos, *Julián Pérez por Benjamín Castillo*
        Saínz de la Peña, José, *Castro quedó atrás*
1971   Acosta Tijero, Alberto, *La pierna artificial y otros cuentos*
        Alcover Herrera, Wilfredo, *Kaktos: Recopilación de cuentos cortos*
        Cabrera, Lydia, *Ayapá: Cuentos de Jicotea*
        Cachán, Manuel, *Cuentos políticos*
        González, Celedonio, *La soledad es una amiga que vendrá*
        Matas, Julio, *Erinia*
        Peña, Humberto J., *Ya no habrá más domingos*
        Quirós, Beltrán de, *Los unos, los otros . . . y el seibo*
        Sánchez-Boudy, José, *Cuentos a luna llena*
1972   Castro, Angel A., *Cuentos yanquis*
        Gutiérrez Kann, Asela, *Las pirañas y otros cuentos cubanos*

Foreign Prose Fiction of the Cuban Revolution

1959   Hawkins, Ward (American), *Kings Will Be Tyrants*
        Herr, Paul (American), *Journey Not to End*
1960   Aguilera Malta, Demetrio (Ecuadorean), *Una cruz en la Sierra Maestra*
        Tully, Andrew (American), *A Race of Rebels*
1962   Ladrón de Guevara, Matilde (Chilean), *Adiós al cañaveral*
        Miller, Warren (American), *Flush Times*

1963 Aguilar Derpich, Juan (Peruvian), *"El majá" o El pérfido Julián*
      Aramayo, X. (Spaniard), *En La Habana ha muerto un turista*
      Martínez Moreno, Carlos (Uruguayan), *El paredón*
1964 Cortázar, Julio (Argentinian), "Reunión" (short story)
      Mases, José Antonio (Spaniard), *Los padrenuestros y el fusil*
1965 Baeza Flores, Antonio (Chilean), *La muerte en el paraíso*
      Hernández, Luisa Josefina (Mexican), *La primera batalla*
      Mases, José Antonio (Spaniard), *La invasión*
1966 Castellanos Velasco, Francisco (Mexican), *Cuando la caña es amarga*
      Gámez, Tana de (Spaniard), *The Yoke and the Star*
      Pellecer, Carlos Manuel (Guatemalan), *Utiles después de muertos*
1967 Uris, Leon (American), *Topaz*
1969 Grimalt, Manuel (Spaniard), *Nadie escribe la historia de la próxima aurora*
      Soto, Pedro Juan (Puerto Rican), *El francotirador*
      Viteri, Eugenia (Ecuadorean), *A 90 millas, solamente*
1970 Baeza Flores, Antonio (Chilean), *La frontera del adiós: Novela del exilio*
1971 Callado, Antônio (Brazilian), *Don Juan's Bar*
1973 Edwards, Jorge (Chilean), *Persona non grata*

BIBLIOGRAPHY

BIBLIOGRAPHY

Cuban Novels of the Revolution

Several volumes that have appeared in previous bibliographies have been omitted for the following reasons:

1. Written by Cubans who left Cuba before 1959 about themes unrelated to the Cuban Revolution: Caridad Bravo Adams (b. 1907), *Flor salvaje* (1960) and twenty-seven other melodramatic novels; Julieta Campos (b. 1932), *Muerta por agua* (1965); and Carlos Zéner (b. 1925), *El rescate* (1965) and *La espiral* (1968).

2. Subliterary sentimentality unrelated to the Revolution: Miguel A. Macau, *Y se salvaba el amor* (1959); Ana María Amador Martz, *Alma hueca* (1960); and Miguel Alfonso, *Clarivel, novela de amor y dolor* (1962).

3. Impossible to locate and never mentioned except in bibliographies: Emma Armenteros, *Guamá* (1964), and Ramón Becali, *Los dioses mendigos* (1965).

4. New editions of pre-1959 novels.

5. Written in 1958 about the Spanish Civil War: Nivaria Tejera (b. 1933), *El barranco* (1959).

6. Written in French by a Cuban living in France and unrelated to the Revolution: Eduardo Manet (b. 1927), *Les étrangers dans la ville* (1960).

7. Anachronistic melodramatic historical novel: Eduardo Benet y Castellón (b. 1878), *Birín* (1962).

8. More aptly classified as autobiography: Miguel Barnet (b. 1941), *Biografía de un cimarrón* (1966).

The Casa de las Américas prize winners are indicated by asterisks.

Agostini, Víctor. *Dos viajes*. Havana: Ediciones R, 1965, 291 pp.

Agüero, Luis. *La vida en dos*. Havana: Casa de las Américas, 1967, 268 pp.

Aguililla, Araceli C. de. *Primeros recuerdos*. Havana: Unión, 1963, 200 pp.

*Alonso, Dora. *Tierra inerme*. Havana: Casa de las Américas, 1961, 202 pp.; 2d ed., Havana: Unión, 1964; 3d ed., in *Cuba ayer y hoy: Dos novelas*, with Daura Olema García's *Maestra voluntaria*. Buenos Aires, 1965, 299 pp.

Amado Blanco, Luis. *Ciudad rebelde*. Barcelona: Nova Terra, 1967, 437 pp.

Aparicio Nogales, Raúl. *Frutos del azote*. Buenos Aires: Palestra, 1961, 128 pp.

Arcocha, Juan. *Los muertos andan solos*. Havana: Ediciones R, 1962, 251 pp.; 2d ed., 1963. For *A Candle in the Wind*, see the section on antirevolutionary novels.

Arenal, Humberto. *Los animales sagrados*. Havana: Instituto del Libro, 1967, 142 pp.

—————. *El sol a plomo*. New York: Las Américas, 1959, 93 pp.; 2d ed., Havana: Cruzada Latinoamericana de Difusión Cultural, 1959, 132 pp.; 3d ed., Mexico City: Nuevo Mundo, 1959, 132 pp. *The Sun Beats Down: A Novella of the Cuban Revolution*. Translated by Joseph M. Bernstein. New York: Hill and Wang, 1959, 96 pp.

Arenas, Reinaldo. *Celestino antes del alba*. Havana: Unión, 1967, 219 pp.; 2d ed., Buenos Aires: Brújula, 1968, 172 pp.; 3d ed., Buenos Aires: Centro Editor de América Latina, 1972.

—————. *El mundo alucinante*. Mexico City: Diógenes, 1969, 222 pp.; *Hallucinations*. Translated by Gordon Brotherston. New York: Harper and Row, 1971, 287 pp.

Barnet, Miguel. *Canción de Rachel*. Havana: Instituto del Libro, 1969, 160 pp.; 2d ed., Buenos Aires: Galerna, 1969, 171 pp.

Becerra Ortega, José. *La novena estación*. Havana: El Siglo XX, 1959, 133 pp.

Buzzi, David. *Los desnudos*. Havana: Unión, 1967, 277 pp.

—————. *Mariana*. Havana: Unión, 1970, 166 pp.

—————. *La religión de los elefantes*. Havana: Unión, 1969, 178 pp.

Cabrera Infante, Guillermo. *Tres tristes tigres*. Barcelona: Seix Barral, 1967, 451 pp.; 2d ed., 1968; 3d ed., 1969; *Trois tristes tigres*. Translated by Albert Bensoussan. Paris: Gallimard, 1970, 463 pp.; *Three Trapped Tigers*. Translated by Donald Gardner and Suzanne Jill Levine. New York: Harper and Row, 1971, 487 pp.

Cárdenas Acuña, Ignacio. *Enigma para un domingo*. Havana: Instituto Cubano del Libro, 1971, 216 pp.

Carpentier, Alejo. "El año 59" (chapter from the unpublished novel of the same name). *Casa de las Américas* 4, no. 26 (October–November 1964): 45–50.

―――. "Los convidados de plata" (chapter from the unpublished novel "El año 59"). *Bohemia*, July 9, 1965, pp. 28–32.

―――. *Los convidados de plata*. Montevideo: Sandino, 1972, 66 pp.

―――. *El recurso del método*. Mexico City: Siglo XXI, 1974, 343 pp.

―――. *El siglo de las luces*. Mexico City: Compañía General de Ediciones, 1962, 300 pp.; 2d ed., 1965; 3d ed., 1966; 4th ed., 1967; Havana: Ediciones R, 1963, 423 pp.; 2d ed., 1965; Havana: Instituto del Libro, 1968; Barcelona: Seix Barral, 1965, 365 pp.; Buenos Aires: Galerna, 1967; *Explosion in a Cathedral*. Translated by John Sturrock. Boston: Little, Brown, 1963, 351 pp., and London: Gollancz, 1963, 351 pp.; *Le Siècle des lumières*. Translated by René L. F. Durand. Paris: Gallimard, 1962, 343 pp.; *Explosion dom kirken*. Translated by Michel Tejn. Copenhagen: Steen Hasselbachs, 1964, 373 pp.; *Explosion in der kathedrale*. Translated by Hermann Stiehl. Frankfurt am Main: Insel, 1964, 379 pp.; *Il Secolo dei lumi*. Translated by Maria Vasta Dazzi. Milan: Longanesi, 1964, 447 pp.; *Detta Upplysta tidervarv*. Translated by Jan Sjögren. Stockholm: Bouviers, 1965, 313 pp.; *Eksplosjon i katedralen*. Translated by Axel S. Seeberg. Oslo: Gyldendal Norsk, 1965, 218 pp.; *Secolul luminilor*. Translated by Ovidiu Constantinescu and María Ioanovici. 2 vols. Bucharest: Pentru Literatura Universala, 1965; *De Guillotine op de voorsteven*. Amsterdam: Meulenhoff, 1966, 316 pp.; *Exsplozja w katedrze*. Translated by Kalina Wojciechowska. Warsaw: Czytelnik, 1966, 509 pp.

Chofre, Francisco. *La Odilea*. Havana: Unión, 1968, 243 pp.

*Cofiño López, Manuel. *La última mujer y el próximo combate*. Havana: Casa de las Américas, 1971, 334 pp.; Mexico City: Siglo XXI, 1972, 328 pp.; Buenos Aires: Centro Editor de América Latina, 1972, 211 pp.

Collazo, Miguel. *El libro fantástico de Oaj*. Havana: Unión, 1966, 107 pp.

―――. *El viaje*. Havana: Unión, 1968, 122 pp.

*Cossío Woodward, Miguel. *Sacchario*. Havana: Casa de las Américas, 1970, 249 pp.

Desnoes, Edmundo. *El cataclismo*. Havana: Ediciones R, 1965, 293 pp.

―――. *Memorias del subdesarrollo*. Havana: Unión, 1965, 101 pp.; 2d ed., Buenos Aires: Galerna, 1968, 145 pp.; *Inconsolable Memories*.

Translated by Edmundo Desnoes. New York: New American Library, 1967, 154 pp., and London: Beutsch, 1968.

———. *No hay problema*. Havana: Ediciones R, 1961, 225 pp.; 2d ed., 1964.

Eguren, Gustavo. *En la cal de las paredes*. Havana: Unión, 1971, 106 pp.

———. *La Robla*. Havana: Unión, 1967, 202 pp.

Feijóo, Samuel. "Jira descomunal." *Islas*, no. 29 (1968), pp. 300–457.

———. *Juan Quinquín en Pueblo Mocho*. Santa Clara: Universidad Central de Las Villas, 1964, 294 pp.

———. "Pancho Ruta y Gil Jocuma." *Islas*, no. 28 (1968), pp. 353–493.

———. *Tumbaga*. Santa Clara: Universidad Central de Las Villas, 1964, 213 pp. A short novel and seven stories.

*Fernández, Pablo Armando. *Los niños se despiden*. Havana: Casa de las Américas, 1968, 547 pp.; 2d ed., Buenos Aires: Centro Editor América Latina, 1972.

González, Reynaldo. *Siempre la muerte, su paso breve*. Havana: Casa de las Américas, 1968, 238 pp.

González de Cascorro, Raúl. *Concentración pública*. Havana: Unión, 1964, 171 pp.

Granados, Manuel. *Adire y el tiempo roto*. Havana: Casa de las Américas, 1967, 350 pp.

Herrera, Mariano R. *Después de la Z*. Havana: Ediciones R, 1964, 118 pp.

Iznaga, Alcides. *Las cercas caminaban*. Havana: Unión, 1970, 188 pp.

Leante, César. *Padres e hijos*. Havana: Unión, 1967, 124 pp.

———. *El perseguido*. Havana: Ediciones R, 1964, 172 pp.

Lezama Lima, José. *Paradiso*. Havana: Unión, 1966, 617 pp.; 2d ed., Mexico City: Era, 1968, 490 pp.; 3d ed., Lima: Paradiso, 1968; 4th ed., Buenos Aires: De la Flor, 1968. *Paradiso: Roman*. Translated by Didier Coste. Paris: Du Seuil, 1971, 573 pp.; *Paradiso*. Translated by Gregory Rabassa. New York: Farrar, Straus and Giroux, 1974.

López-Nussa, Leonel. *Recuerdos del 36*. Havana: Unión, 1967, 194 pp.

———. *Tabaco*. Santa Clara: Universidad Central de Las Villas, 1963, 257 pp.

Lorenzo Fuentes, José. *El sol ese enemigo*. Havana: Ediciones R, 1962, 111 pp.

———. *Viento de enero*. Havana: Instituto del Libro, 1968, 216 pp.

Manet, Eduardo. *Un cri sur le rivage*. Paris: Julliard, 1963, 237 pp.

Navarro, Noel. *Los caminos de la noche*. Havana: Granma, 1967, 203 pp.

————. *Los días de nuestra angustia.* Havana: Ediciones R, 1962, 383 pp.

————. *El plano inclinado.* Havana: Instituto del Libro, 1968, 158 pp.

————. *Zona de silencio.* Havana: Unión, 1971, 189 pp.

*Olema García, Daura. *Maestra voluntaria.* Havana: Casa de las Américas, 1962, 148 pp.; 2d ed., in *Cuba ayer y hoy: Dos novelas,* with Dora Alonso's *Tierra inerme.* Buenos Aires, 1965, 299 pp.

Ortega, Gregorio. *Reportaje de las vísperas.* Havana: Unión, 1967, 167 pp.

*Otero, Lisandro. *En ciudad semejante.* Havana: Unión, 1970, 392 pp.

————. *Pasión de Urbino.* Buenos Aires: J. Alvarez, 1966, 107 pp.; 2d ed., Havana: Instituto del Libro, 1967, 88 pp.

————. *La situación.* Havana: Casa de las Américas, 1963, 317 pp.

Perera Soto, Hilda. *Mañana es 26.* Havana: Lázaro Hnos., 1960, 227 pp.

Piñeiro, Abelardo. *El descanso.* Havana: Unión, 1962, 201 pp.

Piñera, Virgilio. *Pequeñas maniobras.* Havana: Ediciones R, 1963, 208 pp.

————. *Presiones y diamantes.* Havana: Unión, 1967, 105 pp.

Pogolotti, Marcelo. *El caserón del Cerro.* Santa Clara: Universidad Central de Las Villas, 1961, 237 pp.

Sarduy, Severo. *Cobra.* Buenos Aires: Sudamericana, 1972, 263 pp.; *Cobra.* Translated by Ph. Sollers. Paris: Du Seuil, 1972, 176 pp.

————. *De donde son los cantantes.* Mexico City: Joaquín Mortiz, 1967, 153 pp.; *Ecrit en dansant.* Translated by E. Cabillon and C. Esteban. Paris: Du Seuil, 1967, 205 pp.; *From Cuba with a Song.* Translated by Suzanne Jill Levine and Hallie D. Taylor. In *Triple Cross,* with Carlos Fuentes's *Holy Place* and José Donoso's *Hell Has No Limits.* New York: E. P. Dutton, 1972.

————. *Gestos.* Barcelona: Seix Barral, 1963, 140 pp.

Sarusky, Jaime. *La búsqueda.* Havana: Ediciones R, 1961, 206 pp.; 2d ed., 1962.

————. *Rebelión en la octava casa.* Havana: Instituto del Libro, 1967, 152 pp.

Soldevilla, Loló. *El farol.* Havana: Ediciones R, 1964, 141 pp.

*Soler Puig, José. *Bertillón 166.* Havana: Ministerio de Educación, 1960, 244 pp.; 2d ed., Havana: Casa de las Américas, 1960, 217 pp.

————. *El derrumbe.* Prologue by José Antonio Portuondo. Santiago de Cuba: Consejo Nacional de Universidades, 1964, 164 pp.

————. *En el año de enero.* Havana: Unión, 1963, 235 pp.

Tejera, Nivaria. *Sonámbulo del sol.* Barcelona: Seix Barral, 1972, 230 pp.

Travieso, Julio. *Para matar al lobo.* Havana: Colección Cocuyo, 1971.

Valdés Vivó, Raúl. *Los negros ciegos*. Havana: Colección Cocuyo, 1971.

Vieta, Ezequiel. *Pailock, el prestidigitador*. Havana: Granma, 1966, 112 pp.

—————. *Vivir en Candonga*. Havana: Unión, 1966, 157 pp.

Annotated Bibliography of Anthologies of the Cuban Short Story

I have omitted Salvador Bueno's 1959 anthology because it is a shorter and only slightly revised edition of his 1953 anthology: Salvador Bueno, *Los mejores cuentos cubanos* (2 vols., Havana: Festival del Libro, 1959, 143 and 168 pp.). The following two anthologies have been omitted because the authors included are not primarily Cubans: *Antología de cuentos de terror y de misterio* (Havana: Instituto del Libro, 1967) and Oscar Hurtado, *Cuentos de ciencia-ficción* (Havana: Instituto del Libro, 1969, 408 pp.). One other anthology has been omitted because of its extreme brevity and because all five stories are taken from the Rogelio Llopis anthology: Edmundo Valadés, "Breve antología de narraciones fantásticas cubanas," *El cuento* 5, no. 39 (November–December 1969): 21–43. The following anthologies are arranged chronologically.

1. AM   Antón Arrufat and Fausto Masó. *Nuevos cuentistas cubanos*. Havana: Casa de las Américas, 1961, 261 pp.

In this first of the post-1959 anthologies, twenty-nine new authors are represented in chronological order, from Víctor Agostini (b. 1908) to Josefina Jacobs (b. 1943?). Brief biobibliographical paragraphs on each author and a general introduction are included. All the stories were written between 1954 and 1958, except for one in 1959. Personal problems in an urban setting with an existentialist mood prevail. The only revolutionary story is "El responsable" (1958) by Armando Entralgo (b. 1937), about two conspirators who take refuge in a room. Of these new writers, the following were to be heard from again in the course of the decade: Calvert Casey, Rogelio Llopis, Edmundo Desnoes, Lisandro Otero, Ambrosio Fornet, César López, Antón Arrufat, Luis Agüero, and Ana María Simó.

2. SCC   *Selección de cuentos cubanos*. Havana: Editorial Nacional de Cuba, 1962, 143 pp.

This volume includes nineteen authors with twenty-one stories, from Jesús Castellanos (1879–1912) to Guillermo Cabrera Infante (b. 1929). Hernández-Catá (1885–1940) and Félix Pita Rodríguez (b. 1909) are the only authors represented by more than one story. Of the twenty-one stories, all except three are in Salvador Bueno's well-known anthology of 1953.

3. DA   Dora Alonso, Salvador Bueno, Calvert Casey, José Lorenzo, and José Rodríguez Feo. *Nuevos cuentos cubanos*. Havana: Unión, 1964, 323 pp.

Contained in this anthology are the twenty-eight best stories published in books and journals, mainly during the first five years of the Revolution. Only ten of these authors are in the Arrufat-Masó anthology. No biobibliographical information or general introduction is given, and the index is incomplete. Six of the stories are related to the Revolution, of which two are quite unusual because of their rural settings: Raúl Aparicio's "Figuras de Valle Capetillo" and Samuel Feijóo's "El soldado Eloy." Seven of the stories are based on personal problems, while twelve may be classified in the realm of fantasy.

4. AF-1   Ambrosio Fornet. *Antología del cuento cubano contemporáneo*. Mexico City: Era, 1967, 241 pp.

This is the first of the anthologies to be published outside Cuba and the best overall anthology of the Cuban short story, starting with Jesús Castellanos and including five authors associated at the time with the Revolution: Guillermo Cabrera Infante, Calvert Casey, Humberto Arenal, Jesús Díaz Rodríguez, and Ana María Simó. It surpasses Salvador Bueno's 1953 anthology in its better choice of stories, the comments of each author on how he writes, and the excellent introduction, which underlines the relationship between the evolution of the short story and other literary genres as well as the historical development of Cuba as seen in Marxist terms. Cuban history is divided into the following six periods: 1902–1912, 1913–1922, 1923–1932, 1933–1947, 1947–1959, and 1959–. Fornet recognizes Carlos Montenegro, Lino Novás Calvo, and Ramón Ferreira, in spite of the fact that they left Cuba shortly after the triumph of the Revolution.

5. RF   José Rodríguez Feo. *Aquí 11 cubanos cuentan*. Montevideo: Arca, 1967, 169 pp.

Except for two stories by Virgilio Piñera and Onelio Jorge Cardoso, this anthology clearly features revolutionary themes: five on the pursuit and torture of conspirators, two on the existentialist mood of prerevolutionary Cuba, and three on the enthusiasm for the successful Revolution. Of the five revolutionary authors represented in the AF-1 anthology, only Ana María Simó is missing, while five others are added: José Lorenzo Fuentes, César Leante, Edmundo Desnoes, Ambrosio Fornet, and Lisandro Otero. Included are brief biobibliographical paragraphs and a brief introduction, which comments on the stories chosen and alludes to the self-imposed thematic censorship and to the "falso moralismo" that ended with the granting of the 1966 short-story prize to Jesús Díaz for *Los años duros*.

6. SC   Sylvia Carranza and María Juana Cazabon. *Cuban Short Stories, 1959–1966*. Havana: Book Institute, 1967, 229 pp.

This collection contains twenty-four stories in English translation, representing twenty-four authors from basically three different generations: seven born between 1908 and 1914, thirteen between 1919 and 1937, and four between 1937 and 1940. Eleven of the stories do not appear in other anthologies. Conspicuous by their absence are defectors Calvert Casey and Guillermo Cabrera Infante as well as their often-anthologized contemporaries: Antonio Benítez, Edmundo Desnoes, Gustavo Eguren, Ambrosio Fornet, Lisandro Otero, and Jaime Sarusky. A thematic classification reveals nine stories in the fantastic vein, five reflecting conditions in prerevolutionary Cuba, four depicting the rural and urban struggle against Batista, and only two taking place in post-1959 Cuba. Each author is introduced by a photograph and a brief bibliography, and each story by a full-page illustration. The brief one-page introduction to the volume and the one-page glossary add little. Prepared for the Montreal World's Fair, it was also published in French.

7. JMC   John Michael Cohen. *Writers in the New Cuba*. Baltimore: Penguin Books, 1967, 191 pp.

Although this anthology contains some poetry, a one-act play, and parts of Fidel Castro's famous June 1961 speech to the intellectuals, the short story does predominate. Of the eleven authors, only Calvert Casey and Ana María Simó have two stories each. Except for Onelio Jorge Cardoso and Virgilio Piñera, all the short-story writers became known after 1959, but only Jesús Díaz's story takes place in post-1959 Cuba. The anthologist was one of the judges in the 1965 poetry competition.

8. UN   UNEAC. "Literatura cubana '67." *Unión* 6, no. 4 (December 1967), 260 pp.

Nine short stories and seven selections from novels in addition to poetry and critical articles on painting, music, prose fiction, poetry, theater, and the cinema are included in this work dedicated to Che Guevara. Six of the prose fiction selections are also found in the Caballero Bonald anthology. Authors not represented in the other anthologies are Octavio Smith (b. 1921), Enrique Oltuski (b. 1930), and Rafael Alcides (b. 1933), the latter with three pages from his as-yet-unpublished novel "Contracastro," which satirizes the Cuban exiles in Miami. The biographical data are very brief.

9. JRF   José Rodríguez Feo. *Cuentos: Antología.* Havana: Unión, 1967, 77 pp.

This short work presents eleven stories written by members of the Hermanos Saíz Brigade. Born between 1930 and 1948, these writers, with the sole exception of David Buzzi Gallego, are not represented in any of the other anthologies. Only four of the stories are related to the Revolution.

10. RLL   Rogelio Llopis. *Cuentos cubanos de lo fantástico y lo extraordinario.* Havana: Unión, 1968, 329 pp.

Thirty-two authors, with as many stories, are divided into this book's seven sections: magic realism; the absurd and the dream world; loss of identity; satire, fable and black humor; the macabre; tall story; and science fiction. Most of Cuba's best writers are represented, from Enrique Labrador Ruiz, Alejo Carpentier, José Lezama Lima, and Virgilio Piñera to Antonio Benítez, Antón Arrufat, and Reinaldo Arenas. A good general introduction and up-to-date bibliographical data are included.

11. CB   José Manuel Caballero Bonald. *Narrativa cubana de la revolución.* Madrid: Alianza, 1968, 258 pp.

This anthology contains twenty-four selections, from works of Alejo Carpentier to Reinaldo Arenas, of which six are chapters from novels. Three of the authors included had left Cuba by the time of publication: Calvert Casey, Guillermo Cabrera Infante, and Severo Sarduy. Included are bio-bibliographical data on each author and a good general introduction based primarily on previous essays by Ambrosio Fornet and José Rodríguez Feo. Seven selections are based on episodes of Batista's last year in power; eight take place after January 1, 1959; while nine are not directly related to the Revolution.

12. JMO   José Miguel Oviedo. *Antología del cuento cubano.* Lima: Paradiso, 1968, 213 pp.

Nineteen stories, from Alejo Carpentier through Reinaldo Arenas, reflect the Peruvian anthologist's high aesthetic criteria. The omission of defectors Guillermo Cabrera Infante and Calvert Casey reflects his political bias. Oviedo presents short bibliographical notes but no introduction and no table of contents. Six of the stories also appear in the CB anthology. Five of the stories are in the fantastic vein.

13. RW   Rodolfo Walsh. *Crónicas de Cuba.* Buenos Aires: Jorge Alvarez, 1969, 253 pp.

In this collection short stories, sections of novels, poems, essays, and "crónicas" are grouped thematically: "The Saga That Was," "The Changes

That Took Place," "Life under the Revolution," "The World of Fantasy," and "Writers and the Revolution." Eleven short stories, from José Lezama Lima's "El juego de las decapitaciones" to Jesús Díaz's "Amor la Plata Alta," are included. The literary quality of the selections is subordinated to thematic considerations.

14. JEM   Julio E. Miranda. *Antología del nuevo cuento cubano.* Caracas: Domingo Fuentes, 1969, 298 pp.

This is a high-quality selection, from Calvert Casey (1924–1969) through Reinaldo Arenas (b. 1943). The four best authors are represented by two stories each—Calvert Casey, Humberto Arenal, Guillermo Cabrera Infante, and Antonio Benítez—while two rarely anthologized authors are also included: Gustavo Eguren (b. 1925) and Nelson Rodríguez (b. 1943). The stories are arranged by themes: "Cuba: El pasado," "El presente revolucionario," "Lo humano universal," and "Ciencia-ficción y absurdo." Brief biobibliographical introductions include the authors' present occupations. The well-documented general introduction presents the relative merits of the novel and the short story with a somewhat excessive partisanship for the latter and, particularly, for science fiction.

15. PR   Germán Piniella and Raúl Rivero. *Punto de partida.* Havana: Instituto del Libro, 1970, 205 pp.

Slightly more than one-half the volume is devoted to fifteen short stories by previously unknown authors, thirteen of whom were born between 1935 and 1950. Of the whole group, only Enrique Cirules has subsequently published his own volume of stories. There are brief biographical notes and a one-page prologue. The second part of the book is devoted to poetry.

16. AF-2.   Ambrosio Fornet. *Cuentos de la Revolución cubana.* Santiago, Chile: Universitaria, 1971, 199 pp.

Fourteen stories are included, of which six had not previously appeared in other anthologies. They are arranged thematically in order to present an overall picture of the Revolution from 1959 on. Major themes are the military victory of 1959, the Bay of Pigs invasion, and the reluctance of the bourgeoisie to accept the Revolution. The work includes only those authors who have become famous since 1959; except for Víctor Agostini (b. 1908), all were born between 1925 and 1943. Contains a brief prologue and biobibliographical paragraphs for each writer.

17. BS   Bernardo Subercaseaux. *Narrativa de la joven Cuba.* Santiago, Chile: Nascimento, 1971, 128 pp.

This anthology presents nine short stories and two nonfiction selections.

Of the nine authors, seven were born between 1941 and 1944, two in 1936 and 1938. Seven of the selections take place in rural areas and only four in Havana. Four deal with the armed struggle against the counterrevolutionaries, two against Batista. Monologues or first-person narration predominate. The style is relatively direct and unadorned, with no phonetic transcriptions of rural dialect. The prologue convincingly distinguishes these young writers from the previous generations by their objectivity, dialogue, optimism, and greater identification with the Revolution.

18. CM   Eduardo Congrains Martín. *Narrativa cubana.* Lima: ECOMA, 1972, 271 pp.

This work is heavily indebted to the 1967 Ambrosio Fornet anthology for the historical prologue and for the selection of eight older authors, from Carlos Montenegro to Onelio Jorge Cardoso. The six authors from the first revolutionary generation (Eguren, Leante, Arenal, Cabrera Infante, Otero, and Buzzi) are represented by stories found, for the most part, in José Miguel Oviedo's Peruvian anthology of 1968. The most original part of Congrains's volume is the third group of nine stories published after 1966 by authors of the first and second revolutionary generations. The three authors anthologized for the first time are Noel Navarro, Enrique Cirules, and Imeldo Alvarez García. One author is conspicuously missing from each of the three groups: Lino Novás Calvo, Calvert Casey, and Norberto Fuentes. Each story is preceded by a brief and at times incomplete biobibliographical note and a short comment on the story. All references to conflicts between the authors and the revolutionary government are avoided, except for a toned-down statement about Cabrera Infante.

19. GL   Cristóbal Garcés Larrea. *Narradores cubanos contemporáneos.* Guayaquil: Colección Ariel, 1973, 189 pp.

Twenty-six authors ranging chronologically from Hernández-Catá (1885–1940) to Jesús Díaz (b. 1941) are included. The most significant difference from previous anthologies is the inclusion of Alejo Carpentier's "Los advertidos." Notable authors omitted are Calvert Casey, Humberto Arenal, and Norberto Fuentes. The prologue is very brief and no biobibliographical data are given.

Cuban Short Stories of the Revolution

Excluded from the following bibliography are collections of popular folk tales and children's literature. The Casa de las Américas prize winners are indicated by asterisks.

Abascal, Jesús. *Soroche y otros cuentos*. Havana: El Puente, 1963, 72 pp.
————. *Staccato*. Havana: Unión, 1967, 60 pp.
Abdo, Ada. *Mateo y las sirenas*. Havana: El Puente, 1964, 27 pp.
Acosta, Leonardo. *Paisajes del hombre*. Havana: Unión, 1967, 101 pp.
Agostini, Víctor. *Bibijaguas*. Havana: Unión, 1963, 119 pp.
Agüero, Luis. *De aquí para allá*. Havana: Ediciones R, 1962, 125 pp.
————. *Primer día del año en la casa de los muertos*. Havana: Unión, 1968.
Alonso, Dora. *Ponolani*. Havana: Granma, 1966, 132 pp.
Alvarez García, Imeldo. *La sonrisa y la otra cabeza*. Havana: Unión, 1971, 130 pp.
Amado Blanco, Luis. *Doña Velorio y otros cuentos*. Santa Clara: Universidad Central de Las Villas, 1960, 263 pp.; Barcelona: Nova Terra, 1970, 220 pp.
Aparicio, Raúl. *Espejos de alinde*. Havana: Unión, 1968, 157 pp.
————. *Hijos del tiempo*. Havana: Unión, 1964, 174 pp.
Arango, Angel. *¿A dónde van los cefalomos?* Havana: Ediciones R, 1964, 86 pp.
————. *El fin del caos llega quietamente*. Havana: Unión, 1971, 109 pp.
————. *El planeta Negro*. Havana: Granma, 1966, 74 pp.
————. *Robotomaquia*. Havana: Unión, 1967, 74 pp.
Arenal, Humberto. *El tiempo ha descendido*. Havana: Ediciones R, 1964, 71 pp.
————. *La vuelta en redondo*. Havana: Ediciones R, 1962, 103 pp.
Arenas, Reynaldo. *Con los ojos cerrados*. Montevideo: Arca, 1972, 133 pp.
Arrufat, Antón. *Mi antagonista y otras observaciones*. Havana: Ediciones R, 1963, 97 pp.
Benítez Rojo, Antonio. *El escudo de hojas secas*. Havana: Unión, 1969, 178 pp.; Buenos Aires: Aditor, 1969, 117 pp.; Buenos Aires: Centro Editor de América Latina, 1972.
*————. *Tute de reyes*. Havana: Casa de las Américas, 1967, 120 pp.
Cabada, Carlos; Juan Luis Herrero; and Agenor Martí. *Cuentos de ciencia ficción*. Prologue by Oscar Hurtado. Havana: Ediciones R, 1964, 157 pp.
Cabrera Infante, Guillermo. *Así en la paz como en la guerra*. Havana: Ediciones R, 1960, 201 pp.; 4th ed., 1964; Montevideo: Alfa, 1968; Barcelona: Seix Barral, 1971, 194 pp.; *Dans la paix comme dans la guerre*. Paris: Gallimard, 1964.
Callejas Ros, Bernardo. *Para aprender a manejar la pistola*. Havana: Comisión de Extensión Universitaria, 1972, 92 pp.

————. *¿Qué vas a cantar ahora?* Havana: Unión, 1971, 139 pp.

Camps, David. *Balance*. Havana: Ediciones R, 1964, 95 pp.

Cardi, Juan Angel. *Relatos de Pueblo Viejo*. Havana: Dirección Política de las Fuerzas Armadas Revolucionarias, 1970, 131 pp.

Cardoso, Onelio Jorge. *Abrir y cerrar los ojos*. Havana: Unión, 1969, 128 pp.

————. *El caballo de coral*. Santa Clara: Universidad Central de Las Villas, 1960, 70 pp.

————. *Cuentos completos*. Havana: Ediciones R, 1960, 229 pp.; 2d ed., 1962; 3d ed., Havana: Unión, 1966, 259 pp.; 4th ed., Havana: Instituto del Libro, 1969, 271 pp.

————. *Gente de pueblo*. Santa Clara: Universidad Central de Las Villas, 1962.

————. *Iba caminando*. Havana: Granma, 1966, 121 pp.

————. *La lechuza ambiciosa*. Santa Clara: Universidad Central de Las Villas, 1960, 12 pp.

————. *La otra muerte del gato*. Havana: Unión, 1964, 72 pp.

————. *El perro*. Havana: La Tertulia, 1964, 18 pp.

Carpentier, Alejo. *El derecho de asilo*. Madrid: Lumen, 1972. "Right of Sanctuary." Translated by Frances Partridge. In *War of Time*, pp. 59–101. New York: Alfred A. Knopf, 1970. Originally published in the French collection *Guerre du temps* (Paris: Gallimard, 1967). The Mexican and Cuban editions of *Guerre del tiempo* do not include "El derecho de asilo" or "The Chosen," which is also contained in the French and American editions (Mexico City: Compañía General de Ediciones, 1958, 1966, 275 pp.; Havana: Unión, 1963, 155 pp.).

Casey, Calvert. *Notas de un simulador*. Barcelona: Seix Barral, 1969, 131 pp.

————. *El regreso*. Havana: Ediciones R, 1962, 124 pp.; 2d ed. enlarged, *El regreso y otros relatos*. Barcelona: Seix Barral, 1967, 212 pp.

Catorce cuentistas. Havana: Casa de las Américas, 1969. Includes four Cubans (Dora Alonso, Manuel Granados, Juan Leyva Guerra, and Alfredo Reyes Trejos) and ten other Latin Americans.

Chacón, Julio A. *Canción militante a tres tiempos*. Havana: Unión, 1972, 111 pp.

Chaplé, Sergio. *Ud. sí puede tener un Buick*. Havana, 1969.

Chinea, Hugo. *Escambray 60*. Havana: Unión, 1970, 46 pp.

Cirules, Enrique. *Los perseguidos*. Havana, 1971.

Cofiño López, Manuel. *Tiempo de cambio*. Havana: Dirección Política de las Fuerzas Armadas Revolucionarias, 1969, 84 pp.

Collazo, Miguel. *Cuentos*. Havana: Casa de las Américas, 1970, 239 pp.

Correa, Arnaldo. *Asesinato por anticipado*. Havana: Granma, 1966, 132 pp.

———. *El primer hombre a Marte*. Havana: Granma, 1967.

Cruz Díaz, Rigoberto. *Postales de mi pueblo*. Havana: Ediciones R, 1964, 125 pp.

Cuevas, Guillermo. *Ni un sí, ni un no: Cuentos y cosas*. Havana: El Puente, 1962, 93 pp.

Daranas, Manuel A. *Tres cuentos*. Havana: 1967, 14 pp.

Desnoes, Edmundo. *Memorias del subdesarrollo*. Buenos Aires: Galerna, 1968, 145 pp. This edition of the novel includes four stories: "Jack y el guagüero," "¡Créalo o no lo crea!" "Yodor," and "What Can I Do?"

Díaz Chávez, Luis. *Pescador sin fortuna*. Havana: Casa de las Américas, 1961, 55 pp.

Díaz Llanillo, Esther. *El castigo*. Havana: Ediciones R, 1966, 91 pp.

*Díaz Rodríguez, Jesús. *Los años duros*. Havana: Casa de las Américas, 1966, 105 pp.; Buenos Aires: Jorge Alvarez, 1967, 124 pp.

Eguren, Gustavo. *Al borde del agua*. Buenos Aires: Centro Editor de América Latina, 1972, 95 pp.

———. *Algo para la palidez y una ventana sobre el regreso*. Havana: Unión, 1969, 142 pp.

Feijóo, Samuel. *Tumbaga*. Santa Clara: Universidad Central de Las Villas, 1964, 213 pp. Besides the title short novel, this volume contains seven short stories.

Fernández, Angel Luis. *La nueva noche*. Havana: El Puente, 1964, 58 pp.

Fernández, José Manuel. *Todo ángel es terrible*. Havana: Ediciones R, 1964, 145 pp.

———. *El tren de las 11:30*. Havana: La Tertulia, 1964, 18 pp.

Ferrer, Surama. *Cuatro cuentos*. Havana: Caballo de Fuego, 1961, 22 pp.

Fuentes Cobas, Norberto. *Cazabandido*. Montevideo: Libros de la Pupila, 1970, 173 pp.

*———. *Condenados de Condado*. Havana: Casa de las Américas, 1968, 170 pp.; 2d ed., Buenos Aires: Centro Editor de América Latina, 1968, 110 pp.

Gallegos Mancera, Eduardo. *Cartas de la prisión, Héctor Mujica: Cuentos de lucha*. Havana: Venceremos, 1965, 86 pp.

García Vega, Lorenzo. *Cetrería del títere*. Santa Clara: Universidad Central de Las Villas, 1960, 180 pp.

Garófalo, José Miguel. *Se dice fácil*. Havana: Unión, 1968, 125 pp.

Gómez, José Jorge. *La corteza y la savia: Cuentos por Baltasar Enero*. Havana: Presencia, 1959, 139 pp.

————. *Los hijos de Abel*. Havana: Presencia, 1964.

González, Reynaldo. *Miel sobre hojuelas*. Havana: Ediciones R, 1963, 115 pp.

*González de Cascorro, Raúl. *Gente de Playa Girón*. Havana: Casa de las Américas, 1962, 110 pp.

————. *La semilla*. Havana: Ediciones R, 1965, 116 pp.

Granados, Manuel. *El viento en la casa sol*. Havana: Unión, 1970, 118 pp.

Guerra, Jorge. *Nueve cuentos por un peso*. Havana: Lex, 1959, 108 pp.

Henríquez, Enrique C. *Sin freno ni silla: 7 cuasirelatos y 9 temas humanos abreviados*. Havana, 1960, 94 pp.

Heras León, Eduardo. *La guerra tuvo seis nombres*. Havana: Unión, 1968, 60 pp.; 2d ed., Mexico City: Bogavante, 1970, 78 pp.

————. *Los pasos en la hierba*. Havana: Casa de las Américas, 1970, 136 pp.

Herrera, Mariano R. *La mutación*. Havana: El Puente, 1962, 61 pp.

Herrero, Juan Luis. *Tigres en el Vedado*. Havana: Unión, 1967, 80 pp.

————; Carlos Cabada; and Agenor Martí. *Cuentos de ciencia ficción*. Prologue by Oscar Hurtado. Havana: Ediciones R, 1964, 157 pp.

Hurtado, Oscar. *Cartas de un juez*. Havana: Ediciones R, 1963, 91 pp.

————. *La ciudad muerta de Korad*. Havana: Ediciones R, 1964.

Juárez Fernández, Bel. *En las lomas de El Purial*. Havana: Ediciones R, 1962, 114 pp.

Labrador Ruiz, Enrique. *Cuentos*. Selection and prologue by Humberto Arenal. Havana: Unión, 1970, 228 pp.

Leante, César. *La rueda y la serpiente*. Havana: Unión, 1969, 120 pp.

Llana, María Elena. *Le reja*. Havana: Ediciones R, 1965, 109 pp.

Llopis, Rogelio. *El buscador de tesoros*. Havana: Unión, 1971, 165 pp.

————. *El fabulista*. Havana: Ediciones R, 1963, 131 pp.

————. *La guerra y los basiliscos*. Havana: Unión, 1962, 97 pp.

López, César. *Circulando el cuadrado*. Havana: Ediciones R, 1963, 113 pp.

Lorenzo Fuentes, José. *Después de la gaviota*. Havana: Casa de las Américas, 1968, 149 pp.

—————. *Maguaraya arriba*. Santa Clara: Universidad Central de Las Villas, 1963, 121 pp.

—————. *El vendedor de días*. Havana: Unión, 1967, 69 pp.

Martí, Agenor; Carlos Cabada; and Juan Luis Herrero. *Cuentos de ciencia ficción*. Havana: Ediciones R, 1964, 157 pp.

Martínez, Angela. *Memorias de un decapitado*. Havana: Ediciones R, 1965, 83 pp.

Matas, Julio. *Catálogo de imprevistos*. Havana: Ediciones R, 1963, 89 pp. See also list of short-story volumes published by Cubans in exile.

Medero, Marinés. *Cuentos y anticuentos de Juan Dolcines*. Havana: Unión, 1966.

Navarro, Noel. *La huella del pulgar*. Havana: Casa de las Américas, 1972, 67 pp.

Nueve cuentistas. Havana: Casa de las Américas, 1970, 165 pp. Includes two Cubans (Nicolás Pérez Delgado and Haydée Pérez García), three Colombians, three Chileans, and one Peruvian.

Ortega, Antonio. *Yemas de cocos y otros cuentos*. Santa Clara: Universidad Central de Las Villas, 1959, 183 pp.

Otero, José Manuel. *El paisaje nunca es el mismo: 10 cuentos*. Havana: Unión, 1963, 96 pp.

—————. *4 cuentos*. Havana: Unión, 1965, 38 pp.

Perera Soto, Hilda. *Cuentos de Adli y Luas*. Havana: Ministerio de Educación, 1960, 67 pp.

—————. *Cuentos de Apolo*. 2d ed. Havana: Lázaro Hnos., 1960, 109 pp.

Piñera, Virgilio. *Cuentos*. Havana: Unión, 1964, 316 pp.

—————. *El que vino a salvarme*. Buenos Aires: Sudamericana, 1970, 299 pp.

Piniella, Germán. *Otra vez al camino*. Havana: Instituto Cubano del Libro, 1971, 62 pp.

—————. *Polífagos*. Havana: Unión, 1967.

Pita Rodríguez, Félix. *Cuentos completos*. Havana: Unión, 1963, 169 pp.

—————. *Esta larga tarea de aprender a morir y otros cuentos*. Godfrey, Ill.: Monticello College Press, 1960, 128 pp.

—————. *Poemas y cuentos*. Havana: Unión, 1965, 295 pp.

Pogolotti, Marcelo. *Detrás del muro*. Mexico City: Costa-Amic, 1963, 227 pp.

Quiñones, Serafín. *Al final del terraplén el sol*. Havana, 1971.

Rodríguez Leyva, Nelson. *El regalo*. Havana: Ediciones R, 1964, 115 pp.

Sáez, Luis Manuel. *El iniciado*. Havana: Unión, 1967.

Sergio, Gil Blas. *Dos hombres*. Havana: La Milagrosa, 1961, 156 pp.

Simó, Ana María. *Las fábulas*. Havana: El Puente, 1962, 82 pp.

Solís, José; Sixto Quintela; Víctor Casaus; and Carlos Quintela. *Voluntario*. Havana: Imprenta Revolucionaria, 1965, 194 pp.

Suárez Solís, Rafael. *Un pueblo donde no pasaba nada (Novela del tiempo quieto)*. Santa Clara: Universidad Central de Las Villas, 1962, 212 pp. A collection of short stories, in spite of the subtitle.

Tamayo, Evora. *Cuentos para abuelas enfermas*. Havana: El Puente, 1964, 46 pp.

————. *La vieja y la mar*. Havana: Ediciones R, 1965, 147 pp.

Travieso, Julio. *Los corderos beben vino*. Havana: Unión, 1970, 99 pp.

————. *Días de guerra*. Granma, 1967, 88 pp.

Valle, Gerardo del. *1/4 fambá y 19 cuentos más*. Havana: Unión, 1967, 210 pp.

Vieta, Ezequiel. *Libro de los epílogos*. Havana: Unión, 1963, 132 pp.

Antirevolutionary Cuban Novels

The following novels published by Cuban exiles are all antirevolutionary except for Luis Ricardo Alonso's *El candidato*, which is unrelated to the Revolution. Although José Sánchez-Boudy's *Los cruzados de la aurora* takes place in the sixteenth century, it is inspired by events in contemporary Cuba.

Alonso, Luis Ricardo. *El candidato*. Barcelona: Destino, 1970, 217 pp.

————. *Los dioses ajenos*. Barcelona: Destino, 1971, 247 pp.

————. *Territorio libre*. Oviedo: Richard Grandio, 1967, 226 pp.; *Territorio libre*. Translated by Alan Brown. London: Owen, 1966, 266 pp.

Arcocha, Juan. *La bala perdida*. Barcelona: Plaza y Janés, 1973, 139 pp.

————. *A Candle in the Wind*. New York: Lyle Stuart, 1967, 187 pp.

————. *Por cuenta propia*. Barcelona: Plaza y Janés, 1970, 232 pp.

Castro, Angel A. *Refugiados*. Zaragoza: Corneta, 1969, 127 pp.; textbook edition, New York: Eliseo Torres, 1971, 127 pp.

Chao Hermida, Francisco. *Un obrero de vanguardia*. Miami: Universal, 1972, 182 pp.

Cobo Sausa, Manuel. *El cielo será nuestro*. Medellín, Col.: Granamérica, 1965, 298 pp.

Díaz-Versón, Salvador. . . . *Ya el mundo oscurece: Novela histórica de la revolución de Cuba*. Mexico City: Botas, 1961, 228 pp.

Entenza, Pedro. *No hay aceras*. Barcelona: Planeta, 1969, 210 pp.

Fernández Camus, Emilio. *Caminos llenos de borrascas*. Madrid: Gráficas Orbe, 1962, 247 pp.

Fowler, Raoul A. *En las garras de la paloma*. Miami, 1967, 232 pp.

Gómez-Kemp, Ramiro. *Los desposeídos*. Miami: Universal, 1972, 92 pp.

González, Celedonio. *Los primos*. Miami: Universal, 1971, 308 pp.

Landa, René G. *De buena cepa*. Miami: Rema Press, 1967, 225 pp.

Linares, Manuel. *Los Ferrández*. Barcelona: Maucci, 1965, 225 pp.

López, Pablo A. *Ayer sin mañana*. Miami: Universal, 1969, 56 pp.

Márquez y de la Cerra, Miguel F. *El gallo cantó*. Río Piedras: Editorial San Juan, 1972, 190 pp.

Montaner, Carlos Alberto. *Perromundo*. Barcelona: Ediciones 29, 1972, 209 pp.

Núñez Pérez, Orlando. *El grito*. San José, C.R.: Victoria, 1966, 132 pp.

Perera, Hilda. *El sitio de nadie*. Barcelona: Planeta, 1972, 329 pp.

Pérez, Jorge T. "Los Buenos." Yankton, S.D., 1970, 94 pp. Mimeographed.

Rivero Collado, Andrés. *Enterrado vivo*. Mexico City: Dinamismo, 1960, 116 pp.

Sánchez-Boudy, José. *Los cruzados de la aurora*. Zaragoza: Cometa, 1972, 159 pp.

———. *Lilayando*. Miami: Universal, 1971, 80 pp.

Sánchez Torrentó, Eugenio. *Francisco Manduley: La historia de un pescador de ranas*. Coral Gables, Fla.: Service Offset Printers, 1965, 70 pp.

Villa, Alvaro de. *El olor de la muerte que viene*. Oviedo: Richard Grandio, 1968, 427 pp.

Short Stories by Cubans in Exile

Unlike the novels written by Cubans in exile, many of the following volumes are totally unrelated to the Revolution, for example, Lydia Cabrera's *Ayapá*. Ramón Ferreira's *Los malos olores de este mundo* includes some short stories that definitely belong to the prorevolutionary literature.

Abella, Lorenzo. *Más allá del espejo*. Puerto Rico: Clavel, 1970.

Acosta Tijero, Alberto. *La pierna artificial y otros cuentos*. New York: Las Américas, 1971, 106 pp.

Alcover Herrera, Wilfredo. *Cuentos cortos*. Miami, 1965, 28 pp.

———. *Kaktos: Recopilación de cuentos cortos*. Miami, 1971.

———. *Recopilación de cuentos cortos*. Miami, 1968, 27 pp.

Alvarez Fuentes, Germán. *Ficciones y realidades*. Oviedo: Gráficas Summa, 1970, 270 pp.

Andino Porro, Alberto. *Polvos y lodos: Cuentos de Cuba.* Madrid: Estudio Myr, 1968, 91 pp.

Brenes, María. *Diez cuentos para un libro.* New York: Las Américas, 1963.

Cabrera, Lydia. *Ayapá: Cuentos de Jicotea.* Miami: Universal, 1971, 269 pp.

Cachán, Manuel. *Cuentos políticos.* New York: Colección Mensaje, 1971, 64 pp.

Casey, Calvert. *Notas de un simulador.* Barcelona: Seix Barral, 1969, 131 pp.

Castro, Angel A. *Cuentos del exilio cubano.* New York: Lectorum, 1970, 96 pp.

——. *Cuentos yanquis.* Edited by Woodrow Moore and Gloria Smith. Miami: Universal, 1972, 110 pp. Five of the nine stories are taken from *Cuentos del exilio cubano.*

Díaz, Pedro Ernesto. *Cuatro cuentos cristianos: Un interrumpido café, El son se fue de Cuba, El niño y la marsopa, El ordenanza y el caballo.* Miami, 1964, 109 pp.

Ferreira López, Ramón. *Los malos olores de este mundo.* Introduction by John Dos Passos. Mexico City: Fondo de Cultura Económica, 1969, 233 pp.

González, Celedonio. *La soledad es una amiga que vendrá.* Miami: Universal, 1971, 92 pp.

Gutiérrez Kann, Asela. *Las pirañas y otros cuentos cubanos.* Miami: Universal, 1972, 160 pp.

León, Joaquín de [pseud.]. *Sin reproche y otros cuentos.* Mexico City: Centauro, 1970, 27 pp.

Martínez Solanas, Gerardo E. *Dos cuentos y dos leyendas.* Mendoza: Talleres Gráficos D'Accurzio, 1964, 59 pp.

Matas, Julio. *Erinia.* Miami: Universal, 1971, 122 pp.

Montaner, Carlos Alberto. *Instantáneas al borde del abismo.* Río Piedras: Editorial San Juan, 1970, 68 pp.

——. *Póker de brujas y otros cuentos.* Bilbao: Vasco-Americana, 1968, 128 pp.

Montes Huidobro, Matías. *La anunciación y otros cuentos cubanos.* Madrid: Gráfica Clemares, 1967, 190 pp.

Novás Calvo, Lino. *Maneras de contar.* New York: Las Américas, 1970, 405 pp.

Peña, Humberto J. *Ya no habrá más domingos.* Miami: Universal, 1971, 144 pp.

Quirós, Beltrán de. *Los unos, los otros . . . y el seibo.* Miami: Universal, 1971, 79 pp.

Ripoll, Carlos. *Julián Pérez por Benjamín Castillo.* New York: Las Américas, 1970, 57 pp.

Rivero Collado, Andrés. *Rojo y negro: Cuentos sobre la tragedia cubana.* Orangeburg, S.C.: Publicaciones Cruzada, 1964, 22 pp.

Saínz de la Peña, José. *Castro quedó atrás.* Miami, 1970.

Sánchez-Boudy, José. *Cuentos a luna llena.* Miami: Universal, 1971, 164 pp.

———. *Cuentos del hombre.* Barcelona: Bosch, 1969, 171 pp.

———. *Cuentos grises.* Barcelona: Bosch, 1966, 165 pp.

Viana, Roberto. *Los que por ti murieron.* Miami, 1961, 64 pp.

Viera Trejo, Bernardo. *Militantes del odio y otros relatos de la revolución cubana.* Miami: AIP, 1964, 153 pp. The title story, pp. 9–76, is really a short novel.

Foreign Prose Fiction of the Cuban Revolution

Aguilar Derpich, Juan [Peruvian]. *"El majá" o El pérfido Julián.* Havana, 1963, 95 pp.

Aguilera Malta, Demetrio [Ecuadorean]. *Una cruz en la Sierra Maestra.* Buenos Aires: Sophos, 1960, 170 pp.

Aramayo, X. [Spaniard]. *En La Habana ha muerto un turista.* Aránzazu, Guipúzcoa: Editorial Franciscana, 1963, 125 pp.

Baeza Flores, Antonio [Chilean]. *La frontera del adiós: Novela del exilio.* San Juan, P.R.: Editorial San Juan, 1970, 322 pp.

———. *La muerte en el paraíso.* Mexico City: Costa-Amic, 1965, 376 pp.

Callado, Antônio [Brazilian]. *Bar Don Juan.* Rio de Janeiro: Editôra Civilização Brasileira, 1971; *Don Juan's Bar.* Translated by Barbara Shelby. New York: Alfred A. Knopf, 1972, 271 pp.

Castellanos Velasco, Francisco [Mexican]. *Cuando la caña es amarga.* Mexico City: Diana, 1966, 311 pp.; 2d ed., 1967.

Cortázar, Julio [Argentinian]. "Reunión." In *Todos los fuegos el fuego.* 10th ed. Buenos Aires: Sudamericana, 1970.

Edwards, Jorge [Chilean]. *Persona non grata.* Barcelona: Barral Editores, 1973, 478 pp.

Gámez, Tana de [Spaniard]. *The Yoke and the Star: A Novel of the Cuban Revolution.* Indianapolis: Bobbs-Merrill, 1966, 309 pp.; *El yugo y la estrella.* Mexico City: Joaquín Mortiz, 1968, 335 pp.

Grimalt, Manuel [Spaniard]. *Nadie escribe la historia de la próxima aurora.*

Andorra la Vella: Editorial Andorra, 1969, 321 pp.

Hawkins, Ward [American]. *Kings Will Be Tyrants*. New York: McGraw-Hill, 1959, 226 pp.

Hernández, Luisa Josefina [Mexican]. *La primera batalla*. Mexico City: Era, 1965, 140 pp.

Herr, Paul [American]. *Journey Not to End*. New York: Bernard Geis Associates, 1961, 250 pp.

Ladrón de Guevara, Matilde [Chilean]. *Adiós al cañaveral: Diario de una mujer en Cuba*. Buenos Aires: Goyanarte, 1962, 282 pp.; 2d ed., 1962; 3d ed., 1964.

Martínez Moreno, Carlos [Uruguayan]. *El paredón*. Barcelona: Seix Barral, 1963, 286 pp.

Mases, José Antonio [Spaniard]. *La invasión*. Barcelona: Plaza y Janés, 1965, 249 pp.

———. *Los padrenuestros y el fusil*. Barcelona: Plaza y Janés, 1964, 261 pp.; 2d ed., 1973.

Miller, Warren [American]. *Flush Times*. Boston: Little, Brown, 1962, 370 pp.

Pellecer, Carlos Manuel [Guatemalan]. *Utiles después de muertos*. Mexico City: Costa-Amic, 1966, 399 pp.; Barcelona, 1969.

Soto, Pedro Juan [Puerto Rican]. *El francotirador*. Mexico City: Joaquín Mortiz, 1969, 297 pp.

Tully, Andrew [American]. *A Race of Rebels*. New York: Simon and Schuster, 1960, 250 pp.

Uris, Leon [American]. *Topaz*. New York: McGraw-Hill, 1967, 341 pp.

Viteri, Eugenia [Ecuadorean]. *A 90 millas, solamente*. Quito: Casa de la Cultura Ecuatoriana, 1969, 192 pp.

Works Consulted

Abella, Rosa. "Bibliografía de la novela publicada en Cuba y en el extranjero por cubanos desde 1959 hasta 1965." *Revista Iberoamericana* 32, no. 62 (July–December 1966): 307–318.

———. "Cinco años de la novela cubana." *Cuadernos del Hombre Libre*, no. 1 (July–September 1966), pp. 9–14; translation in English, *The Carrel* (University of Miami Library) 7, no. 1 (June 1966): 17–21.

Acosta, Leonardo. "Benítez gana la partida." *Casa de las Américas* 8, no. 45 (November–December 1967): 166–169.

Agüero, Luis. "La novela de la Revolución." *Casa de las Américas* 4, nos. 22–23 (January–April 1964): 60–67.

Alzola, Concepción T. "Muerte y órbita de Calvert Casey (1924–1969)." *Exilio*, no. 5 (Summer 1971), pp. 117–124.

Aparicio, Raúl. "Acotación a *Los desnudos.*" *Unión* 6, no. 3 (July–September 1967): 124–131.

Arcocha, José Antonio. "Dicotomías: Lezama Lima y Cabrera Infante." *Aportes*, no. 11 (January 1969), pp. 59–65.

Arenas, Reinaldo. "Celestino y yo." *Unión* 6, no. 3 (July–September 1967): 119.

Arrom, J. J. "Research in Latin American Literature: The State of the Art (A Round Table)." *Latin American Research Review* 6, no. 2 (Summer 1971): 85–124.

Arrufat, Antón. *Los siete contra Tebas.* Havana: Unión, 1968.

Atia, Marina. *Alejo Carpentier: 45 años de trabajo intelectual, recopilación bibliográfica.* Havana: Biblioteca Nacional José Martí, 1966.

Benedetti, Mario. *Cuaderno cubano.* Montevideo: Arca, 1969.

Benítez Rojo, Antonio. "Otros padres, otros hijos" [review of César Leante's *Padres e hijos*]. *Casa de las Américas* 9, no. 50 (September–October 1968): 183–184.

―――. Review of *Abrir y cerrar los ojos* by Onelio J. Cardoso. *Casa de las Américas* 11, no. 61 (July–August 1970): 171–173.

―――. Review of *Condenados de Condado* by Norberto Fuentes. *Casa de las Américas* 9, no. 49 (July–August 1968): 158–160.

―――. Review of *En ciudad semejante* by Lisandro Otero. *Casa de las Américas* 11, nos. 65–66 (March–June 1971): 161–163.

―――. Review of *Para matar al lobo* by Julio Travieso. *Casa de las Américas* 12, no. 71 (March–April 1972): 107–108.

Blanco, Lucien. *Los orígenes de la revolución china.* Translated by Martín Sagrera from the French (*Les Origines de la Révolution chinoise*, Paris: Gallimard, 1967). Caracas: Tiempo Nuevo, 1970.

Bravet, Rogelio Luis. Review of *Los muertos andan solos* by Juan Arcocha. *Bohemia*, January 11, 1963, p. 18.

Bueno, Salvador. "Alejo Carpentier y su concepto de la historia." In *El ensayo y la crítica literaria en Iberoamérica*, Instituto Internacional de Literatura Iberoamericana, pp. 257–263. Toronto: University of Toronto Press, 1970.

————. "Cuba, Hoy: Novela." *Insula*, nos. 260–261 (July–August 1968), pp. 1, 21, 24.

————. "Los temas de la novela cubana." *Asomante* 16, no. 4 (October–December 1960): 39–48.

————. Review of *En ciudad semejante* by Lisandro Otero. *Sin Nombre* 2, no. 1 (September 1971): 89–91.

Cabrera Infante, Guillermo [G. Caín]. *Un oficio del siglo XX*. Havana: Ediciones R, 1963.

Capote, Truman. "Miriam." In *A Tree of Night and Other Stories*. New York: Random House, 1945.

Cardenal, Ernesto. *En Cuba*. Buenos Aires: Carlos Lohlé, 1972.

Carpentier, Hortense, and Janet Brof. *Doors and Mirrors: Fiction and Poetry from Spanish America (1920–1970)*. New York: Grossman, 1972.

Casal, Lourdes. "A Bibliography of Cuban Creative Literature: 1958–71." *Cuban Studies Newsletter* 2, no. 2 (June 1972).

————. *El caso Padilla: Literatura y revolución en Cuba*. Miami: Universal, 1971.

————. "The Cuban Novel, 1959–1969: An Annotated Bibliography." *Abraxas* 1, no. 1 (Fall 1970): 77–92.

————. "Literature and Society." In *Revolutionary Change in Cuba*, edited by Carmelo Mesa-Lago, pp. 447–469. Pittsburgh: University of Pittsburgh Press, 1971.

————. "La novela en Cuba, 1959–1967: Una introducción." *Exilio*, Fall-Winter 1969–Spring 1970, pp. 184–217.

Castro, Fidel. *Palabras a los intelectuales*. Havana: Consejo Nacional de Cultura, 1961.

"China hoy." *Revista de la Universidad de México* 25, no. 1 (September 1971).

Cofiño López, Manuel. Interview. *La Gaceta de Cuba*, nos. 90–91 (March–April 1971).

Collazos, Oscar; Julio Cortázar; and Mario Vargas Llosa. *Literatura en la revolución y revolución en la literatura*. Mexico City: Siglo XXI, 1970.

Cortázar, Julio, et al. *Cuba por argentinos*. Buenos Aires: Merlín, 1968.

————. "Policrítica en la hora de los chacales." *Casa de las Américas* 12, no. 67 (July–August 1971): 157–161.

————. *Ultimo round*. Mexico City: Siglo XXI, 1969.

————. *La vuelta al día en ochenta mundos*. Mexico City: Siglo XXI, 1967.

Coulthard, Gabriel R. "Cuban Literary Prizes for 1963." *Caribbean Studies*

4, no. 4 (January 1965): 3–10, 48–55.

———. "The Situation of the Writer in Contemporary Cuba." *Caribbean Studies* 7, no. 1 (April 1967): 23–25.

Dalton, Roque; René Depestre; Edmundo Desnoes; Roberto Fernández Retamar; Ambrosio Fornet; and Carlos María Gutiérrez. *El intelectual y la sociedad*. Mexico City: Siglo XXI, 1969.

Desnoes, Edmundo. *Punto de vista*. Havana: Instituto del Libro, 1967.

———. Review of *Un día en la vida de Iván Denisovich* by Alexander Solzhenitsyn. *Casa de las Américas* 4, no. 24 (January–April 1964): 99–102.

Díaz, Filiberto. "Cuba y su literatura." *Mundo Nuevo*, nos. 39–40 (September–October 1969), pp. 83–86.

Diego, Eliseo. "Sobre *Celestino antes del alba*." *Casa de las Américas* 8, no. 45 (November–December 1967): 162–166.

Drummond, Rose B. "The Cuban Revolutionary Novel, 1959–1969." M.A. thesis, University of California at Los Angeles. 1971.

Dumont, René. *Cuba ¿es socialista?* Caracas: Tiempo Nuevo, 1970.

Ehrmann, Jacques, ed. *Literature and Revolution*. [1st ed., 1967] Boston: Beacon Press, 1970.

Ellis, Keith. "La literatura cubana y la revolución." *The Canadian Forum* 48, no. 576 (January 1969): 224–226.

Fagen, Richard. *The Transformation of Political Culture in Cuba*. Stanford: Stanford University Press, 1969.

Feito, Francisco E. "Severo Sarduy en la actual narrativa hispanoamericana." *El Urogallo* 2, no. 8 (March–April 1971): 94–97.

Fell, Claude. "Rencontre avec Alejo Carpentier." *Les Langues Modernes* 59, no. 3 (May–June 1965): 101–108.

Fernández Retamar, Roberto. "Les intellectuels et la révolution." *Les Lettres Nouvelles* [special issue], December 1967–January 1968, pp. 40–61.

Fornet, Ambrosio. Review of *Sacchario*. *Casa de las Américas* 11, no. 64 (January–February 1971): 183.

———. *En tres y dos*. Havana: Ediciones R, 1964.

Fort, Gilberto V. *The Cuban Revolution of Fidel Castro: An Annotated Bibliography*. Library Series, no. 34. Lawrence: University of Kansas, 1969.

Foster, David W. "A Bibliography of the Fiction of Carpentier, Cabrera Infante, and Lezama Lima: Works and Criticism." *Abraxas* 1, no. 3 (Spring 1971): 305–310.

Franqui, Carlos. *Cuba: El libro de los doce.* Mexico City: Era, 1966.

Gallagher, David. "The Literary Life in Cuba." *The New York Review of Books,* May 23, 1968, pp. 37–41.

García, Eligio. "Los relatos de Cabrera Infante." *Imagen,* August 22–29, 1970, sec. 2, pp. 4–5.

García Alzola, Ernesto. "La novela cubana en el siglo XX." In *Panorama de la literatura cubana: Conferencias,* pp. 183–207. Havana: Universidad de La Habana, 1970.

García Márquez, Gabriel. *Cien años de soledad.* 3d ed. Buenos Aires: Sudamericana, 1967.

García Vega, Lorenzo. *Antología de la novela cubana.* Havana: Ministerio de Educación, 1960.

Giacomán, Helmy, ed. *Homenaje a Alejo Carpentier: Variaciones interpretativas en torno a su obra.* New York: Las Américas, 1970.

Gifford, Henry. *The Novel in Russia from Pushkin to Pasternak.* New York: Harper and Row, 1965.

González, Reynaldo. "La palabra, el mito, el mito de la palabra" [Review of Pablo Armando Fernández's *Los niños se despiden*]. *Casa de las Américas* 9, no. 49 (July–August 1968): 147–154.

González-Cruz, Luis F. "The Art of Julio Matas." *Latin American Literary Review* 1, no. 1 (Fall 1972): 125–128.

González Echevarría, Roberto. "Para una bibliografía de y sobre Severo Sarduy (1955–71)." *Revista Iberoamericana* 38, no. 79 (April–June 1972): 333–343.

———. "Son de La Habana: La ruta de Severo Sarduy." *Revista Iberoamericana* 37, nos. 76–77 (July–December 1971): 725–740.

Guevara, Ernesto Che. *Obra revolucionaria.* [1st ed., 1967] 4th ed. Mexico City: Era, 1971.

Hasse, Federico. "Filiberto o el último compilador." *Mundo Nuevo,* no. 46 (April 1970), pp. 63–74.

Hauser, Arnold. *The Social History of Art.* 4 vols. New York: Vintage Books, n.d. [First U.S. edition, New York: Alfred Knopf, 1951.]

Hayward, Max, and Patricia Blake. *Dissonant Voices in Soviet Literature.* New York: Harper and Row, 1964.

Henríquez Ureña, Camila. "La literatura cubana en la Revolución." In *Panorama de la literatura cubana: Conferencias,* pp. 211–239. Havana, 1970.

Karol, K. S. *Guerrillas in Power: The Course of the Cuban Revolution.* New York: Hill and Wang, 1970.

Lane, Helen R. Review of *Hallucinations (El mundo alucinante)* by Reynaldo Arenas. *New York Times Book Review*. August 29, 1971, pp. 4, 20.

Lezama Lima, José. *La expresión americana*. [1st ed., 1957] Santiago: Universitaria, 1969.

Lihn, Enrique. [Article on the Cuban government's new policy toward literature.] *Siempre*, December 8, 1971, p. iii.

Llopis, Rogelio. Review of *El escudo de hojas secas* by Antonio Benítez. *Casa de las Américas* 11, no. 62 (September–October 1970) : 199–201.

––––––. Review of *Pequeñas maniobras* by Virgilio Piñera. *Casa de las Américas* 5, no. 24 (January–April 1964) : 107.

Lockwood, Lee. Review of *Guerrillas in Power* by K. S. Karol. *New York Times Book Review Section*, January 24, 1971, p. 3.

López Segrera, Francisco. "Psicoanálisis de una generación: III." *Revista de la Biblioteca Nacional José Martí* 12, no. 2 (May–August 1970) : 101–152.

Luchting, Wolfgang A. "Los rabdomantes." *Mundo Nuevo*, no. 47 (March 1970), pp. 64–71.

Lukács, Georg. *Realism in Our Time: Literature and the Class Struggle*. [1st ed., 1956] New York: Harper and Row, 1964.

Mao Tse-tung. *Speeches*. Peking: Foreign Language Press, 1967.

Marinello, Juan. "Sobre nuestra crítica literaria." *Vida Universitaria* 21, no. 219 (May–June 1970) : 43–48.

Mario, José. "Allen Ginsberg en La Habana." *Mundo Nuevo*, no. 34 (April 1969), pp. 48–54.

––––––. "La narrativa cubana de la Revolución." *Mundo Nuevo*, no. 41 (November 1969), pp. 75–79.

Masó, Fausto. "Literatura y revolución en Cuba." *Mundo Nuevo*, no. 32 (February 1969), pp. 50–54.

Menton, Seymour. "The Cuban Novel of the Revolution: A Decade of Growing National Consciousness." In *The Cry of Home: Cultural Nationalism and the Modern Writer*, edited by H. Ernest Lewald, pp. 320–333. Knoxville: University of Tennessee Press, 1972.

––––––. "La novela de la Revolución cubana." *Cuadernos Americanos* 23, no. 1 (January–February 1964) : 231–241.

––––––. "The Short Story of the Cuban Revolution, 1959–1969." *Studies in Short Fiction*, no. 1 (Winter 1971) : 32–43.

Mesa-Lago, Carmelo, ed. *Revolutionary Change in Cuba.* Pittsburgh: University of Pittsburgh Press, 1971.

Mier, José Servando Teresa de. *Memorias.* Mexico City: Porrúa, 1946.

Miranda, Julio E. *Nueva literatura cubana.* Madrid: Taurus, 1971.

————. "El nuevo pensamiento cubano." *El Urogallo* 2, no. 8 (March–April 1971): 84–93.

————. "Sobre la narrativa cubana." *Cuadernos hispanoamericanos,* no. 246 (June 1970), pp. 641–654.

Molina-Foix, Vicente. "En la muerte de Calvert Casey." *Insula,* nos. 272–273 (July–August 1969), p. 40.

Montaner, Carlos A. *Diez años de Revolución cubana.* Río Piedras, P.R.: Editorial San Juan, 1970.

Müller-Bergh, Klaus. "Alejo Carpentier: Autor y obra en su época." *Revista Iberoamericana* 33, no. 63 (January–July 1967): 9–43.

Nelson, Lowry. *Cuba: The Measure of a Revolution.* Minneapolis: University of Minnesota Press, 1972.

Orfila Reynal, Arnaldo. Letter to the editor. *Siempre,* June 9, 1971, pp. 8, 69.

Ortega, Julio. *La contemplación y la fiesta.* Caracas: Monte Avila, 1969. On Lezama Lima, Cabrera Infante, and Sarduy, see pp. 77–116, 171–182, 205–210.

————. *Relato de la utopía: Notas sobre narrativa cubana de la Revolución.* Barcelona: La Gaya Ciencia, 1973.

————. Review of *Cazabandido* and *Condenados de Condado* by Norberto Fuentes. *Libre* (Paris), no. 2 (December–February 1971–1972), pp. 146–151.

————. "Sobre narrativa cubana actual." *Nueva Narrativa Hispanoamericana* 2, no. 1 (January 1972): 65–87.

Otero, Lisandro. "El escritor en la Revolución cubana." *Casa de las Américas* 6, nos. 36–37 (May–August 1966): 203–209.

————. "Notas sobre la funcionalidad de la cultura." *Casa de las Américas* 12, no. 68 (September–October 1971): 94–107.

Padilla, Heberto. *Fuera del juego.* Barcelona: El Bardo, 1970.

————. "Intervención en la Unión de Escritores y Artistas Cubanos." *Casa de las Américas* 11, nos. 65–66 (March–June 1971): 191–203.

Peraza-Sarausa, Fermín. *Personalidades cubanas (1957–67).* 10 vols. Gainesville: University of Florida Press, 1964–1967.

————. *Revolutionary Cuba: A Bibliographical Guide*. Coral Gables: University of Miami Press, 1967.

Pita Rodríguez, Félix. "Ho Chi Minh y la función del escritor." *Islas*, no. 37 (September–December 1970), pp. 103–114.

————. "La poesía combatiente de Vietnam." *Islas*, no. 37 (September–December 1970), pp. 59–75.

Pogolotti, Graziella. *Examen de conciencia*. Havana: Unión, 1965.

Portuondo, José Antonio. "Corrientes literarias en Cuba." *Cuadernos Americanos* 26, no. 4 (July–August 1967): 193–213.

————. *Crítica de la época y otros ensayos*. Santa Clara: Universidad Central de Las Villas, 1965.

————. Prologue to *El derrumbe* by José Soler Puig. Santiago: Universidad de Oriente, 1964.

————. Prologue to *Tengo* by Nicolás Guillén. Santa Clara: Universidad Central de Las Villas, 1964.

————. Review of *La última mujer y el próximo combate* by Manuel Cofiño López. *Casa de las Américas* 12, no. 71 (March–April 1972): 105–106.

Rama, Angel. Interview. *Imagen*, May 9–16, 1972, sec. 2, pp. 4–5.

Rodríguez Feo, José. "Breve recuento de la narrativa cubana." *Unión* 6, no. 4 (December 1967): 131–136.

Rodríguez Monegal, Emir. *El arte de narrar*. Caracas: Monte Avila, 1968. For interviews with Cabrera Infante and Sarduy, see pp. 49–80, 269–292.

————. "Estructura y significaciones de *Tres tristes tigres*." *Sur*, no. 320 (September–October 1969), pp. 38–51.

————. "Lo real y lo maravilloso en *El reino de este mundo*." *Revista Iberoamericana* 37, nos. 76–77 (July–December 1971): 619–649.

————. Note on the journal *Amaru*. *Mundo Nuevo*, no. 12 (June 1967), p. 91.

————. "*Paradiso* en su contexto." *Mundo Nuevo*, no. 24 (June 1968), pp. 40–44.

Rojas, Manuel. Review of *La última mujer y el próximo combate* by Manuel Cofiño López. *Casa de las Américas* 12, no. 67 (July–August 1971): 172–173.

Rutherford, John. *Mexican Society during the Revolution: A Literary Approach*. Oxford: Clarendon Press, 1971.

Sábato, Ernesto. *Claves políticas*. Buenos Aires: "El Escarabajo de Oro" y Rodolfo Alonso, 1971.

Salper, Roberta. "Literature and Revolution in Cuba." *Monthly Review*, October 1970, pp. 15–30.

Sánchez, Julio C. "Bibliografía de la novela cubana." *Islas*, no. 3 (September–December 1960), pp. 321–356.

Sánchez-Boudy, José. *La nueva novela hispanoamericana y tres tristes tigres.* Miami: Universal, 1971.

Sarduy, Severo. "Homenaje a Lezama." *Mundo Nuevo*, no. 24 (June 1968), pp. 4–17.

Schanzer, George. "Carpentier Fallen from Grace." *Hispania* 51, no. 1 (March 1968): 188.

Schulman, Ivan A. "*La situación* y *Gestos*: Dos técnicas y dos visiones de la realidad cubana." *Duquesne Hispanic Review* 5, no. 3 (1967): 121–133.

Skinner, Eugene R. "Archetypal Patterns in Four Novels of Alejo Carpentier." Doctoral dissertation, University of Kansas, 1969.

Suárez, Luis. Interview with Alejo Carpentier. *Siempre*, November 20, 1963.

Thomas, Hugh. *Cuba: The Pursuit of Freedom.* New York: Harper and Row, 1971.

Torriente, Loló de la. "La política cultural y los escritores y artistas cubanos." *Cuadernos Americanos* 22, no. 5 (September–October 1963): 78–89.

Uslar Pietri, Arturo. "La lluvia." In *Red, cuentos.* Caracas: Elite, 1936.

Valdés, Nelson P., and Edwin Lieuwen. *The Cuban Revolution: A Research-Study Guide (1959–69).* Albuquerque: University of New Mexico Press, 1971.

Valle-Arizpe, Artemio de. *Fray Servando.* Buenos Aires: Espasa-Calpe, 1951.

Vargas Llosa, Mario, and Emir Rodríguez Monegal. "Sobre el *Paradiso* de Lezama." *Mundo Nuevo*, no. 16 (October 1967), pp. 89–95.

Yglesias, José. *In the Fist of the Revolution: Life in a Cuban Country Town.* New York: Pantheon Books, 1968.

INDEX